# Gardening Basics For Canadians For Dummies

# Typical Number of Frost-Free Days

Gardeners who grow tender vegetables and annual flowers need to know when, on average, the growing season in their area begins in spring and ends in fall, and how many days there are in between. No one wants to lose plants to frost. Growing seasons are based on historical data and are only approximate. To be extra careful, you can plant or transplant temperature-sensitive plants ten days after the dates given here.

| Location | Last Frost Date | First Frost Date | Typical Number of Frost-Free Days |
|---|---|---|---|
| St. John's | June 2 | October 12 | 132 |
| Halifax | May 6 | October 20 | 167 |
| Montreal | May 3 | October 7 | 157 |
| Toronto | May 9 | October 6 | 150 |
| Winnipeg | May 25 | September 22 | 120 |
| Regina | May 21 | September 10 | 112 |
| Calgary | May 23 | September 15 | 115 |
| Yellowknife | May 27 | September 15 | 111 |
| Whitehorse | June 11 | August 25 | 75 |
| Vancouver | March 28 | November 5 | 222 |
| Victoria | March 1 | December 1 | 275 |

For more Canadian locations, go to tdc.ca/canadian_frost_dates.htm.

# Key Measurement Conversions

A lot of measuring goes on in gardening. Here's a helpful basic conversion chart.

| Type of Measurement | Metric to U.S. Customary Units | U.S. Customary to Metric Units |
|---|---|---|
| Distance | 1 centimetre = 0.39 inch | 1 inch = 2.54 centimetres |
| | 1 metre = 3.28 feet = 1.09 yards | 1 yard = 3 feet = 0.91 metre |
| Area | 1 square metre = 10.76 square feet | 1 square foot = 0.09 square metre |
| Volume, liquid | 1 litre = 1.06 quarts = 0.26 gallon | 1 gallon = 4 quarts = 3.79 litres |
| Volume, dry | 1 litre = 0.91 quart = 0.23 gallon | 1 gallon = 4 quarts = 4.41 litres |
| Mass/weight | 1 kilogram = 2.21 pounds | 1 pound = 0.45 kilogram |
| | 1 gram = 0.04 ounce | 1 ounce = 28.35 grams |

*For Dummies: Bestselling Book Series for Beginners*

# Gardening Basics For Canadians For Dummies®

Cheat Sheet

## Picking Plants Made for the Shade

Here's a list of plants for those areas of your garden that receive limited sunlight. Keep this list with you when you go to the garden centre to help you decide what you want for your shady oasis. Although we've used common names throughout the book, botanical names are listed in parentheses here because sometimes nurseries arrange their plants alphabetically according to botanical name. For perennials, the plant's hardiness zone is also listed.

### Annuals

Amethyst flower *(Browallia)*

Black-eyed Susan vine *(Thunbergia alata)*

Canterbury bells *(Campanula medium)*

Coleus *(Coleus* spp.)

Flowering tobacco *(Nicotiana alata)*

Forget-me-not *(Myosotis sylvatica)*

Impatiens *(Impatiens* spp.)

Lobelia *(Lobelia* spp.)

Love-in-a-mist *(Nigella damascena)*

Monkey flower *(Mimulus hybridus)*

Scarlet sage *(Salvia splendens)*

Wax begonia *(Begonia semperflorens-cultorum)*

Wishbone flower *(Torenia fournieri)*

### Perennials

Bear's-breech *(Acanthus spinosus):* Zone 5

Bee balm *(Monarda* spp.): Zone 4

Bellflower *(Campanula* spp.*):* Zone 5

Bergenia *(Bergenia cordifolia):* Zone 4

Bleeding heart *(Dicentra spectabilis):* Zone 2

Columbine *(Aquilegia* spp.): Zone 3

False spirea *(Astilbe* spp.): Zone 4

Globeflower *(Trollius* spp.): Zone 2

Hosta *(Hosta* spp.): Zone 3

Lady's-mantle *(Alchemilla mollis):* Zone 4

Lungwort *(Pulmonaria* spp.): Zone 4

Meadow rue *(Thalictrum* spp.): Zone 5

Siberian iris *(Iris sibirica):* Zone 4

## For Dummies: Bestselling Book Series for Beginners

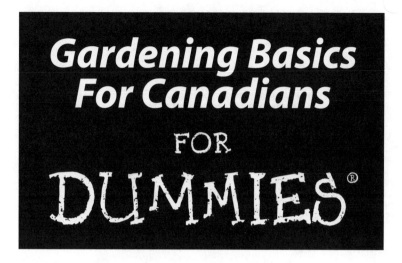

# Gardening Basics For Canadians

## FOR

# DUMMIES®

**by Liz Primeau**
**The Editors of *Canadian Gardening***
**Steven A. Frowine**
**The Editors of the National**
**Gardening Association**

WILEY

John Wiley & Sons Canada, Ltd.

**Gardening Basics For Canadians For Dummies®**

Published by
**John Wiley & Sons Canada, Ltd.**
6045 Freemont Boulevard.
Mississauga, ON L5R 4J3
www.wiley.com

**Library and Archives Canada Cataloguing in Publication Data**
**Primeau, Liz**
　　　　**Gardening basics for Canadians for dummies / Liz Primeau, Steven A. Frowine**
**Includes index.**
**ISBN 978-0-470-15491-5**
　　　　1. Gardening—Canada. 2. Landscape gardening—Canada.
**I. Frowine, Steven A. II. Title.**
**SB453.3C2P752 2008　　　　635.9'0971　　　　C2007-907463-4**

Printed in Canada

1 2 3 4 5 TRI 11 10 09 08

Distributed in Canada by John Wiley & Sons Canada, Ltd.

For general information on John Wiley & Sons Canada, Ltd., including all books published by Wiley Publishing, Inc., please call our warehouse, Tel 1-800-567-4797. For reseller information, including discounts and premium sales, please call our sales department, Tel 416-646-7992. For press review copies, author interviews, or other publicity information, please contact our marketing department, Tel 416-646-4584, Fax 416-236-4448.

For authorization to photocopy items for corporate, personal, or educational use, please contact in writing The Canadian Copyright Licensing Agency (Access Copyright). For an Access Copyright license, visit www.accesscopyright.ca or call toll-free, 1-800-893-5777.

WILEY

# About the Authors

**Liz Primeau** has been a lover of the natural world and a gardener since her teens. While working as an editor and writer at several Canadian magazines, she continued to dig and plant in her suburban garden. Her hobby reached obsessive levels when she became *Canadian Gardening* magazine's first editor in 1990, a position she held for nearly a decade. During the late '90s, she was host of HGTV's popular *Canadian Gardening Television*. Liz is a featured speaker at garden conferences, trade shows, and garden clubs, and is the author of *Front Yard Gardens* (Firefly Books) as well as editor of several titles for *Canadian Gardening*.

**Canadian Gardening** is Canada's most popular national gardening magazine. Since it began publishing in 1990, it's been an informative and entertaining source for new and experienced gardeners alike. For more information about the magazine and for gardening tips and information, visit www. canadiangardening.com.

**Steven A. Frowine** was a plant nut even as a child. Since then, his love and sometimes obsession for outdoor and indoor plants has continued to grow. He worked in various horticultural jobs before and during high school and college. Steve has a bachelor's and a master's degree in horticulture from Ohio State University and Cornell, respectively.

His first job after graduate school was to set up a professional gardeners' program at Pacific Tropical Botanical Garden (now the National Tropical Botanical Garden) on Kauai, Hawaii. He later held other professional horticultural positions at Cleveland Botanical Garden and Pittsburgh Civic Garden Center. At Missouri Botanical Garden, he served as chairman of indoor horticulture.

Steve served as an executive at top horticultural businesses including W. Atlee Burpee Company, White Flower Farm, and International Gardening Products. Steve is sought out as a lecturer and has delivered hundreds of talks throughout the United States. His presentations are noted for his excellent photography, his knowledge of the subject, and his sense of humour. He has appeared on various American TV shows and writes extensively, authoring many articles for horticultural trade and consumer magazines.

He has served on the boards of various professional organizations, including the National Gardening Association, Garden Writers of America, and the American Association of Botanical Gardens and Arboreta. Steve served on the Visiting Committee of Longwood Gardens for six years.

Steve enjoys all plants and has a particular fondness for orchids. He wrote *Orchids For Dummies* (Wiley) as well as *Fragrant Orchids* and *Miniature Orchids* (Timber Press).

Steve is now president of his own horticultural consulting firm, where he works with various companies in the green industry on writing, photography, marketing, and public relations issues.

**The National Gardening Association (NGA),** founded in 1973 and operating within the United States, is a not-for-profit leader in plant-based education. The organization is esteemed for its award-winning Web sites and newsletters, grants and curricula for youth gardens, and research for the lawn-and-garden industry. NGA's mission is to advance the personal, community, and educational benefits of gardening by supporting gardeners, communities, and teachers with information and resources. For more information, please visit www.garden.org.

# Dedication

This book is for all new and veteran gardeners who have discovered or are about to realize the lifelong wonders and pleasures of gardening and the plant world. Please remember that gardening isn't primarily about an end result but about the therapeutic aspects of the journey itself. Enjoy the process, and don't rush it. Let gardening become an integral part of your life. You'll be much richer for it.

# Authors' Acknowledgements

**From Liz:** *Gardening Basics For Canadians For Dummies* wouldn't exist without a second pair of eyes, the very capable Tina Forrester. Tina checked facts and caught spelling mistakes, and offered her sage advice when called upon. Tina is a pro.

I'd also like to say how much I appreciate the support of the capable and easygoing Robert Hickey, who oversaw the project and was a joy to work with. Copy editor Andrea Douglas ensured that every sentence was just right, and Pamela Vokey kept the whole project running smoothly. Many thanks also to Janet Davis, who always has hundreds of just-right photos to choose from and generously loans out her light box so the choice can be made at one's leisure.

Thanks also to the many experts in gardening who answered knotty questions and passed along their wisdom. There are too many to thank individually, but you know who you are.

**From Steven:** Simply put, this book wouldn't be possible without the help and advice of Teri Dunn. I am deeply indebted to her.

Natalie Harris, my project editor, was a joy to work with. She cheerfully kept me on track and shepherded the myriad parts of this book to completion, so without her, this work wouldn't have made it to print.

I've been pleased and privileged over the years to witness the good works of the National Gardening Association (NGA). Thanks to this organization, I received the opportunity to produce this book. I hope it does justice to their mission of bringing the joys of gardening to all.

Charlie Nardozzi, a horticulturist with the National Gardening Association, was generous with his time in reviewing and making helpful suggestions for each of the chapters. It was super having a person with his gardening experience looking over my shoulder.

Putting together a detailed outline for a book takes much time and thought. For this book, Michael MacCaskey tackled this important job. Hats off to him for his thoroughness.

As with any book project, the spouse or companion of the writer suffers from neglect. My wife, Sascha, never wavered in her patience and understanding. She has always been supportive and loving, and I'm lucky to have her as my wife!

And last, I mustn't forget Zoe and Ginger, our two dogs, who always kept me company and face every day with enthusiasm.

## Publisher's Acknowledgements

We're proud of this book; please send us your comments at `canadapt@wiley.com`.

Some of the people who helped bring this book to market include the following:

*Acquisitions, Editorial, and Media Development*

**Project Editor:** Natalie Faye Harris, US edition

**Editor:** Robert Hickey

**Copy Editor:** Andrea Douglas, Colbourne Communications

**Cover Photos:** © Jim Cummins/Corbis

**Interior Photos:** © Janet Davis

**Cartoons:** Rich Tennant (`www.the5thwave.com`)

*Composition Services*

**Project Coordinators:** Lynsey Stanford, Pamela Vokey

**Layout and Graphics:** Reuben W. Davis, Alissa D. Ellet, Ronald Terry

**Proofreaders:** Laura Bowman, Todd Lothery

**Indexer:** Belle Wong

---

*John Wiley & Sons Canada, Ltd.*

**Bill Zerter,** Chief Operating Officer

**Jennifer Smith,** Vice-President and Publisher, Professional and Trade Division

*Publishing and Editorial for Consumer Dummies*

**Diane Graves Steele,** Vice President and Publisher, Consumer Dummies

**Joyce Pepple,** Acquisitions Director, Consumer Dummies

**Kristin A. Cocks,** Product Development Director, Consumer Dummies

**Michael Spring,** Vice President and Publisher, Travel

**Kelly Regan,** Editorial Director, Travel

*Publishing for Technology Dummies*

**Andy Cummings,** Vice President and Publisher, Dummies Technology/General User

*Composition Services*

**Gerry Fahey,** Vice President of Production Services

**Debbie Stailey,** Director of Composition Services

# Contents at a Glance

# Table of Contents

# Introduction

· · · · · · · · · · · · · · · · · · · · · · · · · · · · · · · · · · · · · · · · · · · · · ·

*A*ren't you lucky! You're entering or are already part of the most popular and rewarding lifelong hobby in Canada. Gardening is a common language that knows no national, socioeconomic, or age boundaries — it's a common thread that binds many of us together. Whether you're discussing your outrageous zucchini harvest or sharing your secret tips for prizewinning roses, you've probably already found that gardeners have an instant bond, no matter what their level of experience.

Because gardening is a huge topic that encompasses a wide field of cultivation interests and disciplines, it's impossible for any one book to cover everything there is to know. However, when you're armed with the gardening basics, like those presented in this book, you're ready for just about anything that the art of gardening can throw at you.

Sure, gardening requires some exertion. But it's healthy exercise. You feel a great sense of accomplishment when the flower beds are weeded, the bulbs are planted, and the seeds are sown. It's primal. And reaping the rewards of your labour — by cutting flowers for your dinner party or fresh herbs for your salad — is a special joy that makes the noisy, electronic stimulation that surrounds us (cars, phones, MP3 players, and the like) seem trivial. Gardening fosters a deep satisfaction that nurtures your body and soul. That's why this book, *Gardening Basics For Canadians For Dummies,* exists. In addition to giving you basic pointers on how to make your gardening as successful and rewarding as possible, it's a celebration of the art and sheer joy of gardening.

## About This Book

In this book, we distill our combined 80 years of gardening experience as well as the knowledge of our gardening friends and the experts we've consulted. We all share our know-how with each other.

We hope you enjoy reading this book as well as discovering something about your new hobby. We try to add a little levity here and there, too. Sometimes gardeners can get too serious about their pursuit, but gardening should relieve anxiety, not add to it. In fact, gardening is mostly fun, even when it's hard work (which, sometimes, it is). But whatever sweat you produce is good, honest sweat, and the results are rewarding. Remember, too, that making mistakes (and you will) isn't a big deal. Gardens recover quickly from our bumbling efforts to care for them. They grow back — sometimes better than before.

Our mission with this book is to bring you gardening success and the inimitable pleasure that comes from it. It's no fun if all your efforts end up in the compost pile.

Following the classic *For Dummies* format, this book gives you the most basic gardening information you need, organized and presented in an easy-to-follow, modular manner. Although you can read it from cover to cover, you don't have to. This book can function as a reference work, so you can jump in, find what you need, and get back to your stand of birch trees or the koi pond or the garden centre — or wherever else you'd like to be.

After reading this book, you may not be an expert, but you'll be well on your way to taking on most gardening tasks with new confidence. Gardening is part science and part art, and how you mix them up is a very personal thing. After getting a handle on the basics presented here, you can move on to develop your own style and techniques that work best for you.

# Conventions Used in This Book

As you advance in gardening, you find that in certain branches of horticulture (like perennials, some trees and shrubs, and orchids), you're confronted with dreaded scientific names (usually Latin, sometimes Greek). People use such names in these plant categories for very legitimate reasons, and you can choose to follow the path to those reasons later. For now, we spare you that step by using common names for plants throughout this book. As is typical of all *For Dummies* books, we also shy away from as much jargon as possible and explain any commonly used terms right away (often in parentheses following the term). New, defined terms may also appear *italic*. Horticulture and gardening can be as technical as any other science, but this isn't a textbook for Horticulture 101!

The Internet is part of life now and can provide oodles of great gardening information, so we include various Web references. Web addresses appear in `monofont`. When this book was printed, some Web addresses may have needed to break across two lines of text. If that happened, rest assured that we haven't put in any extra characters (such as hyphens) to indicate the break. When using one of these Web addresses, just type exactly what you see in this book, pretending that the line break isn't there.

# What You're Not to Read

If you're short on time and just want to get down to the nitty-gritty, skip the stuff in the grey boxes. We include this sidebar information for those of you who want to know the *whys* of everything or who just want to dig deeper.

# *Foolish Assumptions*

Because you're reading this book, we assume that you, like us, really love gardening. Here are some other things we assume regarding your possible background and interest in gardening:

- ✔ You've seen other folks' gardens that have inspired you, so now you want to bring your own gardening skill to the next level.

- ✔ You're concerned about maintaining a healthy diet and want to grow some of your own herbs, fruits, and vegetables.

- ✔ Your lawn is looking on the tattered side, so you want to spruce it up a bit.

- ✔ You've moved into a new place, and the landscaping is nonexistent or dreadful, so you want to change it.

- ✔ You love outdoor living, and you want to improve the space around you.

- ✔ You like the idea of gardening, but don't know where to start.

# *How This Book Is Organized*

The basic goal of every chapter is to give you the information you need to go out and create a garden, or at least plant something, no matter what your level of experience. You may already know a lot about roses, for example, but perhaps you want information on how to start an annual flower bed; the chapters in this book can help out in that regard. Even if your primary interest is in growing roses or day lilies, or in setting up a basic vegetable garden, you can find useful information in every chapter that you can apply to your planting project.

This book includes six parts, which are further divided into chapters. Check out the following sections for an overview of what you can find in each part.

## *Part 1: Preparing Yourself (And Your Garden) for Planting*

Sometimes just getting started can be the hardest part. In this part of the book, your wheels begin turning. Chapter 1 introduces you to the main garden players — annuals, perennials, trees, shrubs, vines, and groundcovers — and explains their roles. Chapter 2 helps you put together your grand plan and gives you some ideas about types of gardens to consider and questions to ask yourself. In Chapter 3, we explain what hardiness zones are and why you should care about them. Chapter 4 puts your spade in the ground with the basics of garden preparation and your plants' basic needs. And having the right garden tools makes a big difference, so Chapter 5 takes all the mystery out of tool selection and use.

# Part II: Flowers and Foliage: Growing for Colour

Foliage is nice, but most people are in gardening for colour. Chapter 6 deals with the almost ever-blooming flowers and frequently dazzling colours of annuals — which ones to choose and how to use them best. Recently, perennials have been the hottest category of plant, probably because of their immense variety and year-after-year performance. These repeat performers are detailed in Chapter 7. Nothing can perk up your spirits after a long winter better than spring-flowering bulbs, or give late colour like the summer-flowering types; that's what Chapter 8 is all about. Chapter 9 introduces you to Canada's — perhaps the world's — favourite flower: the rose. In this chapter, you find tips on which roses are easiest to grow and which are most fragrant.

# Part III: Stretching Your Garden beyond Its Boundaries: The Permanent Landscape

The lawn frames everything in the garden and is the family playground during the summer. Chapter 10 can help you grow a lawn that you can be proud of. Trees and shrubs are considered to be the "bones" of the garden because they define its shape and are present for many years. We introduce you to the foundation plants that best suit your needs in Chapter 11. And don't forget vines and groundcovers — they can serve as the icing on your garden cake; see Chapter 12.

# Part IV: Producing Your Own Produce

What can possibly match the flavour of your own warm, vine-ripened tomatoes? Or fresh, ripe strawberries and raspberries? That's what Part IV is about: homegrown produce. It's healthy and delicious. Veggies start off this part in Chapter 13, followed by Chapter 14 on the pleasures of how to grow and enjoy herbs. And Chapter 15 shows you how you can have all the fruits and berries you want.

## Part V: Designing Special and Fun Gardens

This part covers what gardening is really all about — fun! Chapter 16 tells you what you need to know about the extremely popular form of gardening that even space-challenged gardeners can enjoy: container gardening. Water gardens have become the rage not only because of the exotic plants they display but also because of the wildlife (including fish and frogs) they provide homes for. Skip to Chapter 17 for details on water gardening.

## Part VI: The Part of Tens

Of course, this wouldn't be a *For Dummies* book without a Part of Tens. This part is where you go when you want information fast. Chapter 18 gives you answers to the ten most commonly asked garden questions. If you're handy and like gardening projects, see Chapter 19. Getting the kids involved in gardening early in life is a great idea, so check out projects they'll love in Chapter 20. Along with the pleasure of gardening comes our responsibility to be good stewards of our land. Chapter 21 gives you some easy-to-follow tips that can make a real, positive difference to our precious and vulnerable environment.

# Icons Used in This Book

Icons are the cute little pictures that show up in the margins of the book, right next to certain blocks of text. Here's what those icons stand for:

This image points out some ecological tips that you can follow and use to ensure that your gardening is truly Earth friendly.

Gardeners sometimes speak their own lingo, which can be a bit confusing for people who are just getting their feet wet (or dirty) in the gardening process. This icon helps to identify and clarify the most common terms you encounter.

This icon points out some major ideas in the book — stuff well worth remembering.

The *Tip* icon flags notable gardening information that even experienced gardeners may not know. This info can save you time and frustration.

This icon alerts you to possible problems to watch out for or avoid. These problems may result in injury or, at the very least, a bad gardening experience.

# Where to Go from Here

A great thing about *For Dummies* books is that you can start anywhere you want — one part or chapter doesn't depend on any other. For example, if you're interested in growing your own fruit, head right to Chapter 15. No need to start anywhere else!

That said, if you feel more comfortable getting a basic grounding (so to speak) in gardening before plunging right in, start with Part I, Chapter 1. If you're reevaluating or starting your garden from scratch, then any of the other chapters in Part I are good places to begin. After that, where you go is really up to you, based on your most pressing gardening needs or pleasures.

# Part I

# Preparing Yourself (And Your Garden) for Planting

The 5th Wave                    By Rich Tennant

©RICHTENNANT

DON'T PULL

SOMETHING

NOT SURE

WAIT AND SEE

DELPH. MAYBE

?

WHO KNOWS?

"That should do it."

## In this part . . .

Ready to do some gardening? Even if you don't think you're ready to get your hands dirty (or if you're not sure), the chapters in Part I can help you get started. These chapters give you an overview of the gardening process. They show you how to set up everything for your dream garden and arm you with the knowledge vital to successful gardening — which plants you can grow in your area and what they need to thrive, how best to take advantage of the gardening space you have, and how to design the right plans and acquire the right tools to make your garden a reality.

# Chapter 1

# Getting Ready for Gardening

*N*o matter what your main gardening interest — be it growing vegetables, making your yard colourful with flowers, picking out just the right tree, or aspiring to have the most gorgeous roses on the block — chances are that you care most about the plants. Sure, gardening can also involve landscaping and lawn care (see the chapters in Part III of this book), or being able to grow your own food (see Part IV), or just having a great excuse to play in the dirt (see Part V), but for most people, the plants make everything worthwhile.

Of course, keeping your plants alive and making them look their best involves a lot of preparation. There's information on caring for your garden plants throughout this book, but if you really want your plants to grow, thrive, and look their absolute best, read through the first few chapters especially.

Okay, yeah, we know you already know you need to plan and prepare your soil to get your garden going, but you *really* just want to read about plants right now, right? In that case, the rest of this chapter is devoted to the most basic explanations of the kinds of plants you may encounter in the world of gardening. Later chapters in this book go into much more detail about the various types of plants, trees, bushes, and vines, but in this one, you get a sense of how plants are similar and how they are different — the first step in turning a brown thumb green. First, though, here's a bit about plant names.

## Playing the Name Game

What's in a name? For gardeners, plenty. Gardening is a blend of horticulture and botany, common names and high science, and the names can get a bit confusing. Whether you're looking at plant anatomy or simply want to know what to call a plant, understanding a bit about naming can help you wade through the aisles, ask better questions, and treat your plants right.

## *Hello, my name is . . . : Getting used to plant nomenclature*

Whenever you're talking about plants, knowing how they're named can help you avoid getting tangled up in the Latin. Generally, when looking for plants and flowers, you encounter two types of names: botanical and common. Read on for some info on how the naming system works, and then *carpe diem — pluck the day!*

### *Botanical names*

The *botanical name* is the proper or scientific name of a plant. It consists of two parts: the genus name and the species name. The *species name* is kind of like your own first name (except it comes last in a plant's botanical name). The *genus name* is similar to your family name (except in botanical names, it comes first). For example, in the plant name *Hosta undulata, Hosta* is the genus name and *undulata* is the species name. *Hosta* describes an entire genus of famous, mostly shade-loving plants named hostas, and *undulata* describes the type of hosta it is — a hosta with an undulating leaf shape.

Sometimes, the botanical name has a third name, right after the species name, known as the variety. A *variety* is a member of the same plant species but looks different enough to warrant its own name, such as *Rosa gallica* var. *officinalis.*

Still another botanical name that sometimes comes up is the *cultivar,* or cultivated variety. Cultivars are usually named by the people who developed or discovered them, and they're often maintained through cuttings, line-bred seed propagation, or tissue culture. In other words, they're cultivated (humans grow, improve, and develop them). An example is *Lychnis coronaria* 'Angel's Blush'.

A *hybrid* plant is the result of the cross-pollination of two genetically different plants, usually of the same species but different varieties. This combination can happen because of cultivation, or it can occur naturally through bee pollination between two different plants.

Botanical names are more common with some types of plants than others. For instance, you frequently run into botanical names with herbaceous plants, trees, and shrubs, but much less so with roses, annuals, and vegetables. You can find botanical names on the plants' labels and in many garden references.

## Sharing names with distant relatives

If you want to be absolutely sure of the plant you're buying, then remember that the botanical or scientific name, including the cultivar name, is the most exact one. Some common names, like common basil, are very specific. All common basil has the same genus and species, *Ocimum basilicum.* However, a common name like daisy is so general that it may not be very helpful, because it can apply to plants very faintly related and found in various genera. For instance, a daisy can be an African daisy (*Arctotis* or *Gerbera*), Dahlberg daisy *(Dyssodia tenuiloba),* English daisy *(Bellis perennis),* painted daisy *(Chrysanthemum coccineum),* Shasta daisy *(Leucanthemum superbum),* and many others. If you're shopping by common names, read labels to make sure the particular kind of plant you're looking at can grow for you.

### Common names

Common names are what you're most likely to encounter when shopping for plants to put in your garden, and they're what you encounter most in this book. You can find these names prominently displayed on seed packets or on seedling trays of plants that are for sale. Common names are kind of like botanical nicknames that gardeners use to describe a certain type of plant without going into a great amount of detail. For example, the *Hosta undulata* fits into the genus *Hosta,* so most gardeners merely refer to these plants under the common name of hostas. And you may know that *Hemerocallis* is actually the genus name for the common day lily, but chances are that most gardeners you encounter just call them day lilies.

## Anatomy 101: Naming plant parts

Beyond recognizing the names of plants, knowing the various parts of plants is also useful. Figure 1-1 shows a nice, healthy perennial plant with the basic parts displayed. You probably already know most of them, but keep these parts in mind, because you need to know them to understand some of the things we discuss in the rest of this book! In the figure, the *taproot* is the main root of the plant; the *stolon,* or *runner,* is a horizontal stem that spreads through the ground to help some perennials propagate.

When you know the parts of plants and the differences among all the plant names you run into, you're ready to get the lowdown on the types of plants out there!

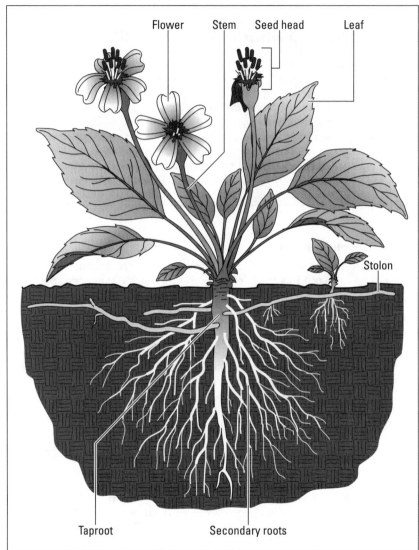

Flower    Stem    Seed head    Leaf

Stolon

**Figure 1-1:**
The basic
parts of a
perennial
plant, above
and below
ground.

Taproot    Secondary roots

# Bringing in Beauty with Flowers (And Foliage)

Flowers are often the first thing that comes to mind when people think of gardening, and they're the first thing people plan to grow when they want to beautify their surroundings. Flowers are marvellous because they come in a huge variety of sizes, colours, and shapes (see Figure 1-2) — and no matter where you live, at least one kind of flowering plant can grow there. Even in Canada's Arctic Region, hundreds of varieties of flowering plants — including the mountain avens, fireweed, and purple saxifrage (the official flowers of the Northwest Territories, Yukon, and Nunavut, respectively) — have adapted to be able to survive and bloom in the tundra.

**Figure 1-2:** Flowers come in a wide variety of sizes and shapes, as these popular flowers show.

Flowers are more than merely the beautiful display they put on, however. If you know the different types of flowers out there, you can take full advantage of displaying them in your own garden. Read on for info on annuals and perennials, as well as a bit on bulbs and roses.

## Amazing annuals

You may already know what annuals are without realizing that you know! These beauties are the flowers, arrayed in flats and pots, for sale every spring down at the garden centre — everything from geraniums to impatiens to marigolds. You bring them home and plunk 'em in the ground, and they get right to work, delivering pretty much continuous colour all summer long. When fall comes, they start to slow down (some may even go to seed); cold weather eventually causes them to wither and die. Game over. (That is, unless you live in a really mild part of Canada; in that case, your "annuals" may become perennials. See "Perennial plants," later in this chapter, for more information.)

For the brief time annuals are growing and pumping out flowers, you get a lot of bang for your buck. A great deal of selection and breeding refinements over the years have made these plants totally reliable. They're hard to kill. Indeed, some of them keep blooming their cheery heads off even when you neglect them.

More sophisticated gardeners have been known to sneer at good old annuals. They're boring. They're *too* perky. They're "plastic plants." These folks may or may not have a point, but hey, annuals are hard to beat if you want a colourful garden.

In the end, the main drawback of annuals is economic: You have to buy new ones every spring. If you're planting a wide area, running out to buy more annuals, year in and year out, can get expensive. Time may also be an issue for you — you may grow sick and tired of getting down on your hands and knees and replanting. (If you're getting to that point, consider planting perennials — see the section later in this chapter.)

You can use annuals

- ✔ To fill an entire flower bed (this popular use is why some places call annuals *bedding plants*)
- ✔ In container displays — in pots, window boxes, patio planter boxes, and more
- ✔ To fill a hanging basket
- ✔ To edge a walkway
- ✔ For "spot colour" in a perennial bed
- ✔ In edging and as decoration for a vegetable or herb garden
- ✔ To cover over, or at least distract from, a fading spring bulb display

If you can't find the info you want on annuals in this chapter, you can get an in-depth look in Chapter 6.

### Caring for and feeding annuals

Luckily, taking proper care of annuals is not rocket science. For the most part, annuals are easygoing, because they're bred to be quite tough and durable. Many annuals can withstand some neglect and still be productive — not that we recommend ignoring them!

Without a doubt, water is an annual's number-one need. All that lusty growth and continuous flowering require fuel. A thirsty plant can't sustain the show for long. Regular, deep soakings are best because they reliably supply water to the roots, which leads to a stress-free life of consistent growth and bud and bloom production. Note that a drying-out plant favours its roots and, to a lesser extent, its leaves in a bid for survival, automatically jettisoning its water-hogging buds and petals (see Chapter 4 for more info on watering).

You can't deny that regular doses of plant food significantly boost your annuals (make sure you apply it according to directions). The leaves become healthier and greener, and you end up with more buds and flowers. (Chapter 4 contains information on fertilizer as well.)

The rather unromantic term of *deadheading* simply refers to the practice of pinching or cutting off spent flowers. Your annuals look nicer when you do this, of course, but removing the flowers also serves another purpose: It thwarts the plant from the energy-intensive process of producing seeds, and the plant responds by diverting its energy back into making more flowers.

### *Favourite annuals*

If you shop earlier in spring (before the garden centre has been picked clean, we mean) or go to a place with a big selection, you see lots of choices. If you find certain types too boring or common, look around for alternatives — one big trend these days is familiar annuals in new colours, even bicolours. Get creative! Have some fun! Here are some popular annuals:

- ✔ **Sun lovers:** Angelonia, California poppy, cleome, cosmos, geranium, lobelia, marigold, million bells, nasturtium, nicotiana, petunia, portulaca, salvia, and zinnia

- ✔ **Shade lovers:** Ageratum, cineraria, coleus, forget-me-not, impatiens, nemophila, pansy, primrose, sweet William, vinca, wax begonia

- ✔ **Unusual, offbeat, but still easy annuals:**

  - • **Eustoma:** A plant with very long-lasting, silklike flowers

  - • **Feverfew:** An annual covered with double, mostly white chrysanthemum-like flowers

  - • **Annual foxglove:** A plant with charming, nodding flowers on a tall spike, adding a dramatic vertical element to any garden

  - • **Honesty (money plant):** An annual grown for its translucent quarter-shaped seed pods that make it choice for dried arrangements

  - • **Larkspur:** A plant that's easy to grow by directly sowing the seeds in your garden in the early spring

  - • **Nemophila:** A plant with sky-blue cup flowers on compact mounded plants

- **Nierembergia:** A ground-hugging plant covered with purple cup-shaped flowers

- **Stock:** An annual with a heavenly fragrance and flowers from white to pink to purple

- **Torenia:** A flower that looks like an open-faced snapdragon on compact plants, in shades of blue, pink, and white; also called wishbone flower because of the shape of the stamen

### Raising annuals from seed

Of course you can raise annuals from seed! Some annuals are simpler to grow than others. Annuals with very small seeds, like snapdragons and begonias, are a bit more of a challenge because you need to start them indoors on a bright windowsill or under fluorescent lights.

Just buy the seed packets in late winter and sow them in flats or pots (particular directions are always on the backs of the packets). Raise the seedlings indoors until spring weather comes and the soil warms up and all danger of frost is past; then move the plants outside.

Some annuals are so fast growing that you can sprinkle their seeds on good soil in late spring, right outside, and they'll quickly sprout and grow. This group includes popular annuals like zinnias, marigolds, and nasturtiums. This process may require you to do some thinning at some point, but otherwise, it's dead easy. Again, consult the back of the seed packet for details. One advantage to this tack is that you can grow some more unconventional or rare annuals. It certainly makes for a more interesting garden!

### Beholding a one-time show

The very definition of an *annual* — a plant that goes from seed to flowering to death in one season, completing its entire life cycle in short order — states that annuals are a one-time show. When it's over, it's over.

## Annuals that aren't really annuals

False annuals are plants with tropical origins, or ones whose parents hail from the tropics, which means that they're actually perennial — more long-lived — somewhere, somewhere warmer, somewhere far away. If you live in one of the mildest parts of Canada, these pseudo-annuals can, at least in theory, be kept going over the winter and live to dress up your garden again next year. Examples of these tropical visitors include the coleus, geranium, salvia, and snapdragon.

If you garden in a cold climate, you can try digging up some favourites or bringing potted annuals inside. Keep the plants in a nonfreezing place, out of direct sunlight, and let them rest. Cut back all spent growth. Start reviving them with water and plant food when spring returns.

However, if despite your best efforts, your wintered-over annuals don't return to their former glory the following spring, accept their fate, pull them out, and replace them with new ones.

# *Perennial plants*

For many gardeners, going from growing annuals to exploring perennials seems to be a natural progression. But remember that you don't have to choose! You can grow both, and indeed, your garden is likely to be the better for the diversity.

So what, exactly, are *perennials?* They're long-lived herbaceous (nonwoody) plants — flowers and herbs, mainly. How long perennials last depends on the plant and the conditions in your garden. But these plants certainly last longer than annuals.

A typical perennial emerges in the spring, grows and often produces flowers and seeds as the seasons progress from spring to summer to fall, and then slows down or dies back in winter. But the plant doesn't actually die; it just rests. The following spring, your perennial returns in glory to repeat the cycle.

Unlike annuals, you don't have to replant perennials every year. Once should be enough — well, if you choose wisely and take good care of your perennials, you ought to get many good years out of them.

Eventually, though, some perennials run out of steam. Their growth gets crowded and they don't seem to flower as well. At this time, you can dig them out and replace them, or you can divide them (perhaps discarding the tired-out centre, or mother plant) and replant well-rooted bits for a fresh new start (Chapter 7 can give you tips on division).

Here are some of the many uses of perennials:

- Creating a colourful bed or border
- Filling an *island bed* (an isolated, self-contained garden, like an island in a sea of lawn)
- Mixing them with annuals to assure summer-long colour

> ✔ Edging a walkway, patio, pool area, or deck
>
> ✔ Interplanting them with roses or other ornamental shrubs to provide year-round interest
>
> ✔ Dressing up an area that was formerly lawn

For the nitty-gritty details on perennials, check out Chapter 7. If you just want the basics, read on.

### Caring for and feeding perennials

The water needs of perennials vary. Some are moisture lovers, others are drought tolerant, and many are somewhere in the middle. Do your homework when choosing plants, not just on what they prefer but on which ones are suitable to the growing conditions in your yard and climate (otherwise, you'll be jumping through hoops trying to please them). Chapter 2 can help you get a grip on how to plan your garden.

One generalization is possible, though: Nothing makes newly planted perennials feel more welcome than does plentiful water. The perennials have gone from a sheltered and confining life in a pot to the wide world of your garden, and water helps sustain the roots and encourages them to establish themselves and expand into their new home.

Many perennials (like most people) enjoy being fed. They respond by growing more robustly and producing more flowers. You're fine with a general, all-purpose garden fertilizer, applied according to the label directions during the height of the growing season. Don't feed your perennials as fall approaches and growth naturally begins to slow. You don't want them producing a fresh new flush of growth that soon gets nipped by a frost. (For some general info on fertilizing, see Chapter 4.)

We have to admit that fertilizing the majority of perennials isn't mandatory. If you plant perennials in soil that suits them (and do your homework when choosing the plants), they may do just fine without fertilizer. Good, organically rich soil, good growing conditions, and regular water can sustain healthy, hearty perennial growth for quite some time. Fertilizing merely supplies a boost in these cases.

### Favourite perennials

Lots of places offer perennials these days. The garden centres in spring and early fall are full of them. Unless the place is especially big or sophisticated, you find mostly common, tried-and-true choices. If you get a taste for the more unusual perennials, or common ones in uncommon colours, turn to mail-order or Internet shopping. What's out there may astound you — thousands and thousands of fascinating and beautiful plants await!

## In on the ground floor: Groundcovers

Low-growing perennial plants may be handy in a flower border (near the front where they won't be blocked from view) or as an edging, but they have another, very practical use: You can plant entire areas with them, and they can form a low-care carpet. They're especially nice for shady areas where lawn won't grow.

Some favourite groundcovers include ajuga, candytuft, creeping phlox, epimedium, ivy, lamium, lily-of-the-valley, pachysandra, sweet woodruff, and verbena.

For details on groundcovers, please turn to Chapter 12.

Here are some favourites:

- **Sun perennials:** Black-eyed Susan, coneflower, coreopsis, day lily, delphinium, gaura, hardy geranium, iris, penstemon, peony, phlox, pincushion flower, poppy, Russian sage, salvia, sedum, and Shasta daisy
- **Shade perennials:** Astilbe, bergenia, bleeding heart, brunnera, ferns, foamflower, goatsbeard, hellebore, heuchera, hosta, Solomon's seal, spiderwort, and violet

### Looking at life span

The life cycle of a perennial depends on various factors, notably the type of plant and whether it's happy in your garden. But you can certainly expect to get a minimum of two years and a maximum of a decade out of the vast majority of perennials. For best results, of course, take good care of them.

Most perennials are slow starters. During their first year in your garden, they tend to invest in developing a good root system. Be patient! After their roots are established, perennials grow and expand, and the flower show gets better with each passing year. You can hurry things along by fertilizing regularly during the height of the growing season (see Chapter 4 for fertilizing details) and getting a head start by planting in the fall.

### Considering fall planting

If you shop for perennials in late summer and get them in the ground a good six weeks or more before the first frost, those plants will definitely have a head start over their spring-planted counterparts. In fall, the soil is still warm and welcoming, and drenching fall rains can help water the new kids. Depending on the severity of your winter, cutting back any new growth and mulching when winter is just around the corner may be good ideas.

For much more on perennials, please turn to Chapter 7.

## Bulbs and roses

Bulbs, which store their food underground, are a richly varied group of plants. The best-known bulbs, like tulips and daffodils, are spring flowering, but these plants represent only the tip of the iceberg. Many other bulbs, like dahlias and lilies, are summer bloomers. What bulbs all have in common is that they're easy to grow and produce plenty of flowers — just provide them a sunny, well-drained spot, stand back, and let them do their thing (see Chapter 8 for info on bulbs).

Although bulbs are quite popular, roses are one of Canada's favourite flowers, and for many reasons. They epitomize romance and come in an impressive range of flower colours, not to mention their inimitable delicious fragrances. Lucky for us, modern rose breeders have worked their wonders on this plant to produce roses that are not only stunningly beautiful but also tough as nails.

Roses are no longer the wimps that gardeners loved to think about growing but were afraid to try because of their reputation for being magnets to every known plant disease and insect pest. Today's varieties are also available in a range of plant habits, from upright to bush forms to those that are ground hugging. Chapter 9 can fill you in on growing roses.

# Gardening for Your Dining Pleasure

For many gardeners, growing food is the real reason for gardening. There really isn't quite anything like the feeling of satisfaction a gardener gets from nurturing and encouraging a tomato plant to put forth the most gorgeous and delicious tomatoes imaginable, or harvesting a healthy and tasty bunch of berries from a tree planted right in the front yard.

Food-bearing plants come in all shapes, sizes, and types, from annuals and perennials, to trees and bushes, to vines that creep along the ground or climb to impressive heights when given the right support. Chapter 13 gives you the information you need to get started on growing your own vegetables. Chapter 14 is devoted to herbs and how you can grow them to enhance the dishes that come out of your kitchen. And Chapter 15 gives you the lowdown on the different kinds of fruit that you can grow and enjoy.

# Working with Woody (Or Viney) Plants

Woody plants consist of shrubs, some vines, and trees. Though we mention this group last in this chapter, it's probably a more important garden element than annuals and perennials simply because of the space that woody plants take up over the long term. You may have inherited some trees and shrubs when you moved into your present home, or you may be considering replacing what you have or installing some new ones. Whatever you're thinking, choose and act wisely. Allow these bigger plants the elbow room, the deeper prepared soil, and the light they may need.

The reason trees, shrubs, and some vines are called *woody plants* is that the bulk of their stems and branches are, well, woody — not herbaceous. This growth doesn't wither or die back in the wintertime. Yes, the leaves, flowers, fruits, berries, and seeds may fade and fall off, but the rest of the plant, its "bones," so to speak, abides. And with each passing year, the main stem or trunk grows another layer thicker, and the plant may add additional branches or woody stems. No wonder woody plants are considered to be more or less permanent, and certainly substantial, parts of a home landscape.

The difference between a shrub (or bush) and a tree can be pretty tenuous. *Shrubs* usually have multiple stems that branch close to the ground, and the plants are often at least as wide as they are tall. *Trees* are usually higher than they are wide, tend to be larger than shrubs, and usually have one or just a few predominant stems or trunks. These definitions become foggier when a very large shrub gets pruned to one stem to look like a tree, or a small tree is trained to have multiple stems and is pruned to be a hedge. In these cases, are they trees or shrubs? Your call is as good as ours!

# Shrubs

You may choose flowering or evergreen shrubs. Both kinds are worthwhile in different ways. Just bear in mind that flowering shrubs tend to have a fairly brief period of glory, and then you're left with only foliage, so pick a shrub whose foliage you like. Good fall colour, leaves, and/or berries may also be factors in your decision. On the other hand, evergreen shrubs, whether broadleaf or needled, are valuable for long-term, consistent green colour and, in many cases, a denser-growing profile.

Favourite shrubs for home landscapes include

- **Flowering:** Azalea, broom, buckeye, burning bush, caragana, daphne, flowering quince, forsythia, fothergilla, hibiscus, hydrangea, mock orange, smoke bush, eastern sweetshrub, witch hazel, and winterberry

- **Broadleaf evergreen (with spring flowers and more-or-less evergreen foliage, some low growing):** Barberry, bearberry, bog rosemary, boxwood, cotoneaster, heath, holly, laurel, mahonia, mountain laurel, pieris, rhododendron, and rock rose

- **Evergreen:** Some cedars, some false cypresses, hemlock, juniper, some pines, some spruces, and yew

Take a look at some of the roles shrubs can play:

- Foundation planting (around the base of your house to add architectural interest, insulation, and security)
- Boundary and hedge plantings (possibly in addition to, or in lieu of, fencing)
- Individual, solo spots of colour (specimen plants)
- Mixed-border citizens for more architectural interest (use a mixture of shrubs, or mix one type of shrub with roses, perennials or vines, or all of these)
- Backdrops for a flower border
- Entryway, poolside, deckside, or privacy plantings

For much more on shrubs, please turn to Chapter 11.

## Trees

Trees can raise your property value, improve air quality, prevent erosion, lower your air-conditioning costs, and provide a handy support for your hammock. Not too shabby, eh?

For most home gardeners, trees in the landscape are often already present but need care and pruning to look good. Or you may be shopping for one or more ornamental or fruiting trees to add. As with shrubs, your options include *deciduous* types (ones that drop their leaves each fall; they may flower and fruit or have berries or seedpods) and *evergreen* ones (with leaves or needles that remain year-round).

Favourite trees for home landscapes include

- **Flowering and deciduous:** Catalpa, dogwood, golden chain tree, horse chestnut, ivory silk tree, Japanese maple, lilac, magnolia, redbud, serviceberry, and stewartia
- **Shade trees:** Ash, basswood, beech, catalpa, elm, ginkgo, honey locust, Kentucky coffee tree, linden, locust, various maples, various oaks, and sour gum
- **Evergreen:** Arborvitae, cedar, cypress, false cypress, fir, hemlock, juniper, pine, spruce, and yew
- **Fruit and nut trees:** Almond, apple, apricot, cherry, chestnut, crabapple, mulberry, peach, pear, plum, quince, serviceberry, and walnut

Trees can play the following roles:

✔ Shade

✔ Privacy (including noise reduction)

✔ Grandeur and substance in the landscape

✔ Food (fruits, berries, and nuts)

✔ Decorative beauty due to foliage (including fall colour!)

✔ Shelter and food for birds and other wild creatures

For much more information on trees in general, please turn to Chapter 11. For info on fruit and nut trees, check out Chapter 15.

# *Vines*

Annual vines such as morning glory, nasturtium, moonflower, gourds, and so on aren't woody, but vines — woody or not — can be a substantial presence in your landscape. Vines like to grow upward, though some need assistance in terms of guidance and/or support.

Some vines are valued mainly for their lush foliage, others for their flower and fruit, with attractive seed heads or berries by fall — all factors that naturally add to their appeal and affect placement and maintenance. Choose vines based on whether and when you want these extra, colour-contributing features. Also, when purchasing, be sure to inquire about predicted mature size!

Some of our favourite vines for home landscapes are

✔ Akebia

✔ Bittersweet

✔ Boston ivy

✔ Clematis

✔ Climbing hydrangea

✔ Climbing roses

✔ Dutchman's pipe

✔ Grape

✔ Honeysuckle

✔ Ivy

✔ Kiwi

✔ Silver lace

✔ Trumpet creeper

✔ Variegated porcelain vine

✔ Virginia creeper

✔ Winter creeper

✔ Wisteria

Roles vines can play include

- Cloaking or disguising a fence (especially if it's unattractive), or just using vines to make it into a more substantial barrier

- Climbing a trellis that's either against a wall or fence or out in the open (if well supported)

- Covering a gazebo to give shade and privacy as well as beauty

- Decorating a pillar, arbour, or pergola, adding shade and beauty as well as making a major contribution to your garden landscape

- Adding extra, vertical colour to your garden (which is especially nice if your garden is small or you want to give it a feeling of enclosure)

- Draping over an outbuilding or shed, an old or dead tree trunk, or another larger structure in need of some softening or disguise

- Providing flowers and edible fruit for decorating and eating

*Note:* Even ridiculously strong vines can't help you swing from tree to tree, namely because they're attached to the ground and not-so-attached at the top. (If you really don't want to stay grounded, Chapter 19 can give you info on installing a tire swing.)

For much more information on vines, please turn to Chapter 12. Climbing roses are addressed in more detail in Chapter 9.

# The World Is Flat: Caring for Your Lawn

Some gardeners love lawn care; others think it's just a necessary chore. Whichever way you feel, one thing can't be denied: Lawns, even small ones, can define a garden. They frame and provide a backdrop for all your other plants. If your lawn looks shabby, unfortunately, the rest of your garden creations just don't look as good.

We appreciate that everyone these days is pressed for time and can't spend the time to manicure their turf like golf course managers do, so in Chapter 10, we give you the basic, nitty-gritty information so that your lawn can do you proud without taking too much time away from the rest of your creative garden pursuits.

# Chapter 2

# Planning Your Own Eden

• • • • • • • • • • • • • • • • • • • • • • • • • • • • • • • • • • • • • • • • • • • • •

## In This Chapter

▶ Working with what you already have

▶ Deciding on your garden style

▶ Staying within your budget

▶ Setting up your garden plans

▶ Hiring a professional

• • • • • • • • • • • • • • • • • • • • • • • • • • • • • • • • • • • • • • • • • • • • •

Consider your ideal garden. Perhaps you know you want a handsome woodland shade garden, but what'll it look like? Or maybe you know you want a sunny cottage garden, but what's your vision? Beginning your garden planning is a bit like shopping for a blue shirt. You know you want a shirt, and you know you want it to be blue, but you still have plenty of options. Now's the time to narrow in on your target.

By assessing your gardening wants, your gardening needs, and what you already have available for your garden, you can come up with the best garden for you. This chapter leads you through the processes that can help you clarify your vision, and shows you how you can start making your dream garden a reality.

# Taking Stock: Evaluating What You Already Have

Observation! That's the very first step. Forget for a moment what's growing in your neighbours' yards or other home landscapes around town that you see and may covet. It's time to take a broader view — it's all part of the assessing process, a process that can lead you to a gorgeous, successful garden of your own. And don't forget that the garden is part of your yard in general. If you incorporate your garden plans into an overall plan for your yard, the yard itself can become a beautiful extension of the garden.

Identifying and spending some time analyzing what you already have are important steps in planning. After all, every yard is different and therefore presents a gardening challenge. You may be surprised, as you ponder, to discover that you can work quite well with what you already have, making seemingly minor changes to major effect.

Start by looking at the big picture. Here are the basic things to look for that affect your overall gardening plans. The following issues directly influence your planting decisions:

- **Local climate:** Over the course of a calendar year, is your area's climate dry or damp? Generally sunny or generally rainy? Do your winters just slow down the growth of many plants or bring almost everything to a temporary halt? In your own garden, do you have different microclimates, like sunny pockets that warm up in February or chilly places that hold frost until late spring? The answers to these questions can tell you which plants are likely to grow easily and which ones may require some extra help. See Chapter 3 for info about Plant Hardiness Zones, as well as microclimates, and how they affect your growing space.

- **Type of soil in your yard:** Consider the natural soil in your area. Is it rather sandy? Clay? Loamy (rich, crumbly, and dark)? Acidic? Alkaline? Does the soil drain rainwater away quickly, or does moisture puddle and linger for days? The answers can help you understand which plants will thrive and which ones will need soil improvements. (If you really don't have any idea what type of soil you have, a simple soil test can tell you — see Chapter 4.)

- **Plants native to your area (or already growing in your yard):** We're not asking that you make your entire garden out of native plants — after all, you may want to distinguish your yard from the surrounding natural landscape. But by finding out which plants (trees, shrubs, grasses, flowers) are native or perform well in your general area — by observing other people's gardens, by visiting parks and botanical gardens, or simply by asking around — you can fill yourself in on what kind of growing conditions you've been dealt.

  When looking at plants, make sure you don't choose *invasive exotics,* which are aggressive non-native plants that can escape your yard and run rampant. Your province or municipality may have its own list of invasive plants or noxious weeds, some of which can't be planted by law. For information and details on what to watch out for, see Chapter 21 or visit www.rbg.ca/cbcn/en/projects/invasives/invade1.html.

And here are some structural considerations for your garden:

- **Permanence of big structures:** Okay, the house stays. The garage and shed, too, although maybe you can move or replace the shed. What about shade trees? Can and should you cut any of them down, or at least prune them? Big branches may be a hazard, and letting more light into a garden is often welcome.

Before you remove a tree, check your local bylaws — some communities require a permit to remove trees more than a certain size.

✔ **Walkways:** It's hard, but not impossible, to change the path of foot traffic if it's currently in the way of your garden space. So take a hard look and be honest. If you add or replace a walking surface, the yard can look immediately nicer and your garden spot may be neatly outlined.

Options for installing a path include gravel, brick, flagstone, and other paving materials. Wandering paths look more graceful and slow down footsteps, but pathways should actually lead somewhere if you want people to use them. Wider paths also slow people down and encourage them to enjoy their surroundings — your beautiful garden.

✔ **Desire for privacy or shelter:** Good fences can make good neighbours, and materials make all the difference. Big, substantial wooden fences do block street noise and unsightly views, but they may also create shade and look unfriendly. A lighter or more open design may be better, perhaps softened with a flowering climbing plant. An alternative is planting living fences of hedges or an informal line of bushes (evergreen or deciduous, with or without fruit and flowers — turn to Chapter 11 for information). Work with what you have to improve your fence's look, or vow to install or replace it with something nicer.

Before making any major changes, consult with neighbours who'll be affected. If you live in a condominium, check the regulations to see what types of gardens are allowed and where they can be planted.

After evaluating the preceding items and the impact they'll have on your future garden, you may find that you have the start of a good plan for forming the boundaries and overall design of your garden.

Don't be intimidated by the beautifully designed and laid-out yards you see in your neighbourhood or admire in the pages of gardening magazines or books. But do steal ideas from them — other gardeners do! The point to remember is that transforming and beautifying your yard yourself, while bringing in outside help only if you think you need it, is perfectly possible. Like any other large project, you'll get further and feel better if you divide it into smaller parts.

## Identifying problems and restrictions

There are certain classic gardening "problems" and, thankfully, myriad solutions. Please don't ever feel overwhelmed — picking out an area to work on and improve and concentrating your efforts can buoy your spirits, and then you can move on to another concern. Our advice is to start first with an area you have the time and money to fix up — preferably an area you'd like to start enjoying sooner rather than later.

The main point is to take action. Address the big issues now, and you'll definitely feel well on your way to having a more beautiful, enjoyable garden. Read on for some basic problems.

### *You have too much shade*

A yard or garden space with a lot of shade is often lamented as forcing too many limitations on gardeners. Never fear! This problem is often much easier to remedy than you may think, usually just by pruning some trees and bushes:

1. **Go out with clippers and/or a small pruning saw to remove all "non-negotiable" branches and twigs — anything obviously dead or diseased, particularly the lower branches of thick trees.**

2. **Go on to thinning — taking out growth that's rubbing against other branches or crowding the interior of a plant.**

3. **Call in a certified arborist or a tree company for anything you can't handle.**

   You need the services of a tree company if you decide to take out an entire tree. Check with local authorities first; in some areas you need permission to cut down trees. In the end? More sun, more light, and more air — a whole new yard!

If a more permanent structure, such as a house or fence, causes your shade problem, you still have more planting options available than you may think. See the chapters in Parts II, III, and IV for a variety of ideas on how to grow in the shade.

 Regardless of whether bushes and shrubs are a shade problem, prune them by removing some or all of the offending thicket to keep your garden (and yard in general) looking good. Try an early-spring pruning foray. This is also the time to do drastic chopping back, say, if you want to reduce a hedge's height; cut no more than one-third at a time — you can prune again next season. Spring pruning encourages new growth, but you can also trim shrubs for shape in late summer, when plants are becoming dormant and won't put on a rush of new growth. This is a good time to trim for appearances, because you've had all summer to assess the garden and know where it looks overgrown or could use some stylistic help.

### *You have too much sun*

If your garden space is sunnier than you'd like, the quick solution is to add human-made items — try an umbrella or two, a pergola (arbour), an outdoor tent, or a retractable awning. For the long term, you can make a planting plan with shade trees (see Chapter 11) and vines that cover trellises and other structures (see Chapter 12).

## *Your yard is too big*

Here are three good ways to reduce that maintenance-demanding, water-hogging lawn and create ideal spaces for gardening:

✔ Create garden beds around the sides of the yard, widening or extending them as you can. Alternatively, create what landscapers call *island beds,* which are flat or mounded beds (in any shape and size you like) in the middle of a lawn.

✔ Add large, sprawling structures that take up a lot of yard space, such as

- Pathways

- A terrace, patio, or deck

- A pool (swimming or ornamental)

- A potting shed or gazebo

Adding garden beds around these structures really spruces things up.

✔ Fence in or otherwise enclose individual "garden rooms" within spaces in your yard. The fence can be an artificial one made of wood or metal, or it can be made of hedges, ornamental grasses, or trellises overhung with vines. Use your imagination!

## *Your yard is too little*

A small yard can seem bigger, more welcoming, and a lot more charming when you employ a few basic gardening techniques. With these methods, you can transform your cozy little yard into the garden of your dreams:

✔ Soften the edges of your lawn so they don't seem so imposing. If you have a fence, you can

- Paint the fence a neutral colour, like mouse grey or stormy blue (bright colours tend to advance and heighten the sense of constriction).

- Add lush vines or climbing roses.

- Adorn the fence with potted plants.

✔ Create a varied layering effect — that is, position different plant types and textures above and behind one another, stepping up to the edges of your yard. To add height and fool the eye into thinking the garden is fuller and more lush than it is, some gardeners display potted plants on a rack or stepladder placed in a bed of perennials and annuals.

✔ Add a focal point — a statue, a small fountain, or one spectacular pot or urn with a big, dramatic plant or showy combination of plants; this focal point draws attention away from the close boundaries.

### *Your soil isn't the type or quality you want*

More often than you may think, poor soil thwarts gardening plans. People just forget or underestimate the importance of having organically rich, well-draining ground to plant in.

To tackle this problem, try growing only those types of plants proven to work in your soil. See what the neighbours are growing in their gardens, or check with the local nursery for the best plants to grow in your area.

You can also amend the soil by digging in better materials, like compost, rotted leaves, or manure (this mixing is sort of like making cake batter, only more work). A rototiller is a handy tool to use for this purpose (see Chapter 5). Remember to work down to a depth of 15 to 20 centimetres (6 to 8 inches) for most garden plants — less for shallow-rooted grass, more for trees and shrubs.

### *You have too many weeds!*

You can attack these unwelcome plants any time of the year, but you'll make faster progress if you start in late fall or early spring and thwart them before or just as they're sprouting. Use a hoe, smother weeds with plastic or mulch, or carefully use a herbicide (check the bylaw section of your municipal government's Web site to see which products have been approved for use in your area), or use some combination of these tactics. Then, in midsummer, make sure you don't let weeds go to seed. Pull them, mow them down, and discard them outside your garden to keep them from coming back.

## *Taking advantage of your yard's assets*

Every garden space has its strengths and its good spots, if only you look, and some of the "problems" we mention in earlier sections can actually be benefits if you see them that way. You can save yourself a lot of time, effort, and grief by identifying these types of spots and working with what you have rather than knocking yourself out to impose an ambitious plan upon your garden space. Go with the flow, in other words! Here are a few examples of conditions you may find within your garden space and how to handle them:

- ✔ **Sunny days:** Bright sunshine is beloved by many plants, especially those with colourful flowers. Rejoice and be glad you have it; then go shopping for a wide range of bright and lively plants. Have fun with colour combinations. Full sun also affords you the opportunity to grow many vegetables, herbs, fruits, and water lilies. See the chapters ahead for details on choosing and growing the types of sun-loving plants that interest you.

✔ **The dark side:** If your lot in life is shade, don't fret. Consider it a gift, a chance to create a cool, soothing, even enchanting oasis. Without direct blasts from the hot sun, plants in a shady area look fresher and crisper for far longer. Wilting and withering in the heat aren't issues, colours don't get washed out, and not only do flowers last longer, but they also add sparkle and definition. For ideas, read the shade-gardening parts of Chapters 6 and 7.

✔ **Dry conditions:** Instead of knocking yourself out trying to provide water for thirsty plants, seek out ones that prosper in drier growing conditions. A nursery that offers native plants (and good-looking cultivars of the same) is a good place to start. You don't have to grow only sedums, coneflowers, and ornamental grasses, though you should check out the amazingly wide range of hybrids in all those varieties before you decide not to. Lots of exciting dry-ground, drought-tolerant plants are available to gardeners these days, including our native prickly pear cactus — a real conversation piece — which grows readily in many parts of Canada and boasts bright blooms in early summer.

✔ **Water:** If your yard's soggy or boggy, stop neglecting the area and letting the weeds grow or trying to dry it out. Instead, grow plants that relish damp ground. Loads of good-looking choices — large and small, tall and ground-covering, flowering and foliage — are available. Try red twig dogwoods, American lindens, marsh marigolds, cardinal flowers, blue flag irises, or Japanese primroses.

# Reclaiming the good garden hiding in your yard

Improving on what you already have in your yard is a quick and easy way to start enjoying a good garden. Timing is often key; that is, make your move at the right time, and the project will be less work and will yield faster results. If the project seems overwhelming, by all means, find or hire help.

To improve a flower bed, rake out all debris, remove all weeds, and add soil amendments in late fall or early spring. Plan what will go in, and remember to avoid overcrowding and to allow for each plant's mature size. Last but not least, mulch the bed to retain moisture and thwart

weeds so the bed will hopefully never get out of hand again.

You can reclaim a vegetable garden, even if it's full of weeds — chances are that the garden still has fairly good soil. Get weeds and debris out of there in fall or early spring, repair or install edging and/or fencing, and then dig in some organic matter for good measure (this step's easier now, before you add plants). Then cover the entire area with black plastic or a thick layer of mulch until you're ready to plant to keep out digging critters and thwart a resurgence of weeds.

# Getting Ideas for Your Garden Space

After you take inventory of your garden space and yard in general, consider what *sort* of garden you want. Before you get bogged down in choosing plants and deciding where to plant them, think in broad terms once again. How do you want to use your garden? What are your needs and expectations? Naming your goals can help you further clarify the details of your plans.

If we had one single, strong piece of advice to give you when deciding what type of garden to create — and we do! — it would be this: Be realistic. Identify, admit, and allow for special uses and considerations. Working within an honest, clear-eyed framework is so much easier. A beautiful garden can grow up around your "givens."

## Gardening with the kids in mind

If you have young children, or if kids are always visiting, plan for them and their antics. A flower border of precious perennials, some of them delicately supported by stakes, will be in constant danger of being trampled if kids ride bikes or play rousing games of soccer nearby. Although placing your raised-bed vegetable garden right in the centre of a sunny lawn may be logical, figure out whether the kids' fun and games can work around it or whether the kids will be running through it.

As parents everywhere know, the key to lowering your frustration level is being flexible. Site the perennials way at the back of the lawn area if you must; shield flowers with a low fence or picnic table or a living barrier, such as a miniature hedge of boxwood or germander; locate that vegetable garden more off to the side; and so on. You get the idea.

With kids' short attention spans and wish for quick gratification, it's unlikely that you'll be able to get the children to help you dig up a new planting area, and it isn't safe or advisable to have them help with pruning projects. But you have plenty of other ways to build your kids' interest in gardening:

- **Raise some easy-to-grow plants for kids.** Favourites include green beans (pole beans, on a teepee, so kids can have a fort inside), nasturtiums, morning glories, mini pumpkins, and sunflowers.

- **Plant things kids love to harvest, whether vegetables or flowers for bouquets.** Just make sure you supervise children, especially if they're using clippers or scissors.

- **Encourage help by putting money in the till.** Don't forget the time-honoured tradition of paying your budding entrepreneurs for pulling weeds — though the going rate is probably no longer a penny a dandelion!

Flip to Chapter 20 for some fun gardening projects for kids.

# *Establishing a good garden for pets*

Contrary to popular belief, pets and gardens are compatible. All you need is some creativity to accommodate both of them. However, because the animal is part of your life, you have to consider meeting his or her needs to be a given when setting out to lay out your yard and garden.

Your biggest concern may be where your pets do their business. Dog and cat urine can create brown spots in lawns (because urine is high in nitrogen), especially when the pet is a creature of habit and returns to the same spot over and over again. Just water the area to dilute, and the problem should go away. Dusting the area with gypsum can also help.

Either bury or scoop pet poop — your decision. Just never add pet waste to a compost pile or a spot where edible plants are growing, because cats and dogs aren't vegetarians, and meat waste products don't belong there. Pet feces can contain harmful bacteria, parasites, or other disease-causing organisms.

Dogs have two basic outdoor needs:

- **Water to drink:** Place a large bowl of fresh water in a spot where your dog can get direct access to it without trampling through valued plants and where no humans will step on it. Replenish the water often, as it may collect debris, dry up, or get too warm if in the sun.

- **Shade to rest in:** Your dog may have his or her own ideas about which shrubs or trees to rest under, but you can influence your pooch's decision by trimming away lower branches so scooting into the spot is easier. You can also create and fill in a "sand beach" area, which allows unfettered and nondestructive digging, if your pooch is a digging sort.

  If you want to have a fenced-in "dog run" area, make sure that it has sheltering shade throughout the day in some part and that the run is in a spot where you can see and/or hear your pet (so you don't forget about your four-legged friend!). Dogs don't like to do their business in the same place where they rest or play, so the run needs to be big enough to allow for both activities.

Outdoor cats need clean, cool water, too, and they also like the sanctuary of a safe, shady spot where they can observe, undetected and undisturbed. Watch where your cats go, and improve the spot for them, if you can, with extra protection (like their own small, simple cat house) and more space. *Note:* The sand beach idea is not for cats; they'll think it's an outdoor litter box!

Sometimes cats use tree trunks as scratching posts; little trees can't tolerate this abuse of their outer bark, so rig a collar of tape or wire to prevent the damage.

If you bring pet birds in cages outside, do so only temporarily — birds tend to be sensitive to cold nights, wind, or hot sun. Make sure they have plenty of water. And don't leave caged birds outdoors unattended. Vermin are sometimes attracted to the feed in their cages, and curious wild birds that can pass on diseases often visit.

If you have pets, be careful about the gardening products you use and where you store them. Plan to keep the critters indoors after fertilizing or spraying until the packaging says it's safe. You may also want to consider what you choose to grow and where you plant it: If animals eat a plant that doesn't agree with them, up it comes — on your living room floor! In some cases, a trip to the vet may be in order. Visit the Government of Canada's Web site at `www.cbif.gc.ca/pls/pp/poison` for more information.

## Creating space for entertainment

A popular trend these days is outdoor rooms or outdoor living, and it's easy to see why. When good weather comes, who can resist hanging out or dining in the fresh air?

Patio gardens, decks, and terraces adjacent to the house (front, side, or back) continue to be popular because you and your guests have easy access to the house. People can easily pop inside for additional food, drink, or supplies; to use the restroom; or to dispose of trash. Screened-in spots may be necessary if you have a mosquito or other bug problem and still want to be comfortable outside. (For ideas on container gardens for patios, see Chapter 16.)

If you want to place your outdoor living space away from the house, such as at a gazebo or under a pergola or in a poolside entertaining area, make sure it's well stocked with beverages and snacks to spare yourself long treks back and forth to the house. Outdoor storage units and shelves should do the trick.

We've witnessed a recent boom in outdoor furniture options — styles as well as materials. From rust-resistant tables, chairs, and benches, to mildew-resistant, quick-drying cushions in bright colours, to handsome but practical umbrellas, you can have a set that looks great even when left out in the sun and rain. Just feast your eyes on the choices at your local home-supply store, big-box retail store, or mail-order gardening supplier. The outdoor lifestyle has never offered so many excellent and attractive choices. Choose stuff that meets your needs, is durable, and has style and colour that match or enhance or set the tone for the surrounding garden. (You may also invest in attractive, fitted covers for everything to protect items from the elements when not in use.)

Outdoor entertainment areas ought to connect to the garden so that although people are enjoying indoor-style comforts and amenities, they're still able to savour the unique joys of being outside. You can incorporate potted plants (both colourful flowers and practical herbs or veggies), set out vases of flowers cut from the garden, add hanging baskets, and plant right up to the perimeters. To create a transition from the outdoor entertainment area to the garden proper (and thus gracefully blend them), repeat elements in both places — use the same or similar plants, or incorporate the same colours or *complementary colours* (red and green, blue and orange, and purple and yellow — colours that are across from each other on the colour wheel).

Add flair and beauty to your outdoor entertaining area with wind chimes, candles, citronella torches, lanterns, or windsocks.

Whatever type of outdoor living space you decide to set up, remember to imagine and then accommodate foot traffic — people will wear a path anyway, so plan for it.

## Designing a sanctuary: The quiet garden retreat

A garden retreat needs to be outside and away from the busy world, where you can relax and gather your thoughts in peace, quiet, and solitude. In a sense, any garden can provide a retreat for the world-weary, nerve-jangled gardener. But some backyard retreats are more soothing than others. Having simple and undemanding landscaping and décor can encourage you to relax, not jump up to attend to garden chores or errant weeds.

You needn't turn your entire garden into a Zen-like space. A special corner or tucked-away nook will do. Privacy, protection, and isolation are key elements of a good retreat. Think about adding a fence or wall to block out sights and, equally important, sounds. Less-solid screens in the shape of trellises, or tall and dense plantings of trees and shrubs, or even a gathering of potted plants can also enclose a space. The idea is to make a garden room accessible yet insulated. For summertime relaxation, consider a shady retreat.

Within the walls of your retreat, make a comfortable place to sit or even recline. A full table-and-chairs set is appropriate if you plan to share the space and enjoy meals or quiet cups of tea. A hammock or a chaise lounge invites reading and relaxing.

Now consider the furnishings — namely, plants and décor:

- ✔ The plants that you choose should be easygoing selections that don't require fussing — for shade, try impatiens; for sun, marigolds or zinnias are good choices. Stick to a simple or even monochromatic colour scheme, one that's soothing to the eye.

✔ Consider a water element, such as a small, tubbed water garden or fountain. The inherently soothing sight and sound of water can help block out distracting noises (see Chapter 17 for water garden ideas).

✔ A judiciously employed ornament — such as a hummingbird feeder, a large clay urn, or a garden statue of St. Fiacre (the patron saint of gardeners) or Buddha — can further the mood. Use simple ornaments that have meaning to you and are in keeping with your theme.

## *Cooking up an edible garden: Gardening for your kitchen*

If you love to cook and enjoy gardening, it's only a matter of time before you long to grow your own produce. A so-called kitchen garden can be modest in size, easy to manage, and produce all the fresh vegetables and herbs you desire. It doesn't need to be extensive or as ambitious as a back-forty vegetable garden. (For help with such a large garden, flip to Chapter 13, remembering that it may require more space and it will require full sun.)

Because a kitchen garden exists for one reason — to generate good things to eat — planting it near your house is best. That way, you can pop out the door, snip the herbs you need or grab a few sun-warmed cherry tomatoes, and put them to immediate use. Ideally, a kitchen or dining-room window overlooks your patch so you aren't likely to forget what's ripe for the taking.

If your goal is to serve healthier and fresher food to your family, go for a variety of classic vegetables and herbs. Even salad skeptics may be won over after they taste a wondrous array of colourful lettuces accompanied by fresh ripe tomatoes. And kids who don't normally enjoy vegetables can discover the joys of fresh, sweet, homegrown peas and carrots.

For more on raising vegetables, consult Chapter 13; we cover herbs in Chapter 14.

## Setting up your garden for international cuisine

Consider what kinds of cuisine you like to cook, and then prepare yourself for an international feast with some of the freshest possible ingredients:

✔ **Asian:** Opt for various herbs and leafy greens, plus certain kinds of eggplant and onions.

✔ **Italian:** Be sure to include tomatoes, oregano, and basil, at the least.

✔ **Mexican:** The easy herb cilantro is a must, as is epazote, and of course, a salsa medley of tomatoes, onions, garlic, and various peppers, hot and mild.

The easiest, most successful kitchen gardens are small and simple. You can always expand later. To get started, we recommend

- ✔ **Keeping it sunny:** At least six hours of full sun per day is essential for good growth and the ripening of almost all vegetables, herbs, and edible flowers. Morning light is preferable to afternoon because it dries the dew (reducing the risk of disease) and is less stressful than the blazing heat of mid-afternoon.

- ✔ **Setting the boundaries:** Stake out a spot using string rigged between wooden sticks, or try a simpler approach: Use your garden hose as a guide. After you establish the garden, you can edge the bed with bricks, stones, or commercial plastic edging. Or dig a roughly 10-centimetre-deep (4-inch-deep) trench all around the edges. The idea is to keep any lawn grass from encroaching on your kitchen garden.

- ✔ **Building raised beds:** If the soil in the appointed spot isn't very good, erect a raised bed from planks standing on edge. Be sure to use untreated lumber, because some wood preservatives may be harmful to edible plants. (Unless you use the more expensive cedar, these wooden sides will eventually rot and need replacing. By then, you may be ready to expand your kitchen garden, anyway.) See Chapter 13 for info on raised beds.

- ✔ **Installing protective barriers:** If you garden in deer, groundhog, or rabbit territory (just to name some of the worst pests), or if you host backyard soccer games, a protective fence around your kitchen garden may be in order. Use poultry wire or wood, and sink the fence into the ground to discourage digging invaders. If the fence doesn't look very attractive, plant fast-growing, lightweight plants to cover it, such as morning glories.

- ✔ **Planting a few containers that are literally at the kitchen door:** Try a small tomato plant surrounded by 'Spicy Globe' basil, a cut-and-come-again mix of lettuces and salad greens, and a container of your favourite herbs.

# *Zeroing In on Your Ideal Garden Style*

After you've determined your basic wants and needs for your garden space, you're ready to decide on its overall style. Gardens come in many types, themes, and moods. Yours can be informal, with less strict boundaries, a more casual look, and a wide variety of plants; or it can be formal, with symmetrical lines, crisp edges, and a limited plant palette. Or it can be one of many variations in between.

Select a style based on the architecture of your house, the lay of the land, or even an idea you saw in a magazine. Your choice also ought to take into consideration the advantages and disadvantages already inherent in your yard and gardening space, as we outline in the first half of this chapter.

A garden is an emotional place for many people — a place of pride and joy, of relaxation, comfort, and meaningful projects. Luckily, a garden's always a work in progress, and you can improve, expand, or totally change some or all of it over time. You should also be open to surprises, like the errant sunflower that pops up near the deck or the herb that self-sows into the roses and ends up looking pretty there. So dream and plan, but be flexible.

## Gardening around a theme

Garden design often goes beyond the types of plants you want to grow and the function you want your garden to have. Thematic elements can also influence the look of a garden. Do you have a soft spot for old-fashioned English rose gardens? Or Japanese Zen gardens? Or even dry, rocky areas filled with sedums, yuccas, and succulents? In the following sections, we list some popular style elements to help you continue clarifying what you may want and need.

If you'd like your garden to be like the styles covered in this book, or like any other of the large variety of garden styles available, be sure to do plenty of research beforehand to make your space look as harmonious and authentic as possible. And don't forget to make sure your space can accommodate the style! Trying to install an outdoor cactus garden in Thunder Bay, Ontario, may not be your best bet.

### Formal gardens

Keep formal gardens simple (see Figure 2-1). Aim for balance and symmetry so the garden has an air of calm elegance. Here are some tips:

- Use strong lines and boundaries, such as groomed hedges, walkways, and perhaps even a reflecting pool.
- Employ single-colour plantings, aiming to match or complement your house colour, fence, or another element.
- Add stylish pots, urns, gazing balls, or statuary. Keep everything in moderation so it doesn't look cluttered.

### Asian gardens

Asian gardens (see Figure 2-2) are usually based on a *garden floor,* or a broad area of raked sand or stones. Choose fine-textured traditional plants, in pots or in the ground. Try dwarf conifers, Japanese maples, iris, azalea, and flowering fruit trees. Then include Asian-style accessories such as stone lanterns, bamboo fencing, a water basin, or even a small "tea house."

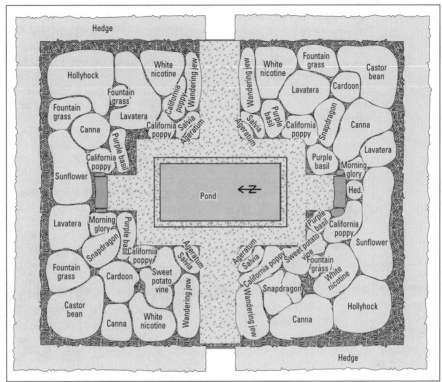

**Figure 2-1:**
A complete plan for a classy, formal garden of annual plants. Common names are presented for plants you may want to consider using.

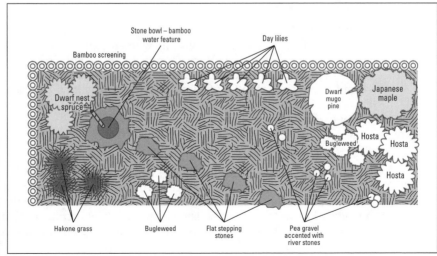

**Figure 2-2:**
A garden plan for an Asian-inspired design.

### Tropical gardens

Put a piece of paradise in your own backyard. Tropical gardens (see Figure 2-3) emphasize lots of big, bold, leafy foliage plants (such as cannas, coleus, hibiscus, and taro) in the ground or in large containers. Use bright flowers in hot colours: yellow, red, and orange, as well as bicolours. Then include a water feature, such as a pool, fountain, or stream. You can add drama with extras: birdhouses or cages, colourful pots, gazing balls, and playful or handcrafted décor and statuary.

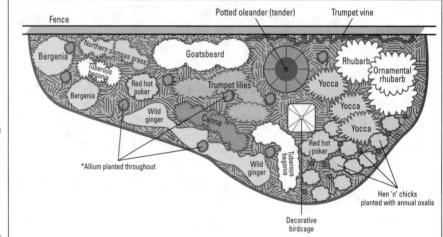

**Figure 2-3:**
A garden plan for a planting with a tropical feel.

### Cottage gardens

Cottage gardens should be overflowing with colourful blooms, so plant these inviting, informal gardens with a generous hand. Include lots of roses and other fragrant plants (including herbs). Keep the plants well tended (remove spent flowers and stems), but allow them to express their natural exuberance. Finally, add some charming touches — a picket fence, an arbour, whimsical birdhouses, or wind chimes.

### Dry-climate gardens

If your area is a little on the parched side, you may want to opt for a dry-climate garden. Employ a naturalistic layout, perhaps with a dry streambed or stone pathways, and choose plants that thrive in hot sun, including but not limited to sedums, yuccas, and succulents. Then strategically place accents of colourful or more water-needy plants in pots or in groups.

### *Woodland gardens*

Woodland gardens, which are often shady, include groundcovers that flower along with spring-blooming bulbs. Both will give lots of colour in spring, before the trees leaf out and when many woodland gardens are at their best. For fall colour, you can plant some native asters and cultivars of goldenrod, which will come into their own once the leaves have fallen.

This type of garden is most practical if you already have a well-treed lot. Tall deciduous hardwoods like oaks, beeches, and maples are ideal, because they provide a high canopy with diffused shade. Seek out diverse forms and colours for the larger plants, from bold hostas to lacy ferns. You can then tuck in non-plant items, such as ornaments and garden furniture, for summer colour and interest.

# *An inspired idea: Perusing books, magazines, and local gardens*

As part of your narrowing-down process, have fun as you gather inspiration. Thumb through back issues of gardening magazines, flagging beautiful photographs and helpful articles. Grab a few of those arguably fluffy gardening magazines you often see at the checkout stand at the grocery store (technically, they're called *SIPs,* or special interest publications). These publications tend to be heavily photo driven and lighter on the actual how-to information, but that's the dreamy stuff you want right now.

Also check the gardening books you already own, both practical ones and coffee-table books, and do the same. Visit a well-stocked bookstore or the book section at a garden centre and do some more prospecting. Buy a few titles if you find something wonderful and useful.

And don't forget the gardens that aren't too far beyond your front door. Bring your camera as you visit your local botanical garden or arboretum, and take advantage of local garden tours. Walk around surrounding neighbourhoods and take pictures of gardens or vignettes that pique your interest.

The object of this exercise is to fill your mind with enticing images of what's possible. You also get to see how other gardeners — in various regions, with different types of yards — have pulled off their woodland garden or cottage garden or whatever you're aiming for. Study their creativity and their solutions; they can help you clarify your vision.

## Tackling the paste-and-ponder method

Some people find their ideas jell best given a little time. If you have an available wall or large bulletin board, try this: Rip out inspirational photos from magazines, gather your photos, and tack them up. Make the display orderly, or make it a collage. Then leave it there and walk by every now and then, pausing to admire and study it. Add to it, shift things around, and take pieces away.

This admittedly informal method can really help clarify your thinking and consolidate your planning, especially if you're a visually oriented person. The paste-and-ponder method also helps you keep your eye on the prize, so leave the board up for a while.

# *Making Sure Costs Don't Outgrow Your Budget*

Having a good garden, or a series of smaller gardens, on your property does cost money. Fencing materials and paving stones aren't cheap. Garden furnishings and décor aren't cheap. Big plants, special small plants, and pots aren't cheap. Potting soil and loam aren't cheap. Fertilizer and pesticides aren't cheap. It all adds up. And, frankly, budgeting is hard when you're dealing with an ongoing project whose look is likely to evolve.

So here's our main advice: Relax. Rome wasn't built in a day. Take small bites, if need be. Tackle one project at a time and see it through, and then move on to the next one. Or divide a large project into sections and allow yourself time — even several seasons or years — to complete it.

One place where you can save money is labour — use yourself, involve your partner or your kids, bribe friends with dinner, or hire neighbourhood kids. And remember that, fortunately, gardening is one of those experiences in life whose journey can be as satisfying as the destination.

Here are some other money-saving gardening ideas:

- ✔ Grow plants from seed.

- ✔ Divide perennials and shrubs and then move the pieces to other parts of your yard (see Chapter 7 for info on how to divide perennials).

- ✔ Get plants from other gardeners — some people may simply give you their unwanted surplus; others will be happy to swap. Join a local garden club, and you may be assured of these transactions!

✔ Make your own compost (see Chapter 4 for tips). And always compost your fall leaves instead of bagging them and sending them off to the local landfill.

✔ Buy from the source, whether it's a special day lily nursery nearby or a local brickyard.

✔ Browse yard sales, junkyards, and antique shops. You may happen across real bargains in garden ornaments as well as pots, gates, trellises, fencing, and so on.

Last but not least, take care of your investments. It's a sad waste to let good, costly plants or garden areas languish or die. The more you know about soil, about planting, about plant care — and this book is chock-full of useful advice — the easier it is to do right by your garden. A thriving garden can repay you many times over.

## Computer-aided design: Embracing your inner (garden) architect

Garden-planning software, formerly the province of professionals, is now available to the general public. Computer programs can take you through entire planning processes and generate detailed plans, alternate plans, and close-up plans. Some come with extensive plant databases. Others offer impressive show-and-grow features to help you visualize what your yard will look like next year, five years from now, and so on.

To use one of these programs, you need

✔ **Time and patience:** You have to study and decipher these programs to understand what they can do, especially if you have no landscaping training. The journey should be as intriguing to you as the destination, or else you'll get frustrated.

✔ **Money:** These programs vary a great deal in their cost. The ones designed for amateurs aren't that expensive and have many of the features you need. If you want a full-blown design program like the professionals use, you're talking about a sizable chunk of change, but it's still cheaper than hiring someone.

✔ **Good equipment:** An old Mac or PC will choke on today's gardening software; you need a powerful machine with plenty of available memory and speed. If the computer runs your kids' video games well (or yours, for that matter), it'll do a decent job with most design programs.

You don't need a fancy large-format or colour printer, though — just burn a disc of your plan, take it down to a good copy shop, and have someone else whip up the visuals.

To find software that suits your skill level and needs, do an Internet search, examine advertisements, order brochures, and of course, talk with anyone you know who's used a program.

# Bringing Your Garden Ideas to Reality

Now's the time to start getting real. Armed with your ideas and goals and wishes, step outside and bring your plans to life. Some gardeners find that the best time to do this step is fall or winter, when you have fewer distractions from overgrown plants and seasonal clutter. The outline and the "bones" of a yard are more evident then. But whenever you do this step, look beyond what's present. Visualize what will change and what will go in.

When you're ready to sketch out your garden plan, you can do it yourself or, if it seems daunting or is simply not your cup of tea, you can hire a licensed professional (see "Getting Professional Help for Your Garden Plans," later in this chapter). Your overall garden plan doesn't have to be precise or perfect. It just has to do what you need it to do — show you your yard so you can plan what you want to put into it.

## Sketching out the yard you have now

Using graph paper and the tools necessary to draft out your garden (see Figure 2-4), draw a plan of your site to scale, allowing one 1-centimetre space for each metre (or one space for each foot). As long as the proportions are accurate, you can use the squares as you wish so you your plan is big enough to see clearly (such as two 1-centimetre spaces for each metre). Plot every feature you find on your site, both natural and those you or your predecessors have put in place. Use a measuring tape to get at least approximate measurements. You may want to indicate areas of sun and shade.

If you'd like, you can also use photography to help sketch out your plans. Photograph panoramic sequences of every part of your property, as well as external features (such as views) you may want to enhance or hide. Paste the photos together to form a wide-angle shot. Enlarge and photocopy your snapshots, if that makes them easier to view.

## Making your drawing match your dream garden

After you've completed the initial drawing of your yard or garden plot to your satisfaction, add the elements for your garden plan. Here are some recommendations:

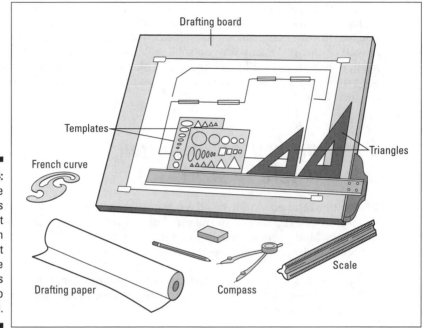

**Figure 2-4:**
There are many ways to draft out your garden plan, but these are the tools you need to get started.

1. **Gather any pictures you're using for inspiration, and prepare a list of your main goals, assets, and limitations.**

   Refer to the earlier section "Taking Stock: Evaluating What You Already Have" for advice on looking at your yard's challenges and advantages. "Getting Ideas for Your Garden Space" can help you focus on your gardening goals.

2. **Study your current plan carefully.**

   Decide which features you want to incorporate into your final plan, which ones you want to highlight, and which ones you want to downplay or remove.

3. **Place a piece of tracing paper over your plan.**

4. **Use a pencil, and sketch in or leave out various features and designs.**

   Try hard to stick to your theme or overall vision, and attempt to be organized (refer to "Zeroing In on Your Ideal Garden Style" for details on themes).

   When designing your garden plan, you don't have to get bogged down in details, listing every plant by name. Instead, penciling in "sun-loving perennials," "blue and yellow bed," or "pots of annuals" may suffice.

After all the elements you've planned for are in place, take a good look at them to make sure the overall drawing matches the initial image of the dream garden you had in your head. If something looks awkward or looks like it needs to be moved or changed in any way, do so! Keep changing that drawing (and redrawing it, if necessary) until you have a final plan that satisfies you. Only when your final plan is in your hands should you prepare yourself to move on to the next step.

## Defining key areas so you know where to start

With your sketched yard in hand, your next steps are to decide which area you want to start with and to roll up your sleeves. As we always advise, tackling everything at once isn't easy and often isn't realistic or affordable. Break big projects down into manageable pieces, and do them one at a time.

Like rooms in a house, a garden area has four major elements. And as in building a house, going from the ground up is best. Tackle the four major elements in this order:

1. **Floor**

   Lawn grass, a groundcover, paving materials, or good, plantable soil

2. **Walls**

   Supplied literally by a wall of your house; by a fence, hedge, or trellis; or by a backdrop of evergreens or shrubs of some kind

## A word in defence of boundary materials

Call us fussy, but we both like enclosures and edgings in a garden, which, in the context of the key areas in this chapter, can be walls or floors or portions thereof. We mean bricks, stones, plastic materials, wood, iron, and of course, living plants.

Enclosures and boundaries distinguish the cultivated area from the wild or neglected areas beyond. They embrace the plants and the people enjoying them. They create a sense of order and intimacy so you can focus on and savour what the garden contains and has to offer your senses.

Boundary materials also set the tone for a garden, making it feel formal or informal, elegant or casual. Wisely chosen, they connect a yard to a house or a yard to the surrounding landscape. They enhance the scene and flatter your plants without stealing the spotlight. Good-quality materials endure for years and look like they belong.

### 3. Ceiling

Can certainly be open sky but may also involve an umbrella, awnings, overarching tree or large-shrub branches, or a pergola with or without a cloak of plants

### 4. Furniture

Literally tables and chairs and benches and the like, but also major containers or garden ornaments and décor

Don't go overboard with garden gnomes and pink flamingoes. Limit yourself to one or two ornaments in the same style and mood, and keep the focus on the sense of space and the living parts of your garden.

# Getting Professional Help for Your Garden Plans

Getting a garden plot ready, especially a large one, isn't easy, and we'll never pretend that it is (we have better uses for our creative energies, such as pretending we're in Hawaii or Mexico). If starting the process makes your head reel, or if you don't have confidence in your design sense, don't worry. Others can do it for you. Contractors can do everything, in fact, from planning on paper to purchasing to digging the holes and planting the plants. You can confer with or hover over them, or wind them up and let them go. You can even stop them at the point where you want to take over.

Also, be honest with yourself when a project is beyond your ability, unsafe for you, or too time-consuming to undertake on your own. Under such circumstances, it's better to go ahead and hire a contractor.

If you decide to get professional landscaping help, be savvy so you get good work and you get what you pay for. Here are some guidelines:

✔ Ask around before you check the Yellow Pages. Word of mouth is an ideal way to find the right person.

✔ Find a minimum of three possible contractors. They should be willing to make an initial appointment that involves assessing and estimating only; be sure to ask whether they charge for this step (and whether, if you go with them, the fee can be credited to the job).

✔ Have some copies of your plans to show the professionals when they arrive, and if need be, hand them over.

✔ Ask for a bid in writing— materials *and* labour estimates, with a clause for addressing unexpected expenses and overruns. To figure out what a reasonable cost is, ask friends and neighbours what they paid, and get estimates from multiple sources.

✔ Check references. Also confirm that the contractor is both licensed and insured.

✔ Pick someone you like and, more important, can communicate with.

✔ Discuss concerns every step of the way — the more communication, the better. If changes come up, be smart and get the revised plans and charges in writing.

✔ Pay in installments — give a deposit, then perhaps pay a second installment or more, and finally, pay the last one when all parties agree the work is complete and satisfactory. Such an arrangement gives the contractor security and a commitment from you but also prevents you from being taken for a large fee if something goes awry.

Overall, just be clear with each other. Have a budget. Get written estimates. Get your agreement (plan, expectations, *and* timetable) in writing. Call or visit references. Check and/or supervise the work.

Start the process of hiring a contractor early if you can. The summer or fall before the spring in which you want the work to begin is an ideal time. Good people have full calendars, and spring commitments are booked very early. Finding the right professional, somebody you can afford or someone nearby, may take some time; you may interview several contractors before settling on one.

## Landscape architects, landscape designers, and garden designers

Landscapes versus gardens, architects versus designers — confusing isn't it? Various names apply to this group of professionals. Although they each perform a service, you may find quite a bit of overlap.

Landscape architects, landscape designers, and garden designers are all professionals, trained in every facet of planning and realizing an outdoor plan. Their scope goes beyond regular backyard gardens or even the landscaping of an estate; many of these folks are capable of laying out a resort, college campus, public park, and so on. They can cope with topography and know how to analyze a site completely, down to its soil and light and existing vegetation. They can design walkways and decks and such in savvy and attractive ways. They can then draw up a design or several alternatives.

In general, *landscape architects* are space planners who may or may not be very knowledgeable about plants. They're mostly called in for very large commercial or institutional projects and where *hardscapes* (any masonry or woodwork like walks, patios, or gazebos) are a substantial part of the job. You may find that landscape designers and garden designers are more familiar with plants suited to your area and may be more attuned to residential-scale projects.

All concerns about cost aside, hiring a landscape architect to do your garden is a marvellous investment. These professionals tend to notice and address elements and problems you may not have thought of; they propose appropriate and attractive solutions; and they have wide knowledge of both plant material and hardscape components. They're the full planning package.

To find one of these experts, you can consult ads, the Internet, or the Yellow Pages. Word of mouth may work. If you know of someone who's used one in your neighbourhood or town, try to visit and ask the owners how the process went, whether they're happy, and perhaps — if asking doesn't seem too tacky — what it all cost. Garden tours in your area may feature professionally done properties, too, which can also lead you to the person who designed a beautiful garden.

## Landscape or general contractors

*Landscape* or *general contractors* are the folks who are usually called in to actually install the job. They do the heavy lifting.

If you're daring (or foolish), you can try to take down a massive shade tree yourself, or regrade a slope, or install an in-ground irrigation system, or lay out and install a flagstone terrace. Before taking this step, think whether the money you're saving will be enough to pay for the chiropractor you may need afterward!

Seriously, if you're not used to this work, you can do a lot of damage to your body and your landscape. Don't be afraid to ask someone for help to create your vision: somebody strong enough, experienced, and knowledgeable; somebody certified, bonded, and insured as well. A reputable contractor has no problem demonstrating his or her qualifications. Getting help isn't wimpy; it's only good sense.

In short, let someone else do the hard jobs and do them safely and correctly the first time. These folks can install all your residential hardscape needs like walks and walls. Save the fun and creative parts for yourself.

To find a landscape or general contractor, check the Yellow Pages; ask neighbours; ask at a garden centre; check ads in the local newspaper; or copy the telephone number or Web site address off a truck parked at another home.

## *Master gardeners*

A *master gardener* isn't someone you hire, but rather someone you can consult and consider a resource. Master gardeners have to follow a certification process. Classes in British Columbia, Saskatchewan, Alberta, Ontario, Nova Scotia, and Yukon train avid home gardeners or anyone else who's interested in horticulture (see the appendix for more information). Something to remember: Courses vary across Canada. Yukon offers one 40-hour course; Nova Scotia offers six courses. In the Prairie and Maritime provinces and in Yukon, master gardeners are government funded, but in Ontario and British Columbia, they're independent, nonprofit organizations.

Certification follows only after the student has completed additional classes and has volunteered a certain number of hours in the community. The volunteering can involve anything from manning the phone help line to assisting with community plantings (including school gardens), holding plant clinics at garden centres, staffing county and provincial fair booths, assisting with horticulture therapy projects, or helping with workshops that educate the public about gardening.

The hours and courses required for certification vary from office to office, province to province. Getting certified doesn't make a person an expert; it just shows that he or she has made a commitment to learning more about and serving in the local horticultural scene.

Master gardeners aren't paid, so you can't really haul them over to your yard and get them to do your work for you. However, they can help you with questions and point you toward helpful resources. And who knows? In time, you may decide to become one yourself.

To find a master gardener, call the nearest provincial office of the Master Gardeners (in Yukon, call the Department of Energy, Mines, and Resources). You can also run an Internet search by typing "Master Gardener" and the name of your province or region into your preferred search engine.

# Chapter 3

# Getting into the Zone —
# Your Garden's Zone

*N*ewcomers to gardening are often baffled by all the talk of zones in gardening magazines, books, and catalogues, and on plant labels. Beginners often hear more-experienced gardeners, garden centre staffers, and professional landscapers tossing around zone terms and numbers as well. You may sense that this zone business is some kind of secret code or language that's hard to remember or tricky to understand. It's not. Zoning is really a simple (if generalized) system for describing climate so you can figure out whether a plant ought to be able to grow where you live.

Most plants grow best in roughly the same temperatures and humidity that human beings enjoy, but some plants like it cooler, some warmer. This chapter helps you to know and navigate the zones so you can put the information to use and pick out the right plants as you plan or add to your garden.

## Different Hardiness Zone Maps for Different Folks

If all that gardeners ever grew were locally adapted plants, you'd have no reason to find out or concern yourself with hardiness zones. But of course, you want it all, right? You want to grow exotic goodies from distant lands or plants from allegedly similar but far-off places.

Indeed, you already do have it all: Peonies come from Asia, tulips hail from Turkey, and strawflowers are from Australia. So after your initial infatuation with a plant that's new to you subsides, you can ask yourself, "Is growing this in my garden possible?" Finding out the plant's appropriate zone gives you an answer.

People commonly use hardiness zone information for trees, shrubs, and perennial plants. Annuals don't get rated, or just don't count, because they live for only one growing season. Hardiness zones are all about survival from one year to the next. (And anything tender grown in a pot can always be moved inside, out of the weather, thus avoiding the issue.)

Just to complicate matters, there are several different zone maps for North Americans, and some are better than others, depending on where you live. For example, most Canadian gardeners refer to the Plant Hardiness Zones of Canada 2000 map, but most people in the northern U.S. use the USDA Plant Hardiness Zone Map. The American Horticultural Society's Plant Heat-Zone Map is more useful for and popular among people in the southern and western United States, and Sunset's Garden Climate Zones map, though complex, serves the western states well.

## *Taking a look at the world's Plant Hardiness Zone maps*

Every part of the world has its own hardiness zones, and most maps are set up the same way.

The Plant Hardiness Zones of Canada 2000 map, for example, is a colour-coded or shaded map, accompanied by a chart that explains the various shades. This book displays the map in the colour section, and you can also see the map (and others) in many places after you become tuned in to it — tacked up on the wall at your local garden centre, printed on the back flyleaf of a gardening book, or tucked into the interior of your favourite gardening catalogue. You can also find it online at sis.agr.gc.ca/cansis/nsdb/climate/hardiness/intro.html.

Canada's Plant Hardiness Zone map shows nine zones, based on average climatic conditions — minimum winter temperatures, length of the frost-free period, summer rainfall, maximum summer temperatures, snow cover, January rainfall, and maximum wind speeds — and the altitude of each area. The harshest zone is Zone 0, and the mildest is Zone 8. In addition, the major zones are further divided into subzones; for example, Zone 4 is split into 4a and 4b.

The most recent USDA Plant Hardiness Zone Map, published by the United States Department of Agriculture, came out in 1990 and is based on climate data gathered at National Weather Service stations throughout the U.S. and at weather stations throughout Canada and Mexico. The USDA map has 11 zones marking the average lowest winter temperatures, with Zones 2 to 10 divided into subzones.

It's helpful for Canadian gardeners to know both the Canadian and USDA zones, because some plants sold here are imported from the U.S. with tags listing the USDA zones only. You can find the USDA Plant Hardiness Zone Map online at `www.usna.usda.gov/Hardzone/ushzmap.html`.

The Hardiness Zone Map of Europe presents a general overview of the European continent and can be broken down further into each European nation and the zones within it. You can see this map online at `www.uk.gardenweb.com/forums/zones/hze.html`.

China's Plant Hardiness Zone map covers arguably the largest and most varied gardening spots in the world. You can view it at `www.backyardgardener.com/zone/china.html`.

Plant Hardiness Zone maps aren't limited to just the Northern Hemisphere of the Earth! You can find online maps for South America and Africa as well. And the Australian government has established a series of maps that many Australian gardeners use to gauge not only planting zones and climates but also rainfall. To view the Plant Hardiness Zone map of Australia, go to `www.anbg.gov.au/hort.research/zones.html`. To see Australia's climate zone map, visit `www.bom.gov.au/climate/environ/travel/map.shtml`.

Traveller beware: If you buy a plant in Victoria or Vancouver that's labelled as a perennial or as "hardy," and you live in a colder zone, say Sudbury, the plant label may apply only to the area where it's sold.

## *Warming up to the heat-zone map*

It's no secret that gardeners in colder climes often envy those who can grow tender plants like bougainvilleas and gardenias in their gardens. But did you know that Canadians can grow plants that tropical and subtropical gardeners can't — such as delphiniums that sulk when the temperature soars, and wisteria and most peonies that refuse to bloom if they don't receive enough winter cold? And our hardy, common lilacs are considered exotic in many parts of the southern U.S.

In many parts of the U.S., it's heat rather than cold that dictates which plants survive from one year to the next. Thus, in 1997 (after years of study and research), the American Horticultural Society released its own map, the AHS Plant Heat-Zone Map. Though it's relatively new and still being tweaked, this map has proven to be quite useful to gardeners in the southern and western U.S. Although the map has little bearing on gardening in Canada, it's interesting to see the climate problems other gardeners face, and it helps to understand overall climate patterns that affect gardening. You can take a look at the Plant Heat-Zone Map by downloading it at `www.ahs.org/publications/heat_ zone_map.htm`.

## Savouring the Sunset zones

Gardeners and garden centres in the western U.S. generally refer to the Sunset climate zones because neither the USDA Plant Hardiness Zone Map nor the AHS Plant Heat-Zone Map gives complete environmental information. Complex and varied terrain and dramatic weather variations conspire to make this particular region unique. So the Sunset Publishing Company, based in the San Francisco area, devised its own Garden Climate Zones map, which you can find online at `www.sunset.com/sunset/garden/article/1,20633, 845218,00.html`. This map is based on five variables — minimum winter temperatures, maximum summer temperatures, the length of the growing season, humidity levels, and rainfall patterns.

Some western Canadians may consider using Sunset's map because its zones extend into southern Canada. However, the Plant Hardiness Zones of Canada 2000 map is more precise because it's based on seven climate variables (refer to the section "Taking a look at the world's Plant Hardiness Zone maps," earlier in this chapter). Three are the same variables used to create the Sunset version. The Sunset map considers humidity levels and rainfall patterns, whereas the Canadian map includes summer rainfall and January rainfall. In addition, the Canadian map considers snow cover and maximum wind speed as well as the altitude of each area.

## Pointing the way: Indicator trees and shrubs

Sometimes people suspect they garden in a slightly warmer or colder zone than the map they consult suggests, and they may be correct. Your garden may exist in a *microclimate* (see "Managing your microclimates," later in this chapter). To help Canadians determine the severity of their climate without using a map, the National Land and Water Information Service has formed lists of indicator trees and shrubs. You can view the list of trees online at `res.agr.ca/cansis/nsdb/climate/ hardiness/trees2000.html` and the list of shrubs at `res.agr.ca/cansis/ nsdb/climate/hardiness/shrubs 2000.html`. To establish which zone your garden is in, look down the lists for the name of a tree or shrub that thrives under similar conditions in your neighbourhood. For example, if you have a healthy dove tree in your back garden, your growing zone is at least as high as Zone 7b, maybe higher. On the other hand, if your area is too harsh for a Norway maple to survive, your zone is lower than Zone 5.

## A hot issue: Global warming and zone changes

In 2006, the U.S. National Arbor Day Foundation released a revision of the USDA Plant Hardiness Zone Map. This revised map, which you can find at www.arborday.org/media/zones.cfm, shows that the U.S. zones have shifted northward since 1990. Some people see this change as a clear sign of global warming; others claim that the Arbor Day Foundation's 15 years of data collection is statistically inconclusive. Most gardening sources in the U.S. still use the USDA's map.

Unfortunately, the National Arbor Day Foundation's map does not include Canada, and comparing Canada's new Plant Hardiness Zones map released in 2000 with the previous one from 1967 can be misleading. The earlier map consisted of ten zones, and the new one has only nine, eight of which are divided into subzones. What's more, the old map is based on temperature. The 2000 version builds on the older one using newer topographic and statistical

mapping techniques, and it factors in variables such as snowfall and snow depth in January as well as elevation.

However, Plant Hardiness Zones seem to have changed in many parts of Canada, too, particularly in the west, where some plants can now grow that never could before. National Resources Canada (NRCan) is currently revising the hardiness zones for more than 2 million varieties of trees, shrubs, and perennials, building a database of climatic profiles that will be mapped for each species, indicating its possible range. NRCan is asking people all over Canada and the U.S. (whether expert or not) to contribute the names of plants surviving at their location. After enough data has been contributed through National Resources Canada's Web site (plant hardiness.gc.ca/ph_main.pl?LANG=en), the department will generate maps and upload them to the Internet.

## Reading Plant Hardiness Zone maps

Take a look at the Plant Hardiness Zones of Canada 2000 map, either in the colour section of this book or online at sis.agr.gc.ca/cansis/nsdb/climate/hardiness/intro.html. Notice that Zone 0a, located at the top, or northernmost, part of the map, is coldest; Zone 8a is at the bottom-left corner, or the southwestern part, and is the warmest. In terms of hardiness zones, Zones 0a and 8a represent the extremes. Excluding Canada's three territories, though, the bulk of the most populated areas fits into Zones 3, 4, 5, and 6. Originally, when the first Plant Hardiness Zones of Canada map was created in 1967, the zones were conceived to be approximately 6°C (10°F) apart.

As you study the map or chart, say you find that you live in Zone 5. So you determine that this means

- ✔ You should be able to grow any tree, shrub, or perennial labelled "hardy to Zone 5."

- ✔ You probably can't grow plants that are less cold-hardy, such as Zone 6 or 7 ones — your colder winters may harm or kill them.

- ✔ You can grow plants labelled for farther north, even more cold-tolerant ones said to be "hardy to Zone 4 or 3."

However, every rule has an exception. Most gardeners can stray one, maybe two zones from their own when making plant choices and the gamble will pay off. See "Zoning Out: Breaking the Zone and Growing Season Rules," later in this chapter.

You often see a plant's projected hardiness zone expressed as a range. For instance, most Clematis hybrids are said to be "hardy in Zones 4 to 8." This statement means anyone gardening in Zones 4, 5, 6, 7, or 8 ought to be able to grow one; the plant should survive your winters.

Basic zones are based on the average annual minimum temperature — in other words, as cold as winter gets. Thus, in the Plant Hardiness Zones of Canada 2000 map, Zone 5's lowest winter temperature (on average) is −29°C (−20°F).

Climatological data comes from the horticulture industry, university researchers, botanic gardens, and so forth. Sometimes when a new plant enters commerce, the zone rating is conservative, but after a while — with more people growing the plant in different areas and with more research — the experts find the plant to be more or less cold-tolerant than they originally thought.

# Fathoming Frost Zones and Growing Seasons

Whether a plant can survive the winter isn't your only concern. You know annuals are going to live for only one season, but you also want to know how long that season will be. After all, you may not be pleased if your dahlias die before flowering or your tomato plants freeze before producing much fruit. Unfortunately, hardiness zones don't tell you much about the length of the growing season. Enter the frost zone map.

Zones are determined not only by temperatures but also by the *climate,* which combines temperature readings, rainfall, humidity, wind, air pressure, and other factors. Climates in frost zone maps are generally determined by *growing season,* the time during which — hold on to your hats — plants add new growth. The last spring frost and the first fall frost bookend the growing season, marking a predictable period of frost-free days. Basically, this time period is your window of opportunity to plant, nurture, and enjoy your home landscape, whether you're growing flowers or edibles. Make the most of it!

If you live in mild areas of Canada, such as Victoria and Vancouver, seven to nine months of the year are likely to be frost free. The rest of us may feel we're not as lucky, but look at it this way: If you have a colder winter, you get a longer break — more time to stop, relax, and regroup to plan for an even better garden next year, after the last frost is past.

The length of a growing season varies somewhat from year to year, but is generally about the same. You probably already have a sense of the length of your growing season, but if you really need to know, finding out is fairly easy. Call your nearest provincial ministry of agriculture's office, ask a knowledgeable gardener or garden centre staffer, or watch your local newspaper for the frost dates (which can vary from one year to the next).

Here's how to calculate your growing season: Suppose you live in Regina, Saskatchewan; your last frost is May 21, and your first fall frost is September 10. That gives you 112 days in which to garden. Or suppose you live in St. John's, Newfoundland; your last frost is June 2, and your first fall one is October 12. You get 131 days of growing.

Winter doesn't mean a gardener can or should be idle in the downtime. You can find plenty to do if you're so inclined to capitalize on the "shoulder seasons." You can be plotting for the future, starting seeds indoors with the plan to put them out in the ground the minute the last spring frost passes; you can be reading and discovering more about plants; you can be fussing with cleaning and sharpening your tools; you can enjoy yourself as you care for indoor plants; and you can be placing orders with mail-order suppliers — all activities that feed into the process and joy of having a wonderful garden.

# Zoning Out: Breaking the Zone and Growing Season Rules

Despite all the zone maps and all the research, hardiness remains an inexact science. Although some plants turn out to be surprisingly tough, others succumb unexpectedly. The easiest thing you can do is to set your sights on plants said to be appropriate for your area. Here are some tips on deciding what you can grow, even if you're not sure about the zone:

- ✔ **Peek at your neighbours' yards.** Chances are that if a type of plant is succeeding nearby, it can grow well, survive, and thrive for you, too.

- ✔ **Buy local.** When you get plants that were raised in your area (not raised in some distant place or coddled in a greenhouse), they're much more likely to handle whatever your local weather dishes out. After all, they've already experienced some of the harsher conditions and survived so the seller can offer them to you. Production fields out back or right nearby are your cue.

✔ **Grow native plants.** Plants that come from your area or region — ones you've seen growing in the wild, perhaps, or certainly in local parks or botanic gardens — are sure to be well adapted and set not only to survive but also to prosper. How do you know whether a plant is native? Ask where you buy, or look it up.

By the way, some local nurseries that promote or segregate native plants may also have tempting *selections* or *cultivars*— improved versions of native plants — for you to choose from (they may have smaller or more-compact sizes, different flower colours, bigger or longer-lasting flowers, and so forth). Keep an eye out.

You can, however, force plants to grow in your hardiness zone or frost zone by taking advantage of *microclimates* (pockets of different growing conditions) or by using tools to extend your growing season. The following sections tell you how you can sometimes beat the zone system.

## Managing your microclimates

Features in your yard, both natural and human made, often modify the overall climate and create small areas with distinctly different environmental conditions (including hardiness zones). Here, your zone rating may go up or down by one or possibly even two levels, changing your planting options.

A *microclimate* (a small, usually isolated area that's warmer, cooler, drier, or wetter than most of its surroundings) can be anywhere from a metre wide to a few hundred metres wide. Examples of a microclimate include a low area, a south-facing area, the north side of your house or other structure, an exposed hilltop, a slope, any enclosed and sheltered area, a spot close to the foundation of your heated basement, and so on.

Look for marked differences in these areas:

✔ **Water:** Proximity to a pond, stream, wet ditch, or the ocean can make temperature fluctuations less dramatic.

✔ **Soil:** Different types of soil can create protective or stressful growing conditions. For instance, clay soils hold moisture and heat, and thus can reduce stress in dry or very cold conditions. Very sandy soils drain well and are great where excessive water is a problem, but in hot and dry conditions, sandy soil can put plants under severe water stress.

✔ **Wind:** Observe how strong the winds are in your garden and how often you get air movement in a particular area. Winds are very drying.

✔ **Temperature:** One spot may be significantly hotter or colder than its surroundings. Note that cold air often flows like water over a landscape, settling in low areas and creating cold pockets.

A useful tool for determining temperature variation is the *maximum-minimum thermometer* (also known as a Six's thermometer). This thermometer can measure the high and low temperatures during a given time and can measure the extremes of temperature in a location. See Figure 3-1.

✔ **Light:** Note dramatic differences in the amount of daily sun and shade. Human-made structures (yours or a neighbour's) and trees can contribute to these changing conditions.

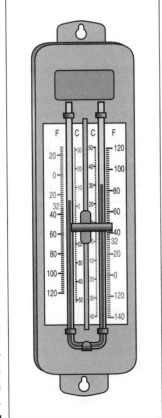

**Figure 3-1:**
A maximum-minimum thermometer gives you an idea of the outdoor temperature ranges in your area.

# Cheating the system: Creating microclimates

Ah, here's where gardeners can and do cheat their zone ratings so they can successfully grow plants they shouldn't be able to and satisfy their zone envy. You can actually create microclimates (see the preceding section for general info on microclimates). Usually, the aim is to raise the temperature. For example, you can create a warm, Zone 8-ish spot in a colder Zone 7 garden by employing a few gardening tricks:

✔ **Safety in numbers:** Planting less-hardy plants in groups helps make them more resilient and better able to withstand temperature extremes and drying winds. The local humidity is likely to be higher in a crowd, too.

✔ **Mulch:** A layer of organically rich mulch moderates soil-temperature fluctuations. Mulch also helps hold in soil moisture so you don't have to worry about a lack of rain or having to water quite as much.

✔ **Heat traps:** These structures help retain heat. Row covers, hot caps, and cold frames (see Figure 3-2) are well-known heat traps used to raise the immediate temperature and/or protect vulnerable plants from cold weather. You can purchase heat traps or build your own.

✔ **Water:** Proximity to water has a moderating effect on temperature, so you may have luck pampering a slightly tender plant by growing it next to a water feature on your property (natural or artificial).

✔ **Wind and sun blocks:** Fences, walls, buildings, and other structures offer shelter from drying winds and blasts of snow. Warmth and humidity can build up close to them, allowing you to coddle a tender plant. Structures often also create more shade, which can be cooling or inhibiting, depending on your plant's needs.

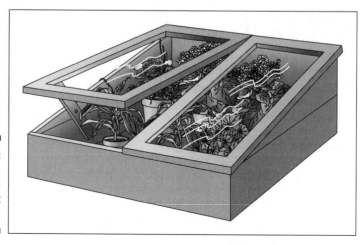

**Figure 3-2:**
Putting a
cold frame
to efficient
use.

## Emergency protection: Keeping Jack Frost at bay

You may find you tried to stretch the growing season a little too far, or perhaps the weather experts missed the mark on the date of the final frost. A big chill is creeping up, and you've already used mulch and blankets as much as you can to keep the plants warm. What's a gardener to do? Try a little emergency frost protection.

Spray vulnerable plants with water to slow or prevent plant injury caused by chilling (as Florida orange growers know all too well when a rare frost threatens). How does this work? Cold, dry air tends to draw the moisture out of leaves and from the ground; the spray of water raises the humidity levels, which in turn reduces moisture loss. Also, in order for water vapour to condense or for water to freeze, the water has to release heat, which in turn warms the plant. The plants need to be kept wet until the danger of freezing has passed; using a sprinkler system is the most practical way.

## *Stretching your growing season*

Maybe it's the rebel in us all. Maybe it's natural restlessness. Maybe it's an urge to make maximum and efficient use of available time. But gardeners do like to try to push the envelope in order to grow more or better or different plants.

You can dig up many tricks and techniques to help stretch your growing season, and you certainly may come up with a few of your own as your experience grows. The following sections describe some favourite rule benders that you can try if appropriate to your garden, your needs, and your climate.

### *Building protection*

If frost will damage a plant, perhaps you can still have it outdoors by shielding it somehow. This idea applies both to setting plants out a bit too early in the spring and to leaving them in the garden later than recommended in the fall.

Use row covers, blankets, burlap, plastic sheeting, or extra mulch (compost, weed-free hay, or pine boughs). Water well; hydrated roots can withstand cold and drought better.

### *Bringing the plants inside*

Potted plants, provided they're not too big or heavy, may be pretty easy to move indoors for a time. Most plants tend to grow less and be less productive, or are unproductive, during the winter months, so you also want to reduce water and plant food. You may even cut the plants back and just keep the pots moist enough to keep the roots alive until spring returns.

Prized plants or special herbs that you want to save can also come inside when you dig them up out of the garden and put them in a pot. Again, they may not grow full force, but you can try to keep them alive. They may experience cooler temperatures inside, but not the hard frost that would damage or kill them outdoors. If you plan to enjoy these plants longer, give them a warm and sunny spot on a windowsill or insulated sunroom. Water and feed moderately, and keep an eye out for pests.

By the way, dried herbs, canned vegetables, and carefully stored (and cured, when applicable) fruits and vegetables all keep the bounty and memory of the garden alive in the off-season. So do dried bouquets and potpourris.

# Chapter 4

# Live Long and Prosper: Giving Plants What They Need

*T*ime to get down and dirty! When you properly prepare the foundation of your garden, making sure plants can get what they need, success follows. The formula's as simple as that.

Well, maybe not so simple. Is your soil already in great condition? Do you have just the right amount of soil nutrients and rainfall so your garden can thrive without any help from you? Not likely! For most people, improving the soil they have and taking charge of garden watering are necessities if they really want their plants to thrive. This chapter tells you how to give plants a boost.

*Remember:* Some of the information in this chapter may seem like common sense, but read each section carefully, anyway. We describe some techniques and tuck in some tips that experienced gardeners use to save plenty of time, grief, and money.

The needs of plants aren't weird or complicated, but you may find that if you omit any of the recommendations in this chapter — either on purpose or unintentionally — trouble can follow. So consider this chapter a bit of a checklist as you get your garden ready for growing! Ready? Here you go. The work you do now can save you a lot of effort later.

Improving a bed or area prior to planting is so much easier than doing so after. Do these tasks early if you can. If you can't, well, then at least make it a practice to dig really fabulous, roomy holes for each plant.

# Let There Be Light!

Every plant needs at least some light in order to grow and prosper, but the amount really varies. Mushrooms (which are actually fungi), for instance, can grow in bins in a dim basement or shed; daisies and water lilies, on the other hand, crave hot, full-on sunshine. Plenty of plants rest in the middle of these two extremes, of course. And some plants, like azaleas and day lilies, grow well enough in less-optimum light, but don't flower well in the shade. In terms of labelling, just remember that *full sun* usually means six or more hours per day; *part-day,* of course, refers to less.

You may assume that flowers drink up the light, but actually, the leaves do most of the work. Leaves are the main "engine room" of a plant. For a plant to operate, thrive, and increase in size, all plant parts (except flowers) need to play their roles in photosynthesis. Roots draw in water, but the real energy production takes place primarily in the foliage. Light helps produce the fuel.

Long hours of plentiful sunlight, with varying angles throughout the day, are important so that every leaf — even the ones lower down on the plant — gets the chance to receive light. The good news is that no matter what light conditions your yard has to offer, at least something should be able to grow there. Sun plants and shade plants are labelled, and of course, gardeners try to accommodate them. If you need plant ideas along these lines, not to worry — the plant chapters in Parts II through IV of this book have plenty of suggestions for you.

The warmth of the sun, even more than actual light, inspires flowers to unfurl. Sunlight from the east (morning light) is considered cooler, and western sun (afternoon light) can be scorching. Many plants prefer a site with some morning sun, even until midday, and late-afternoon shade. Other plants are able to endure even the hottest conditions. A plant's tolerance, of course, varies by region. You can place the same plant in a sunnier spot if you live up north than you can if you're farther south.

If you have plants growing in a spot that receives a blast of late-afternoon sun, be sure to monitor their water needs closely so they don't dry out. If you find the plants are struggling, you can help them by installing something to cast a shadow, such as an arbour, or by planting a tree or large shrub in just the right spot. Even companion perennials or annuals planted nearby can cast enough shade to bring needed relief.

Here are some signs that indicate a plant is getting too much sun:

- Flower petals dry out.
- Leaf edges look burnt or dried.
- Flower colour looks faded or washed out.
- Plant starts to flag.

And here are signs that tell you a plant isn't getting enough light:

- Growth is sparse.
- Stems are lanky and spindly.
- Distances between leaves, where they're attached to the stems, are especially wide.
- Flower buds are fewer, and, thus, there are fewer flowers.
- Plant leans toward the light source.

Some of figuring out the proper location is trial and error — you're aware that roses like a full day of sun, but you really want that bush to go in the nook that gets afternoon shade. Give the spot a try. If the plant's unhappy, you can always move it to a more appropriate spot.

# *Facing the Fertilizer Facts*

*Fertilizing* — that is, supplying your plants with supplemental minerals — is an important part of gardening. We address the specific needs of specific types of plants in their respective chapters. What follows here isn't the last word on the subject, but rather a quick introduction. A well-timed dose of fertilizer really boosts a plant. You can't argue with success!

Just as a healthy diet allows a person or animal to prosper, a good and appropriate supply of nutrients keeps a plant healthy and happy. Plants have complex systems in need of chemicals to help them produce their own foods. The three primary plant-growth elements, or nutrients, are as follows:

- **N (nitrogen):** Enhances stem and leaf growth (for most plants, nitrogen ends up being the most important nutrient)
- **P (phosphorus):** Contributes to flower production, fruit production, seed production, and root growth
- **K (potassium):** Ensures general vigour; helps plants resist disease

An all-purpose, balanced formulation contributes to overall plant health. These top-three nutrients are usually listed on the back labels of bags of fertilizer that you can buy in any garden supply store, and they're usually listed in order as numbers on the package (N-P-K). A *balanced* fertilizer (one that contains these three most important elements — nitrogen, phosphorus, and potassium) may show up as 5-10-5 or even 5-10-10. Nitrogen-heavy lawn fertilizer usually has a high first number. You can find plenty of other variations, depending on the intended use of the fertilizer.

A fertilizer label often tells you which kind of fertilizer is best for your particular garden. If in doubt about your garden's exact needs, talk to someone at your local garden nursery or supply store. Chances are that their own garden needs aren't much different from yours!

Certain plants demand more or less of the top-three nutrients (for instance, lawn grass loves nitrogen best — consult Chapter 10 if you need to know more about that). But most garden flowers are not specialists, which is why generally fertile soil is desirable and why all-purpose fertilizer is most commonly recommended.

Good soil also contains secondary nutrients, like calcium, magnesium, and sulphur, as well as some trace elements, called *micronutrients,* that enhance plant health and growth. You usually don't have to add these nutrients to the soil. However, soil tests sometimes indicate that gardeners should add micronutrients or secondary nutrients, especially calcium (see "Figuring out your soil's pH" for info on soil tests).

Fertilizing good soil is often optional. If you have fertile, organically rich soil, many of your plants may do just fine without it — particularly if you develop the habit of amending the soil regularly (once or twice a year) with more organic matter. If your garden soil is organically rich, it's fertile and thus has the major elements. If not, or if you're pushing your plants to peak performance, you can use plant food or fertilizer, natural or organic, to supply or supplement these important nutrients.

Constantly fertilizing lousy soil isn't a good idea. Not only is it a lot of work and expense for you, but it's also a losing battle. Salts build up, plants are never really healthy in the long term, and the soil texture remains poor. You're far better off increasing the organic matter and just using fertilizer as a nutrient boost for your plants — if they need it. *Organic matter* — once-living material that releases nutrients as it decays — includes compost, dehydrated manure, chopped leaves, damp peat moss, and ground-up bark.

Depending on what type of fertilizer you use, how much you use, the plant in question, and so forth, the effects of adding fertilizer can be impressive — but they're not instant. Wait two weeks to a month before assessing the results.

## Adding organic matter with cover crops

If you have a large flower bed or big vegetable garden, one fairly easy and undeniably efficient way to give it a dose of organic matter is to plant a *cover crop* — plants that you grow for the sole purpose of maintaining and improving the land to prepare the garden for next year. A cover crop planted in early spring provides plentiful organic matter and limits erosion. Good choices include annual rye, buckwheat, and clover. Buckwheat grows fast and out-competes the weeds in a vegetable garden; then when you till it under in fall, it enriches the soil with organic matter over the winter. Sow the cover crop according to the directions on the bag and let the plants grow. Whatever cover crop you choose, it should be planted thickly enough to hog the area and sufficiently thwart weeds.

Alternatively, sow the cover crop in early fall and till the remains of the plants under in spring. Good choices include winter barley and winter rye. ***For spring planting:** When the plants are about a foot high and are still soft and green, dig them in (if practical) or till with a rear-mounted rotary tiller (see Chapter 5 for information on rototillers). Then let the plants decompose. ***For fall planting:** Plant in early fall and let winter kill the crop. The plants will decompose at least somewhat, with or without snow cover. Till the area in spring, when the ground is workable again. Wait a few weeks before planting the area.

"Feed the soil, not the plants!" is an old gardening adage, and frankly, these are words to live by, folks. You can't go wrong taking the time and effort to build up soil fertility and structure at least once a year, or more often if the opportunity presents itself. Dig in organic matter, add it to every planting hole (except when planting trees and shrubs), *top-dress* (sprinkle some on the soil surface at planting time), and *side-dress* (deliver more over the root zone midseason). Why? Because plants and soil organisms like to eat nutrients up and ask for more.

## *What to feed: The great natural versus chemical debate*

Quite honestly, only you can decide which plant food is convenient and successful for your own garden. A plant doesn't know the difference between one form of an element such as nitrogen and another — it's nitrogen in any case. Some gardeners swear by one fertilizer and use only that kind; other gardeners use a variety of fertilizers. The only way to know which fertilizer you should use is through personal trial and error. That said, you need to know a few things about natural and chemical fertilizers to help you make your decision. Check out Table 4-1 for a side-by-side comparison.

| Table 4-1 | Differences between Natural and Chemical Fertilizers | |
|---|---|---|
| *Trait* | *Natural Fertilizers* | *Chemical Fertilizers* |
| Form | Are organically based; examples include compost (homemade or store bought), manure, fish emulsion, blood meal, bone meal, and liquid seaweed | Come in various forms, including granules, powders, and concentrated liquids; examples include bagged and boxed fertilizers in various formulations, including Miracle-Gro and Osmocote |
| Cost and maintenance | Pound for pound, are generally more expensive in terms of the amount of fertilizer they provide, but they also improve the soil and tend to last longer than chemical fertilizers | Are usually affordable and easy to maintain |
| Effects on soil | Tend to improve soil texture and quality | Don't contribute to long-term soil fertility |
| Presence of secondary nutrients and micronutrients | Can include beneficial minor elements | May or may not contain these nutrients; check the label |
| Effect on organisms | Feed helpful soil organisms | Usually have a neutral effect |
| Rate of release | Tend to release nutrients slowly, so plants aren't damaged, but results aren't always as dramatic | Are a fast-acting way to jump start plant performance but must be applied correctly so they don't injure or burn your plants; special slow-release chemical fertilizers are the exception |

## When to feed your garden

Whether you're using store-bought or natural fertilizer, such as compost or manure, most plants like to be fertilized at planting time, just to get off to a good start. Thereafter, you may fertilize again on a monthly basis. Reduce or stop in late summer (except for annuals). Fertilizer inspires fresh new growth, and you don't want new growth in fall — it's a time for plants to slow down and approach dormancy, and cold weather can damage new growth. (You should, however, feed the *lawn* in autumn to stimulate root growth; feeding grass in the spring pushes excess leaf growth that the roots can't support — see Chapter 10 for details on lawns.) Again, for advice on specific plants, read more in the Parts II through IV of this book.

If you're using store-bought or chemical fertilizer, read the label to figure out how to deliver the fertilizer and how much to use. Some fertilizers work best if you dig them right into the soil; others are better delivered in dilute form when you water. The label can also tell you how much to use per square foot or metre and how often to apply. For bagged organic fertilizer, read the label; otherwise, do some research on your own.

More is not better! (Though if you're fertilizing with compost, using too much is almost impossible — see the following section.) Plant fertilizer is like aspirin. The right amount is beneficial; too much is harmful. So don't get carried away. Remember that some fertilizers are types of salt, and high concentrations of any salt can kill plants. Always read the label and follow the directions carefully. To get the amounts right, you may have to pull out the tape measure and figure out how much area of lawn or garden you need to cover.

Some gardeners like to fertilize their plants half as much, twice as often. That's perfectly okay. Just make sure you dilute properly and get your measurements right. (Gardeners often use this technique with roses and many houseplants.)

# Compost: More than Just a Fertilizer

Yeah, we talk about compost in the fertilizer section also, but compost is useful and necessary to your garden in so many ways other than as plain fertilizer. Because it's organically rich, with good texture, compost is just about the best thing you can add to soil. What works best really depends on the type and fertility of your native soil, but you can't go wrong digging in quite a lot of compost. Compost lightens heavy clay soil and gives needed substance to sandy soil. And less-extreme soils can still benefit.

In any event, having half-compost and half-native soil isn't excessive. Some really keen vegetable gardeners forgo native soil altogether and use 100 percent compost to grow incredible crops. Using solely compost is most feasible in raised beds. Roots relish it. You can get healthier, happier plants.

Don't use soggy or overly dry compost. Compost should be fully decayed, dark in colour, and crumbly in texture. This issue is more significant with homemade compost than with the bagged, store-bought sort. For homemade, you're fine if you take it from the bottom of the pile (most store-bought composters have a convenient hatch there). See Chapter 13 for info on how to make your own compost.

Whether you're planting a new rose, a young perennial, a handful of bulbs, or a bunch of annuals, always dig a hole both deeper and wider than the root ball. This practice gives you an opportunity to make a great new home for the plant, an area the roots can eagerly expand into. Either scoop some compost into the bottom of the hole (where a lot of root growth occurs) or mix compost with the native soil (try a 50-50 mix).

Skip this step of mixing in organic matter for trees and shrubs. The latest studies show that trees and most shrubs do better in the long run if you keep the plants in native soil; in amended soil, they may not grow past the planting hole. However, if you plant them in native soil, they can easily grow beyond the planting hole. (Flip to Chapter 11 for info on trees and shrubs.)

In general, potted plants like a lighter medium. Go ahead and put a handful or two of compost in along with the potting soil, but don't be heavy-handed. Chapter 16 can fill you in on container gardening.

Quite a few gardeners make their own compost, a process that can take three months to a year to complete. Many gardeners also use a compost bin, like the wooden one in Figure 4-1, for this process, though you can just pile the compost in an isolated and sectioned-off portion of your yard. Keep your compost pile slightly damp but not soggy. Stirring or turning the material every few weeks can speed up the decomposition process. When the compost is dark brown, is cool to the touch, and has a pleasant "earthy" smell, it's ready to use.

Good material choices for mixing and making your own compost include

- Chopped-up leaves (smaller pieces decompose more quickly)
- Young weeds that have not gone to seed
- Old lettuce or other salad greens
- Prunings from healthy plants

**Figure 4-1:**
Many gardeners find wooden compost bins attractive and easy to use.

Don't compost any weeds that have gone to seed, any diseased plants, or any plants that have been sprayed with herbicides. Also, animal fats and spoiled meat aren't recommended and often attract rodents.

# Demystifying Soil pH

The *pH* (you can find various arguments about exactly what pH stands for) is the measure of your soil's acidity, and it's often a huge area of debate among gardeners. We try to keep this discussion simple so your head doesn't spin, especially if you have little or no acquaintance with chemistry.

A soil pH that's too low means the soil's too acidic, and a pH that's too high means the soil is alkaline. Generally speaking, you want your soil pH to be on the *slightly* acidic side for the vast majority of garden plants. Extremes are rarely good. The pH scale ranges from acidic to alkaline — 0 to 14, with 7 as neutral. The really good news is that many soils are fairly close to neutral.

Acidic or alkaline soil isn't bad soil or bad for plant growth per se. But the minerals in the soil that are important to plant growth and health have a tough time getting to the plants when the pH isn't right for the particular plant. Scientists have discovered that beneficial soil bacteria don't function well unless the soil pH is relatively close to neutral. These bacteria are important because they break down organic matter and make sure nutrients are in forms that plants can use.

Of course, some plants prefer or are well-adapted to pH levels that are a little more acidic or a little more alkaline, and some soils are naturally so. When in doubt, you can take your cue from the native plants.

Examples of plants that like acidic soil include blueberries, azaleas, rhododendrons, most other broadleaf evergreens, and heather. So in the Maritime provinces, where many soils are acidic, you see wild blueberry plants. And if gardeners in that region want to grow blueberry bushes (albeit improved, bigger-sized fruit varieties), they're likely to have good luck.

Examples of plants that like alkaline soil include penstemon, dianthus, baby's breath, and beets. So in the Prairie provinces, where many soils are more alkaline, you see native penstemons. And if gardeners in that region want to grow these flowers (native species or improved selections), they're likely to be successful.

## Figuring out your soil's pH

You can do a little detective work by observing which native plants are thriving in your yard, and then confirming that they have a preference one way or another.

Or you can run a soil test — use either an inexpensive kit or arrange one of those more-intense tests where you take soil samples from various parts of your yard and then mail the dirt in to a lab. The benefit to doing this more-intense test is that the lab report not only tells you the pH (and a few other useful things, like the nutrient levels in your soil) but also gives you specific recommendations on how to improve or alter your soil. Check the appendix for some soil-testing services, or your province's agricultural office may be able to run the tests for you at a minimal cost or suggest an accredited lab.

## Adjusting your soil's pH

Of course you can adjust your soil's pH! Gardeners do it all the time when they know their lot in life is extreme soil, or even when they're just trying to please some special fussy plant. It's not a big deal. You just dig in something that nudges the pH in the direction you want it to go:

✔ **If your soil is too acidic:** If you need to raise the pH, dig in dolomitic limestone (a mined product that contains calcium and magnesium carbonate), bone meal, or wood ashes.

How much? We knew you were going to ask that! The answer has to do with how much ground you want to alter or improve. If a test shows you really need to adjust the pH (and we strongly recommend you get that lab-analyzed soil test), the lab can give you tailored directions on what to do and how much amendment(s) to add. Just so you know, though, the general guideline for adding dolomitic limestone is between 2.3 and 4.5 kilograms (5 and 10 pounds) per 10 square metres (100 square feet) of garden area.

✔ **If your soil is too alkaline:** To lower the pH, dig in some acidic organic matter such as peat moss, sawdust, well-chopped leaves from oak trees, or pine needles. Alternatively, you can add calcium sulphate, iron sulphate, aluminum sulphate, or powdered sulphur.

If you don't let the sawdust, leaves, or pine needles decompose somewhat before adding them to the soil, they can leach nitrogen from the soil as they break down. And too much peat moss can waterlog the soil as well as make it quite acidic. Consider adding no more than one part of organic amendment to three parts soil. You need professional advice on application rates if you decide to go with powdered sulphur or other additives.

# Much Ado about Mulch

Mulching is a good gardening habit, but is not mandatory. But, oh boy, do the benefits make it worth the effort! A really good job of mulching your garden usually

✔ Inhibits weed germination and growth (not only are weeds unsightly, but they also steal resources from your plants!)

✔ Holds in soil moisture, protecting your plants from drying out so fast

✔ Moderates soil-temperature fluctuations (this benefit is especially valuable during that turbulent-weather period in spring when you don't want your plants to be stressed)

✔ Protects plant roots from winter cold and helps prevent *frost-heaving*, in which plants are literally pushed out of the ground by the natural expansion and contraction of the soil as it cools off and heats up

✔ Helps keep plant roots cooler in the heat of summer

✔ Adds a bit of welcome nutrition (depending on which mulch you use) to your garden as it breaks down

Sound like good enough reasons to use mulch? Yeah, we knew you'd be convinced. Read on for the lowdown on mulches.

## *Knowing your mulches*

First of all, we can't name any "right" or "best" mulch. Benefits vary in different climates and parts of the country. Some mulches are free, found right in your own backyard; you can purchase others locally. Experiment to find out what you and your plants prefer.

Table 4-2 provides the basic information you need to know about some of the more popular options.

| Table 4-2 | Comparing Mulching Options | |
|---|---|---|
| *Type of Mulch* | *Advantages* | *Concerns* |
| Grass clippings | Are cheap, readily available, and easy to apply | Decay quickly, so you have to replenish them often; if you use weed killer or nitrogen-heavy fertilizer on your lawn, it may adversely affect other parts of the garden; can turn slimy if you apply more than 2.5 cm (1 in.) or so at a time; if the grass went to seed before you cut it, the grass seeds can germinate in your garden beds (yikes!) |

*(continued)*

### Table 4-2 *(continued)*

| Type of Mulch | Advantages | Concerns |
|---|---|---|
| Wood or bark chips | Look neat and attractive; stay where you put them; are slow to decay | Pine bark mulch is fairly acidic, which you may or may not want for your garden; if you apply it too deeply (more than 7.5 cm/3 in.) or apply a deep layer up against tree and shrub trunks, you may create a hiding spot for a bark-damaging rodent, especially during winter |
| Decaying leaves | Smother weeds very well; help hold in soil moisture | Are not especially attractive; if leaves contain seeds, they can germinate and become a weed problem; if the leaves are soft, like maple leaves, the mulch can mat; if they're acidic (oak especially), they can lower your garden soil's pH |
| Compost | Is free and plentiful if you have your own compost pile; adds nutrients to the soil as it breaks down | Makes a good place for weeds to take hold; fresh compost (especially if it contains manure or grass clippings) can burn plants |
| Peat moss | Looks neat and tidy; is versatile — also functions as a soil amendment | Can be expensive; if dry, will repel water or wick up moisture from the soil; becomes crusty over time |
| Straw | Is cheap and easy to apply | Is so light that it can blow or drift away; may harbour rodents, especially over the winter months; isn't very attractive for ornamental plantings |
| Hay | Is cheap and easy to apply | May harbour rodents, especially over the winter months; isn't very attractive for ornamental plantings; probably contains weed seeds |

| Type of Mulch | Advantages | Concerns |
|---|---|---|
| Gravel, pebbles, or stones | Have a nice, neat look (though not "natural"); are easy to apply; won't wash away easily and will last a long time; don't need to be replenished over the course of a season in colder climates | Can allow weeds to sneak through; provide no benefits to the soil |
| Plastic (garden plastic, black plastic) | Keeps weeds at bay; holds soil moisture and warmth in | Watering and feeding is hard (you need to cut openings for plants); can be difficult to apply unless you're doing an entire area at one time; isn't very attractive |

## *How to apply mulch — and how much*

If you're ready to start applying mulch to your garden, here's what you need to know to ensure you get the best possible use of your mulch:

✓ **When you plant:** Applying mulch right after planting something is easy. Use a shovel or scoop with a trowel. Spread the mulch over the root-zone area but not flush up against a plant's base or main stem (which can smother it or invite pests or disease).

Depth depends on the sort of plant. Annuals and perennials are fine with 2.5 centimetres (an inch) or so of mulch; shrubs, roses, and trees need 7.5 to 10 centimetres (3 to 4 inches) or more.

✓ **During the growing season:** Add more mulch midway through the growing season or whenever you notice it's depleted.

You may have to get down on your knees or wriggle around a bit as you try to deliver it where it's needed without harming the plant or its neighbours. Again, use less for smaller plants, more for bigger ones.

✓ **In the fall or for winter protection:** Depending on the severity of your winters and the amount of snow cover you expect (a blanket of snow can act like protective mulch, actually), you want to cover an overwintering plant well.

You can cut down perennials first and then practically bury them under several centimetres of mulch. But don't apply mulch until the ground has frozen — the goal is to keep the cold in and not allow warm winter days or erratic springs to thaw the soil even a bit, which may fool plants into thinking it's time to start growing. You don't have to be careful to keep mulch away from the crown as you were in summer, because the plant is no longer growing actively. In really cold areas, use 15 centimetres (6 inches) or more around the bases of roses and shrubs.

*Remember:* These amounts are guidelines only. You have to tailor them to your climate, growing season, and specific plants.

 To limit erosion, don't excavate large areas on a slope too early in the spring without planting or at least mulching right away. Otherwise, rainy weather can cause washouts.

# Water, Water Everywhere: Tackling Watering Issues

Sure, without moisture, plants die. Everyone knows that. But you may not know why water is so incredibly vital. The answer is threefold, actually:

- Sufficient water pressure within plant tissues creates *turgor,* or rigidity, so the plant can stand up. A plant without turgor pressure collapses.
- Water keeps nutrients flowing through the soil, the roots, and the plant parts as they should; it keeps the show going.
- The chemical process of photosynthesis — which you no doubt remember from biology class in school — involves the plant using light, carbon dioxide, and water to make sugar (a pretty impressive trick). Without photosynthesis, plants can't grow or develop flowers or fruit.

Keeping a close eye on your plants is easier said than done, of course, but the following sections tell you what you need to know, to keep in mind, and to watch out for when evaluating just how much moisture your garden needs.

## Providing plants with the right amount of moisture

How do you make sure your garden has the right amount of moisture? Relying on natural rainfall would be nice and easy, but natural rainfall is difficult to count on (though it does kindly water your garden for you from time to time). Gardeners always seem to have to supplement the moisture, a little or a lot. You just need to keep an eye on things and pay attention to your plants. Read on for the warning signs that tell you when there's too much or too little water.

### On the dry side

If you know what to look for, you can figure out your plants' watering needs. Plants actually prioritize when water-stressed, so look for these early warning signs that indicate a plant isn't getting enough water:

1. **Flower petals and buds (or fruit if it has developed) are jettisoned.**

   These are the first parts of a plant to go because making and maintaining them takes so much energy and water.

2. **Leaves shrivel.**

3. **Stems flop.**

4. **Roots go limp underground.**

Obviously, if your garden is in this condition, it needs more water.

### Bogged down

Telling when a plant doesn't have enough water may seem to be a snap, but keep in mind that there's definitely such a thing as too much water. If puddles form in your garden, or an area of it's quite soggy, all the pores in the soil fill. When this happens, no free oxygen, which needs to get to the roots, is in the soil (See "Air! Air! Plants Need Air!" later in this chapter).

Meanwhile, some plant diseases (like mildew and blight) travel via water and can easily develop and spread in soaked conditions. Sodden roots blacken and rot, and all the above-ground growth subsequently dies. Garden plants in these circumstances, of course, need less water. See "Dealing with drainage problems" later in the chapter to find out what to do.

Unfortunately, an overwatered plant looks the same as one that's underwatered! The reason is that an overwatered plant is actually suffering from dehydration because the roots have been damaged by too much water (actually, too little oxygen, because the water has displaced the oxygen); the roots can't absorb water, so the plant wilts. One difference is that overwatered plants don't recover from wilt when you apply additional water, but underwatered ones generally do.

## Determining which watering system to use

The amount of water your garden needs depends on what kind of soil you're using, what your climate is like, and what kinds of plants you have. Shallow-rooted plants, for example, need more water than deep-rooted ones for the simple reason that they're closer to the soil surface, which dries out more quickly in the heat of the sun. Deep roots can reach the more consistently damp lower soil layers.

For many gardeners, getting enough water to their gardens is the biggest gardening challenge. If you're crunched for time or have a large area to water, installing in-ground sprinklers and irrigation systems may be a good idea.

Employing the use of a regular watering system, such as drip irrigation or an in-ground system, is the best approach to ensuring a consistent moisture cycle to grow happy, healthy plants. However, in-ground watering systems tend to be expensive and should be installed by professionals. If you're looking for suppliers of irrigation systems, the companies listed in the appendix may be a good starting point.

Of course, you can always water your garden yourself, by hand, and that's a great way to do it, because you can personally inspect each plant. For details about equipment like soaker hoses and portable sprinklers to help you with your watering, check out Chapter 5.

Whether you water by hand or use a system, here are some things you may want to keep in mind:

- Watering your garden early in the morning, before the sun is fully overhead, is usually best. Watering at night can make plants susceptible to diseases that cause them to rot.

- Some plants in your garden, such as melons, may require more water than others, in which case, watering by hand is probably best.

- If you don't have an outdoor spigot close to your garden for convenient hose hookup and watering, a rain barrel may be a good substitute for keeping water close to your garden. Various mail-order suppliers sell rain barrels.

  Make sure you get a barrel that's tall enough so pets can't get in, or put on covers to reduce drowning risks to pets and children. To keep mosquitoes out, use Aquabac, a product that comes in granular or liquid form and contains a type of bacteria harmless to humans but deadly to mosquito larvae.

- Usually, watering the soil rather than the leaves is best because the roots are what absorb water, and they're in the soil. Also, wetting the leaves can result in more disease problems. Still, on a very hot or windy day, watering the leaves can reduce wilt and lower leaf temperatures.

- Unless you have a very large garden, sprinkler heads that you attach to garden hoses are usually better suited to lawns than gardens. If you decide to use one, make sure the sprinkler covers the entire garden area evenly and doesn't water things you don't want watered, like your lawn furniture or windows.

- No matter what kind of garden you have or which watering system you use, infrequent deep soakings are better than frequent shallow waterings.

## Deciding whether you need professional help

Valves, risers, timers, controllers, moisture sensors, and pipes, oh my! If thinking about all these parts and how they should go together makes your head spin, hire someone who's done it hundreds of times. Find such a contractor via your local garden centre, in the Yellow Pages, or through a reference from a friend or neighbour. (Get a written estimate for the work, labour, and parts, and check references.)

However, if you're an affirmed do-it-yourselfer, handy, and confident, by all means, install your watering system yourself. Check with your local utility companies — gas, water, and electric — (if the system's underground) before doing any digging to avoid costly and potentially dangerous accidents. Detailed information and advice is available (where else?) in *Lawn Care For Dummies* (Wiley), by Lance Walheim and the editors of the National Gardening Association.

## *Cutting back on watering*

Even if you don't live in an area experiencing drought, you don't want to waste water, no matter what you pay for it or how much you have to use. Remember that for the most efficient delivery, water in early to mid-morning — after the dew has dried but before the heat of the day sets in and much of the water evaporates. And mulch, mulch, mulch individual plants and entire beds to hold in the water right by the roots, where plants most need and appreciate it. We go into more detail about mulch earlier in the chapter in "Much Ado about Mulch."

Wherever possible, build up a basin of mounded-up dirt or mulch around the edge of the root ball of each plant at planting time. Water goes right in the basin and soaks directly down into the root system instead of running off onto the lawn or driveway or elsewhere where it isn't needed.

The method of delivery can also save water: In-ground irrigation systems are wonderfully efficient, as we mention earlier in the chapter, and soaker hoses are also good. A good drip system doesn't produce any appreciable runoff on slopes. Although some sprinklers are good, others are very wasteful. Check out mail-order catalogues that specialize in sprinklers. They're filled with good information on how to choose the right ones.

Depending on what kind of soil you have and how well it absorbs, you may find it worthwhile to run the water slowly rather than quickly, and perhaps ten minutes on, ten minutes off — either or both of these techniques often drenches an area quite efficiently with little waste.

Rain gauges are useful for measuring water when you apply it with overhead sprinklers. For drip systems, run them for an hour or two and then dig down into the soil around the plant to see how far down and wide the moisture has penetrated. Run the system longer if it hasn't yet penetrated deep enough to reach the root zone. After you do this exercise a few times, you should know how long to run the system each time you water.

Another way to cut back on the amount of watering you need to do is to use drought-tolerant plants in your garden. Gardeners in the Prairie provinces are particularly good at this type of gardening, largely through necessity. Drought-tolerant plants include cacti (yes, many are native to Canada!), succulents, rock roses, native dryland plants and their cultivars (such as penstemon and gaura), and deep-rooted perennials like prairie natives and their cultivars (such as baptisia, liatris, black-eyed Susans, and purple coneflowers).

## *Dealing with drainage problems*

You know you have a drainage problem in your garden when heavy or even moderate rain leaves puddles that take forever to drain. Or you may find out, to your dismay, that under a shallow top layer of okay soil in your yard is a stubborn layer of *hardpan* (most people discover this water-resistant barrier — often packed clay — when they dig a deeper-than-usual hole for planting a big shrub or a tree).

Really damp areas (especially during humid periods or in shady spots) are slow to evaporate water, whether from rain or from your sprinkler. Then plant diseases can get started, particularly on foliage. The answer here is to try to improve the air circulation: Prune overhanging growth and give individual plants more elbow room. And when you're in charge of watering, supply it to the roots instead of allowing it to splash the entire plant.

Obviously, bad drainage isn't good for any garden plant, including trees and shrubs. If you're smart or lucky, you can deal with the problem before you plant or redo an area. Here are some options, from the simple to the high-tech:

- **Try improving the soil.** Dig in lots of organic matter. Soil with high organic-matter content allows excess moisture to drain through while absorbing needed water. Sounds paradoxical, but it's true. (For info on improving soil with compost, check out the earlier section titled "Compost: More than Just a Fertilizer.")

- **Build and garden in raised beds.** You control the soil within, and thus it drains well and your plants are happy. Problem averted.

- **Create a rain garden or a bog garden, and plant only water-loving plants.** Water-loving trees and plants include maples, willows, astilbe, ferns, filipendula, bee balm, mint, some irises, and canna.

✔ **Route water flow away from the garden area.** Just get out there with a trowel or shovel and create some diversion channels. Of course, you don't want to send the problem to another important part of the yard, or foist unwanted, excess water on your neighbour. Send it down the driveway and onto the street, or into the gutter. This water needs to head for the storm drains. (If this plan isn't practical, dig a hole nearby, fill it with gravel, and route the channel there.)

Fertilizer runoff can harm rivers and streams, so if you use fertilizers, be especially careful that you don't use excessive amounts and that you apply it at recommended times so the plants use the nutrients rapidly. See the earlier section "Facing the Fertilizer Facts" for info on proper application.

✔ **Make a gravel channel.** Follow the advice about rerouting water flow, but dig the channel somewhat deeper and fill it with crushed gravel or pebbles. You can hide some or all of it from view by scooping a little soil over it. It'll still do its job of slowly but surely taking the water away.

✔ **Use perforated plastic pipes, lightly or deeply buried, to divert the water to where you want it to go.** Home supply stores sell pipes specifically for this purpose. These pipes usually come in various forms and sizes of plastic; clay tiling is also available, but it's too heavy and expensive for most homeowners.

✔ **Think about drainage tiles, a French drain, or a curtain drain as options if the problem is severe and you can't seem to solve it.** Installing one of these systems can be a very expensive and involved process. Hire someone experienced to advise you, explain the options, and install.

# Air! Air! Plants Need Air!

A sometimes overlooked necessity for plant life is air (and not just carbon dioxide). Without air, plants struggle and perish. Yes, the free oxygen in the air is part of the photosynthesis recipe, produced by the plants themselves, but there's another practical reason why plants need air: Air movement around your plants prevents disease, especially fungal diseases that gain a foothold when the air is too "close" and humid and when wet leaves can't dry or don't dry quickly.

Underground, oxygen between the particles of soil is important. Plant roots, or more accurately, their little root hairs, are busy. They take in that oxygen, absorb water, and then release carbon dioxide. If this process is thwarted, as in waterlogged soil, the roots can't function properly, they begin to rot, and the plant surely suffers.

We're not suggesting you set up a fan out there in your garden, but here's what you can do to make sure your plants are getting plenty of air:

- ✔ **Don't let soil get compacted.** If the ground is quite wet, don't walk on it or dig in it. Loose soil is airy soil.

- ✔ **Add organic matter.** Mixing in organic matter, especially in dense clay soil — something we keep harping on, we know, but it's so important — helps keep soil aerated.

- ✔ **Never kill an earthworm.** Earthworms help break up and aerate your soil. Rejoice in their presence! Welcome them!

- ✔ **Make sure your garden is well drained.** (See the preceding section on drainage.)

- ✔ **Don't crowd your plants together in the garden bed if they're susceptible to mildew or black spot.** Give everyone a little elbow room!

# Chapter 5

# Gathering Your Gardening Gear

*Y*ou can find deep and abiding pleasure in a good tool, in finding and using the right equipment for the job at hand. This statement is as true for gardening as it is for, say, cooking or woodworking. In this chapter, we take a look at the tools you probably need (and want) to aid you with your gardening, and we advise you on their selection and care.

Here's where you get to roll up your sleeves at last and get into the really satisfying work that's the heart and soul of successful gardening. High-quality, well-chosen tools allow you to put your plans into action! This chapter covers the most common and general tools you likely need for successful gardening, and it includes pointers on how to pick the best ones. (We list some suppliers in the appendix, in case you need a starting point.)

The difference between the right garden tool and the wrong garden tool is the difference between back-breaking labour and joyful efficiency.

## Digging Those, Er, Digging Tools

Dogs (and kids) often dig for no apparent reason, for the sheer pleasure of getting deeper into the ground and letting the dirt fly. Gardeners, on the other hand, dig with a purpose — to create a new planting bed or hole, to create a trench, or to harvest a delicious, homegrown root vegetable. Nonetheless, gardeners have the right to have fun in the dirt! And having fun turning the soil is possible when you have the right tool.

# Getting down with shovels and spades

Shovels and spades are digging tools, and you may be astounded at the array available. "Necessity is the mother of invention," as the adage goes, and never is this truer than in the great variety of shovels in the world. Each one was invented by someone with a specific kind of digging in mind. However, generally speaking, digging tools fall into two main types: shovels and spades. Choosing a shovel or spade requires matching it to your needs — the sort of soil it'll be digging, plus your own height and body strength.

What's the difference between a shovel and a spade? Well, generally, it comes down to the shape of the digging edges:

- **Shovels have rounded edges.** The rounded tip is meant to allow easy, swordlike penetration of a variety of soils and materials. Shovels also have dishes to hold dirt, and you want a shovel with a dish that's reliably strong and firm enough not to bend.

- **Spades have squared edges.** The main purpose of this digging tool is to lift, move, and throw with ease. Spades are supposed to be easier than shovels on your back — just slightly flex your knees and thrust the spade in and out of the pile of leaves, compost, or topsoil you're working on. (Spades are also good for mixing concrete and delivering it neatly to its appointed spot.)

When you go shovel or spade shopping, you may observe various grades and prices. You get what you pay for, folks. A so-called "homeowner" or "economy" shovel looks good enough, but it may not stand up to tougher jobs or rocks in the ground. A "contractor" shovel, on the other hand, has a thicker blade made of forged steel and strong attachments where the blade meets the handle. Be sure to pay close attention to the labels to know what kind of shovel you're looking at. You can usually find shovels and spades in a range of qualities at a single store.

Shovels and spades made of forged steel (as are axe heads or hammer heads) are the best. Stamped shovels and spades are okay for lighter jobs, but because their blades are cut from a single thickness of metal, they're not as strong or tailored to do a heavy job.

To determine whether a shovel or spade is well made, examine it where its parts come together (assuming the tool you're contemplating is not all one piece). The longer the *socket,* the part that holds the shaft to the head, the stronger the tool will be. Rivets and welding points are weak spots, though often necessary. Avoid any tool with sloppy workmanship. The following sections outline the features to look for.

## A strong shaft

The reason the shaft is straight is simple: Bends or curves create weak points or stress points. Do check that the tool you're thinking of buying has a perfectly straight shaft. Material is equally important. A label that says "solid hardwood shaft," although desirable, is also rather vague. You want a strong, solid, splinter-resistant wood; ash is considered the best, with hickory in second place. Maple is okay, too, though it's heavier and can break in unpredictable ways.

Painted shafts? No doubt they're attractive in their jaunty colours and smooth textures, but beware: A coat of paint on a shovel's shaft may be hiding weaknesses or flaws, such as knots or grafted pieces of wood. Better to go with a plain, unadorned model so you can see what you're getting (and paint it yourself at home, if you like).

Metal (including steel) and fibreglass shafts are also available. Though these shafts can be quite strong and weather-tough, and superior to cheap woods like pine, their drawback is that when they bend or break, the tool is finished. And either of these materials may transport uncomfortable or numbing vibrations into your hands and arms. Also, metal tools can be darn cold during the winter (and they conduct electricity if you happen to hit electrical live wires — yikes!).

## The correct handle

You need good leverage; the right grip, well designed and durably constructed, delivers just that. Seek a comfortable fit for your hand, and peer closely at the rivets that attach the handle to be sure they're neatly installed and flush. You're likely to see the classic D-handle most often, usually made of durable but lightweight plastic (which can and does crack or break down over the years due to use and exposure to sunlight, though you can certainly get many good years out of it). A good handle is easy and comfortable to hang on to, especially during twisting and lifting motions.

A variation on the D-handle is the so-called YD-handle, which is longer and potentially sturdier. The two sides of the handle converge in a *Y,* and a crosspiece of wood (usually metal-reinforced) joins them. This design has the advantage of dissipating twisting forces.

Last but not least is the T-handle, which is excellent for two-handed pushing work, such as with the shallow-angled spades that gardeners use to edge planting beds or peel off turf or topsoil. The drawback is that the impact of your digging travels straight into your wrist, so look for a coated handle or wear gloves to alleviate the shock, at least somewhat.

### A good angle, or cant

*Cant* refers to the angle between the head of the spade or shovel and the ground. A lower angle is best for digging and holding soil; a steeper angle is better suited to lifting and tossing soil and other materials. To check the cant, place the tool on the ground and see how flat it lies.

### A well-designed frog

The *frog* is an open-backed tube or socket, meant to fit the head of the tool to the shaft. The frog is vulnerable to collecting dirt along its length, so unless you assiduously clean your shovel after every use, the dirt eventually starts to rot the wooden handle. Some shovels have metal welded over this area to prevent dirt from getting in, which helps, although the front side is still a point of weakness.

## Trowels: More than just little shovels

A good trowel is an indispensable gardening friend, with you through thick and thin for many years. Consider everything we say here, but definitely pick a trowel that feels right to you when you hold and use it. As with shovels and spades, many different kinds of trowels are on the market. You have plenty of choices, so be sure to pay attention to the labels at the store and ask for assistance if you have trouble determining which trowel is right for you.

As you may gather by reading about shovels in the preceding section, good-quality materials make for a more effective, longer-lasting trowel. The blade (from cheapest on up to best) can be made from

- Stamped metal
- Aluminum
- Forged carbon steel or (no rust!) stainless steel

Top-of-the-line trowels feature a carbon steel blade that's epoxy-coated to resist wear and rust. As for the handle, good, strong wood is what you want — ash or hickory is best. Avoid cheap trowels made of lightweight materials, because they seem to bend or even break at the slightest challenge.

A sign of a quality trowel, one that can stand lots of use, is one whose wooden handle meets its metal blade in a strong and lasting manner so it won't bend or break, of course. Cheap ones employ a simple tang-and-ferrule design. The *ferrule* is the circular clamp that holds the blade to the handle, and the *tang*, or *shank*, is the part of the blade extending into and usually through the ferrule.

After a while, the ferrule tends to loosen and rattle around on the trowel's shank. This statement is not to criticize all tang-and-ferrule attachments; good, solidly anchored ones exist and are sometimes even reinforced with rivets. The alternative is getting a one-piece metal trowel.

The one-piece metal trowels may send tiring shockwaves into your hands as you work and be icy cold to the touch, but clever manufacturers have solved this problem by coating the handle with rubber or PVC plastic. For other types, seek a smooth wooden handle so you don't get splinters or blisters. In any event, you should be able to squeeze the handle comfortably, with little stress to your wrist.

Some trowels have a hole drilled into the very top part of the handle, perhaps with a string or leather thong loop for hanging and storing the tool when it's not in use. Though this feature may seem frivolous, it can be a handy extra if you're the sort of person who needs to be reminded to bring your gardening tools indoors and clean them up after use. Another feature you may appreciate is a ruler stamped or etched into the blade — built-in rulers are helpful when you're planting various sorts of bulbs or other flowers that require varying planting depths.

## Garden forks: Not for dining!

Although not an essential garden tool, many gardeners come to find that a garden fork is quite handy and more agile than a spade or shovel for some digging jobs. You drive this shovel-size tool into the soil and then pull back on the handle and rock it to break and loosen the soil. Garden forks are useful for digging up bulbs and root crops, including onions and potatoes; they're also good for scooping jobs (moving compost or hay from one spot to another, for instance). Garden forks tend to be shorter than pitchforks and have shorter, flatter tines.

Yes, you can find many different kinds of garden forks, though you'll notice that the four-tine model is standard. As with shovels and trowels, pay close attention to what the labels say, and ask a store clerk for assistance if you need help determining which type of fork is right for you.

A strong ash or hickory handle is desirable. As for the prongs, they'd better be strong — stamped or forged steel or high-carbon steel, maybe slightly incurved to resist the temptation to bend, with tines that taper to a point. Solid-socket construction where the handle meets the tines is critical because this tool can really take a beating in use, and you don't want it to bend or break.

You want widely spaced tines on your garden fork so you expend less effort when digging.

---

# Taking care of your things: Garden tool maintenance

Use those skills you picked up in kindergarten — make sure you pick up after yourself and clean up your things! Keep your tools out of the weather, no matter what they're made of, and bring them indoors after use. Otherwise, dampness causes wood to rot, and exposure to sunlight breaks down plastic parts. Plus you don't want anyone running over your tools on foot or with a bicycle or vehicle — for their safety as well as for the good of the tool itself. And make sure you store sharp objects away from where kids or pets can get to them.

Keep tools clean. Tools are always going to have some dirt, soil, or other material adhering to their blades after a project, but take the time to hose or wipe them off — this simple step really, really prolongs a digging tool's life. Just make sure the tool is dry before storing, because many tools are made of high-carbon steel, which rusts easily if not coated in rust-resistant material.

---

## *Dabbling in dibbles (or dibbers) for poking holes*

A *dibble* (or *dibber*) can be a very helpful tool to have. Essentially, it's a hand-held poking tool that creates a planting hole in the ground. The tool is generally cylindrical and comes to a point, somewhat like a stubby, sharpened pencil; larger ones may have a curved handle. End to end, the dibble may be up to 25 or 30 centimetres (10 or 12 inches) long. Fat dibbles are popular for bulb planting or for creating a hole for a larger seedling, while skinny ones are great for planting seeds or for setting out smaller seedlings.

Why bother with dibbles? Because like any good tool, a dibble makes a project easier — your hand becomes much slower to tire. You can purchase one of many examples available from your local garden supplier, or you can make your own by sharpening a broken hoe, shovel, or broom handle. For small jobs, you can use a sharpened pencil or wooden dowel.

Though a simple tool, a good dibble is often a two-part item. The top half, or handle, allows for a comfortable grip, so it's usually made from wood or strong, durable plastic. If designed well, you should be able to grab the dibble almost like a pistol or screw gun, which reduces stress to your hand and wrist as you work. In any event, the bottom digging or prodding half is best made out of strong, stiff metal such as carbon steel.

## Chemical warfare: Pesticides

The use of chemicals to control pests — including weeds, insects, rodents, fungi, and microorganisms — is a very complicated subject that varies in its regulations across the country (check the bylaw section of your municipal government's Web site to see which products have been approved for use in your area). Luckily, most chemicals sold to consumers are relatively safe. The most toxic ones have been taken off the market or are available only to certified appliers. Visit `www.pestcontrolcanada.`

`com/pesticides.htm` for general pesticide info and a pesticide database. For information from Health Canada's Pest Management Regulatory Agency, check out `www.pmra-arla.gc.ca/english/consum/consum-e.html`.

You can also look through the plant-specific chapters for more info on using pesticides and other methods of pest control.

Some dibbles have a hollow tip so that when the tool penetrates soil, the dibble captures displaced soil so you can set it aside. However, if you're working in clay, this type of tool probably isn't your best bet, because the soil tends to get stuck in the hollow and can be difficult to remove.

Owing to its smaller size and the scope of appropriate planting projects (namely, planting bulbs or seedlings), you shouldn't be stooping or bending when using your dibble. Sit or squat on the ground, or kneel. This position also allows you to keep an eye on hole depth. Don't get carried away, lazy, or tired and start plunking things into too-deep holes!

# Clues to Quality Cultivating Tools

What exactly is cultivating, anyway? After all, this is *gardening* we're talking about, not *farming*. All *cultivating* really means in this context is stirring up the soil and fighting weeds. These jobs, quite honestly, always seem to go hand in hand. You need to do them for the good of the soil and the survival and prosperity of your garden plants. Cultivating tools exist to make the job easier and more efficient, regardless of whether you're tending a vegetable garden or a flower bed.

Removing whatever is growing in a spot (whether weeds or wild plants or old lawn, or whatever) creates open ground — which, like a good gardener, you should improve prior to planting (refer to Chapter 4). So you do everything you're supposed to do, and then what happens? A crust forms. Water may puddle and seedlings may strain to poke through. You need to gently break it up, and that's where cultivating tools come in.

**GARDEN JARGON**

---

## Putting an oscillating hoe to use

An *oscillating hoe* (also known as an action hoe, hula hoe, or stirrup hoe) looks different from the average hoe. Rather than ending in a solid piece of sharp metal, this hoe has a shallow open box (like a cookie cutter) of double-edged blades, and it moves about 13 millimetres (½ inch) back and forth as you push or pull it. Thus, the tool can cut in two directions and is also self-cleaning (debris slips off with each back-and-forth motion). Oscillating hoes are especially effective for combating established weeds in heavy soil.

This sort of hoe is amazingly easy and fun to use, almost relaxing or hypnotic. The blade may be as big as 18 centimetres (7 inches) across or as small as 5 centimetres (2 inches) across.

---

Weeds love freshly cleared ground. They're fast; they're aggressive. They creep in, or birds and other animals deliver them. Seeds that had been slumbering below the surface now have the light, warmth, and moisture they need to sprout. However they arrive, weeds elbow out the plants you want and hog all the resources to boot. What to do? Mulch if you can (refer to Chapter 4 for details) and cultivate!

## *Ho, ho, hoes*

All sorts of hoes are available, and the one or ones you choose to invest in is partly a matter of what you feel comfortable using and what you need them for. For maximum efficiency, both pushing and pulling action is desirable. At any rate, hoes tend to be long-handled, which is fine, but the blade also needs to be right for the place where you use it. If you'll be working in cramped spaces, like the rows of a vegetable or herb garden, pick a narrow-bladed one, of course. About 15 centimetres (6 inches) wide is standard.

A good hoe isn't a lightweight or wimpy tool — you mean business! Choose a hoe with a strong, durable hardwood handle (such as hickory or ash). Forged steel is standard for the blade. If either of these parts gets worn out or damaged, replacing it is an option. As for the point of attachment, the handle should be snug and secure in a hole in the top of the blade, even reinforced with rivets, so there's no risk of its falling off.

**REMEMBER**

Sharpness counts! Your hoe will be sharp when you first bring it home. But you have to keep it so, or else it'll do a sloppy or damaging job. File it often to maintain its bevelled edge.

**TIP**

Hoes do a better job on ground that has recently been watered or rained upon — the weed roots they're meant to tear out depart damp ground much more easily and completely than those in dry soil.

## *Weeding out poor weeders to get to the best*

Unlike the hoe, or a layer of smothering mulch or black plastic, a weeder is a hand tool, a clever hand-held weapon in the war on weeds. You can usually take out the invading marauders one at a time. As such, using a weeder is better than attacking the enemy with your bare hands. You can use the same vigour — or frothing rage, if it comes to that! — but a weeding tool makes your efforts more productive. A good weeder helps you extract the entire plant (as you know from dandelions and other weeds, leaving a bit of root behind usually means that the war isn't over yet).

Make an effort to match the weeder to the weed, because some tools are specialists. You need a single blade with a forked end, for example, to get plants with taproots out. And the "mini-hoe" action of a typical hand-held weeder works best on shallow-rooted and well-hidden weeds where your aim is merely to slice off the above ground parts of the plants. Personally, we don't find weeders with rotary blades to be very useful.

Because weeders go into the difficult zones of tough soil and tenacious root systems and may contend with daunting obstructions, including rocks and other impediments, they need to be both very tough and somewhat flexible or resilient. Steel is best, of course, though not all steel is created equal. Sturdy gauge steel is fine, and stamped steel is adequate, but if you want a truly powerful and long-lasting weapon, spend your money on a higher-quality forged steel weeder.

Most weeders are meant to be used down on the ground, as close to their quarry as possible. This means you have to sit, kneel, or squat, which reduces strain on your back and allows you to bring maximum force to the job at hand. If the ground is damp or uncomfortable for you, do your weeding perched on a mat or kneeling on one of those nifty low gardening stools.

Take out weeds earlier rather than later, because smaller weeds are always easier to attack. Work when the ground is damp from rain or a recent watering, and you should find the job much easier.

# *Making the Right Cut with Cutting Tools*

So many great cutting tools are available for gardeners! This area has seen remarkable innovation in recent years, making everything from harvesting flowers and fruit to major pruning jobs neater and more efficient than ever before. Treat yourself to some good cutting tools — they make life (and plant, tree, and shrub maintenance) so much easier.

Keep 'em clean. As with digging tools, or any garden tool at all, for that matter, cutting tools get dirty with use. If you're good about cleaning them after each use, or at least when grit, sap, or pitch builds up on their blades, they'll serve you much better and for much longer.

For information on how to prune and trim trees and shrubs, see Chapter 11.

## Getting a handle on hand pruners

Many serious gardeners value hand pruners, also popularly known as *secateurs,* above all else — they carry these hand-held cutters everywhere (in a special belt holster or tucked in their back pocket) and are reluctant to lend them. Why? A good pair fits your hand comfortably and takes care of a wide range of gardening jobs — from snipping off the spent stems from last year's perennials to cutting roses for a vase to cutting away a pesky sucker to trimming a favourite shrub or ornamental tree. In a word, pruners are handy!

In general, hand pruners are intended for use on branches 13 to 19 millimetres (½ to ¾ of an inch) in diameter (depending on the type of pruner) — which covers a lot of gardening cutting jobs, actually. If a branch is thicker, your pruners and your hands will strain and the pruners won't be able to do a good job.

The best pruner handles are designed to absorb shock but are still lightweight and strong. Usually, they're made of aluminum alloy and coated with a smooth, durable vinyl (usually red!). The more-expensive hand pruners come in left- and right-handed models.

As for the blades, you want tempered carbon steel. This type of blade starts off sharp and then needs to be sharpened by you or someone else (which is never expensive) from time to time to maintain the bevel, but it'll hold up well and last a long time. You usually use a whetstone for sharpening, though you may be able to find gadgets made for sharpening pruners that can make the job much easier. Sometimes just replacing nicked blades is easier. Better hand pruners have replacement cutting blades that you can purchase.

Here are some other considerations to keep in mind when you're looking for a good hand pruner:

✔ If you're investing in a good, professional-grade pruner, you may one day want to replace the blades rather than the entire tool. Discern when you buy whether the pruner's blades are replaceable.

✔ A safety latch is very important so the clippers don't spring open when you don't want them to, such as when they're not in use or when they're lodged in your pocket. A good pruner should click in and out of position easily, ideally with a flick of your thumb.

✔ The spring that holds the pivot, keeping it tense, should operate smoothly, without catching, without hesitation. Try it out a few times to make sure.

✔ Some pruners have a nifty feature on the bottom blade: a groove that helps carry sap and pitch away from the tool. You should be in the habit of cleaning your pruners after every use anyway, but this little extra feature certainly helps.

Though you may feel like dozens of different kinds of hand pruners line the store shelves, the tools are really all variations on two themes — *bypass pruners* and *anvil pruners*. Both types are approximately the same size but operate differently:

✔ **Bypass pruners:** By far the most common, these pruners use a scissor action that makes neat, even, shave-close slices, thanks to a bevelled cutting blade.

✔ **Anvil pruners:** This style of pruner earns its name because the cutting blade comes down on a slender, noncutting "anvil" blade, so a flush cut isn't possible. This tool is right for cutting very tough or dead wood. Some anvil-style pruners have a ratcheting action, which makes cutting easier. These pruners are usually cheaper than the bypass types.

## *Hedging your bets on hedge shears*

The basic design of hedge shears has changed a little over the years to become even more efficient than ever before. Basically, you're looking at a tool that's from 30 to 60 centimetres (1 to 2 feet) long from tip to handle's end (unless you get an especially long-handled model). This form allows the average-size person to slice away while standing comfortably. These cutters are meant to be used to trim hedges, whether evergreen or deciduous; they're too big and unwieldy for spot-cutting jobs or regular pruning.

The shafts are either light, but tough, tubular steel or heavier hardwood, usually with cushioned grips to make your work more comfortable and your grip more secure. The cutting blades are long and sharp, the cutting edge is ideally bevelled, and the base (near the fulcrum) may have serrations for those occasions when you encounter especially tough branches.

You can get better results and longer use from your hedge shears if the blades are tough, drop-forged carbon steel. Check also that the point where the cutting blades meet the handles is secure and tough.

The blades of hedge shears vary in design. Wavy-edged ones help keep branches in place as you work without gathering dirt or roughening the cut. Serrated-edged ones can tame unruly stems of wayward shrubs by holding them while you cut.

Assuming you can run a cord from a power source out to your hedge or to other shrubs that need occasional shearing, electric hedge trimmers are worth considering. Electric-powered shears can often do a neater and faster job than manual shears, which may be important to you if you have a lot of hedge to cut or are striving for a formal, tidy look. But before using any power tool, make sure to check out the safety tips in "Safety first: Controlling your power tools (so they don't control you)," later in this chapter.

## Branching out with loppers

A lopper is a sort of in-between cutting tool. By that, we mean a lopper is what you reach for when a branch is too thick for a hand pruner yet too leggy to be managed with a saw. In these cases, which come up more often than you may think, there's no better tool for the job than a lopper.

A good pair of loppers has long, strong shafts of steel, fibreglass, or hardwood. At the ends, where you grip them, you want either vinyl or rubber handles, just to alleviate vibrations from cutting and to make the work more comfortable. At the top, the curved hook and blade ought to be tough metal such as forged carbon steel — sharp, of course, and bevelled. The point where the shafts and the hook and blade come together needs to be strong and secure; look for strong, stout pins or rivets, as well as rubber bumpers.

Use loppers on wayward vines, on overgrown shrubs and hedges, and on small ornamental or fruit trees. You may find loppers especially handy if you have to reach into the greenery or work in tight quarters. Employ a pair of loppers when you need to cut something 5 centimetres (2 inches) in diameter or less. Some of the special ratcheted types can tackle somewhat larger material.

## Moving up to pruning saws

The pruning saw is such a simple tool that people tend to underestimate it. The first thing you need to know about pruning saws is *accept no substitutes*. Don't use any household or carpenter's saw in its place. Those tools aren't curved — a feature of the pruning saw you can immediately appreciate when you use it. Plus the blade may be too thick, which chews up the branch instead of severing it, or the cutting teeth may not be right for the branch you want to cut. Invest in the saw that's meant for gardening! Pruning saws are never expensive, and you won't be sorry.

Use a pruning saw on branches that won't yield easily to loppers — basically, anything over 8 centimetres (3 inches) or so. You can manage thicker branches using the standard three-way cut (see Chapter 11 for details).

If a job seems too big for your pruning saw — if you feel in the slightest that you're overmatched or in danger — hire someone else to do the job or use a chainsaw instead (see the upcoming section "Chewing through chores with chainsaws").

End to end, a typical pruning saw is between 35 and 50 centimetres (14 and 20 inches) long. Some shorter folding saws are handy for smaller jobs and are easy to carry in your pocket. The handle is traditionally of pistol grip design so you can hold and wield it securely and safely; it's usually wood, but it may be tough plastic. As for the blade, seek something that's rust-resistant and strong, such as tempered steel alloy. Look closely at the teeth — you want *tri-edge* blades (the ones with three bevels), because this shape makes the fastest, neatest cuts. Plain lance-toothed pruning saws are still around and are admittedly cheaper, but the cutting can be rough going.

What's the advantage of a folding saw? It's simply a safety feature, eliminating the need for a scabbard of some kind for carrying or storing the saw when it's not in use. Beware of cheap folding saws, though! A well-designed folding saw locks securely in both the open and closed positions.

The *bow saw,* which is a D-shaped saw, is bigger and more formidable, up to 90 centimetres (3 feet) long and intended only for bigger pruning jobs on larger branches. Bow saws let you use both a push and pull cut. The frame should be of rigid steel so the blade is kept taut (or you can tighten it before each use).

# Putting Power Tools to Use

Plenty of power tools are designed to make certain gardening chores faster and easier, but go easy on purchasing many of them. For small gardens, they can be overkill, and many of these tools are noisy, which can really detract from what's supposed to be a relaxing and quiet pursuit.

In this section, we describe some powered garden tools that you may find useful. Many of them make the work go much faster than the hand-powered alternatives. Just be sure not to buy a tool that's too big for the job — the purchase may end up being too expensive and too daunting. (For information on lawn mowers, see Chapter 10.)

## *Safety first: Controlling your power tools (so they don't control you)*

When using power tools in your yard, you have to take precautions to protect yourself from harm:

✔ Wear appropriate clothing (long sleeves, long pants, and steel-capped boots), eye protection, and perhaps ear protection as well.

✔ Read the manual so you understand how the machine operates.

✔ Make sure you know how to turn the tool off before you turn it on.

✔ Make adjustments only when the tool is off.

✔ Be careful to avoid burns — some tools become hot as you use them.

Obviously, when a tool is not in use, it should be safely stowed indoors, out of the path of foot traffic; make sure you have it secured, in its off position, and sheathed or covered if it has sharp parts. Here are some more safety tips:

✔ **For gas-powered tools:** Double-check that there are no leaks (sniff!). Store extra fuel in containers intended for that purpose; then label these containers and keep them out of the way in a cool, dry spot.

✔ **For electric-powered tools:** Always use a circuit breaker; check the cord often for signs of wear or damage to the insulation or connectors. If you need an extension cord to run the tool out to the project spot, get one of those bright-orange ones so the cord is readily visible to you and others.

✔ **For tools in general:** Service the tool annually (at season's end is best; surely by early spring). If you don't know how to or don't want to, hiring someone else to do it isn't expensive. Wipe or scrub the entire exterior clean and drain all fuel at the season's end. Sharpen dull edges and replace worn parts.

## *Chewing through chores with chainsaws*

Chances are you don't need a big, powerful chainsaw like the ones road-clearing crews use. Plenty of good, smaller-size ones are suitable for home-owners — some are gas-powered (they have two-stroke engines), and some are electric-powered (which have the advantage of being quieter). Either way, confirm that important safety features are present, namely

✔ A two-handed switch

✔ A chain brake that triggers if the saw kicks back

Although a chainsaw can be invaluable, it can also destroy hedges that were meant to be trimmed with hedge shears and can do major damage to you if you don't show it respect!

## Working with weed trimmers and weed whackers

Weed trimmers and weed whackers can do a lot of different things around your yard and garden: They can cut grass (especially in tricky, hard-to-reach spots like under a fence and along edges and borders) and trim weeds and light brush (for info on lawn care, check out Chapter 10).

These useful tools come in different sizes and varying rates of power. They also come in three forms:

- ✔ **Gas-powered:** Noisy but effective and portable; they tend to be heavier than other types, but weight can vary a great deal depending on the power of the unit

- ✔ **Corded electric:** Less powerful but not as loud, and it may be just fine for your needs; your extension cord may limit where you can go

- ✔ **Battery-operated:** The quietest and least powerful (running out of juice after around 30 minutes), but very portable

The less-expensive string trimmers employ a rapidly spinning nylon string that does the cutting but wears away slightly as you work (as more string is fed out), so be sure to keep a backup supply or backup coil on hand. Fancier trimmers have a two-line system that reduces cutting time. Superior, usually gas-powered, models use fixed plastic blades.

Be careful about operating weed trimmers or whackers near trees, because they can bite into the trunk, making a wound that not only looks bad but also may contribute to the tree's decline (especially if it's a small, skinny tree).

## Tilling soil with rototillers

Consider the rotary tiller, or rototiller: You may need one of these soil-eating machines if you're going to create a large new flower bed or a vegetable garden (or to install a new lawn) — any project too daunting to undertake by hand.

If your property is large or you like to keep busy with large projects and tend to revise them every year or so, you may want to consider buying a tiller. But for most situations, you're better off renting what you need (check the Yellow Pages under "Equipment Rentals" or "Rental Services"). The only drawback to renting, or borrowing from a neighbour for that matter, is that the tool may not be well maintained, which slows down the work or may be dangerous. Here's how tillers compare:

- **Full-size tillers:** These beasts are for the bigger jobs. They're heavy, and figuring out how to navigate and control them takes some strength and practice. But the powerful spinning tines do a great job of chewing up soil, mixing in compost or other amendments, and spitting everything out to create a fluffy, loose, wonderful planting bed. The tines may be in front, in the middle, or in the rear.

  These tillers come in various sizes. For heavy-duty jobs like cultivating heavy soil for the first time, the larger tillers are more practical. The larger tillers are really intended for very substantial row crop gardens that are 1,000 square metres (¼ of an acre) or so. For frequent use, after the initial cultivation, the smaller tillers are usually fine and are much easier to handle.

- **Hand-held mini tillers:** These lightweight helpers come either gas-powered (two- or four-cycle engine) or electric (120-volt, much quieter); typically, they weigh 9 kilograms (20 pounds) or less. Choose an electric mini tiller based on how far from an outlet you'll be. These tools are suitable for smaller-scale projects and do a fine job of mixing amendments into the soil. Plus, you can control them so you don't go where you don't want to go and don't stray into the root zones of established shrubs or perennials.

Turning over the soil inevitably brings dormant weed seeds to the surface, where they're only too happy to germinate and start growing. And if you till any weeds, alive or dead, into the ground, you may release and churn up their seeds as well. Your best bet is to try to clear an area of weeds *before* you do any tilling.

# Rolling Out the Wheelbarrows and Carts

You may be wondering whether you actually need a wheelbarrow or cart — they're kinda big! Well, even in a small garden, wheelbarrows and carts are handy mainly for hauling. In other words, they save your back and reduce the number of trips you make back and forth.

You can haul weeds, prunings, leaves, grass clippings, soil or soil amendments (including compost, mulch, or sand), rocks or gravel, firewood, or even harvested veggies (in those bumper-crop years!). Wheelbarrows and carts help out when you want to take a pile of tools, or pots or flats of plants, or both, to a project area. You can even use carts and wheelbarrows to mix various amendments — like you'd mix cake batter — before dumping the load into a garden bed or filling your decorative planting pots. Last but not least, some people get a kick out of parking one in a visible spot and displaying things (such as flowering annuals or Halloween pumpkins) above ground level, where they're more noticeable.

Steel trays are tough and strong but can rust over time because exposure to moisture in a garden setting is unavoidable; therefore, consider a wheelbarrow or cart that's coated with a baked epoxy finish, or choose a sturdy plastic one. Wood can absorb moisture over time and rot, so make sure that the wood of your cart has been treated with rot-retardant material. No wheelbarrow or cart is forever, especially if it sees heavy use. Many choices of wheelbarrow or cart are available, but here are the truly important things to consider when shopping for one:

- ✔ **Capacity:** Make your choice based on the purpose you want to use it for. A 140-litre (5-cubic-foot) wheelbarrow is wonderful if you plan to do major hauling, but if your garden is smaller, your needs are modest, or you don't mind making more trips back and forth, a smaller-size wheelbarrow or cart may be just fine.

- ✔ **High or low edges:** As with capacity, choosing between these features depends on what you're planning to haul. If the material is loose or spillable, higher sides are preferable. Just remember that you have to contend with the high sides when you put stuff in and take it out again.

  If possible, stand next to the cart or wheelbarrow you're considering with a shovel in your hand and try a dry run — if the motion is awkward or uncomfortable, you need a smaller cart or something with lower sides.

- ✔ **Wheel(s):** Wheelbarrows tend to have a single wheel at the front — this trait makes them eminently manoeuvrable even in tight spots. Carts and wagons, on the other hand, have two to four wheels — they're less manoeuvrable but more stable. So think how you're going to use your hauling device before you buy.

  One final note on wheels: You get what you pay for. It isn't just that cheap tires may go flat one fine day or maybe every year or so, which can be a real nuisance. Better, thicker, treaded tires do last longer, but they also turn more easily and absorb shock when you're trundling over uneven terrain.

- ✔ **Handles:** Handles are for more than steering when you're moving through the yard, though of course you'll appreciate a comfortable, coated grip. On a well-designed wheelbarrow, the handles do the work, with the wheel acting as a fulcrum, and the whole arrangement spares you heavy lifting. On a well-designed cart, handles clear the bed enough so that you can shift the entire thing around comfortably.

- ✔ **Pouring end:** To help you get the contents out of the bed (even on lazy Saturday mornings), a wheelbarrow often has a tapered lip at the front end. A cart may have a front "gate" that folds down or lifts out, which can be handy.

# Wading through Wondrous Watering Tools

Well, you *know* you need to water your garden, but what you may not know is that you have quite a range of options. If you match the watering tool to the job, your plants will do better and, just as important, you won't waste water.

The watering tools we describe in this section are actual tools, not whole watering systems. Most in-ground watering systems really should be installed by a professional.

## Hoses

The good old garden hose — it saves time and steps. You can just drag it out to the right spot, turn it on, let it go, and then come back later. Coil it up when it's not in use. Keep it for years. Simple, right?

Well, not always. Cheap hoses and older ones have an annoying flaw: They kink and tangle. If you aren't watching, you can waste water and sometimes harm plants as the hose lashes around. Then you have the problem of hoses that crack, burst, and leak after being left out in the sun or run over by the car, or that just break down after what seems like not very much use. Read on for some important considerations when buying a garden hose.

### Materials and construction

The best, most long-lived hose is one that's composed of layers. The inner layer needs to be flexible, a smooth rubber or synthetic tube. To protect the inner layer and give it toughness, it's covered or coated with at least one outer layer of nylon fabric or mesh. The outer skin beyond that, the part you touch and see, needs to be of a material that doesn't break down after prolonged exposure to sun and weather. It also needs to resist punctures and scratches. Usually, the outer layer is vinyl, or a vinyl-rubber blend, and it's often green or black. Multilayered hoses may seem a bit fatter or heavier than the inexpensive alternatives, but as usual, you get what you pay for.

The standard, vinyl-coated, layered hose comes in different forms: namely three-ply, four-ply, and five-ply. As with anything, heavier-duty versions, like the five-ply, are more expensive. Heavier-duty hoses don't kink as often, can take higher water pressures, and last longer. For occasional watering jobs, the lower ply works fine; for more frequent use and a longer life, go with the higher ply.

Other types of hoses include

- ✔ **The soaker, or leaky, hose:** This hose "sweats" water slowly out along its entire length via tiny holes.
- ✔ **The flat hose:** Made of cotton canvas, the flat hose is lightweight and compact.
- ✔ **The patio hose:** The end of the patio hose is designed to attach to a sink faucet.

One more thing to look for when hose shopping: The fittings at the ends need to be of good quality also. Their job is to attach seamlessly to a faucet (or sprinkler, if at the other end) without leaking or spraying. How do you judge quality? If the fittings are cast brass rather than cheap metal, they're built to last. A stamped, galvanized steel fitting never seems to hold up over time.

### Sizes

The most common hose size is 16 millimetres (⅝ of an inch) in diameter, which works very well with typical municipal water pressure (2.1 to 3.5 kilograms per square centimetre, or 30 to 50 pounds per square inch). You may have cause to go down to 13 millimetres (½ inch) or up to 2.5 centimetres (1 inch) — the skinnier one delivers water more slowly; the fatter one, more quickly.

Length depends on how far you have to make the hose reach. For flexibility, you may want to buy your hose in 8-metre (25-foot) segments rather than longer lengths and then join them together as needed for different areas of the garden. Remember that shorter lengths are lighter and thus easier to lug around.

### Storage and placement accessories

Coils and hose caddies are useful accessories to have. You see, a hose comes coiled and stores well coiled in its original direction and loop size — in other words, a hose has *coil memory*. Letting the hose return to this state when not in use is better for the hose's longevity.

## Repairing a hose

Hoses seem to undergo more abuse than just about any other type of gardening tool, and chances are that sooner or later you're going to find yourself owning a hose with some end or thread damage. When this happens, determine whether repairing the hose end is worth the trouble. If the hose wasn't cheap and the damage is minor, by all means, give it a try. The following figure shows you how to fix a hose end.

For hoses that develop leaks, patch kits are available wherever hoses are sold. Patch only when the hose is completely dry.

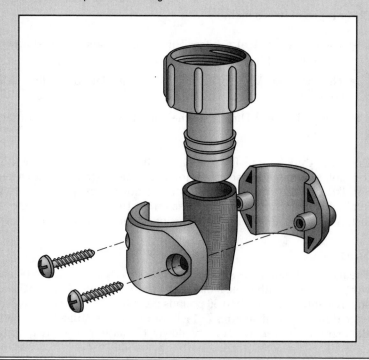

A hose guide is a simple but worthwhile gadget. A stake anchors the guide in the ground or in predrilled holes in your patio or pathway, and it holds the hose in place, even along curves or around corners. In this way, the hose can't stray onto a path or across your garden plants.

## *Nozzles*

An awful lot of hose accessories are out there. Rarely are they expensive, so you can give one a try and see how you, and your plants, like it. Here are some of the common ones; they all screw on to the end of a standard hose:

✔ **Watering wand:** This gadget extends your reach for watering hanging baskets or irrigating the back of a deep flower bed. The *rose,* or head, at the end of the wand delivers the water in a gentle, drenching spray. The watering wand is also good for watering potted plants and seedlings if you keep the water pressure low so you don't dislodge the little plants. Get a wand with a thumb-operated on-off valve so you can move from plant to plant without wetting things you don't mean to or wasting water.

✔ **Jet-spray nozzle:** Usually brass, this tool focuses water into a strong, stiff spray. It's ideal for hosing off muddy tools and boots or cleaning a walkway or driveway.

✔ **Adjustable round nozzle:** A refinement of the jet-spray nozzle, this nozzle can also deliver a softer spray right on down to a mist — all by twisting it until the water is coming out the way you want.

✔ **Misting head:** Though small, this tool can be a bit pricier because it usually comes in brass or brass-coated die-cast metal. It delivers water in a fine mist, perfect for little emerging seedlings.

✔ **Pistol-grip nozzle:** Usually made of tough, UV-resistant plastic, this nozzle is a favourite among gardeners because you can vary the intensity of the spray by applying pressure to the trigger, and thus use it throughout your garden.

✔ **Fan head:** This tool delivers a drenching sweep of water from its broad, broom-head-like end, making it a good choice for bigger watering projects like irrigating a newly planted shrub or rosebush.

✔ **Multiple-head nozzle:** These nozzles are showing up more frequently on the market. They have several types of nozzles built into one head and are quite handy.

## Hose-end sprinklers

Here's another way to put your good hose to work: A hose-end sprinkler is designed to screw into a standard hose and rest on the ground wherever you drag it and set it down; it then delivers water in a spray pattern in the immediate area. Clever designers have come up with all sorts of nifty alternatives, so you'll have no trouble finding a sprinkler you like and that suits the lay of your particular landscape. Here's a rundown of the common ones:

✔ **Fixed-spray sprinkler:** These sprinklers are the simplest types and are perfectly satisfactory for watering small areas. They deliver a fine, soft rain, rather casually (that is, without a super-reliable pattern).

Use fixed-spray sprinklers on the lawn or for watering flower beds and shrubs; they're less effective under trees because they fling water up into the branches, where it's neither needed nor especially appreciated. You may have to run the water on low or get a heavier model if it tends to flip over on its side or upside down, a common problem.

- **Whirlybird sprinkler:** A spring-loaded arm breaks the shooting stream of water into droplets as it snaps back into place, which makes this sprinkler revolve. This deceptively simple design can actually accomplish a very thorough watering job in a circular shape.

- **Rain tower:** The rain tower is just an impulse sprinkler like the whirlybird, but it's elevated on an adjustable tripod contraption so it can water a broad circle. Therefore, it's terrific for watering large areas of tall plants, such as a corn patch or vegetable garden.

- **Oscillating sprinkler:** You have to set or assign these sprinklers their job, which can be a full swing from left to right and back again, or a half swing to the left or right, or just a held, stationary position. Oscillating sprinklers are marvellous for watering lawns and broad plantings. Splurge on the more expensive units; they last much longer and offer a greater range of settings that can make your watering more accurate and efficient. Compared to a whirlybird sprinkler, oscillating sprinklers tend to lose a lot of water to evaporation.

- **Tractor (travelling) sprinkler:** The tractor sprinkler is a little more high-tech, at least for a homeowner. The small water-driven tractor scoots slowly across a lawn, using the laid-out hose as a guide. Meanwhile, a simple revolving sprinkler mounted on top does the watering. Some models have three speeds, for lighter to deeper watering.

## Water timers

If you have a good idea how much watering your plants need but can't be there to do it, the water timer's for you. Though they're no bigger than coffee cans, some of these gadgets contain a small computer that you can program for watering time and duration. Others have a clever intermittent feature that delivers the water in on-off cycles (for instance, five minutes on followed by a ten-minute rest) over a period of time (say, three hours) before shutting off automatically. Watering in cycles allows the soil to efficiently absorb the water with far less runoff and evaporation.

The fancy battery-operated types with all the settings are handy if you need lots of features, but if you're after simplicity and dependability, you can't beat the spring-operated ones. One end of the timer attaches to the faucet, the other to the hose end — you have no batteries or wires to worry about.

Some timers are more elaborate (and expensive) than others, so have a clear idea of your needs as well as your technological savvy when you go shopping. You can find water timers wherever gardening supplies are sold, as well as at specialty greenhouse supply companies.

Water timers are most often used with professionally installed sprinkler systems (refer to Chapter 4).

# Part II
# Flowers and Foliage: Growing for Colour

The 5th Wave    By Rich Tennant

"The next time you order flowering bulbs, I suggest you have them express mailed."

# In this part . . .

The first thing many people notice when looking at a garden is colour, be it yellow, blue, red, pink, or various shades of green. The chapters in Part II introduce you to the wonderful sources of gardening colour that the plant world supplies: annuals, perennials, flowering bulbs, and roses. Although it's easy to think only of flowers when you're looking to give your garden an impressive colour palette, these chapters also introduce you to the great possibilities that foliage plants, such as hostas, can provide. As you read about these plants, be sure to jot down information about the ones that interest you. When you start shopping for them for your own garden, you may find that the plants you've picked out appear even more beautiful and interesting face to, er, plant!

# Chapter 6

# Growing Annuals: Adding Yearly Variety to Your Garden

*F*or sheer flower power, annuals are hard to beat. Because they have to complete their entire life cycle in one growing season — which is the technical definition of the term *annual* — these plants work fast. They go from seed or seedling to full-grown plant, bursting with flowers, in short order, delivering colour when and where you need it.

This chapter can help you choose and place annuals in your garden. It also fills you in on their basic care requirements so you can get the most out of them. Gardening with annuals is, more than ever, easy and rewarding.

## Finding Flowers That Fit Your Garden

Modern-day annuals are impressive indeed. They've been bred to produce abundant flowers and lush foliage throughout the heart of the growing season. They rush to flowering because their means of reproduction is by seed. And to get there, the flowers must come first. This great output guarantees bountiful garden colour and also makes most annuals great for bouquets. By the time fall comes and seeds form (if they do, before frost), the plants are spent and they die. By then, though, you should certainly have had your money's worth! Annuals are very gracious guests. Figure 6-1 gives you an idea of how an annual progresses through life.

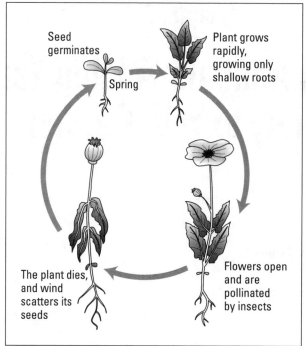

**Figure 6-1:**
Following an annual's life cycle, from seed germination to seed production.

Seed germinates

Spring

Plant grows rapidly, growing only shallow roots

Flowers open and are pollinated by insects

The plant dies, and wind scatters its seeds

Not surprisingly, a huge range of annuals is on the market, and more annuals arrive every year. Demand is market driven, innovation pushes on, and the upshot is that you can choose from many, many different annuals — no matter where you live, no matter what growing conditions your garden offers. The variety of annuals allows you to find countless plants that are specific to warm or cool weather. (For more info about annuals that love sun or shade, check out "Deciding where to plant annuals," later in this chapter.)

## Some like it hot: Warm-weather annuals

Lots of annuals thrive in hot summer weather, tolerating even periods of prolonged drought in style. Many annuals have this preference because their predecessors, or ancestors if you will, originated in warm, tropical climates with long growing seasons. All plant breeders did was capitalize on or preserve these qualities while improving the plants' appearance or expanding the colour range.

Some warm-weather annuals are actually perennial in some regions but are used as annuals in other areas because they're not hardy there (they don't survive the winter). For instance, the snapdragon can be a perennial in warm climates, like in the southern United States, but it's used as an annual farther north. Some tropical plants are also commonly used for temporary display.

Examples of favourite warm-weather annuals include impatiens, Madagascar periwinkle, zinnias, and marigolds.

## Some annuals like it cool

Some annuals have their origins in areas with colder winters and mild but not blazingly hot summers. Plant breeders have stepped in to improve these plants' flower production (the more blooms, the merrier!), add new colours, and select for compact plant *habit* (shapes or forms). The result is a huge range of good, tough plants that Canadian gardeners with short growing seasons can count on. Examples of favourite cool-weather annuals include cleome (spider flower), pansy, Johnny jump-ups (a type of viola), trailing lobelia, and calendula (pot marigolds).

 Annuals that like cool weather are often fine choices for the parts of your garden where shade prevails. The shelter of a fence, pergola (a type of arbour — see Chapter 12), porch, or overhanging tree keeps the plants cooler, preserving their flower colour, prolonging bloom time, and protecting the plants from drying out in the hot sunshine.

# Mixing and Matching Annuals

Fun and creative combinations, of form as well as colour, are so easy with annuals! Assuming you plant them in a hospitable spot, they're so eager to grow and so certain to bloom that you can be artistic with confidence. The following sections tell you how you can design your annual bed with respect to the shape of the plant, colour, and scent. Figure 6-2 shows an example of how to set up a flower bed of annuals.

For more info on designing a flower bed, refer to Chapter 2.

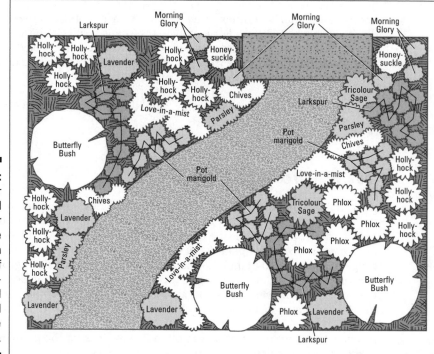

**Figure 6-2:**
An idea for
an annual
flower
bed. The
common
names of
recom-
mended
annual
plants are
shown.

# Good habits: Taking advantage
# of shape, height, and structure

Contrary to popular belief, not all annuals are little bloom-studded muffins.
Hardly! Try to install annuals with a range of growth habit — variety is the
spice of life! Check out Table 6-1 for some of your options.

| Table 6-1 | Appearance and Habits of Annuals | |
|---|---|---|
| *Type* | *Description* | *Examples* |
| Low growers | These annuals can create a carpet in your flower beds, not only covering open ground or making a "skirt" at the base of taller plants, but also generally spilling over and softening the edges while adding welcome interest and colour. | Fan flower, sweet alyssum, million bells, and portulaca |

The structure of a formal garden can be created with plants, such as the box-wood outlining the rose beds, at right. The fountain in the centre is a focal point that draws the eye. (Chapter 2)

Vegetable and herb gardens can be formal or casual. At left, onions and kohlrabi grow with sunflowers, zinnias, and poppies. Below, an arched willow arbour and stepping stone path complement a herb garden. (Chapter 2)

Gardens designed for family activities require a firm surface to hold furniture, as well as plants to soften hard edges. (Chapter 2)

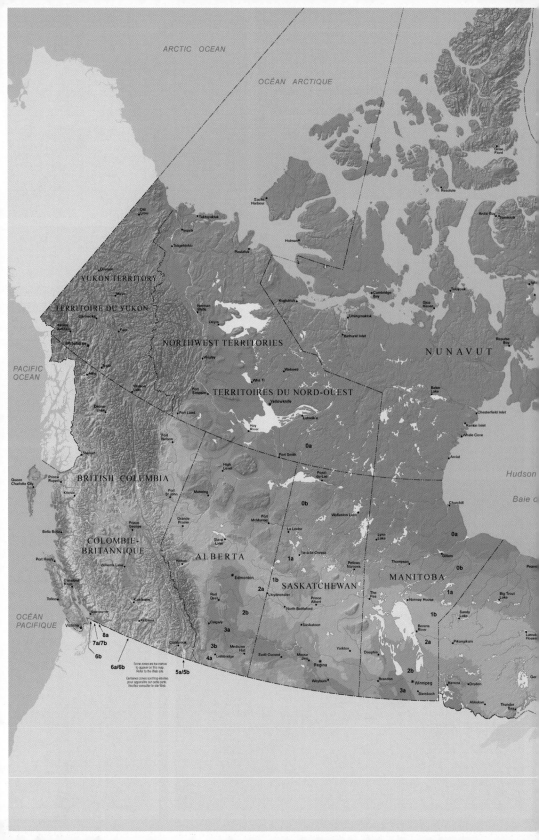

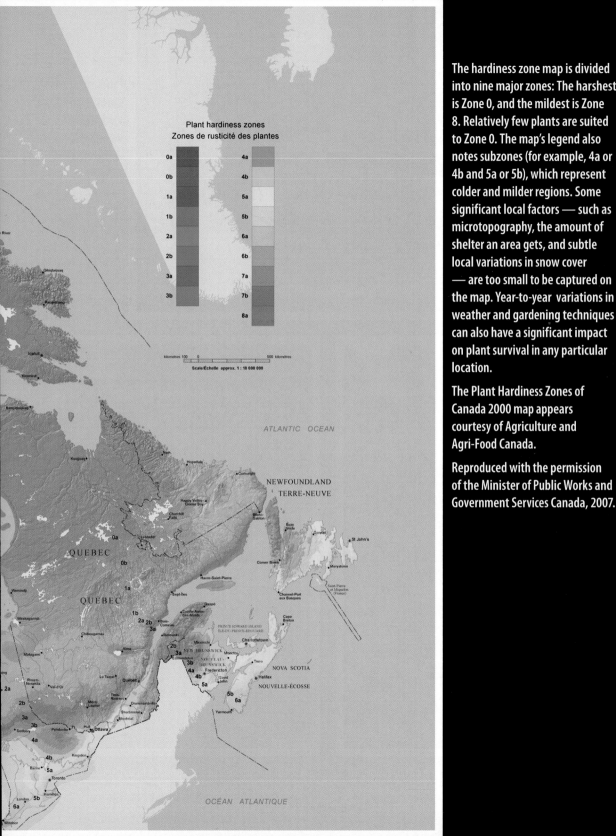

Plant hardiness zones
Zones de rusticité des plantes

| | |
|---|---|
| 0a | 4a |
| 0b | 4b |
| 1a | 5a |
| 1b | 5b |
| 2a | 6a |
| 2b | 6b |
| 3a | 7a |
| 3b | 7b |
| | 8a |

kilometres 100    0                    500 kilometres
Scale/Échelle  approx. 1 : 10 000 000

The hardiness zone map is divided into nine major zones: The harshest is Zone 0, and the mildest is Zone 8. Relatively few plants are suited to Zone 0. The map's legend also notes subzones (for example, 4a or 4b and 5a or 5b), which represent colder and milder regions. Some significant local factors — such as microtopography, the amount of shelter an area gets, and subtle local variations in snow cover — are too small to be captured on the map. Year-to-year  variations in weather and gardening techniques can also have a significant impact on plant survival in any particular location.

The Plant Hardiness Zones of Canada 2000 map appears courtesy of Agriculture and Agri-Food Canada.

Reproduced with the permission of the Minister of Public Works and Government Services Canada, 2007.

A pleasant, plant-surrounded spot near the house is the best choice for an outdoor dining area. (Chapter 2)

Don't overlook the potential of a side path leading to the back of your house. Above, a profusion of plants, including Japanese maple and tall pink lavatera, welcomes visitors. (Chapter 2)

Colour is king in an early summer bed of gorgeous annual larkspur and allium 'Giganteum'. Larkspur can be grown from seed, and it likes a bit of shade. (Chapters 6 and 8)

Perennials show well when planted in large patches that spread and weave together. Stick to two or three colours for the best effect. At left, yellow rudbeckia 'Horizon' blends with blue ageratum, and a few tiny yellow zinnias poke their heads through. In the late-summer bed, below, 'Vintage Wine' coneflower combines with 'Little Spire' Russian sage. (Chapter 7)

The seed heads of ornamental grasses such as miscanthus appear in late summer and early fall and last for winter interest. Cut the grass nearly to the ground in spring to allow for new growth. (Chapter 7)

Showy Oriental poppies — this one is 'Victoria Louise' — bloom in scarlet, rose, pink, or white in early spring. The foliage dies back in midsummer. (Chapter 7)

Rooftop gardens are growing in popularity. But we advise you to get professional help before creating your own rooftop garden, to make sure that your roof can carry the weight and that you use the right underlay materials. In this raised garden grow hostas, grasses, and liatris. (Chapter 7)

A front-yard garden can replace your lawn, and it requires less irrigation and care. At left, deschampsia and other ornamental grasses grow with liatris, purple coneflower, and goldenrod. (Chapter 7)

Solomon's seal (left) and European wild ginger (below), a groundcover, both prefer shady conditions. (Chapters 7 and 12)

Allium is an ornamental member of the onion family. The 25-centimetre (10-inch) bloom of 'Globemaster' allium shines in the late-May garden and lasts for up to four weeks. (Chapter 8)

Daffodils are good choices for making a planned garden or woodland look natural. Plant daffodils in groups of different varieties about 7.5 centimetres (3 inches) apart, and the bulbs will multiply over the years, creating natural-looking clumps. (Chapter 8)

'Pink Impression' is a tall, elegant Darwin tulip that blooms in mid-spring. It also makes a good cut flower. (Chapter 8)

A beautifully tended lawn edged with a symmetrically trimmed boxwood never goes out of style. (Chapter 10)

| Type | Description | Examples |
| --- | --- | --- |
| Spiky growers | Spires of pretty flowers, whether loose and airy or dense and commanding, are wonderful punctuation marks in a display. They break up monotony, standing out from the crowd even as they keep the eye moving. | Snapdragon, larkspur, and salvia |
| Petite, compact annuals | These little cuties pack a lot of appeal into a small space, making them perfect for containers (small pots as well as window boxes or big, deck-side planter boxes), edgings out in the garden proper, or in any spot that needs reliable coverage that'll be viewed at close range. | Trailing lobelia, diascia, small pansies, and nierembergia |
| Mound formers | The mainstay of many garden displays, plants with a lower-growing, rounded habit are valuable because they fill in their allotted space so well and are handsome when viewed from any angle. Closely planted, they're excellent for edging or masses of dependable colour. | California poppy, geranium, impatiens, nasturtium, petunias, and French marigold |
| Big annuals | Count on an impressive show and lots of colour — quickly! This sort of annual is wonderful for fence-side, along a wall of the house or garage, or in your entryway garden. | Sunflower, cleome, zinnia, and flowering tobacco |
| Great annuals that range from small to tall | These annuals have such a range in height that no matter what your needs, you can probably find one that fits. | Zinnia and marigold |
| Leafy plants | Don't forget foliage! So-called *foliage annuals* may flower, but their main attraction is their handsome, colourful leaves. Rimmed, variegated, striped, splashed, or dappled; red, maroon, white, yellow, cream, or chartreuse — you can find all sorts of varieties and opportunities to make exciting, stand-out displays with these plants. | Coleus or grey dusty miller for texture and muted colour |

Here are some good ideas for making annual diversity work for you in your garden displays:

✔ **Small in front, medium in the middle, and tall in back:** This tried-and-true guideline works because plants don't block one another from view, and the stepping-up effect simply looks great and adds dimension to your flower bed. This setup makes a display look full and is especially effective in small or tight spaces. Thus, for island beds (in the middle of your lawn, say) or containers, you want small plants on the edges, then medium plants, and finally, tall ones in the centre. See Figure 6-3 for an idea of how to vary heights in your flower bed.

✔ **Repetition and balance:** Plant so that one plant habit (or form) recurs at regular intervals in the display. This touch supplies continuity and naturally looks pleasing. Vary what happens in between plantings of your chosen habit, if you wish.

✔ **Simplicity:** The smaller the area is, the more important it is to avoid clutter. Use several or many of one kind of plant, together. Or stick to one sort of plant habit but vary the types of plants or the colours.

**Figure 6-3:**
You can add dimension to a flower bed by planting short annuals in the front and tall ones in the rear.

Annuals are great fill-ins among smaller, newly planted perennials to provide fast colour during your garden's first season. The following year, the perennials will come into their own and fill the space formerly occupied by the annuals. Many gardeners also use annuals, sometimes in pots, to fill in spaces after perennials have bloomed and they've cut back the plants to allow for new, fresh growth.

## Combining colours

As a painter or interior decorator may say, with justifiable envy, "Wow, what a palette!" Annuals come in literally every colour of the rainbow, and the only limit is your imagination. If you want to be absolutely sure of a splashy display, you can use the following principles.

However, sometimes rules are made to be broken, or sometimes a combination idea happens accidentally or just occurs to you. Not only are annuals reliable, but they're also forgiving. So feel free to try anything, removing or shifting plants around as you fine-tune your display. Yes, you can move an annual from one place to another without much trauma (just get all or most of the root system when you do, and water the plant well in its new home until it adjusts).

Throwing a bunch of flowers together in a flower bed or container can make an arrangement look like a lively bouquet, or it can look like a hodgepodge. So try to decide on a mood or focus, and then stick to it. Here are some useful colour principles you can try:

- **Go for the bold:** Mix annuals in bright primary shades of red, yellow, and blue. Ideally, they're of the same colour intensity so one doesn't steal the spotlight. Yellow zinnias and blue calibrachoa are a stunning combo.

- **Hot, hot, hot!** Compose an exciting, traffic-stopping display out of any or all of the following: hot pink, bright orange, ruby red, magenta, and bright purple. Try some bright orange marigolds combined with purple petunias.

- **Soft and sweet:** If you like romantic, soothing pastels, go for colours of similar strength or intensity; combine pale yellow, lavender, pink, baby blue, and cream rather than white. A tranquil pairing is lemon-coloured osteospermum with powder blue verbenas.

- **Aim for contrast:** Colours considered opposites (complementary colours) — such as orange and blue, yellow and purple, and red and green — look terrific together. Orange nasturtiums topped with blue salvias is a good choice.

- **Use neutral hues:** These colours go with everything and thus make a cool, calming filler in a display that may otherwise look busy or cluttered; try cream, beige, silver, or grey (supplied by foliage, if not flowers). An occasional white-flowered annual is also welcome in colour-filled layouts. Silver-leafed foliage plants like the dusty millers are great combined with any white-flowered plants such as angelonias or petunias.

## Designing annual beds for fragrance

Annuals are already dependable in terms of growth and flowering, so if you love to walk outside and take in sweet scents or pick scented bouquets, designing for fragrance is totally doable.

If you're buying seed packets, information on whether the annuals are fragrant can be found in the fine print. If you're shopping for plants and they don't have flowers yet, check the tags or ask. If you'd prefer to trust your own nose, buy larger, blooming annuals. (But realize that petals or buds may fall off during the journey home or shortly after transplanting. Don't worry — the plants will soon generate more!)

Blooms that open later in the day or remain open in the evening hours are often fragrant, relying on their sweet aroma to entice pollinators (usually night-flying moths). Examples of late (in the day) bloomers include flowering tobacco, four o'clocks, heliotrope, angel's trumpet, and moonflower.

Our favourite fragrant annuals include flowering tobacco, stock, heliotrope, angel's trumpet, wallflower, sweet pea (especially the old-fashioned or heirloom varieties), and scented geraniums.

Here's how to make sure you, your family, and anyone who visits notices and enjoys your fragrant annuals:

- **Strategic placement:** Cluster annuals in pots and place them on or near places where people gather, such as a patio table, the sides of deck or porch steps, or even in a hanging basket.
- **Strength in numbers:** Don't use just one plant! The more you grow, especially if they're near one another, the stronger their scent will be.
- **Ample space between different plants:** Although each plant may have a delightful fragrance on its own, variety can produce clashing odours.
- **Sufficient watering:** Flower fragrance cells reside in petals, and foliage fragrance cells are in the leaves, of course. These cells stay healthy and swollen to maximum size when you keep an aromatic plant well watered. If guests are coming over, water well shortly before they arrive.
- **Shelter from the wind:** A little windbreak (from a fence, deck corner, or even a garden bench or vine-draped trellis) can help prevent fragrance from dissipating.
- **Focus on the evening hours:** White-flowered fragrant annuals — especially flowering tobacco and the dramatic moonflower vine — waft their most powerful scent into the night. (Their white flowers also show up better in limited light.) So situate them near the deck, patio, or dining area where you'll be enjoying dusk outdoors.

# Buying Annuals

Because annuals are a one-shot deal — that is, good for only one growing season — you have to buy new ones each spring. You have two options: seed packets and nursery starts. The following sections explain the differences.

## Starting with seed packets

The almighty seed is the symbol of a new beginning. Buying your annuals as seed packets gives you four important advantages:

✔ **You can get an earlier start.** Starting seeds indoors takes time and space, but it's not at all difficult — and it's a great way to chase away the winter blues.

✔ **Variety!** Thanks to a broader selection in the seed-packet world, you can grow unusual annuals or new and different colours of popular ones. Look in seed catalogues that come in late winter, or browse the company Web sites. You have all sorts of wonderful choices — better than you'll find in a garden centre!

✔ **Quantity!** Any given seed packet can contain 100 or more seeds. Even with some attrition, using seed packets is a great way to grow a whole lot of plants.

✔ **It's inexpensive.** Sure, experienced gardeners bemoan the rising cost of seeds over the years, but really, buying seeds is still the best deal in town, always substantially cheaper than buying young plants.

Be sure to shop early for best selection, and always check the packet to make sure the seeds are fresh. (The packets should be stamped with an expiration date of later this year or next year, or they should say "Packed for [current year]" — see Figure 6-4.) Store the packets in a cool, dry place so the seeds aren't tempted to germinate until you're ready to sow them in flats. For details on how to sow seeds, see Chapter 13.

For a listing of some mail-order seed and flower companies, check out the appendix.

**Figure 6-4:**
Packets of fresh seeds contain planting information, details about the plant, and packing dates.

$1.39
**Lobelia**
'Crystal Palace'
*Lobelia erinus*

Annual
Blooms spring to fall frost
Spreads 12"
2" tall
Sun
Low growing ground cover with intensely rich, deep blue flowers, massed over the top of the plant

net weight
125 mg

To open: Peel this flap back.
Peel back side and bottom flaps
to find additional information
on inside packet!

*'Crystal Palace' Lobelia catches your eye with dazzling, vibrant, dark blue flowers.*

**When to plant outside:** Spring after average last day of frost. In mild winter areas, sow late summer for winter color.

**When to start inside:** 8-10 weeks before last frost. This is the recommended method since Lobelia takes a long time to germinate.

**Important! Read inside of packet for more specific information.
See top flap for directions.**

Packed for 1998

7  36210  00011  9

## Starting with nursery, well, starts

You generally see nursery starts at garden centres in mid- to late spring. Small annual plants are generally sold in four-packs or larger packs, with each cell holding a single young plant. These plants were raised from seed or from cuttings in a greenhouse, so they need a little TLC (shelter from cold and wind, and regular water so they don't dry out) when you get them home.

Here's what to check before buying nursery starts:

- ✔ **Labels:** Labels should contain useful information, such as flower colour and mature plant size, as well as the name of the plant.

- ✔ **Blooms:** A blooming plant may be more attractive, and it lets you check that the colour is what you want, but the flowers take energy away from the roots. When you get the plant home, cut or pick off any flowers or buds.

- ✔ **Well-rooted plants:** Pop or wiggle a plant out of its cell to check the rooting. If the seedling promptly falls out of the soil mix, it hasn't been in the cell or pot long enough. If you see a mass of white roots, the plant has been in the cell too long and is stressed.

- ✔ **Healthy appearance:** Is the foliage crisp and green? Just a few yellowing and bedraggled leaves aren't necessarily a problem — you can pinch those off. But you should look in the crown and the *nodes* (where the leaves or leaf stalks meet the main stem) for insect pests or signs of them.

# An Annual Event: The Whens, Wheres, and Hows of Planting

Well, of course, in most Canadian gardens, annuals bloom in the summer months — they start in late spring and don't quit till the fall frosts begin. But some lucky gardeners in milder areas of British Columbia with longer growing seasons can enjoy some annuals, especially those that are frost tolerant, for a much longer period. Your growing conditions and climate dictate how soon the show gets started, how long it lasts, and where and how you should plant your annuals.

## Filling in the garden after the last frost

If you live in an area with a long growing season — say seven months — you can go ahead and sow some annual seeds straight into the ground, secure in the knowledge that they'll sprout, grow up, and start pumping out flowers, all in plenty of time. This approach is generally easy and cheap, but it doesn't work well with annuals that need a really long time to germinate and develop — such as annuals with small seeds, like petunias and impatiens. For these plants, or if you live in an area with a short summer, either start the seeds inside or buy seedlings.

Freezing weather kills, or at least severely damages, most annuals. Therefore, the trick is to know your last spring frost date and your first fall frost date — these dates bookend the annual-gardening year. (If you don't know your area's frost dates, ask an employee at a local garden centre or a more experienced gardener, or check out www.tdc.ca/canadian_frost_dates.htm. Note that the dates are averages; they can vary somewhat from one year to the next.) You can refer to Chapter 3 for more information on plant zones and growing seasons.

### *Planting in late spring*

The majority of annuals are frost sensitive. In other words, a freeze can damage or kill them. Frigid temperatures also make annuals much more susceptible to disease damage. If small seedlings are damaged by cold, they may never quite recover. Don't risk it: Plant your new annuals in the ground only after all danger of frost is past. Many gardeners think the rule is to plant on the Victoria Day weekend (on or about May 24), but don't you believe it: In some areas, you can plant earlier; in other parts, you may get a hard frost in early June. Use this guideline with plants you're putting in containers, too (though you can bring the pots indoors on chilly nights if you have to — see Chapter 16 for info on container gardening).

Gardening fever hits us all on the first warm spring day. But warm *air* isn't necessarily what you're waiting for — warm *soil* is. If the ground is still semi-frozen or soggy from thawing cycles or drenching spring rains, it's better to wait another week or two. No, you don't have to take the soil's temperature before proceeding. Just remember the wise advice of garden author Roger Swain: Don't put plants in a bed you yourself wouldn't be willing to lie on!

### *Planting annuals later in the season*

Of course you can plant later in the season! Plant and replant all summer long if you want, and into early fall if you garden in a mild climate. As long as the plants are willing and able to grow and produce flowers, why not?

Because blazing hot weather is stressful, avoid planting during such spells, or at least coddle the newcomers with plentiful water and some sheltering shade until they get established. A dose of all-purpose fertilizer (applied according to the instructions and rates on the container) may also hasten latecomers along.

# Deciding where to plant annuals

By and large, annuals are resilient plants that tolerate a wide range of growing conditions. But some have preferences for more or less sun, and these specialists allow you to dress up such areas for maximum impact.

### Planting in the sun

Full-on, warm sunshine inspires many annuals to grow robustly and generate loads of flowers. You can always tell if a sun-loving annual isn't getting enough light, because its stems become leggy and lean toward the light source, and flower production is disappointing. So let them have it! How much is enough? Six to eight hours a day suits most. Favourite annuals for sun include cosmos, nasturtiums, zinnias, marigolds, verbenas, clary and mealycup sages, and cornflowers.

### Planting in the shade

Banish gloom in your yard's dim and tree-shaded areas with shade-loving annuals. Plenty do just fine in shade or partial shade. Indeed, their flowers last longer without the stress of the sun beating down on them. White and yellow flowers really add sparkle, individually or massed. Our favourite annuals for shade or partial shade include tuberous and fibrous begonias, impatiens, fuchsias, heliotropes, lobelias, nicotianas, love-in-a-mists, and torenias.

If your shade areas have poor soil or are laced with tree and shrub roots, don't despair. Instead, just display the plants in pots, setting them here and there or in clusters. Or dig holes in the ground and stick the plants — pots and all — into the holes. Doing so makes changing them easy, too. (A clever idea: Hook hanging baskets over tree branches and fill them with shade-tolerant annuals.)

# Getting annuals in the ground

Annuals are simple to plant. Just follow the label directions for spacing, and dig a hole deeper and wider than the root ball. Add some compost to the hole or mix the native soil with organic matter (refer to Chapter 4 for details). If desired, you can add some dry fertilizer in the planting hole and water it in, or you can fertilize the annual after planting (check out the upcoming "Fertilizing" section).

Annuals are most frequently sold in *market packs,* in which four or so plants are each in separate cells. Merely turn the pack upside down and gently push each plant out of its cell from the bottom. Don't pull them out from the top because the stem may break off from the roots. After removing the plants from the packet, plant them in the ground so that their rooting mass is slightly below the soil surface. Firm the soil around the plants, and then water them in well.

# Feeding the Flower Power: Taking Care of Annuals

Although annuals are usually so full of gusto and not much slows them down as they hurtle from spring planting into the summer months, don't assume they're no-care plants. Low-care, yes, but they're not to be neglected. Attend to their basic needs, and they'll do you proud. Pamper them a little, and your yard can be a showplace.

## Watering

Sufficient water is always important for growing plants, but even more so for productive annuals; consider it fuel for the ongoing show. Moisture hydrates the roots, plumps up the leaves, makes buds swell and open, and sustains the flowers. Don't allow your annuals to wilt before being revived, or they'll be stressed out and unable to perform their best. Regular watering is ideal. Keep the following in mind when setting up a watering schedule for your annuals:

- ✔ **Spring watering:** If your area gets normal, drenching spring rainfall, your newly transplanted-into-the-garden annuals may not need supplemental water from you. But remember how important early watering is — it encourages the roots to gain a foothold in their new home before the plant can properly turn its attention to growth and flowering. So water on day one and then keep an eye on things in the ensuing days and weeks.

- ✔ **Summer watering:** Established annuals tend to be pretty tough and often forgive your watering lapses. But they'll certainly be healthier and look much better if you give them water at regular intervals and nurture them through periods of drought.

- ✔ **Fall watering:** In some areas, rainfall may take care of your annuals at this time of year. But if not, continue to water as needed so your annuals look terrific right up to the finish line (for most plants, the first frost).

Your best watering methods depend on how many annuals you have and how close together they are. Options range from a gentle spray from a watering can to soaker hoses to a sprinkler. Watering in the morning hours is best, so that the water can soak in and hydrate the annuals through the hot midday.

## Fertilizing

Strictly speaking, fertilizing annuals isn't necessary, but for best performance, it's highly recommended. Remember, annuals are high-energy plants that respond impressively if you fertilize them regularly (refer to Chapter 4 for more information on fertilizing).

The effects of adding plant food can be dramatic but not instant. Keep an eye on your annuals for a week or two, or even three, before concluding that you've given them enough fertilizer.

By and large, annuals lap up nutrients eagerly and use this extra nutrition to produce more and healthier growth and to bloom like gangbusters. So you'll be amply rewarded for your efforts!

## Mulching

Adding a layer of mulch 2.5 to 5 centimetres (1 to 2 inches) deep around the base of your annuals is a great idea. Mulch keeps encroaching weeds at bay and conserves soil moisture. Plus it looks nice! Favourite mulching materials include bark chips, shredded bark, straw, pine needles, grass clippings, and shredded tree leaves. Keep the mulch at least 2.5 centimetres (1 inch) away from the stem to keep insects and disease from getting into the plant. For more info on types of mulch, refer to Chapter 4.

## Grooming

Like any other garden plant, an annual looks better if you stop by every now and then to give it some personal attention — some grooming. Annuals soon replace pinched-off, bedraggled leaves with new ones.

Plant diseases and insects are harboured in wilted, browned, spotted, or yellowed leaves (indeed, pests and disease may have caused the damage). So always get rid of those unhealthy leaves when you see them, and don't forget to scoop up any that have fallen at the base of your plants. Such tidiness can arrest a problem or even clear it up.

You can get more flowers through *deadheading,* or removing spent blossoms. Annuals aim to go to seed, and when you cut flowers for bouquets or remove spent blossoms, you're thwarting this natural process. The plant responds by generating more buds and flowers. If you're diligent, the plant may never get a chance to go to seed.

## Dealing with annual pests

Annuals that were healthy when you brought them home and that you planted in an appropriate spot with adequate moisture rarely develop any problems. Annuals are pretty tough by nature. That said, sometimes one or many hungry bugs show up to dine on your display. This section gives you the basics on the most common culprits, along with some advice on how to battle them. Of course, if things get bad enough, you can just yank out the plants and buy new ones — though just to be safe, put the replacements in a different spot.

## Aphids

Aphids come in all colours and are often prevalent, so people tend to worry about them too much. It's easy enough to rub these plant-sucking insects out, literally, by squishing them with your fingers. Or hose them off with a strong spray of water. Some companies sell ladybugs as natural aphid controls, though ladybugs aren't too dependable — keeping them in your yard is a challenge.

## Cutworms

Cutworms are actually moth larvae. These little fellows rest in your garden soil by day and emerge by night to dine on your annuals, especially newly planted, juicy ones. A clever and safe control is to press a collar of cardboard around the plants. The cardboard collar should go 2.5 to 5 centimetres (1 to 2 inches) into the ground and 5 to 8 centimetres (2 to 3 inches) above ground level; in a pinch you could use a 170-gram or 6-ounce tuna fish or cat food tin with both ends removed — they're not as deep, but will serve the purpose. The natural growth of your annuals may soon hide this barrier from view.

## Japanese beetles

If you live anywhere from Manitoba to the Maritimes, you've probably seen Japanese beetles — they're approximately fingernail-sized and copper-coloured, with green heads and legs. They eat all plant parts, though chewed-up leaves are their hallmark. Hand-pick Japanese beetles (a great money-making project for your kids!) and drown them in a bucket of soapy water. Western gardeners, beware: These nasty little pests are on the move and will be in your area before you know it.

## Slugs and snails

Ravenous and disgusting creatures, slugs and snails can decimate your annual flower beds and even get into container displays. If you don't catch these pests in the act, you'll certainly spot their giveaway slime trails. These critters are mainly active at night, and they especially relish damp conditions.

Watering early in the day and spacing plants so they aren't crowded may help, but sterner measures are necessary if you have many snails and slugs and they persist. You can set traps that you buy down at the garden centre, or sink pie trays of cheap beer into the ground. Alternatively, protect your plants with barriers of copper strips or sharp *diatomaceous earth* (fossilized algae — again, available where gardening supplies are sold) — slugs and snails won't cross these. A relatively harmless pelletized form of iron phosphate sold as Sluggo is a safe and effective control.

Don't pour salt on slugs; salt can damage your plants. Also, some slug and snail products, like metaldehyde and iron sulfate, can be poisonous to pets. Opt for the safer controls first.

### Spider mites

You may not spot the actual culprits — spider mites are really tiny reddish, brownish, or yellow spiderlike pests — but you may see their webs on the leaves of your annuals. These pests are particularly prevalent when the weather is hot and the soil is dry. Combat them by picking off and destroying affected foliage, rinsing or spraying surviving leaves, or spraying the mites with insecticidal soap.

# Chapter 7

# Growing Perennials: Plants That Make a Comeback

* * * * * * * * * * * * * * * * * * * * * * * * * * * * * * * * * * * * * * * * * * * * * * * *

## In This Chapter

▶ Examining perennials

▶ Designing a perennial garden

▶ Getting perennials of your own

▶ Putting plants in the ground for the long haul

▶ Keeping perennials happy

* * * * * * * * * * * * * * * * * * * * * * * * * * * * * * * * * * * * * * * * * * * * * * * *

*P*erennials are flowering plants that are meant to last — several years, at least, and sometimes much longer. So ideally, they're a wise and practical "one-time investment," unlike the annuals you have to buy and replant every year; therein lies their great appeal and value.

Yes, you may have detected a note of hedging. Perhaps you've even heard the old gardener's joke: "A perennial is a plant that had it lived, would've bloomed year after year." After you go to the effort of acquainting yourself with handsome perennials and bringing them home, you sure don't want them to totally miss the boat and turn out to be expensive annuals!

Don't worry. Get your perennials off on the right foot and give them the care they need to thrive (it's perfectly easy), and you won't be disappointed; you'll be thrilled. This chapter can arm you with the basics so you can be a successful and happy perennial gardener!

# Looking at Perennials, the Repeat Performers

The broadest definition of a *perennial plant* simply states that it's a *herbaceous,* or nonwoody, plant — as opposed to, say, a shrub or tree (see Chapter 11) — that lasts a couple years or more. Perennials, like lilies and daffodils, can be bulbs (Chapter 8 contains info on bulbs). Herbaceous perennials are plants that have foliage that dies back to the ground, and new foliage and shoots sprout from their overwintering roots next spring.

Perennial plants are a wonderfully varied group, quite possibly the most varied group a gardener can work with. No matter where you live or what your growing conditions are (climate, soil type, sun or shade), you have plenty of plants to choose from. So which perennials should you include in your garden? Start off by knowing which general group can work best for you: hardy perennials or tender perennials.

## Hardy perennials

The broad group of hardy perennials is justly popular in colder climates (they're generally appropriate for gardens in Plant Hardiness Zones 3–8 — refer to Chapter 3 for details on hardiness zones). These plants emerge each spring, producing foliage and flowers. Come fall, their top growth dies down and the show is over for the year. But their roots live on underground, waiting to revive and do it all again when warm weather returns.

Popular examples of hardy perennials include aster, columbine, coneflower, day lily, delphinium, mums, penstemon, peony, phlox, and Shasta daisy.

## Tender perennials

Contrary to popular belief, the upper parts of the Northern Hemisphere don't have the corner on perennials. Lots of plants from milder climes (say, the southern U.S. and warmer areas, right down into the tropics) also meet the perennial description. These more tender repeat performers also burst forth in the warm spring weather of their climates, enjoy the summer months, and then slow down or die back in the fall, their roots still very much alive. They return in glory when the year cycles around to springtime again.

Obviously, you can grow tender perennials with impunity if you live in a mild-climate area. However, others can enjoy them, too: Gardeners in Canada's warmest climes can often get the tender treasures through winter right in their gardens. But perennials need to be kept alive with good winter protection (see the section titled "Preparing perennials for winter," later in this chapter, for more details on other methods). A more expensive alternative is to leave your tender perennials in the garden to perish over the winter — which makes them essentially annuals and means you'll have to buy new ones next spring if you want repeat performances of these plants.

Popular examples of tender perennials include angelonia, coleus, gerbera, geraniums, sweet potato vines, four o'clocks, impatiens, and pentas.

# Planning a Long-Term Strategy for Your Perennial Garden

So many great perennials are available that one of the great joys — and challenges — of growing them is combining different kinds in plantings. Here's the challenge: Because different perennials bloom at different times, and because of their relatively slow growth compared to annuals, gardening with perennials usually involves some advance planning to get what gardeners call *continuous bloom* — in other words, a garden that has something in bloom all through the season. You need to plan so that you can get the most bang for your buck and get the exciting look you want, when you want it.

Don't be intimidated by perennials. If you're displeased with a result, you're still in better shape than a painter. Instead of throwing out the canvas, you can simply pull out or move a plant, or even replace it with something else until the result looks great. And while you're waiting for perennials to take hold, you can fill in the bare spots with some annuals (refer to Chapter 6) or bulbs (see Chapter 8).

That said, perennial gardening doesn't have to be a hit-or-miss operation. You can gather information from others, using their knowledge and ideas. Copy or approximate combinations of perennials that you like, or borrow a good idea as a jumping-off point. Inspiration is all around you — in books, gardening magazines, and other gardens, both public and private. Above all, have fun! Perennial gardening is a very enjoyable hobby, with a broad and forgiving learning curve.

## Choreography: Timing perennial blooming

Although some perennials bloom for long periods during the summer, others do not. They have a period of glory that peaks for a week or several weeks, and then the show subsides.

Gardeners have lots of ways to find out in advance when a perennial will bloom and for approximately how long. Look up your chosen perennial in a gardening reference book. Do research on the Internet. Check a print or online gardening catalogue (bearing in mind, however, that some merchants may exaggerate!). Look on the plant's tag or label. Ask a garden-centre staffer or someone who's a member of a gardening club. Best of all, ask someone in your area who's already growing your perennial of choice, because performance varies by climate and even soil conditions.

Nature being as flexible and fickle as it sometimes is, your perennial show may run longer or shorter than you'd originally planned; some plants' time of bloom may change from year to year, depending on the weather; or you may end up with some overlapping bloom you hadn't expected. However, coordinating plants to share the stage at *approximately* the same time works. You can fine-tune later, after you've basked in your early successes.

Perennials fall into several different categories of bloomers. See Table 7-1 for a rundown of perennials in terms of when they bloom, remembering that these aren't hard and fast rules. Some blooming times will overlap.

| Table 7-1 | When Perennials Bloom | |
|---|---|---|
| *Blooming Time* | *Description* | *Examples* |
| Spring bloomers | These babies are quick studies. They tend to emerge with the bulbs, generating colourful flowers early in the growing season. Afterward, the foliage may remain for a while or die down completely until next year. | Basket-of-gold, bleeding heart, columbine, forget-me-not, hellebore, pasque flower, and Solomon's seal |
| Early summer bloomers | Use these plants to bridge the gap that sometimes occurs between the first splash of spring and the full-on summer flowers. | Dianthus, peony, coral bell, lupine, foxglove, lady's mantle, globe flower, and poppy |
| Midsummer bloomers | The glory of high summer! Midsummer bloomers begin growing with warm weather and finally show off their flowers when summer is in full swing. | Black-eyed Susan, crocosmia, day lily, Shasta daisy, delphinium, and hardy geranium |
| Late summer–fall bloomers | These flowers are a welcome sight just when the weather seems too hot and the garden looks tuckered out. | Boltonia, obedient plant, monkshood, stonecrop, Russian sage, and Japanese anemone |

| Blooming Time | Description | Examples |
|---|---|---|
| Fall bloomers | The gardening year's last hurrah can be quite colourful, and if you have bright fall tree foliage, the combined effect can be really fabulous. | Aster, dahlia, goldenrod, mum, and sedum |
| Long-blooming perennials | For a show of long-term colour without too much planning, look for perennials with a long bloom period (it could be a spring, summer, or late-summer-into-fall bloomer) or those that come in several varieties with different bloom periods. Create a bed of day lilies, for example, with early, mid-season, or late-season cultivars. Mix and match various colours and forms. Most long-term bloomers tend to be sun lovers, so grow them in an open area of good soil, and take good care of them so they will perform at their best. | Plants with several varieties that bloom at different periods: bellflower, astilbe, coreopsis, day lily, lily, phlox, and veronica<br><br>Plants with long blooming periods: blanket flower, bugbane, purple coneflower, columbine, gaura, veronica, bistorta superba, mallow, lungwort, sea holly, turtlehead, and yarrow |

# The living palette: Keeping colours in mind

As with annuals (refer to Chapter 6), colour is one of the best parts of perennial gardening — the fun, creative, and satisfying part! Realize that for any given plant that you like, it probably comes in different flower colours (and sometimes, as with the numerous hostas, in different leaf colours), which gives you even more options. There are few absolute colour rules today, but you can refer to Chapter 6 for ideas on the types of colour combinations you'd like to try.

# Designing perennial beds and borders

The most common way to display perennials is together, in a large flower bed or, space permitting, a long border either of meandering form or with firm boundaries. Quite honestly, these methods of growing perennials are purely practical: You can prepare the soil, plant them together, and care for them together (see the upcoming sections "Planting Perennials" and "Show the Love: Taking Care of Your Perennials").

Here are some basic layout tips and techniques that professional garden designers use, which can be easily transferred to your own garden (for additional planning advice, refer to Chapter 2):

- ✔ **Plan to be in scale.** Some sense of proportion among your home, garage, and/or shed (whatever's nearest to the proposed perennial garden) is key. A big house, for instance, does best with wider beds and taller plants; a smaller one is better served by a series of smaller beds and lower-growing plants.

- ✔ **Match garden style with structures.** A casual bungalow, cottage, or one-level home likes an informal perennial garden with curving boundaries; a larger or more imposing home, or one with strong architectural elements and lines, needs a more formal, straighter-edged approach.

- ✔ **Try a dress rehearsal.** Lay out the lines of your proposed garden in advance with a hose, outdoor electrical cord, rope, or even chalk or flour. Set potted plants or lawn chairs or whatever here and there within the lines' bounds as stand-ins (these items should match the perennials in terms of mature height and bulk, not the size of the plants you buy). Stand back and assess. Tinker with the plan until you're satisfied, and then sketch it on paper so you can remember it on planting day.

After you have your perennial garden's layout planned, you're ready to begin your plant selection. In addition to choosing plants for the bloom times and colours, take these points into consideration when choosing your perennials:

- ✔ **Consider height and width.** Perennial gardeners have to be patient and be able to imagine the future, because new plants are small. Find out your chosen plants' expected mature sizes and allow them enough elbow room in your plan. Plan to position taller-growing plants to the back of a traditional border or to the centre of an island bed; array lower growers at their feet. If you need help visualizing, some software programs let you see what your garden will look like as plants mature.

- ✔ **Mix it up.** Nature loves diversity, and the variety looks great — it keeps the eye moving even as it lets individual plants stand out. So intersperse a variety of plant forms, from spiky ones to mound formers. But don't mix things up so much that the plan is too busy and tires the eye. Plan to have several of one type of plant in groups throughout your border or island bed.

- ✔ **Match the plant to the growing conditions.** Save yourself a lot of grief and wasted money and effort by choosing plants that are clearly labelled as sun lovers or shade lovers, as the case may be in your intended site. Figure 7-1 gives you an example of a shade garden, and Figure 7-2 shows a sun garden plan, each with appropriate plants labelled for the two different types of gardens.

As for soil conditions, some perennials like the dirt rich and moist; others like it dry and only moderately fertile. Do your homework here, too. (Of course, you can improve or alter the existing soil conditions if you like. Refer to Chapter 4 for advice.) If you have a dry garden, you may want to consider the plan in Figure 7-3. Or if you have very rocky soil, you can take advantage of the situation by creating a perennial rock garden.

**Figure 7-1:**
If you have a shade-filled area for planting, such as one beneath a group of trees, try a garden plan such as this one.

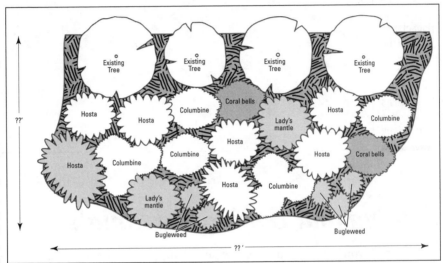

**Figure 7-2:**
If your yard gets a lot of direct sunlight, here's a garden plan that accents grasses and perennials and will truly give you a great day in the sun!

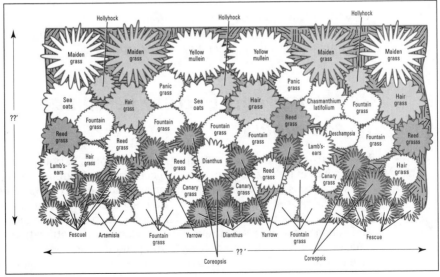

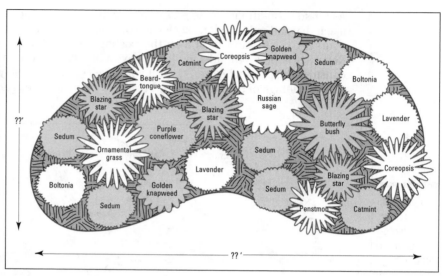

**Figure 7-3:**
Dry gardens can still be beautiful with the right plants, like the drought-tolerant perennial beauties included in this plan.

# Finding and Buying Perennials

If you have a clear idea of which plants you want, you're ready to go get them. You can acquire a perennial plant in many different ways, but this section covers the most common methods.

Very few gardeners grow perennials from seed — it takes too long, and most gardeners want only a few plants of each variety. Besides, the best varieties today are clones, and you can't grow them from seed.

## To the market: Getting perennials in containers

You can usually purchase partially grown perennials in pots, and they come in a variety of pot sizes, from a mere 5 centimetres (2 inches) on up to 22 litres (5 gallons). Both mail-order nurseries and local retailers sell perennials in containers (see the next section, "Buying perennials through mail order," for info on mail-order perennials). The larger the plant is, the more mature — and expensive — it is, and the more immediate your gratification. However, a smaller plant can catch up quickly if you plant it in an appropriate site and give it good care. Consider also how big of a hole you want to dig.

Here are some important tips to remember so you can be sure of getting a good potted plant:

- **Buy a healthy plant.** Examine the entire plant:
  - Look above and below the leaves as well as along the stems for signs of insect or disease damage. A few yellowing leaves are fine.
  - Examine the crown for signs of rot (no good, obviously) and fresh new shoots (very good).
  - Pop the plant out of its pot and examine the roots. They should be crisp and viable, often white or brown, not wiry, wry, limp, or black. Avoid pot-bound plants.

- **Choose a plant that's not yet in bloom.** Some growers force plants into early bloom so they'll look good at the stores, but don't be seduced! The trip home in your car or the adjustment to the transplanting process often causes blossoming perennials to jettison expendable growth; in other words, they ditch petals and unfurling buds.

  If your new plant sheds its flowers on the way home, make sure to plant the perennial well and care for it; it may bloom again soon enough. However, many perennials don't rebloom, so the show may be over until next year. You're best off choosing a plant that's conserving its energy.

- **Don't buy out of season.** Bargain perennials aren't always a bargain. Those plants for sale in midsummer have a stressful time establishing themselves; fall-planted ones may do just fine or may succumb to winter's cold (see "Fall planting," ahead).

- **Have a few alternatives in mind.** You can't always get what you want, but with all your options, you can find something that works.

## Buying perennials through mail order

Buying through mail order can be very convenient. You can shop from a catalogue or on a Web site in the dead of winter, or in the middle of the night in your jammies. Also, you can spend plenty of time thinking over your plans. After all, mail-order companies often carry a broader range of varieties than do local providers. And after you order your plants, they're delivered to your door at the right time to be planted — all without standing in line!

Just make sure to pick out a company that's been in business for a while, that's able to answer your phone or e-mail questions, and that your gardening friends have had good experiences with. You can start your search with some of the companies listed in the appendix.

The following sections outline how the plants may look after their trip through the mail. Or you can check out "Preparing for the actual planting" for info on how to treat the plants after they arrive.

### *Potted plants, ready for action*

Some mail-order nurseries ship small perennials in small pots. If you get a live-plant shipment, open it immediately upon arrival, even if you're not going to plant anything that very day. Inspect the plants as we describe in the preceding section, and quarantine any plants of questionable quality. Call the nursery immediately if you see a problem so you can work out a refund, merchandise credit, or replacement.

Small potted plants aren't necessarily baby perennials. Such young plants take too long to grow, and mail-order nurseries want you to jump right in and enjoy your garden. So the small plants nurseries ship out tend to be 2-year-old, field-grown plants that have simply had a haircut of their top growth prior to shipping. A good, strong root system is what you want. Don't worry: Fresh, new top growth will soon follow!

### *Their roots are showing: Dormant, bareroot perennials*

Bareroot perennials are the typical mail-order product. Selling perennials this way is simply more practical for some plants for a variety of reasons. For instance, baby's breath and baptisia have root systems that are sensitive to being moved in and out of the ground and various pots too many times. Other perennials, like day lilies and peonies, have large root systems that don't fit well in smaller pots. Bareroot plants are also dormant and lightweight, which makes shipping them cheaper and less risky.

Like potted mail-order plants, bareroot ones are usually 2-year-old, field-harvested plants. They were probably dug up the previous fall, just as they became dormant, and kept in climate-controlled cold storage until spring shipping season. Bareroot plants consist of a hearty root system and some trimmed-down stems; little or no leaf growth should be evident.

# *Acquiring free divisions from other gardeners*

If you're a practical or frugal person, you may gladly accept gift plants from friends and neighbours. Usually, free divisions are surplus plants, which means that these plants have been growing a little too well in their garden of origin. This is good news for you — it means the plants are in robust good health, and it also means that sort of plant probably really thrives in your area.

You can also obtain divisions from mature plants already growing in your yard, if you're creating a new gardening bed or expanding an old one. See the section "Dividing perennials" for information on how to separate your plants, and check out "Preparing for the actual planting" for advice on how to treat your divisions after you receive them.

# Planting Perennials

Perennials are probably the hottest topic these days among garden enthusiasts and plant suppliers. As a result, information about how to select and plant them abounds. Reputable garden centres have knowledgeable salespeople, and universities, garden centres, and public libraries sponsor various workshops and lecture programs about perennials. If you need more information than you find in this chapter, check out these sources and the books in your public library or local bookstore.

## Figuring out where to plant perennials

Good news — there's a perennial for almost any growing situation your yard can dish up. Make a match between the conditions you have to offer and the known characteristics of a plant, and you're halfway there. A little care from you on planting day and beyond, and your perennials are sure to thrive.

### Sunny locations

Lots of perennials adore sunshine. They grow more compactly when they get enough sun (as opposed to becoming lanky or leaning toward the light source), and they produce more and better flowers.

*Full sun* means six or more hours of sun per day. If you have to choose between a spot with morning sun and a spot with afternoon sun, most sun-loving perennials seem to do better with the afternoon site. This situation varies somewhat according to the situation in your garden. If your garden is west- or south-facing in one of the warmer parts of Canada — like Victoria, British Columbia, or Ontario's Niagara Region — some plants that like a bit of shade may droop. On the other hand, if you live in a cooler area — like Edmonton, Alberta, or northern Quebec — full sun will definitely be required for the same plant. Because sun can be drying, either choose dryland natives or help out the plants with regular watering and by adding moisture-conserving mulch around their root systems.

Favourite sun perennials include artemisia, armeria, basket-of-gold, blanket flower, coneflower, coreopsis, delphinium, gaura, lavender, penstemon, peony, sea holly, and yarrow.

### Shady spots

Judging from many gardening books and magazines, a beautiful garden is full of sunshine and flowers, and those of us with shade are doomed to a dull and boring display. Not so! Many perennials prefer shade, prospering in a range of conditions ranging from deepest woodland gloom to areas of dappled or filtered light to those that get morning sun and afternoon shade.

Not only that, but many plants appropriate for shade have beautiful leaves — you can find amazing variety in shape, texture, and even colour. And you may be pleasantly surprised to know that plenty of shade plants produce attractive flowers.

Shade is actually a benefit to many plants. Lack of direct sun means their leaves look healthy and lush, without burned edges or tips, without drying out or wilting. Sunlight also tends to bleach out the beauty of variegated leaves (leaves that are marked or rimmed in white, cream, or gold), whereas in shade, such foliage thrives and lights up the scene. Shelter from the sun's hot rays also preserves flower colour.

Favourite shade perennials include astilbe, bugleweed, bergenia, bleeding heart, brunnera, coral bells, corydalis, many ferns, goatsbeard, hellebore, hosta, lady's mantle, lamium, lily-of-the-valley, lungwort, Solomon's seal, and sweet woodruff.

### Dry soil

If sandy, gritty, or fast-draining soil is your lot, growing a fabulous perennial garden is still possible. Save yourself a lot of blood, sweat, and tears by working with what you have. Sure, digging in some organic matter at planting time (and on an annual basis) is good advice to follow when you can, but your gardening life can be a lot easier if you go native. You don't have to pour on water you don't have, and you may be delighted with the easy maintenance and attractive look.

That's right: Go native. Perennials native to dry ground are your best bets. Before you protest that they aren't attractive or are probably weeds, take a fresh look. Peruse the offerings at a local nursery that specializes in indigenous plants. Visit a public garden or botanical garden with displays of natives. Your eyes will be opened. Botanists and horticulturists feel your pain and have been working hard over the years to find out which native perennials adapt best to gardens and which ones are prettiest. There are even selections or cultivated varieties (cultivars) that are significant improvements over their wild parents — new flower colours and bigger, longer-lasting flowers on more-compact, handsome plants.

Favourite dry-soil perennials include black-eyed Susan, blanket flower, baptisia, butterflyweed, evening primrose, gaura, penstemon, phormium (a tender perennial in Canada), and yarrow. And don't overlook cacti and succulents — cacti are native to many parts of Canada, and well-stocked, native-plant nurseries (see the appendix for some mail-order sources) reveal their astounding range and beauty. Their siblings, the succulents — from common types like hens 'n' chicks to tender echeveria — are also easily available locally or by mail order.

### Wet soil

Soggy, boggy ground is usually written off as a lost area or a liability. But what if that damp side yard, wet back forty, or perpetually muddy roadside ditch was to come alive with handsome leaves and blooming colour? It's certainly possible. A host of plants actually like wet feet; a little research can point you to the ones that are a match for your problem spot's conditions.

You may have to wade in prior to planting to get the spot ready. Bring your rubber boots and create a hospitable open area with gusto and determination! Yank out most or all of the existing vegetation so it doesn't compete with the desirable incoming perennials. If warranted and practical, dig a drainage trench to route excess water away from the spot. Perhaps dig in some organic matter to improve soil fertility and drainage, if only a little.

After you've planted the area with appropriate moisture-loving perennials, not much more should be required. The plants' basic need — water — is already present. If the plants are happy, they'll increase over time, reducing the need for weeding or, indeed, any intervention on your part. If they grow too lushly, why, you can rip out and discard or give away the extra plants.

Cardinal flower, day lilies, forget-me-not, Japanese primrose, marsh marigold, and turtlehead are good plants for wet soil. Don't apologize for the wet soil: Go ahead, call it a bog garden! And if you're ambitious, make the boggy area the entry to a new water garden — see Chapter 17 for details on ponds.

### Clay soil: Soggy soil at its worst

If your yard has clay soil, you already know it. Slick and soggy in wet weather and nearly impenetrable in dry, clay soil is actually composed of lots of densely packed, very tiny particles. Clay leaves little space for air and water to circulate, and the result is heavy ground that drains poorly. Needless to say, many perennials — or rather, their roots — have a hard go of it in such conditions (and so does your shovel or trowel, for that matter).

Clay soil does have some advantages, believe it or not. This soil is often fairly fertile because it holds nutrients and water so well. And of course, it's slower to dry out in hot weather, which can help your plants.

At any rate, if clay is your lot in life, you have three options:

✔ **Improve the soil's structure.** Add organic matter. Doing so can help lighten and aerate the area, making it more hospitable to perennials and other plants and allowing water to drain away better. Dig organic matter in often and deeply — compost and/or well-rotted manure are up to the job. (For details on soil improvement, refer to Chapter 4.)

✔ **Go with what you have.** Plant clay-tolerant perennials such as beebalm, cardinal flower, chrysogonum, epimedium, many ferns, gunnera, Japanese iris, Japanese primrose, marsh marigold, monkshood, turtlehead, gentian, or spiderwort.

✔ **Bypass it.** Grow your perennials in raised beds (see Chapter 13) or pots (Chapter 16).

## Deciding when to plant perennials

Perennials tend to be rather tough and forgiving plants in terms of picking the right time to plant them, but generally, most people plant perennials in either the spring or the fall.

Perhaps the best way to know when to plant perennials is to know when *not* to plant them. For example, avoid planting perennials in stressful conditions, or you'll, as the saying goes, reap what you sow. No-no times include

✔ Any blazing hot day

✔ Any time of drought

✔ Any time when frost is predicted

✔ Any time when the ground is soggy or still frozen

✔ Right after a deluging storm or flood

Read on for some seasonal planting advice.

### Spring planting

Springtime is the preferred time to plant perennials for good reason. All the conditions these plants relish and respond to are in place: warming soil, warm sunshine, longer days, moist ground, and regular rainfall. Roots quest into the ground, taking up water and nutrients to fuel growth, and *top growth* — foliage, stems, and flowers — surges forth.

When getting ready for spring planting, make sure you do the following:

1. **Harden the plants off.**

   Just as you wouldn't plunk a new goldfish into its tank without letting it adjust to the water temperature, you don't want to give your perennials an environmental shock. Let new plants adjust to life outdoors for a few days or a week by setting them in a sheltered spot, such as on the porch or against the semishady side of the house. Start the plants off for just a few hours, and increase the time until they're outdoors 24/7. (But bring perennials indoors or cover them if there's a threat of a late frost.) Cover them with a single layer of newspaper to reduce the light intensity and wind exposure.

2. **Choose a cool, cloudy, or damp day to plant, or plant in late afternoon.**

   The hottest part of the day (midday to early afternoon) is a bit stressful to both you and the plants!

3. **Plant in good soil, create a basin of soil or mulch around each plant, and give the plant and soil a good watering.**

   Check that the water drains in where you want it.

4. **Mulch after planting.**

   Not only does this step hold in soil moisture and moderate the effects of fickle, fluctuating spring temperatures, but it also keeps weeds at bay (they love to grow this time of year, too).

Here are some things perennials find very unpleasant. During spring planting, do not

✔ **Handle the plants roughly.**

✔ **Plunk a root-bound plant into the ground.** Either tease apart the roots a bit or lightly score the sides with a sharp knife, which inspires new root growth. *Then* you may place the perennial in its planting hole.

✔ **Plant perennials in waterlogged ground, or drench them right after planting.** A moderate dose of water is a needed drink; too much water prohibits oxygen from getting to the roots, and the plants literally drown or rot.

### *Fall planting*

Autumn turns out to be a fine time to plant many perennials in temperate climates. The soil and air are cooler and sunlight is less intense, so the weather's less stressful for newcomer plants. Competition from weeds isn't likely to be a big problem, either.

In some regions, rainfall becomes more regular, too, which helps provide the moisture the perennials need to start good root growth. And their roots *do* grow — the plants simply aren't programmed to start producing lots of new leaves or flowers at this time of year. Yes, the perennials will soon head into winter dormancy, but fall planting often gives these perennials a head start over their spring-planted counterparts.

When spring rolls around, you may notice the difference. The fall-planted perennials should be raring to grow, larger and more robust. You can expect a good show. All this, plus you won't have to elbow through crowds at the garden centre. You now know something that many gardeners don't. Seize this opportunity!

Fall planting also applies to perennials you want to dig up and move to a new spot, and to *dividing* perennials (taking strong, rooted pieces of overgrown plants).

When getting ready for fall planting, make sure you do the following:

✔ Buy good, strong plants. These plants have the best chance to establish themselves in your garden.

✔ Mulch a little at planting time, about 1.3 to 2.5 centimetres (½ to 1 inch), to hold in soil moisture and warmth; mulch even more as winter arrives, another 5 to 8 centimetres (2 to 3 inches) after the ground freezes, to protect the plants during the cold months. (For more info on mulching options, refer to Chapter 4.)

✔ Cut back the top growth, just to further urge the plant to concentrate on root growth.

Here are some things to *avoid* during fall planting:

✔ **Fertilizing:** Fertilizing inspires a fresh spurt of young shoots and leaves, which are vulnerable to cold damage. You want perennials to enter dormancy for the winter.

✔ **Plant late bloomers:** Late bloomers (like asters, mums, black-eyed Susan, and perennial ornamental grasses) are better planted in spring.

Make doubly sure, before you find out the hard way, which plants relish fall planting and which do not. You can always double-check at wherever you buy perennials in the fall. Reputable nurseries don't sell plants that resent being planted this time of year. Some fall-planting favourites are day lilies, peonies, oriental poppies, and rhizomatous iris (for info on plants with rhizomes and bulbs, see Chapter 8).

## Preparing for the actual planting

How to plant your perennials has a lot to do with how you acquired them, whether by mail order, from the local nursery, or as a division from a fellow gardener.

If you purchased your plants by mail order as pots or bare roots, here's what to do when they're delivered to your home:

1. **Unpack the plants immediately, and then inspect them.**

   As with potted plants, you want to be on the lookout for obvious problems of pests or rot. And you want to see crisp roots. You shouldn't see any green stem or leaf growth yet, or at least not much.

2. **Hold the plants in a cool, dark place until you're ready to plant them — perhaps for a few days or a week at the most.**

   The refrigerator is also fine. Mist them lightly if they seem dry.

If you can't plant your mail-order perennials right away, pot them, water well, and care for them in a sheltered location.

3. **On planting day, rehydrate the roots by soaking them in a bucket of tepid water for a few hours.**

Here's how to handle plant divisions (see "Dividing perennials," later in this chapter, for info on doing the separation):

- ✔ **Keep plant divisions moist.** Don't let them dry out! This idea is especially important if you're not prepared to plant the divisions in your garden right away. Place them in a plastic bag or box and then sprinkle on some water or temporarily pot them; water well.

- ✔ **Clean them up.** Clip off or tug out weeds and limp, yellowing, or damaged foliage. Cut off flowering stalks (don't worry, they'll generate new ones soon enough). Right now, you just want the divisions to devote their energy to establishing their roots in your garden.

- ✔ **Plant in a prepared area and then keep an eye on them.** Don't just toss divisions on the ground and hope for the best, even if your friend characterized them as tough guys. They need time, water, and weeding to get their legs under them.

See the preceding section for seasonally specific planting tips. For advice on planting perennials that come from a local store or supplier, please refer to the planting instructions for annuals in Chapter 6.

# Show the Love: Taking Care of Your Perennials

Generally, perennials require the same type of care as annuals (refer to Chapter 6), with a few modifications that depend on the type and size of your perennials. Mature perennials can grow quite large and may require some help in staying upright, or they may need to be trimmed down or separated if they grow too large or crowded for their space. They also attract fewer pests than annuals, but they do attract the critters. Here's some advice on how to handle all these basic perennial care issues.

## Supporting with stakes or rings

Because some perennials are tall, or tall and broad, a little support is a good thing. It not only keeps the plant more in bounds and manageable, but it also prevents the plant from keeling over under its own weight. You've been waiting for those flowers — don't let them cast downward or flop on the ground!

Using a stouter or larger support than you think you need never hurts — if your perennials are healthy and happy, they're probably going to need it.

Resourceful gardeners like to rig their own plant supports, and certainly, nothing's wrong with bending some old coat hangers or recycling sticks and stakes of various kinds, including tree branches or twigs. But your local garden centre or home store or favourite mail-order catalogue may well have a perfectly affordable alternative, like the ones shown in Figure 7-4, saving you the time and effort.

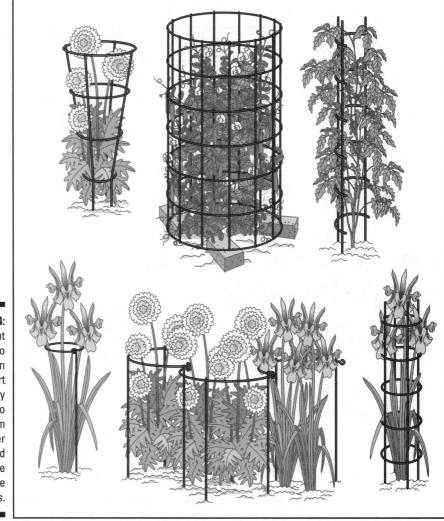

**Figure 7-4:**
Plant supports do more than support plants; they can also help them grow better and produce more blooms.

Here are a few important tips to remember about using perennial supports:

- ✔ **Install early.** Press a *peony hoop* (a ring on legs that's useful for many more perennials than just peonies) over the plant well before it reaches the hoop's height. This way, you can centre the support right over the plant, and when the perennial does grow as expected, the stems, leaves, and flowers will froth over the hoop and hide it from view — without a struggle. Early installation also reduces the risk of damaging the root system as you poke the support in.

- ✔ **Press the support in deeply.** At first, the support may be equal to the job, but as the plant grows ever larger, the stake or hoop may lean or slump. Anchoring the support deeply at the outset can make the support more stable and stronger. A foot or more into the ground is usually best, depending on the plant.

- ✔ **Help out with ties.** As the plant grows, check on it and fasten the stem or stems to the support at regular intervals. To avoid abrading the plant tissue, use soft material (not wire — try string or cloth); if you loop it once around the stem and create a second loop for attaching to the support, the plant will be able to move in a breeze but still be held gently but firmly to its appointed place. (Use green string or cloth, and you'll hardly be able to see it.)

- ✔ **Be tidy!** Remove and store or discard the support at season's end. This step will also remind you to cut back the perennial (and mulch if your winters are cold). With a season's experience under your belt, you know whether the support is the right one for the job and thus worth saving or replacing. If you need something more substantial, add it to your springtime shopping list.

You really don't know whether a perennial needs support until you grow it. Whether a support is necessary depends not only on the type of plant but also on cultural conditions — a plant that may be self-supporting in full sun in a protected location may need to be staked if grown in a shady spot or one with a lot of wind. Perennials that do need support need it every year.

## *Practising good grooming habits*

Perennials look better with a little grooming, but don't feel you have to fuss over them constantly. Just remove dead or damaged stems, wayward ones, or ones that are crowding others. The same goes for foliage that doesn't look good. And always clip or snap off stems at ground level (beheaded and short stems don't look good). You can pinch off smaller branching stems or individual leaves.

Spring and summer, when perennials are growing, are the best times to groom. The grooming doesn't traumatize the plant, and new growth can soon fill in and hide your cuts.

## Off with its head! Deadheading your plant

*Deadheading* is just a gardening term that refers to the practice of removing spent flowers or flower heads. Not only does it leave your perennials looking nicer, but it also encourages more blooms. Deadheading works by thwarting the plant's natural inclination to go from flower to seed and thus finish up for the year. If you deadhead, the chemical messages that put the seeding process in motion are stopped and the plant redirects its energies into

making more buds and thus more flowers. You can keep a perennial in bloom a lot longer by doing this.

So make a habit of deadheading your perennials every time you walk by. Toss the faded flowers on the compost pile. Or bring your clippers along and cut bouquets while the flowers are still in their prime — cutting fresh flowers now has the same effect as deadheading later!

## Dividing perennials

A number of perennials need periodic dividing. You know when yours do because the plants are growing in ever-denser clumps and the flower show isn't as prolific as it was in previous years. The interior of the clump, in particular, may become disappointingly unproductive.

Luckily, rejuvenation is both possible and easy! Just look at Figure 7-5 and follow these steps:

1. **Dig up the clump, taking care to get as much of it as possible without damage.**

   Most roots are in the top 30 centimetres (12 inches) of soil, and the root's mass is usually the diameter of the plant plus 8 to 15 centimetres (3 to 6 inches) beyond the plant. For digging and transplanting, going larger than these measurements isn't necessary.

2. **Cut or cleanly break the clump into two or more pieces (divisions), each with an obvious growing point and some roots.**

   Work on the clump quickly so the plant parts don't dry out too much (you can cover them with a tarp or mist them occasionally if need be). Discard any unproductive portions and any shrivelled or rotten parts. Leave the roots surrounded with the soil to protect the root hairs from drying out and becoming damaged.

3. **Replant the new pieces, some in the same spot and the others elsewhere in your garden (or give them away to other gardeners).**

   Water the divisions in well, and look in on them regularly. They should generate new, smaller, vigorous plants.

**Figure 7-5:**
Two different methods for dividing a perennial. The method on the right is recommended for plants with thick or dense root structures.

Here are some tips for division success:

✔ Good timing is important to give the new pieces the best chance of prospering. Early spring is usual, but you can divide some plants (notably poppies and peonies) in the fall.

✔ You can pry apart fibrous-rooted perennials with your bare hands; all others require sharp, strong, clean tools that are equal to the job: a stout knife, a trowel, or even two spades or gardening forks braced back to back.

✔ Plant in good (fertile and well-drained) soil. Perhaps the original spot could use a dose of organic matter before you return pieces to it; when planting elsewhere in your yard, prepare a bed in advance so you can move quickly. (Refer to Chapter 4 for info on soil amendment.)

## Preparing perennials for winter

If you live in a cold area and want to overwinter your tender perennials, dig up the roots or entire plants and bring them indoors to a nonfreezing spot to spend a few months as dormant or semidormant houseplants. Pot the plants in any good soil, and grow them in a cool (5°C–10°C, or 40°F–50°F) and bright area. Keep them barely moist. The idea here is to just keep them alive until you can plant them back outside after the danger of next spring's frost is over. Then with warmer temperatures and brighter light, they'll spring back to life.

You can also trim and prune your perennials and use mulch to protect them through the winter (refer to Chapter 4 for more information on mulch).

# Dealing with perennial pests and diseases

Good news — perennials aren't especially pest-prone. If they're growing in an appropriate spot with elbow room and you water regularly, they're in good shape. And healthy plants are your best defence against potential problems.

There are but a handful of common perennial-garden pests. Read on for their descriptions and some ways to control them:

- ✔ **Aphids:** These small whitish critters congregate on stems and nodes, sucking the life out of your plants. A strong spray from a hose can dislodge them. Ladybugs can also make a quick meal of aphids, so don't get rid of these helpers.

- ✔ **Black vine weevils (taxus beetles):** In late spring and early summer, these critters are harmless pupae resting in your soil. Then the adults emerge and eat the foliage of dozens of perennials (and lay eggs for the next generation while they're at it). The telltale sign is notched leaf edges, especially lower down on the plant where the insects find more shelter. Starting in early fall, the newly hatched grubs eat roots.

  Launch your counterattack in fall by releasing beneficial nematodes (roundworms), available from well-stocked garden centres and mail-order sources; apply according to label directions. Other pesticides are registered for controlling these creatures; check with your provincial ministry of agriculture for more information.

- ✔ **Leaf miners:** These bugs form brown or tan or clear traceries — tunnels or channels — on affected leaves but rarely kill the plant. Just remove and discard affected leaves, and the plant will generate new ones.

- ✔ **Root nematodes (roundworms):** Affected plants develop severely distorted growth. Rip the plants out and discard them before the problem spreads.

- ✔ **Voles:** These little rodents slip out of their underground tunnels when you're not looking and nibble on your perennials, especially the leaves but also roots, seeds, and bulbs. They're a bit larger than mice, with a shorter tail and smaller ears. You can try trapping them with a baited mousetrap, but the best deterrent is a cat who's a good hunter. Castor oil as a repellent works fairly well (see the sidebar "A slick trick for keeping out moles and voles"). You can also surround plants with small moats of sharp gravel.

As for diseases, they, too, are mercifully few on healthy perennials. You may encounter mildew or other fungal diseases. These problems appear as spots or a powdery coating on leaves, and severely affected plants may have distorted growth and buds that fail to open. If the problem is bad, tear out the plants or resort to spraying with a fungicide.

# A slick trick for keeping out moles and voles

If you're having problems with moles (or other small animals), try using this formula to drive them out of your yard:

- ✔ 60 millilitres (¼ cup) castor oil

- ✔ 30 millilitres (2 tablespoons) liquid detergent soap

- ✔ 90 millilitres (6 tablespoons) water

Blend the castor oil and soap together in a blender (they won't mix properly otherwise). Add the water and then blend again. Store this mix in a container till needed.

When you're ready to apply the solution to the area where the moles are active, mix 30 millilitres (2 tablespoons) of the solution into 3.8 litres (1 gallon) of water. Pour the liquid into the problem area (all over the affected area, not just down the holes).

If fungal problems are chronic in your garden, your best line of defence is good air circulation, particularly in hot, humid summer weather. Also, be sure to pick off and discard sick leaves and clean up fallen affected leaves around the base of your plants. Regular, even watering right at the roots (that is, not splashing the leaves) is also wise.

Of course, an easy way to prevent both pests and diseases is not to grow vulnerable plants! You can deliberately seek out varieties touted as resistant.

# Chapter 8

# Brightening Up the Garden with Bulbs

- - - - - - - - - - - - - - - - - - - - - - - - - - - - - - - - - - - - - - - -

## In This Chapter

▶ Finding out what bulbs are

▶ Planting different kinds of flowers together

▶ Selecting and purchasing bulbs

▶ Putting bulbs in the ground

▶ Caring for bulbs

- - - - - - - - - - - - - - - - - - - - - - - - - - - - - - - - - - - - - - - -

*P*lant them, forget them, and wait to be surprised and delighted! Along with perennials, bulbs provide some of the earliest colour in gardens. They can also provide some of the latest colour: Suppliers sell bulbs for all growing seasons — spring through fall — not just early spring. This chapter explores all you need to know about choosing, planting, and caring for these beauties.

## Shedding Light on Bulbs

A *bulb* is a structure that grows underground; it stores food during its dormancy and then supplies energy for an emerging plant. You know what bulbs are if you buy onions or garlic at the grocery store. Good ones are dense and have some heft to them plus a thin papery skin for protection; as bulbs age, their robustness diminishes and they dry out. They sometimes begin to sprout the beginnings of green leaves out of their tops. Gardeners also consider foods like potatoes, sweet potatoes, ginger, and water chestnuts to be bulbs.

Garden bulbs are actually much the same as the ones you find at the grocery store. Good ones have some plumpness and density because they're full of healthy, moisture-filled plant tissue. They really are a package of life! With the right conditions, and in time, they're sure to generate leaves — and the big payoff, gorgeous flowers.

# Defining terms: Bulbs aren't always, well, bulbs

When you shop for garden bulbs, you may immediately notice some variations on the underground-storage theme. The minor but key differences are worth knowing because they affect not only what sort of plants the bulbs produce but also how to divide them to get more plants. Here's a rundown of some of the plant structures that gardeners call bulbs:

- **True bulbs:** Bulbs are composed of concentric fleshy scales, or layers, which are actually modified leaves (see Figure 8-1). Yes, just like an onion. At the base of a true bulb is a *basal plate,* the place from which the roots grow. Examples of true bulbs include allium (flowering onion), amaryllis, daffodil, hyacinth, and tulip. Interestingly, when you cut a bulb in half, you can see the future plant parts — stem, leaves, flowers.

  Offsets that you can pry off and plant may appear (see Figure 8-2). In some cases, notably with lilies, you can grow new plants from individual scales.

- **Corms:** These structures resemble true bulbs somewhat, with a growing point on top and a basal plate at the bottom (see Figure 8-3). However, they don't have the clasping modified leaves; technically, corms are swollen underground stems. Also, they use up their store of food in one growing season — though new little *cormels* (baby corms) often appear atop the old one to carry on. Examples of corms include autumn crocus, crocus, crocosmia, freesia, and gladiolus.

**Figure 8-1:**
As you can see from the protective layers in this cross section, a bulb is really a plant in a protective package.

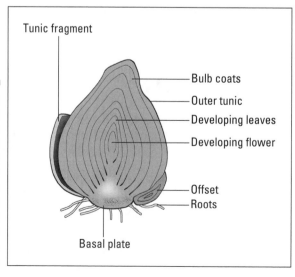

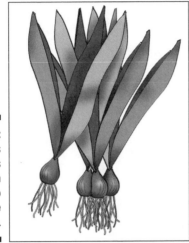

**Figure 8-2:**
True bulbs
form offsets
that you can
pull apart to
form more
plants.

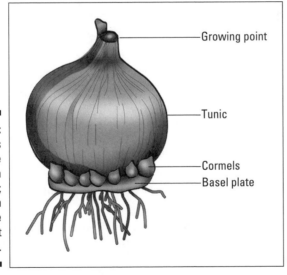

Growing point

Tunic

Cormels
Basel plate

**Figure 8-3:**
Corms
resemble
true bulbs in
many ways;
this corm
has little
cormels at
its base.

> ✔ **Rhizomes:** Rhizomes are thickened stems that grow horizontally; the roots grow down from the underside (see Figure 8-4). The tip tends to have a primary growing point, though productive side-buds are common, and you can cut them off and plant the buds individually. Examples of rhizomes include agapanthus, bearded iris and many other irises, canna, and lily-of-the-valley.

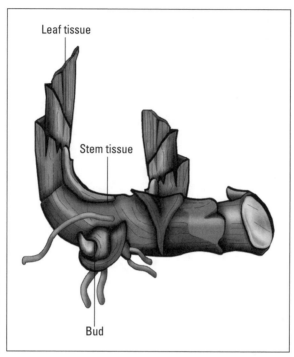

Leaf tissue

Stem tissue

**Figure 8-4:**
Rhizomes
grow
sideways.

Bud

✔ **Tubers:** Tubers are swollen stem bases. Roots grow from their sides as well as their bases, and you may see multiple productive buds. A classic example of a tuber is the potato. Other examples include most anemone, tuberous begonia, caladium, cyclamen, dahlia, and gloxinia.

The way to divide tubers varies by the type — dahlias, cyclamen, and gloxinia involve different methods. Generally, you want to cut the tuber so that each piece contains a bud.

✔ **Tuberous roots:** These structures are in fact roots, not modified stems (see Figure 8-5). Fibrous roots, like fingers, radiate outward from a central point. You can easily divide these roots to get more plants, making sure, of course, that each piece has at least one bud on it. Examples include alstromeria, clivia, foxtail lily, and ranunculus.

Many gardeners discuss the differences between hardy bulbs and tender bulbs. Unfortunately, making the distinction isn't easy, because a tender bulb in one climate (like Zone 4) may be a hardy one in Zone 7. Generally, *hardy bulbs* can survive wintering in the ground without too much trouble, whereas *tender bulbs* have to be dug up and stored. Your local nursery can help you determine which bulbs are considered hardy in your area.

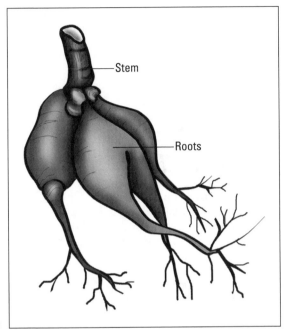

Stem

Roots

**Figure 8-5:**
Tuberous
roots look
like swollen
roots.

# *The time of the season: Looking at early and late bloomers*

Many bulbs bloom in springtime — those bulbs are the most familiar and beloved to gardeners in Canada. However, fewer but no-less-pretty ones make their show in summer or even fall. See "Getting Down and Dirty: Planting Bulbs" for examples of these types of bulbs.

The terms *early, mid-season,* and *late* abound in bulb descriptions. All this naming system means is that some bulbs burst forth earlier rather than later — all during the springtime. A month or more of time can separate the first snowdrop from the first tulip or the first tulip from the last tulip. The expected bloom time is worth knowing so you can plan for continuous colour or set up attractive colour duos or spectacular full-bed shows.

The reason people plant most spring-blooming bulbs in the fall is not just so the plants can get a head start on root growth. These bulbs also need a period of cold (so obligingly supplied by a winter in the ground) to maintain their biological clocks. The warmer, thawed-out but moist soil of spring, not to mention the warm sun above, coaxes them at last to burst into their full and glorious potential. Spring-blooming bulbs like tulips are so sought after that in North American mild-winter regions, like southern California and Texas, gardeners can buy a limited selection of prechilled bulbs to transplant to their gardens. Some ambitious gardeners in these parts even refrigerate bulbs for a specified period (at least eight weeks) and then plant them in their gardens in late winter or early spring.

## Getting acquainted with the most popular bulbs

You can find many different types of bulbs, but they all have one thing in common: They're packages of life just waiting to be planted. They differ from seeds in that they contain within them the beginnings of leaves, stems, and flowers. All they need is to be planted and watered, and the growth process can begin.

The common spring-flowering bulbs include tulips (Figure 8-6), noted for their impressive range of blooming times, flower types, and colours; daffodils, some of the most rugged and easiest to grow of all bulbs, also with a wide range of flowering times; and lilies, which can bloom from late spring to early fall if you plant different varieties. Check out the colour insert for a look at some of these bulb superstars, and see the following sections for advice on how to let them take the spotlight in your garden plans. In this chapter, we also introduce you to some lesser-known players that are well worth your while.

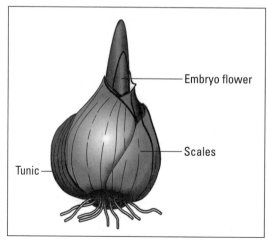

**Figure 8-6:**
A tulip bulb, waiting to flower.

Embryo flower

Scales

Tunic

# Social Mixers: Choosing to Combine Your Bulbs

A lone bulb isn't much of a show; nor, in truth, is a scattering or a row of a mere dozen. Bulbs are meant to be planted, enjoyed, and shown off in generous numbers. The more, the merrier!

This need for company isn't just because bulbs are small plants. In fact, some plants can grow fairly tall and even sport big, dramatic flowers. The case for putting in lots of bulbs, in sweeps or mix-and-match displays, is compelling: The whole is inevitably greater than the sum of the parts. Flowering bulbs simply look fabulous in groups; their natural exuberance is multiplied.

Read on for some design ideas (for general info on designing a garden, refer to Chapter 2).

## Combining various types of tulips

If the only tulips you know are the classic red ones lining a neighbour's walk-way, you're in for a treat. The world of tulips is amazingly varied. You can find a wonderful range of hues, from royal purple to golden yellow to shell pink to pure ivory white. There are also many fabulous bicolours, especially the smashing red-and-yellow and pink-and-green ones. Forms also vary, from the popular goblet-shaped flowers (mainly the *Darwin hybrids*) to those that resemble plush peonies or elegant lilies. Some tulips have flared or fluted petals or petals with fringed edges. Some are nearly knee-high; others are surprisingly low to the ground. All tulips are equally easy to grow.

But before you get carried away with an ambitious planting scheme, remember also that although tulips are always spring bloomers, they don't all bloom at the same time. You can find everything from "single early" to "double late" tulips, and you have to take these designations into account if you want your plans to work out. Check out the following tips for different types of displays:

- ✔ **For single-colour displays:** Use a large quantity of the same exact tulip variety, and plant them closely.

- ✔ **For mixed-colour displays:** Stick to a theme, such as pastel or bold colours. Tuck in a few bicolours that tie the display together. Of course, if you have lots of space, going for the full rainbow can be fun, but to be effective, such a show needs to have a generous number of tulips in every hue.

- ✔ **For a longer-lasting show:** Research the bloom times so you get a range. Then mix up the varieties throughout the display so it doesn't look unbalanced and so something is always in bloom.

> ✔ **For smaller areas or pots:** Choose tulips of different heights, and place the taller ones in the middle. That way, you can distinguish each one, and the variety and complexity of the show give it more splash.

Don't plant your tulip display in a shady spot. Some spring bloomers don't mind, but tulips do.

## Mixing up your daffodils

Daffodils simply don't have the colour range that tulips do, but they do offer a fresh elegance in their whites, creams, yellows, oranges, and near pinks. Daffodils come in about a dozen different forms, too, which aficionados call *divisions.* These varieties include the ever-popular trumpet forms; little ones that bloom in clusters; daffodils with tiny, almost flat trumpets; and flowers with trumpets that have so many petals they hardly seem like daffodils at all.

A great feature of daffodils is that nothing likes to eat them! Not squirrels, not mice, not voles, not rabbits, not deer!

And many daffodils are scented. Most have a light, sweet perfume that's not overpowering. (If you're after knock-your-socks-off fragrance, check out the jonquil type of daffodils.) To capitalize on fragrant daffodils, plant them in quantity so they can make an impression. Or at least plant enough so you can spare some for bouquets and enjoy that wafting sweetness indoors. Here are some tips for choosing daffodils:

> ✔ **For single-colour displays:** Daffodils whose petals and trumpet are both the same colour, all white or all yellow, make excellent massed displays, lovely in their simplicity. For a little more definition, you can seek out a few differently named varieties in the colour you like. Varied forms can make such a display more intriguing.
>
> ✔ **For mixed-colour displays:** A planting devoted entirely to yellow-and-orange bicolour daffodils is a lot of fun. You can tuck in a few solids just to keep things interesting. Another idea is to mix the white-petalled, so-called pink-trumpeted daffodils with some plain whites.
>
> Blending all the colours and forms doesn't tend to work well, because the pastel daffodils jar against the bolder hues, and a mix of varied forms often looks too busy.
>
> ✔ **For a longer-lasting show:** Situate daffodils in an area that gets part-day shade or filtered light.
>
> ✔ **For smaller areas or pots:** You're best off devoting a limited area to a single variety or two compatible ones. Miniature growing varieties are also a perfect choice.

Don't mix daffodils of differing bloom times. When a daffodil is done blooming, you need to let the leaves die down (so they can replenish the bulb's energy stores for next year's show), and sometimes it seems to take forever. Having some yellowing or drying leaves among up-and-coming bloomers doesn't look good at all!

## Combining different kinds of bulbs

Ah, combining different kinds of bulbs is the most fun of all! A great coordinated burst of flowers is such a thrill to behold, especially after a long, cold winter. For maximum impact, you want a range of colours, sizes, shapes, heights, and bloom times. See Figure 8-7 for a mixed garden.

You can pull off a daring combination of bulbs in two ways. The easy way is to buy the mixes offered by bulb merchants, often at quantity-discounted prices. The merchants do all the planning work for you; all you have to do is plant. If you're more of a do-it-yourselfer or you have some specific or creative ideas, by all means, research and make your own mix. All the information you need is on the bin or bag label or in the catalogue descriptions. Exercise your creativity and design your own plan.

Here are a few tips for success:

- ✔ **Make growing conditions as good as they can be.** With properly drained soil and good lighting conditions, bulbs have the best chance of performing their best. (See the upcoming "How to plant bulbs" section; the needs of most bulbs aren't that different.)

- ✔ **Buy good bulbs and plant them promptly.** Cheap, poor-quality bulbs or ones that sit around drying out for too long before going in the ground are bound to be a disappointment, thwarting your vision for a colourful display.

- ✔ **Planting at different depths is okay.** Different bulbs are supposed to be planted at different depths, so a mixed planting will be pocked with some deep and some shallow — like a holiday fruitcake. That's fine, just so long as you don't plant one bulb right over another (and even if you do, the lower one will probably find a way around the obstruction and poke up and bloom anyway). See Figure 8-8.

- ✔ **Casual is better than formal.** Mixed plantings that are laid out in neat patterns can be done, but they run the risk of looking rather stilted. A variety of bulbs cast about informally ends up looking livelier.

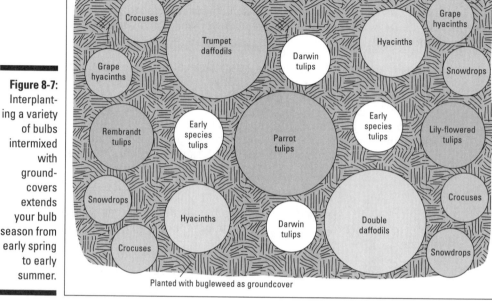

**Figure 8-7:** Interplanting a variety of bulbs intermixed with groundcovers extends your bulb season from early spring to early summer.

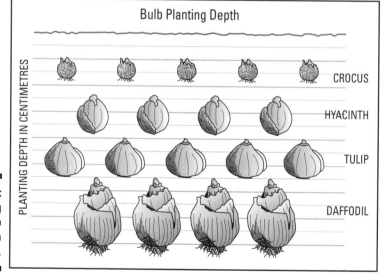

**Figure 8-8:** Planting bulb varieties in layers.

---

## A daffodil by any other name . . .

What's the difference between a daffodil and a narcissus? None! *Narcissus* is the Latin name for the genus common to all daffodils.

Jonquil, another common name ascribed to daffodils, is proper only when you're referring to a particular type, or division (Division 7), of daffodil

called *jonquilla*. Essentially, the name refers to the species *Narcissus jonquilla* and its hybrids. These plants are the ones that have multiple flowers to a stem, and the blooms are usually very fragrant. In other words, all jonquils are daffodils, but not all daffodils are jonquils.

---

# *The Search: Where to Get Your Bulbs*

Making a successful, beautiful bulb display doesn't begin at planting time. It begins when you go bulb shopping or bulb swapping. Neighbours can be a great resource for extra bulbs when they're dividing their bulbs. But do be picky: Free bulbs aren't a bargain if they aren't strong and healthy or if they're simply too small.

Bulb quality can vary, so starting with good ones is important. Here's what to look for:

- ✔ **Appearance:** A fresh, good-quality bulb is plump and clean, without obvious damage to its outer layers. Avoid bulbs with disfiguring dents or blemishes, which can let in rot-inducing bacteria. Bulbs may contain a small amount of green penicillin mould, which is rarely harmful. Some bulbs, like anemone and ranunculus, always look dried up.

- ✔ **Heft:** Pick up a bulb and handle it for a moment. Then pick up a few others from the same basket or bin (of the same variety) and compare their weights. Bulbs that feel lightweight relative to their peers are likely to be dried out and not viable (they may even be last season's leftovers, for all you know). While you're at it, gently squeeze the bulb. A squishy texture indicates rot, but a good, firm feel means the bulb has sufficient moisture content.

- ✔ **Size:** With bulbs, bigger is better. A larger bulb has more stored reserves and therefore can produce larger flowers, and more of them, on more substantial stems. You get what you pay for; you can get incredible deals on bulbs, but they may be too young and small to bloom.

## Buying bulbs from home stores and nurseries

You can buy bulbs in so many places these days. If you're a novice and need some planting information, want top-size bulbs, and need help with your selection, garden centres and nurseries are often your best choice. Home centres have reasonable selections but usually sell smaller bulbs, and they rarely provide much gardening information. Here are the advantages of buying bulbs in person:

- **Instant gratification and impulse buying:** You can get the bulbs you want, or come across others that tempt you, and then buy them on the spot.

- **Immediate planting:** Shopping and planting on the same day is an option if you have the time and are feeling gung-ho.

- **The chance to observe the bulbs:** You can handle the merchandise before buying, checking the bulbs' appearance, heft, and size.

And here are the drawbacks:

- **Poor storage conditions:** Normal display-rack or display-box conditions aren't ideal for bulbs. Some may dry out; others may sprout prematurely. The smaller the bulb, the faster it dries out. In spring, summer-blooming bulbs are often displayed in home stores for weeks, if not months, before the soil is warm enough for planting them.

- **Lack of variety:** Selection isn't all that varied.

Buy spring-blooming bulbs early for late-summer to early-fall planting. That way, the bulbs are fresh and in the best condition, and you have the biggest selection.

- **Questionable contents in the bin:** Bulbs may get into the wrong bin as customers pick through them. You may end up with the wrong colour or a completely different type of bulb.

When selecting your bulbs, read bin or packaging labels with care so you know the names of what you're buying as well as something about the plants — like how tall they get, when they bloom, whether they grow in sun or shade, and how far apart and deep to plant them.

## Purchasing bulbs through mail order

Sometimes you just don't have enough time to get to a retail store, or you want a particular variety of bulb that's not commonly found in your local garden centre or home supply store. This is when buying from a mail-order supplier can be a real advantage.

Here are the perks of sending away for your bulbs:

- ✔ **Quality:** Mail-order bulbs are frequently bigger and fresher. Every step of the way, from climate-controlled storage to the cushioned box they arrive at your door in, mail-order bulbs get premium treatment.

- ✔ **Selection:** Catalogues and Web sites devoted especially to bulbs are impressive: You can browse beautiful bulbs you've never seen at your local garden centre. Suppliers usually offer a selection of cutting-edge varieties as well, because bulb merchants often work directly with Dutch growers to get the new and improved bulb varieties that sometimes aren't produced in enough quantity to be distributed by mass merchants.

Take a look at the disadvantages:

- ✔ **Wait time:** There's a lag between the time you place your order and the day you receive your bulbs.

  When you order the bulbs matters. If you order bulbs in spring or summer to be sent the coming fall, you may wait many weeks. If you order them in the fall, delivery usually takes just a few weeks, and some-times less. The wait time also depends on the supplier. If the seller grows the bulbs (as is the case with many lilies) or has the bulbs in his or her warehouse in Canada, the bulbs are usually shipped faster than if they have to be sent to you directly from Holland.

- ✔ **Inability to inspect the merchandise:** You can't handle or inspect your bulbs until they arrive. However, all reputable mail-order suppliers guar-antee their wares and will replace bulbs or refund your money if the bulbs don't meet your expectations. Find and read the guarantee and return policies, just in case you have to use them.

Check out the resources in the appendix at the back of this book if you want a list of some mail-order companies to consider. And look for deals — larger quantities and mixes are often discounted.

# Getting Down and Dirty: Planting Bulbs

There's a right time for everything in gardening. The general rule for bulbs is to buy and plant them as soon as they're available in the market. That's when bulbs are most viable. Many mail-order companies ship their bulbs during planting season only, and it's best to plant them as soon after you receive them as possible.

## Keeping your cool: The skinny on forcing bulbs

*Forcing* bulbs may sound cruel, but the term merely means that you're encouraging the plants to bloom early by treating them in a special way. You can force potted bulbs into early bloom, but they still need 8 to 16 weeks to chill (generally, the larger the bulb, the longer the chilling time). Place the bulbs in the fridge, in an unheated garage that doesn't freeze, on chilly basement stairs, or in a *cold frame* (a wooden or concrete-block box buried in the outside soil during the cold months). Some of the easiest and most popular bulbs to force are paperwhites.

As soon as you pot the bulbs you want to force, you have to keep them cool and the soil lightly damp. If the soil dries out, their roots won't form, and if the temperatures are too warm, the bulbs may end up being *blind* (meaning the flower buds inside never develop), or the flower buds will *blast* (they grow, but shrivel on the stem and never develop into full blossoms).

Forcing spring bulbs has two stages, and the first is the rooting period. For the rooting stage, place the potted bulbs in any cool (5°C–10°C/40°F–50°F), dark spot for 10 to 16 weeks. Some varieties take longer than others. Don't worry if the temperatures aren't in this range every day; the temperature range is just the ideal. The important point is that the bulbs are in a cool, not freezing, place to root. A refrigerator is perfect.

*Tip:* Before moving the potted bulbs to the next stage, look at the drainage holes in the pots.

Roots should be growing out of the holes; if they aren't, put the potted bulbs back into a cool, dark area until they are. One of the most common ways people fail in this game is by not allowing the bulbs to root sufficiently before going to the next stage. Alternatively, the bulbs may be ready to come out of the big chill when you see at least 2.5 centimetres (1 inch) of top growth and the bulbs don't move when you try to wiggle them by hand.

After the bulbs are well rooted, you can move them to the growing phase, where the foliage starts to grow and the bulbs eventually bloom. First, you want the bulbs to adjust to warmer temperatures and higher light, so place the rooted bulbs in their containers in a cool, bright spot that's around 16°C (60°F) for a few weeks. Remember to keep the soil lightly moist. Next, move the bulbs to an area that's slightly warmer — 18°C–20°C (about 65°F–68°F) — and very bright to finish the plant's growing cycle. A sunny, south-facing windowsill is fine. Turn the pots a quarter turn each day; otherwise, the stems will lean toward the light. You can also place the bulbs so their foliage is about a decimetre (a few inches) from a two-tube, or preferably four-tube, fluorescent light fixture.

The bulbs should bloom in about three to four weeks. The blossoms will last longer if you move the bulbs to a spot that's cool (16°C–17°C/61°F–63°F) and not quite as bright (without direct sunlight).

## When to plant bulbs

Bulbs aren't instant-gratification plants. They need some time in the ground before they send forth stem, foliage, and flowers. But they're not inert when they're in the ground, of course. They're generating root growth, which will help nourish the show as well as anchor the plants in place.

The following sections explain what different types of bulbs require, depending on when they bloom.

### Planting spring-blooming bulbs

Spring-blooming bulbs require a chilling period. They're dormant when you get them, and they break dormancy only after the chilling. Winter conveniently supplies this necessary cold period! That's why you put the bulbs in the ground the fall before you want them to bloom.

### Planting summer-blooming bulbs

Most summer bloomers, such as gladioli, calla lilies, cannas, dahlias, tuberous begonias, and crocosmias, love warm soil and toasty summer sun. If you garden in a mild climate (Zone 8 — see Chapter 3), you can plant these bulbs in the early spring and expect flowers by summer. But in most parts of Canada, early-spring planting isn't feasible. Instead, wait until late spring or early summer — the same time locals plant tomatoes outside. A better idea is to start bulbs early indoors in a warm spot and care for them until the danger of frost has passed; then you can move the plants outdoors. Many bulbs need a long growing season to produce those flowers you hanker after, and they need the indoor start.

In either case, regular doses of all-purpose fertilizer (applied according to label directions) can nudge your plants into faster, more robust growth and more and better flowers.

To get flowers earlier and longer from these summer bloomers, visit a nursery in late spring or early summer (or place your order then with a mail-order house, either via catalogue or Web site) to buy a larger, prestarted plant.

### Planting fall-blooming bulbs

Spring gets all the attention, to be sure, but some bulbs bloom from late summer into fall, and they're gorgeous and easy to grow — they're also a wonderful sight to behold when the gardening year is winding down. Among this group are the autumn crocuses (*Colchicum autumnale* — actually no relation to true crocuses — and *Crocus speciosus*), winter daffodil (*Sternbergia*), Guernsey lily *(Nerine bowdenii)*, saffron crocus *(Crocus sativus)*, and even a species of snowdrops *(Galanthus reginae-olgae)* that's hardy in Zone 8. If your local garden centre doesn't have these, look for them in specialty bulb catalogues or on gardening Web sites.

 Some late-blooming bulbs have a different dormant period than spring-blooming bulbs: spring into summer. These bulbs are offered for sale while they're dormant. Thus, you plant them in mid- to late summer, and they wake up in the earth and bloom within a few weeks. Nerine (hardy to Zone 8) and Sternbergia (hardy to Zones 7 and 8) are two examples of late-blooming bulbs that can be grown in the warmest parts of Canada. Some hardier bulbs, like the colchicum and autumn crocus (Zone 5; available for planting in late summer) send up their leaves in spring, and then the leaves die back and the flowers appear without leaves in fall. Lycoris (Zone 5), also known as the resurrection lily or magic lily, blooms in late summer or early fall and is usually available for planting in spring. But be sure to mark the spot where you plant summer- and fall-blooming bulbs so you don't forget them by the next spring — when the leaves die back and disappear, it's easy to plant a new perennial or annual on top of them.

Many tender, late-blooming bulbs are available, but because they aren't hardy enough to winter over in most Canadian gardens and need a long growing period to bloom, they need to be started indoors in spring (when the bulbs are available) and grown in pots outdoors. Examples include tuberose and hymenocallis.

## Where to plant bulbs

Bulbs are some of the least demanding of all plants, but they appreciate your efforts to give them as good a growing area as possible (with well-drained soil). If you're careful about planting your bulbs, they'll reward your efforts with years of bountiful flowers.

### Flower beds

Flowering bulbs are very happy in prepared flower beds. They receive the good, loose soil they relish and the elbow room they need. Here are two good approaches:

✔ **Bedding schemes:** Perhaps you've seen these beds in public display gardens: broad areas devoted to nothing but, say, tulips. The mass of colour can be very impressive. You can do the same at home. Pick an open spot, choose a large amount of the same or very similar bulbs (in terms of colour, height, and/or bloom time), and plant them fairly close together.

✔ **Mixed beds:** Bulbs are only part of the show in a mixed bed; they can share the stage with early-blooming perennials (refer to Chapter 7), some colourful annuals (refer to Chapter 6), and perhaps a few sheltering shrubs (see Chapter 11). The overall show never declines: Whether you're waiting for the bulbs to burst into bloom or waiting for their fading foliage to die down, you always have something to look at and enjoy.

### Containers

Growing bulbs in containers outdoors can only be done successfully in some parts of Canada, notably in southern Ontario and British Columbia. In most other areas, the winters are so cold that the pots freeze solid and the bulbs turn to mush. But if you live in a relatively mild area, say, Zone 5 or Zone 6, it's worth trying: Use a fairly large container; plant bulbs in autumn, when you would usually put them in the ground, and when it gets really cold, move them into the garage or a protected place beside the house. You can also insulate the pots with leaves held in place around the pots with chicken wire. When the bulbs come into bloom, place the pots front and centre on your porch or patio.

## Naturalizing: Plants gone wild

*Naturalizing* is just a gardening term (and a rather sensible one, actually) to describe bulbs usually planted in large informal drifts, where they remain undisturbed and multiply. You can naturalize in a grassy area, under fruit trees or other deciduous trees, at the edge of a wooded area, or on an embankment. You want a semiwild area, because the bulb foliage should be able to die down undisturbed after the plants finish blooming. Over time, the bulbs tend to increase their numbers, spreading out the show with each passing year, with virtually no effort from you.

To begin, invest in a large amount of good-quality bulbs. On planting day, literally toss them out over the chosen area and plant them where they land. This display ends up looking more spontaneous and, well, natural.

An easier solution is to buy pots of forced bulbs at the supermarket in spring and then group them in large planters. As the blooms begin to fade away, just remove them and then replace them with new pots — it's the lazy gardener's way. Most gardeners think that forced bulbs won't bloom again, and so they discard them. But we've turned them out of their pots right into the garden, as soon as the soil can be dug, and allowed the leaves to ripen off naturally, adding a little 5-10-5 water-soluble fertilizer to help them along (refer to Chapter 4 for info on fertilizer grades). It may take a couple of years for growth to appear, but most bulbs will eventually grace your garden with more bloom.

Soil in pots dries out faster than garden-bed soil. Keep your potted bulbs watered. Consistent water (that is, every day or two instead of only when the plants are gasping) leads to a healthier, longer-lasting show. For ideas and tips for container gardening, consult Chapter 16.

## *How to plant bulbs*

Planting bulbs is simple. But before you start, be sure the chosen spot has fertile, well-draining soil. Bulbs rot in soggy ground and struggle in sandy soil; the addition of some organic matter eases these problems considerably. Follow these planting steps for the best results:

1. **Dig the hole.**

   If you're planting only a few bulbs or you're spot planting (tucking bulbs in among other plants in a mixed bed), use a trowel. Various bulb planters are on the market, but frankly, neither of us find them very useful unless the soil is loose. If you're planting lots of bulbs, break out the shovel and make a trench.

Not all bulbs are the same size, so not all bulbs should be planted at the same depth. The general rule is *three times as deep as the bulb's height.* This guideline varies a bit based on your soil type. In sandier soils, you can plant a little deeper; in heavy clay soils, a little shallower. If you forget how deep to plant your bulbs, consult the bulb supplier's label or catalogue. Too shallow, and your bulbs may poke their heads above the soil surface too early and get damaged by wintry weather; too deep, and they'll take longer to emerge.

Roots grow out of the bottom of the bulb, so the quality of the soil underneath it is more important than what you pack the hole with. If you're amending the soil with organic material like compost or sphagnum moss (refer to Chapter 4), dig somewhat-deeper-than-recommended holes so you can accommodate this addition.

The bulbs' distance apart varies with the type of bulb and the sort of display you have in mind. If you crowd the bulbs underground, the eventual show may suffer. Certainly, don't let the bulbs touch one another. The general rule is *at least three bulb widths apart "on centre"* (from the centre of one bulb to the centre of the next). But experience can tell you what the bulbs you've chosen tolerate and how dense you like your displays.

**2. Add a fertilizer.**

Use a fertilizer that has a higher phosphorus number, such as a 5-10-5 fertilizer (refer to Chapter 4 for info on fertilizer grades). Phosphorus (the *P* in the N-P-K on fertilizer labels) is important for the root growth as well as flower production. Just sprinkle the fertilizer in the bottom of the hole and then scratch it in so it mixes with the soil a bit. (For more on choosing and using fertilizer, see "Fertilizing your bulbs," later in this chapter.)

If the ground is bone dry, water a day or so before planting so the ground is damp but not muddy when you're planting bulbs. If you want to wait to fertilize, you can scratch the fertilizer into the surface of the soil in the spring as the bulbs are growing.

**3. Put the bulb in the hole (see Figure 8-9).**

You want the *nose,* or growing point, to point up, and the roots, or basal plate from which they'll grow, to point down. (If you can't tell, plant the bulb on its side — the plant will figure it out in due course! Botanists call this nifty skill *gravitropism.*) Make sure the bottom of the bulb is in contact with soil; if you leave an air pocket, the roots can dry out and the bulb won't grow or won't grow very well.

**4. Backfill and water.**

As you scoop soil back into the hole, firmly press it in place to prevent air pockets. Water well (some settling will occur) and then add a bit more soil as needed.

Indicate where you've planted your bulbs so you don't plant other flowers in the same place. Mark the locations with permanent nonrusting, nonrotting labels, like those made of zinc or copper.

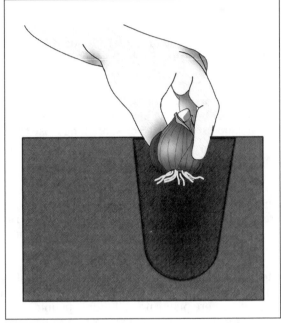

**Figure 8-9:**
Securely
place the
bulb's basal
plate
against the
bottom of
the hole.

# Taking Care of Bulbs

Because bulbs come as a package of life — that is, with the embryonic plant and flower within, plus stored food to fuel their growth — they demand little from you, the gardener. With a little tender, loving care — not a lot — they can do their thing and be wonderfully reliable.

## Watering your bulbs

Just like grocery-store onions, bulbs rot with too much moisture. And yet, they need water to generate roots and get growing. But don't fret — there's no mystery or careful balancing act. Just grow bulbs in well-drained soil; they can use the water they need, and any excess moisture should drain away.

Fall-planted, spring-flowering bulbs have it easy if you live where fall rains water them in and spring rains wake them up. (Of course, in an uncharacteristic dry spell, you can provide supplemental water.) Summer and fall bloomers appreciate water most when they're beginning to emerge, and again when they open their flower buds. Water at these times only if the soil is dry.

# Fertilizing your bulbs

Although newly planted bulbs have all the stored foods they need to perform the following spring, annual fertilizing can help keep this show going year after year.

A general-purpose fertilizer works fine for bulbs. A higher phosphorus content is often recommended simply because it inspires root growth as well as flower production. So go ahead and use the 5-10-5 or something close to this ratio.

People often recommend bone meal for bulbs, with its approximate formulation of 2.5-24-0. Alas, modern-day, store-bought bone meal is highly sanitized, and its benefits are questionable. Nonetheless, some bulb enthusiasts swear by it. This natural material tends to be very slow to release it nutrients, so some gardeners prefer using *super phosphate* instead; this material is rock phosphate that has been treated with sulfuric acid to make it more soluble. It's 20 percent phosphorous (0-20-0).

Some people debate over where to place the fertilizer. In the hole? On the soil surface (top-dressing)? The case for adding plant food to the planting hole is that it's right at the roots, where plants need it (some people are concerned that direct contact with fertilizer can burn a bulb or its roots, but not all bulbs are so fragile). The case for soil-surface feeding is that the nutrition can filter into the growing area more gradually.

What to do? Try whichever way is more convenient for you, and then judge the results. You can always switch methods.

You need to fertilize only once, and you have three opportunities to do so:

- **At planting time (usually in the fall):** This option is described in the previous "How to plant bulbs" section. Even though the flower is already in embryo form within the bulb, fertilizing at planting time gets the bulbs off to a good start.

- **As growth starts, usually in early spring:** This fertilizing improves the current season's display. Individual plants will be more robust, with brighter, longer-lasting blooms.

- **At post-bloom:** While the foliage dies down naturally, this little boost sends food down to the bulb to fuel next year's show.

The standard application rate for fertilizer is about 15 millilitres (a tablespoon) or a small handful per square foot, but read the label on the fertilizer package for exact directions. Apply fertilizer to damp ground. Water it in afterwards if there's no rain so it penetrates the soil and gets to the root zone. Or use a water-soluble fertilizer that you water in around the bulb.

# Mulching

Mulch helps keep down weeds, can add organic matter to the soil, retains moisture, and stabilizes the soil temperatures. Stable soil temperatures are important so the bulbs don't sprout too soon and risk getting freezing damage from a late spring cold snap.

Shredded leaves, compost, or bark chips are all fine choices for mulch. Sprinkle it lightly around your bulbs just after planting them or when they're up and growing. And add some more mulch after the show is completely over.

# Caring for fading leaves

After bulbs bloom, the foliage tends to linger. Eventually it starts to yellow, then brown, and finally gives up the ghost — a process that can take many weeks. This stage is not a pretty sight, but don't interfere! The plant is busy sending food from the leaves down to the bulb to fuel next year's show. Cutting off the leaves before they naturally die back diminishes next year's display.

Some gardeners bend over the offending, fading leaves and cinch them with a rubber band or piece of string. Some even braid them! Both of these tacks don't really solve the ugliness problem, and they thwart the refuelling process. It also looks odd, so don't waste your time.

If you just can't stand to watch your bulb foliage die down, you have two choices:

- ✔ **Tear out the entire bulb — ugly, fading leaves and all.** Plant new bulbs at the appropriate time.

  Don't use this method with bulbs like autumn crocuses or naked ladies (a common name for colchicum), which don't send up their leaves at the same time as their flowers. You'll be tearing out their fall blooms, too.

- ✔ **Hide, or at least distract from, the process.** Plant perennials with strong, emerging foliage in the area (refer to Chapter 7), or tuck in some annuals (Chapter 6). Here are some recommended companions and cover-ups:

  - Basket-of-gold (*Aurinia*)

  - Bleeding heart (*Dicentra*)

  - Bugleweed (*Ajuga*)

  - Day lilies (*Hemerocallis*)

  - False rockcress (*Aubrieta*)

  - Forget-me-not (*Myosotis*)

• Spurge *(Euphorbia)*

• Violets or pansies *(Viola)*

## Fighting bulb pests

If you were a rodent tunnelling around underground and you came across a nice, plump bulb, how could you resist? The main predators of bulbs are mice and voles (not moles, actually — moles are carnivorous, dining on insects and worms and such; mice and voles may use the tunnels of moles). Squirrels and chipmunks are more likely to sniff out the tasty treats above ground and dig up your bulbs, sometimes strewing remnants about your yard. In spring, they love the tender bits of stem just under the flower and are likely to nip them off for a gourmet meal. These rascally rodents are enough to make even the most mild-mannered gardener homicidal.

Rodents love tulips and crocuses, but they avoid daffodils and fritillaries (these bulbs are poisonous, and the critters seem to know it). Here are some strategies for keeping your bed of bulbs rodent free:

✔ Fill each planting hole with small, sharp gravel.

✔ Make a "cage" of screen or hardware cloth, fill it with soil, plant your bulbs inside it, and then bury it at the correct depth.

✔ Make a raised bed especially for bulbs. This bed should be about 30 centimetres (1 foot) deep. The bottom layer, at least 5 centimetres (2 inches) thick, should be small, sharp gravel. To accommodate the bulb's roots, at least 15 centimetres (6 inches) of good soil can go over the gravel. Plant the bulbs and cover them with 5 centimetres (2 inches) of gravel or even sand. Last, lay a thick layer of mulch (hay, pine needles, or shredded leaves) up to 15 centimetres (6 inches) over everything. Remember to rake off the mulch when spring comes.

✔ Prior to planting, spray your bulbs with a foul-tasting repellent marketed for this purpose. Two common brands are Ro-pel and Critter Ridder. Let the bulbs dry before planting. Spray Ro-pel or Critter Ridder right on the stems and flower buds in spring to keep the little varmints away. Castor oil is also a common, safe, and reasonably effective repellent that you can apply to the bulbs and/or the ground they grow in.

# Chapter 9

# Coming Up Roses

. . . . . . . . . . . . . . . . . . . . . . . . . . . . . . . . . . . . . . . . . . .

. . . . . . . . . . . . . . . . . . . . . . . . . . . . . . . . . . . . . . . . . . .

*W*hat can roses do for you? Just about anything (well, anything becoming to a plant). They're long-lived plants, they deliver plentiful and gorgeous colour, and you get to pick your own bouquets to enjoy indoors (or give away to your dazzled friends!). And many roses are deliciously, seductively scented. The colour pages of this book contain some beautiful pictures of rose varieties that may be just right for your garden.

Of course roses are beautiful — in fact, roses, traditional symbols of beauty, are arguably the most gorgeous blossoms that exist! They certainly look wonderful in a corsage or vase. There, you can't help but admire their form and notice they're fairly long lasting off the bush. But here's a secret gardeners know: There's so much more to roses — different flower forms, different colours, different scents (some are quite fragrant, others are fruity or spicy), and even different plant forms.

All this can be yours — really! This chapter tells you what you need to know about choosing, planting, and caring for roses. There's nothing quite like enjoying the pride and pleasure of your very own roses!

## What Makes a Rose Be a Rose Be a Rose

Officially, roses are shrubs of the genus *Rosa,* but growers weren't completely content with bushes. Roses now come in a huge array of sizes and forms. This unique and splendid variability means that if you like roses, you can display them in all sorts of settings.

Some roses are large stand-alone bushes, capable of being the main showpiece of a large garden. Some are dense enough to form impenetrable hedges (when planted in a row), an attractive way to get a living fence. Other types of roses, although still bushy, are compact enough to find a home in a mixed flower bed or to thrive in a container. Some roses even have a spreading form and are low-growing enough to serve as groundcovers on embankments or curb strips. And don't forget the climbers and ramblers — some of these roses can cover your shed or garage if you let them; others naturally remain a manageable size as they drape their loveliness over a simple garden arch.

Ever-popular miniatures range from patio-planter-box or hanging-basket size all the way down to little peewees that you can tuck into small decorative pots, alone or with other plants. Some enthusiasts like to tuck the miniatures right in the ground — not their traditional use, but why not? They certainly add a reliable splash of colour in any sunny bed.

The trick is to choose the right rose for the spot you have in mind. The following sections cover some important options for you.

## Checking out blooming habits

Back when roses were first introduced into cultivation, they tended to throw a great late-spring or early-summer show. And then it was over. Gardeners didn't see this tendency as a problem. People were so taken with the beauty and fragrance of the rose blossoms that they didn't complain. These early rose varieties were usually full petalled (full of so many petals that you could rarely see the centre of the rose) and richly fragrant.

Many spring bloomers are still in commerce to this day, and they're well worth growing. Spring bloomers are full of splendour and romance, their short period of glory notwithstanding. They're generally called *old garden* or *vintage* roses. Sometimes their French- or Italian-sounding name is a give-away. (For more information on these lovelies, read the upcoming "Species and old garden roses" section.)

Roses that don't just bloom in late spring or early summer and then finish are a modern development. (The year 1867 was the benchmark, with the introduction of the first hybrid tea rose, 'La France'.) Repeat-bloom roses don't actually bloom nonstop; if you observe carefully, you may notice that they cycle in and out of bloom.

Assured blooming cycles, shortened gaps between them, and longer-lasting blossoms are all the result of a long, complex, and varied genetic background and many different and protracted breeding programs taking place in many countries. All you really need to know is that many modern roses can produce blossoms for you all summer long and often well into fall. How many other flowering shrubs, or even flowering perennials, can claim that?

# Looking at hardiness

Don't worry about hardiness! Generally speaking, roses run the gamut of hardiness, and you can find varieties that can grow almost anywhere in North America, from Plant Hardiness Zones 2 or 3 to Zone 8. Some roses tolerate colder winters and can grow in the Prairies and northern Canada, right up to Yukon; others prosper in mild climates. Just as with any important plant purchase, you should make sure that the rose of your choice is considered hardy in your area (refer to Chapter 3 for info on Plant Hardiness Zones).

Also, just as with any other important plant purchase, you may be willing and able to pamper a marginally hardy rose plant. Winter mulching is important, especially with *grafted roses* (roses with cold-hardy roots and a less-tough rose variety grown on top). Details about when and how to do this care, and what material to use, are ahead in the section "Maximizing winter hardiness."

# Identifying the various rose types

Look closely at the plant tag or catalogue description to find out what type, or class, of rose you're considering. Among the numerous, widely used, and generally recognized types, you can find genuine differences. Know what you want and what you're buying! Read on to see your options, and look at the colour photo pages for pictures of some of these varieties.

## Hybrid teas

Because hybrid tea roses are so widely grown, they're perhaps the first type of rose that comes to mind when you think *rose*. They're surely the queens of the rose world, with their handsome growth habit and elegant flowers. Hybrid teas come in medium to tall bushes and usually have a distinctive vase-shaped profile. Elegant pointed buds precede the big, gorgeous, refined-looking flowers that usually grow one to a stem. These flowers are often bred with long cutting stems, so hybrid teas are great for bouquets. They bloom continuously throughout the growing season.

## Floribundas

Shorter and more compact than the ubiquitous hybrid teas, floribundas are — as you may guess from their name — cluster bloomers. This quality makes them excellent landscaping roses, in groups with one another or as part of mixed flower beds. They're also good choices for small spaces and small gardens. Floribundas were bred to be hardier than hybrid teas, so they're better choices for most Canadian climates, where they don't need the pampering that hybrid teas do.

Floribundas also remain in bloom all summer. In any given cluster, you may observe some flowers in bud, some partially open, and some as fully open blossoms. This staggering keeps the show going and also makes for variety in a homegrown bouquet.

### Grandifloras

A grandiflora is a big, upright-growing plant with large blossoms. The flowers appear in clusters, as with a floribunda. A cross between hybrid teas and floribundas, grandifloras are hardier than the teas but not as cold tolerant as floribundas. These plants bloom all summer. Some experts consider them to be a subclass of the hybrid tea.

### Polyanthas

Polyanthas are similar to floribundas but are technically older and less-intensely bred. Polyanthas have a compact, shrubby habit — they're a bit informal, but charming. Their smaller flowers, which the plants produce in profusion, remain in force all summer long.

### Species and old garden roses

*Species* are, as you may guess, old, historic roses that survive to this day because some enthusiasts deemed them worth preserving and perpetuating. They're the wild forebears of modern roses, and they exhibit admirable vigour, natural toughness, and casual, exuberant beauty. Yes, they tend to bloom only in spring. You may have a niche for these classics, or you may leave them to the fanatics. The best way to decide is to view one for yourself.

*Old garden roses* are historical roses that generally bloom only once a season, in late spring or early summer for a few glorious weeks. Sometimes referred to as *vintage, heirloom,* or *antique roses,* some old garden roses are species, which means they grow in gardens today the same as they grew in nature; others are hybrids of the species, or newer human-designed varieties. You can assume that the historical roses that didn't survive either were not very tough or were replaced by improved versions. As you may also guess, a number of excellent vintage roses have contributed their qualities to other sorts of worthy rose hybrids.

So grow these survivors with confidence. The best selections are at specialty nurseries. See the source list (in the appendix) for some places to try.

You should know that this group includes numerous subcategories: albas, Bourbons, centifolias (cabbage roses), China roses, damasks, gallicas, hybrid musks, hybrid perpetuals, moss, noisettes, Portland, Scotch, and tea roses. Whew! How can you sort through this bounty? Our advice is to read the individual descriptions or visit the nursery and then pick the one that captures your heart, no matter what it's called.

### David Austin roses, or English roses

Starting in 1963, British nurseryman David Austin electrified the rose world by successfully combining beautiful, full-petalled, richly fragrant old garden roses with modern ones to produce attractive, romantic plants. Many of these plants also feature improved disease resistance and a much longer blooming period. Today other breeders have waded in and contributed, so the more proper term is *English roses.*

### Shrub roses, or hedge roses

*Shrub roses,* or *hedge roses,* turn out to be catch-all terms for "lots of roses." To warrant the title, the rose should have a big, broad, shrubby habit; good weather resilience (be cold hardy but also able to tolerate hot, humid summers); disease resistance; and less-refined but often quite pretty, and frequently fragrant, flowers. Shrub roses are bred to be covered with blooms throughout the summer months.

But wait — there's more. This group of roses has subgroups that are distinctively different from one another. Here are the more widely available ones:

- **Buck roses:** The late Dr. Griffith Buck, a horticulture professor at Iowa State University in Ames, succeeded in selecting and developing attractive shrub roses that are genuinely low maintenance and able to tolerate the notoriously cold winters, fickle springs, and blazingly hot and humid summers of many parts of Canada and the American Midwest.

- **Explorer and Parkland roses:** These roses have been developed in Canada by breeders working for Agriculture and Agri-Food Canada to withstand the rigours of Canadian winters. Most are hardy to Zone 3, some even to Zone 2. The Explorers are named after — what else — famous explorers. The Parklands often, but not always, have *Morden* in their names, after the Morden Research Station in Manitoba where they were developed. For more details on these roses, see the sidebar "Why Canadian is often best."

- **Meidiland roses:** Weather tough and disease resistant, these French-bred roses tend to form relatively compact plants no more than 1.2 metres (4 feet) high and wide so that less pruning is necessary. The flowers are pretty and sometimes scented.

- **Rugosa roses:** Originally hailing from Asia, these coarse-leaved, extremely thorny bushes are now a common sight in many parts of North America. They're among the hardiest of roses, withstanding temperatures down to –37°C (–35°F) with little protection. Their flowers tend to be single (with just a few petals and blossoms that open rather flat), but they come in bright shades of pink, red, maroon, and white. And best of all, they're intensely fragrant, with a scent that's undeniably spicy. The *rose hips* (the fruit of the rose plant) that follow in fall tend to be big and bright, which makes the bushes look perky and festive until the birds eat all the hips.

Yes, the plant breeders have waded in, mainly to improve the flowers (double rugosas, for instance, sport more petals per flower). Rugosas make excellent, low-care hedges.

## Miniatures

Miniatures sport small leaves, small buds, and small flowers — all in scale with one another. These little rosebushes are cute and perky, ideal for pots but also sometimes a colourful touch added to a mixed flower bed or planted in a ribbon as an edging. Their diminutive size belies the fact that they're very tough and are often more winter hardy than their larger counterparts.

## Tree roses, or standards

If you read *Alice in Wonderland* as a child, or more accurately, studied the illustrations, you know the tree roses, or standards! They look like compact, continuous-blooming shrubs atop tall, bare stems, like fancy living lollipops. Because they look formal, they're a grand sight flanking an entryway or walkway, or growing by a swimming pool, alongside a deck, or in any formal garden area. Gardeners often display them in large pots, but you can certainly plant them in the ground. They're not winter hardy, however; in cold parts of Canada, you may have to bury them completely, tops and all, or overwinter the plant indoors or in a cold storage area. (See "Maximizing winter hardiness," later in this chapter.)

But what is a tree rose, exactly? Basically, it's a rose — usually a hybrid tea, a floribunda, or even a miniature rose — grafted onto a bare stem. Essentially, it's a two-part plant (or a three-part, if the bare stem has been grafted onto a special rootstock). Basically, the grafting simply lets you get many familiar roses — a 'Peace' or 'Queen Elizabeth,' for instance — in tree form. Such details aren't ultimately that important for you, the consumer. Just choose a plant that looks well done and appears healthy.

## Climbers and ramblers

Long, pliable *canes* (stems) are the main characteristic of the climbers and ramblers; this trait allows you to train these roses on a support such as a tree, trellis, fence, or archway. Although older rambling roses bloom just once every spring, modern ones can go all summer. Be warned that although ramblers are very vigorous — they can grow up to 6 metres (20 feet) tall — they aren't reliably hardy in most of Canada because they don't resist temperatures below about 12°C (–10°F).

These plants aren't technically vines that climb, because they have no way to attach themselves well to a support. They need your help and guidance — use judiciously placed nonbonding ties (strips of cloth are ideal). For advice on how to encourage climbing growth, see "Using roses as vines," later in this chapter.

## Why Canadian is often best

Explorer and Parkland roses are extremely hardy because they were bred to survive regions as cold as Zones 2 and 3. You always get a good show — all of the current year's shoots flower, even if the canes are killed to the ground and have to regenerate each year. These roses are generally heavy bloomers — some flower all summer — and they grow on their own roots, in shades of pinks and reds, whites through yellows.

What's the difference between Parklands and Explorers? Essentially, Parklands are bred from the native species *Rosa arkansa,* and the original Explorers were based on rugosa types. Other species have been bred into their genetic makeup and have passed along their disease resistance and repeat blooming characteristics to each type.

### *Groundcover and landscape roses*

In recent years, rose breeders have been working on groundcover and land-scape roses (the free-flowering Flower Carpet series is widely available; the Pavement series is perhaps hardier and equally floriferous; like the others, the hardy Knock Out series, a recent arrival on the horticultural scene, comes in many shades of red and blushing or shocking pink, and boasts purplish-green leaves in fall). These plants are simply low-growing roses that tend to sprawl outward rather than upward. With dense growth, some thorniness, and scads of pretty flowers all summer, they're an outstanding landscaping solution if you love roses and have a broad, open strip in need of coverage — a hill or embankment, say, or a sunny side yard, or an area you want to route foot traffic around rather than through.

# Deciding Where to Put Your Roses

Roses have become more sociable! Although some lovers of these special flowers enjoy planting them in beds by themselves (so gardeners can give the plants special care and make them more accessible for cutting), other folks have decided to let them join company with the other garden players — herbaceous perennials, bulbs, and shrubs. The choice is yours.

## Planning your beds and borders

Ah, beds and borders are surely the most popular and beautiful way to show off your roses. When you invite a rose or several roses into your garden, don't just plunk them into the ground at random. Instead, plan to create splendid beds that incorporate roses into your landscape or mixed flower beds. Your plan can be as elaborate as the one shown in Figure 9-1, or as simple as creating a small bed of three or four types of roses.

**Figure 9-1:**
A large,
classic plan
for a very
elaborate
rose garden.
The blank
sections
indicate
where each
rosebush
will be
planted.

Apply a few landscaping tricks and techniques, and the results can be quite splendid:

- ✔ **Let the sun shine in.** Roses love sun — at least six hours a day. Their foliage is denser and healthier in full sun, and flowers are more plentiful. So the appointed spot can't be shaded by nearby shrubs, a fence, or the house. (Or if it is, hopefully the shade happens in the early morning or late in the day.)

- ✔ **Pick the site — it should have ample elbow room so the plant can grow freely and healthily.** The rosebush shouldn't block or be blocked by other plants. Roses need space so that air can move freely around them. Location is a fairly important garden decision!

✔ **Match the rose to the spot.** Consider mature height and width (whoever sells the plant to you should be able to provide this info if it's not on the tag). You're going to love and cherish this plant, so it's sure to reach its full potential in, say, two or three years.

✔ **Let big plants come first when selecting plant locations.** If you're planning for your bed or border to have other flowers — perennials and annuals — chances are your rosebush or bushes will be among the larger players. If you're working with a newly cleared area, no problem; just reserve a corner or a back spot that can accommodate the plant's mature size. If the rose is a new addition to an existing display, you may have to coldheartedly remove plants that'll be in the way (transplant them elsewhere in your yard, or give them away so you don't feel so guilty).

✔ **Match your garden.** Use your eyes, nose, and heart. Choose something gorgeous. Pick a colour that you like. A rose will be in bloom over a long period, unlike some of your perennials or shrubs, so it needs to be a colour you can live with and enjoy over a long period — something that'll go with nearby plants or be a hue you can build a display around.

✔ **Consider colour.** Roses are red (and pink and yellow and cream and orange and white and purple and so on). Because many roses bloom all summer — and lustily if they're happy and healthy — their blossoms' colour becomes a major contribution to any mixed-flower bed or border. Here are some favourite schemes:

  • **Romantic pastel:** White, cream, pink, and pale yellow roses

  • **Hotshots:** Red, crimson, maroon, orange, and bicolours of these

  • **Bright lights:** Pure whites and bold yellows

If you want to find out more about landscaping with roses or landscaping in general, check out the book *Landscaping For Dummies,* by Phillip Giroux, Bob Beckstrom, Lance Walheim, and the editors of the U.S. National Gardening Association (Wiley).

## Using roses as groundcovers

Roses may not be the first plants that spring to mind when you're in search of a good groundcover, but if the site is sunny, you can do it! The plants may never be as low as, say, a carpet of vinca or pachysandra. But low-growing roses, no more than 30 or 60 centimetres (1 or 2 feet) high, can grow just as dense, prevent erosion, hold weeds at bay, and generally fill in a broad area quite nicely.

Unlike traditional groundcover choices (see Chapter 12), your ground-covering rosebushes will be full of colourful flowers for most or all of the summer — an appealing sight! Their thorniness, whether light or thick, can also be an asset. Nobody, not even the cat, will try to walk through!

Of course, you want to use roses that are either specifically bred for or singled out as groundcovers because they are low-growing spreaders. Here are some good ones to look for:

- ✔ **'Charles Albanel':** Medium red
- ✔ **'Fairy Dance':** Medium red
- ✔ **Flower Carpet series:** White, red, pinks, yellow, coral
- ✔ **'Jeeper's Creeper':** Single white
- ✔ **'Lavender Dream':** Deep pink
- ✔ **Pavement series:** White, pinks, purple, salmon, red
- ✔ **'Red Cascade':** Red
- ✔ **'Red Ribbons':** Red
- ✔ **'Seafoam':** White
- ✔ **'The Fairy':** Pink
- ✔ **'Yesterday':** Medium pink

Alternatively, certain enterprising gardeners have found that some climbing and rambling roses can easily be induced to sprawl along the ground. You just have to anchor, or peg down, the canes at regular intervals so they go where you want them to go. (A 30-centimetre, or foot-long, piece of sturdy wire, such as a piece of a coat hanger, may be bent into a *U* shape and pressed into the ground over a stem — this technique works great! Do this anchoring in winter or early spring, though, when seeing what you're doing is easier.) Try one of the following types:

- ✔ **'Dortmund':** Red
- ✔ **'New Dawn':** Pink
- ✔ *Rosa banksiae lutea:* Yellow

## Screening with roses

Why not have a living fence of roses? Wisely chosen and properly spaced, a screen of rosebushes can do everything you ask: block unsightly views (of a street, neighbour's yard, trashcan, or storage area); diminish noise; keep out intruders (hooray for thorns!); keep pets or children in (again, hooray for thorns!); or define a boundary. You get all this, plus the look is more informal, more colourful, and far prettier than any wooden or metal fence could hope to be!

Roses suitable for this screening job are easy to find. Recommended screen roses include Simplicity hedge roses (many colours), 'Bonica' (pink and white), any rugosa rose, and any of the very hardy 'Morden' shrub roses. The light pink Explorer 'Jens Munk' is an excellent barrier plant at 1.5–1.8 metres (5–6 feet), but it's a devil to prune: It's attacked more gardeners than intruders. 'Stanwell Perpetual' is a bushy 1.2-metre (4-foot) rose in a pretty pink that makes a not-too-daunting lower barrier. If they're not specifically touted as *screen roses,* here's what to look for:

- ✔ **Dense growth habit:** So they fill in and crowd out weeds

- ✔ **Thorniness:** For safety and security

- ✔ **Flowers that appear all over the entire plant, not just at the top:** For a uniform show (fragrance is also a plus, if you plan to be nearby to enjoy it; otherwise, it's optional)

- ✔ **Low care requirements:** Because a screen or hedge isn't something you want to pamper or fuss over; you want both disease and pest resistance and minimal pruning

## Using roses as vines

Climbing roses are great choices where you want extra colour or lack space. If your garden is horizontally challenged, go up! Although you can choose from many flowering vines — clematis, trumpet creeper, and honeysuckle, to name but a few — there's nothing quite like a rose to bring real lushness and bountiful colour. If you choose a modern climber, the colour can last most or all of the summer. And choosing a climber with fragrance can double your pleasure.

A trellis or arbour is the traditional choice as a vine support (and certainly you want a strong one — flimsy plastic is not equal to the job); use a support that's out in the open or against a wall, fence, or porch. (For more information on vines and supports, flip to Chapter 12.) You have other appealing options as well:

- ✔ A wire or wooden arch, standing alone or as a continuation of your garden fence
- ✔ A stand-alone pillar or post
- ✔ A teepee
- ✔ A pergola (arbour)
- ✔ A side of the porch
- ✔ An open-design fence
- ✔ A dead tree that's too much trouble to dig out
- ✔ A gazebo

GARDEN JARGON

## Grafted versus own-root roses

When you go rose shopping, you may notice that roses are labelled as grafted or own-root roses. Lately, the growing trend goes toward more own-root roses. What's this all about?

A *grafted rose* is actually two plants: the stems (or *canes*) of one plant and the root system of another. In grafting, horticulturists play around with a sort of Frankenstein assembly — they take a piece of one plant, attach it to a closely related plant, and then encourage the parts to grow together. Ideally, a grafted rose is the combination of a weather-tough, vigorous root-stock and a possibly more frail but desirable and attractive *scion,* or top.

A grafted rose plant has a telltale knob, bulge, or bump low down on the stem right above the root system. Certain rootstocks have been used to confer vigour, uniformity, disease resistance, or adaptability to certain types of soil. However, the rootstock may generate suckers (errant canes) — or leaves and even flowers — that look nothing like the main plant; a bitter or snow-less winter can kill the top and leave you with only the rootstock rose (in which case, you may as well rip out the entire plant and discard it).

An *own-root rose,* on the other hand, is entirely one plant and one plant only. The rose is raised from a cutting, and it grows on its own roots. You can recognize these plants because they bear no sign of a graft at the point where the canes meet the roots; the seller also proudly labels the plant as *own root.* If you prune an own-root rose low or if winter damages it, it'll resprout true to type — that is, as itself, as expected. Winter damage, although unfortunate, is not a disaster. And you don't get suckers. Own-root roses are often (but not always) longer lived than their grafted coun-terparts. On the other hand, plant vigour and productivity (the amount of foliage and flowers) vary. Some own-root hybrid tea roses, in partic-ular, are not as tough or uniform as their grafted counterparts.

How do you decide? If you have cold, harsh win-ters, you may be better off with own-root roses. Elsewhere, you can grow either type and judge the results for yourself, which vary according to the rose variety. Some rose lovers are even will-ing to treat tender roses (such as hybrid teas) as annuals, enjoying their special cultivar all summer while knowing it can't possibly survive the harsh winter in their garden.

# Buying the Best Roses

At garden centres, in large retail stores, or even sometimes arrayed out in front of your local grocery store, you've probably seen potted roses for sale. They may be in a plastic pot, a sturdy cardboard box, or even a plastic polybag. These forms certainly aren't the only ways to get roses: You can also buy them bareroot, as we describe in "Purchasing a bareroot rose," though with bareroot roses, you don't get the instant gratification of having a rosebud almost ready to bloom, as is usual with a potted plant.

*Where* you get your rose may be a more important consideration than the way the plant is sold. Potted or bareroot, the rose at the nursery is a good bet because you can personally inspect it for quality and health. You can also get the staff to help you select and evaluate the plants you want.

## Getting a potted rose

Plastic pot, cardboard box, or plastic polybag — what's common to plants sold in containers is that the plants show growth on top and their roots are in the soil mix below. Here are the real advantages of getting a potted rose:

- ✔ You can see and inspect the plant before deciding to buy it.
- ✔ If you want, you can take it right home and plant it that day.

However, buying potted roses has disadvantages, too. Depending on the place where you buy it, the plant may not be well cared for (it may be getting too much hot sun and not enough water, for instance). It could also be root-bound, especially if it's been in the same pot too long.

Here are some things to check when picking out a potted rose:

- ✔ **Labels:** Is it labelled with its name and planting/care instructions?
- ✔ **Flowers:** Is it in bloom? (***Note:*** Travelling home, and the trauma of transplanting, may cause a rose plant to jettison its flowers; you're better off buying one that's only in bud if you want quick colour.)
- ✔ **Stems and roots:** Do the stems look plump, green, and healthy? Are the roots plump, white, and healthy? (To check roots, probe them with your finger or temporarily pop the entire plant out of the pot.)
- ✔ **Signs of disease and pests:** Are there signs of insect pests or diseases, such as webs or yellowed or black-spotted leaves? (See the section titled "War of the roses: Tackling rose pests" for details.)

## Purchasing a bareroot rose

Bareroot roses (see Figure 9-2) come partially or fully bagged or boxed. When you look inside the wrapping or container, you see plain stems and roots, perhaps along with some wood shavings or other slightly moisture-retaining material. Fear not! A bareroot plant is a dormant plant, and this appearance is normal.

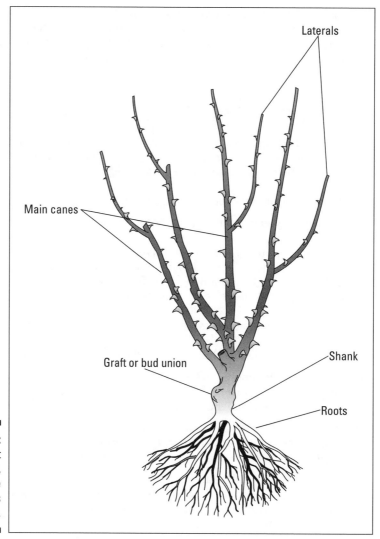

Laterals

Main canes

Graft or bud union

Shank

Roots

**Figure 9-2:**
A bareroot
rose plant,
showing the
various
parts.

Buying roses in this form gives you several advantages. Because bareroot
plants are dormant, you get to put them in the ground earlier (in mid-spring,
as soon as the soil is workable). And because they've never been cramped
into a pot, the roots are likely to be in good condition and ready to go into
the ground. Bareroot roses also tend to be cheaper than potted ones; cost
is definitely a consideration when you're putting in a hedge or boundary
planting and need to buy many roses.

# Exposing the truth about bareroot rose grades

A plant is rated on the number and thickness of its *canes* (stems); the Canadian Nursery Trades Association sets these standards, and all reputable rose suppliers adhere to them. Here's how the ratings compare:

✔ **Grade No. 1:** The best bareroot rose: A bigger, more vigorous and sturdy plant with more numerous and thicker canes

✔ **Grade No. 1½:** A midway rating, for a rose that's not as robust as a Grade 1 but still has more and thicker canes than a Grade 2

✔ **Grade No. 2:** The bargain rose — this lowest rating indicates a smaller, younger plant; it's still worth growing, but it'll take longer to reach maturity

The disadvantage to getting bareroot roses is that they may be harder to find (though you can always order them by mail). Also, they aren't going to leaf out and make buds right away; they spend their early days in the ground on root growth.

Here are some things to check when picking out a bareroot rose:

✔ **Name and instructions:** Is it labelled with its name and planting/care instructions?

✔ **Plant quality rating:** Is it labelled with its grade? The grade tells you about the number of canes the plant has and their thickness (see the "Exposing the truth about bareroot rose grades" sidebar).

✔ **Cane condition:** The canes should be thick, succulent, and green but not quite leafing out. Are the stems viable? They should be flexible and crunchy, not brown or black (if only a few are discoloured, just snip them off).

✔ **Moisture:** Have the packaging and/or the roots dried out? Dried-out plants mean trouble ahead.

Even though bareroot roses are dormant, you still have to protect their roots. Lay the newly opened plants in a shallow trench and then cover the roots with dirt if you can't plant them immediately upon receiving them. When you're ready to go, see the section titled "Planting bareroot roses," later in this chapter.

If you buy through mail order, the plant will be bareroot, because dormant plants are safer to ship (and because this form is lightweight compared to a potted plant). You have to shop via a colourful printed or online catalogue, place an order, and then wait for delivery, but the selection is likely to be far broader than what you find at any local nursery. Mail order is the way to go if you desire a specific rose, something special or rare.

Worried about arrival? Don't be. Mail-order nurseries have sophisticated weather-watch programs, and the companies don't ship until conditions are safe. After all, suppliers want you to be a happy customer. You can see the appendix of this book for a list of good mail-order companies.

# Planting Your Roses

Deciding when and where to plant your roses is easy: A sunny spot is key, because roses adore sunlight. A full day, or at least six hours of sunlight a day, is best for roses. And unless you live in a really mild climate, you need to plant your roses at the beginning of the growing season. High summer is too stressful, and fall is too late. The ground should be *workable* — that is, thawed and warmed up, and not soggy. And of course, you probably don't want to plant roses too close to your water faucet or anything else you use regularly, unless you don't mind dodging thorns.

Because bareroot roses are dormant plants, they can go into the ground in early spring. They should make a slower and better-paced transition into life in your garden as the season ramps up.

Plant a potted rose early in the growing season (late spring or early summer) — about the time you generally find them for sale. Plant soon after the last frost. But don't wait too long, simply because hot summer weather stresses a freshly transplanted plant.

Good soil is also very important; it should be rich in organic matter and drain well. If your soil is lacking, import some good loam (rich, crumbly soil) and compost, or at least mix the existing soil half-and-half with premium soil. (Refer to Chapter 4 for garden preparation.)

*How* to plant roses is a bit more complicated than when or where, but here we give you the basics.

## Putting containerized roses in the ground

When planting roses that come in containers, your first order of business is preparing the hole:

1. **Eyeball the pot the rose came in and then dig a hole a bit wider and deeper.**

   You can set the pot in, plant and all, to check for the right depth. Remember, you want the *bud union* (the point at which the bud is joined to the shank — refer to Figure 9-2) to be below the soil level. In southern Ontario and coastal British Columbia, the bud union can be placed just beneath the soil surface, to 5 centimetres (2 inches). In areas where there is severe freezing, the bud union should be planted up to 15 centimetres (6 inches) below the surface.

2. **Loosen the soil on the sides and in the bottom of the hole, using your fingers or a trowel.**

   This way, the roots can head outward and downward more easily when they're ready.

Then prepare the plant:

1. **Water the plant well — until liquid runs out the bottom of the pot — before planting.**

2. **Groom the top half of the plant.**

   Clip off damaged stems, flowers, and buds. Leave on as much good foliage as you can. You can cut down to the highest five- or seven-leaflet leaf group. Cut down to an outward-facing set of leaves to encourage new growth away from the centre of the plant.

3. **Run a butter knife, ruler, or other similar flat object all the way around the inside edge of the pot to loosen the plant.**

   Squeezing the container sometimes helps. Gently pop the rose out.

And here's how to plant:

1. **Rake your fingers up and down along the rootball to loosen the soil and roots.**

   Don't fret if a few roots break off.

2. **Take a moment to help it further if the rose is really root-bound.**

   Score the sides of the dense rootball with a sharp knife, up and down, in two or three places. Don't make a deep cut — just ½ inch in is fine. This step stimulates new root growth.

3. **Hold the plant by the rootball (not the top growth), set it into the prepared hole, and then backfill good soil around it.**

4. **Make a basin of soil or mulch around the plant when you're done; then water.**

   The basin should be about 30 to 46 centimetres (12 to 18 inches) in diameter so the water it collects soaks in directly over the root zone of the rose. This basin makes for easier watering (which you should do right now — give it a good soaking). If the plant settles too low in the hole after the watering, wiggle it back up.

# Planting bareroot roses

If you're ready to plant, you begin, as usual, with digging (if you can't plant right away, see "Purchasing a bareroot rose," earlier in this chapter, for info on how to keep the roots viable). When digging the hole for bareroot roses, you have to accommodate roots that are currently open to the air. Here's how to prepare the hole for bareroot roses:

1. **Dig at least 30 centimetres (1 foot) deep, and perhaps a little wider, so you can accommodate the rose's roots without cramping, pushing, or bending them.**

   As with containerized roses (refer to "Putting containerized roses in the ground"), the bud union should be placed 5 centimetres (2 inches) below the soil surface in mild-winter areas, or up to 15 centimetres (6 inches) below the surface in very cold locations.

2. **Loosen the soil on the sides and in the bottom of the hole, using your fingers or a trowel.**

   This way, the roots can head outward and downward more easily when they're ready.

3. **Mound up a cone of soil in the middle of the hole on which to rest the plant.**

   This method is much easier than trying to sift soil back in around the roots as you go.

Bareroot roses are a little unique, because you especially want to encourage new growth from the dormant plant. Here's how to prepare the plant:

1. **Slide the plant out of its protective sleeve, pick off any packing material, and then groom it.**

   Cut off any damaged, black, or rotten stems or roots (see the upcoming "Grooming" section for details).

2. **Shorten all the canes to about 20 centimetres (8 inches) long.**

   This step reduces stress on the plant when it goes into the ground. Don't worry — it'll surge into growth pretty fast! Make each cut at a 45-degree angle to an outside *eye* (the swollen bump on the stem) to direct new growth outward.

3. **Shorten the roots with a little 2.5-centimetre (1-inch) haircut.**

   This step will stimulate new growth.

4. **Rehydrate the plant.**

   Stick the roots in a bucket of lukewarm water for a few hours before planting to help it plump up.

Here's how to plant bareroot roses:

1. **Hold the plant in one hand atop the centre mound and spread the roots out over the mound.**

2. **Backfill good soil in and around the plant, pressing down lightly as you go, to eliminate air pockets.**

3. **Make a 30- to 46-centimetre (12- to 18-inch) basin of soil or mulch around the plant when you're done.**

   This step makes watering easier. Give the plant a good soaking! If it settles too low in the hole after the watering, wiggle the plant back up.

# Taking Care of Your Roses

Roses have a reputation for being difficult to care for, but don't be intimidated. Roses are actually quite middle-of-the-road, horticulturally speaking, in terms of their needs. This section gives you the basics, but realize that if you forget or muff something, the plants are surprisingly forgiving. Just get back on track. Consider reading *Roses For Canadians For Dummies,* by Douglas Green, Lance Walheim, and the editors of *Canadian Gardening* magazine and the U.S. National Gardening Association (Wiley), if you want even more information on rose care.

## Watering

Roses like and need water. The rule of green thumb is to make sure roses get about 5 centimetres (2 inches) a week. Like so many other garden plants, deep soakings are much better than frequent, shallow waterings. Set the hose at the foot of the rose (hopefully, you created a nice basin when you planted it — see the preceding planting sections) and let water trickle in. Or if you have a big bed of roses or roses and companions, use a soaker hose or install an in-ground system (Chapter 5 can fill you in on watering tools). All these methods are good because the water gets right to the roots. You prevent waste, and you don't splash water on the foliage (as a sprinkler does), which invites fungal diseases.

## Fertilizing

Unless your soil is fabulously fertile, adding some supplemental fertilizer for your roses is a good idea. Fertilizer inspires robust growth and more flowers. Also, a well-nourished plant is healthier and is thus less likely to succumb to stress, disease, or insect attacks.

Use an all-purpose garden fertilizer because it has balanced amounts of N (nitrogen), P (phosphorus), and K (potassium). Fertilizers touted especially for roses are fine but not mandatory. In spring, as the plant emerges from dormancy, you can water with 15 millilitres (a tablespoon) of Epsom salts (magnesium sulfate) dissolved in a gallon of water to promote strong canes.

Always water before applying fertilizer so the plant is plumped up and under no stress. Watering also helps deliver the food more evenly and more gradually. You can also water right after feeding your roses, to help move the nutrients into the root zone faster. Better still, water with a hose-end "deep root" fertilizer attachment.

*Foliar* (leaf) feeding is another way to supplement your roses' fertilizing program. Use any water-soluble fertilizer, mix it up in a tank sprayer or sprinkling can, and apply so that it just drips from the foliage. This form of fertilizing is seldom sufficient for all the nutrient needs of roses, but it's a nice pick-me-up in addition to your regular fertilizing program. Fertilize early enough in the day so the water has time to evaporate — wet leaves can invite fungal disease.

## Keeping roses in shape

Cutting off dead or damaged canes, removing spent flowers, and doing some pruning can keep your roses looking sharp. The following sections tell you how to make sure your flowers stay presentable.

### Grooming

Using sharp clippers, you can spruce up your rosebushes whenever something unattractive about the plant catches your critical eye. We're not talking about major shaping cuts here (see the upcoming "Pruning" section), just tidiness. Here's stuff you can cut out any time you see it:

- **Dead wood:** Remove dead canes down to the ground level.

- **Damaged wood:** Cut the plant back into about 2.5 centimetres (1 inch) of healthy wood.

- **Misplaced stems:** Take off stems that are rubbing together (choose one and spare the other), stems that are taking off in the wrong direction, and stems that are trailing on the ground.

- **Suckers:** In a grafted plant, these errant canes emerge from below the bud union (the bulge at the base of the bush, now below the soil). The suckers look different from the rest of the bush — they're often smoother, straighter, and lighter in colour. Another clue: They sprout leaves and occasionally mongrel flowers that look nothing like the main bush. Off with their heads! (Well, more precisely, cut them off flush to the ground.)

### Deadheading and tidying up leaves

*Deadheading* is just a gardening term for cutting or snapping off spent flowers. The plant looks better when you get rid of them. Also, because the goal of all flowering plants is to stop flowering and produce seed (in the case of rose-bushes, to make rose hips), deadheading thwarts the process. So the plant is fooled into making more flowers. Deadhead away!

Whenever you see badly damaged, diseased, or dead leaves, remove them. To be on the safe side, throw them in the trash rather than in the compost pile. Otherwise, the leaves may spread disease.

### Pruning

Unlike the grooming cuts we describe in the previous "Grooming" section, actual pruning has a timing requirement. Early spring is best, about six weeks before the usual date of the last spring frost in your area. Too early, and your overeager cuts may lead to frost damage. Pruning is pretty straight-forward. Don't forget your tough leather gloves and maybe a good, thick, long-sleeved shirt.

1. **Remove all non-negotiable growth.**

   This step means making all the grooming cuts described in the "Grooming" section, if you haven't attended to them already. Some winters are hard on rosebushes, so early spring is a fine time to cut out the parts that'll never recover or come back to life.

2. **Thin the plants.**

   The easiest way to thin is to clip out the crowds of twiggy, thinner growth. That may be sufficient, or it can at least allow to you stand back and assess the plant's density and form better.

3. **Shape.**

   Aim for a balanced-looking plant with evenly distributed canes, with the centre of the plant somewhat open.

When pruning roses, use clean, sharp clippers, and cut at a 45-degree angle. Cut near a *bud eye*, the tiny brownish or reddish bump on the stem (not to be confused with a thorn). Experts advise cutting 6 millimetres (¼ inch) above a bud eye so the bud eye doesn't dry out. Figure 9-3 shows you a typical rose-bush before and after pruning.

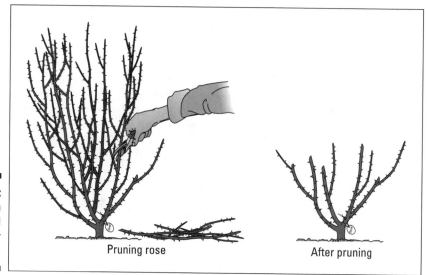

**Figure 9-3:**
A rosebush
before and
after
pruning.

Pruning rose                    After pruning

Beyond the basics of pruning roses, here are specific pruning tips for certain rose types (see the earlier section "Identifying the various rose types" for info on how some of them differ):

- **Hybrid teas and grandifloras:** Prune every early spring. After removing dead wood — and you may have a lot of it after a really cold winter — cut back almost all the canes, sparing the five or so best ones. The goal is to channel the plant's energies into only a few canes for better flower production.

- **Old garden or heirloom roses:** Do *not* prune in early spring, or you may remove the coming show. Restrict your cuts to cosmetic trimming and shaping right after they finish blooming.

- **Shrub roses:** You can cut vigorous shoots originating near the ground back by about a third in early spring. Branches coming off shrub roses can be shortened to about 30 centimetres (1 foot) long. And keep after the twiggy growth, or you may have an impenetrable thicket in a few years.

- **Minis:** Spare the minis — they're so small already. After removing dead wood, shape miniature roses lightly in early spring, and maybe take out old stems every few years to make way for newcomers.

- **Tree roses:** Clip and shape tree roses in early spring and immediately after flowering. Vigorous growth, unchecked, makes for a top-heavy, unwieldy plant.

- **Climbing roses:** Many climbing roses bloom on last year's wood, so prune only what you need for maintaining the shape you want — the process is similar to what you use for old garden or heirloom roses.

# *Maximizing winter hardiness*

A lovely, prize rosebush really may need and deserve a little tender, loving care heading into winter. You can take your protection cues from experienced gardeners in your neighbourhood — ask them what they do and when, as well as what they use. Here's some general advice that'll do the trick for most iffy rosebushes in most areas:

- ✔ **Give the plant a good soaking in late fall before the ground really freezes so it heads into winter well hydrated.**

- ✔ **Stop deadheading.** Consider leaving the rose hips on in late fall to induce dormancy (and feed wild birds).

- ✔ **Remove all dead leaves in late fall.** Removing the leaves gets rid of disease spores that may be on the leaves; otherwise, these spores can overwinter and start a new disease outbreak the following year.

- ✔ **Consider fall pruning.** With tender roses, some gardeners prune canes back to stop winter winds from whipping the canes about and causing damage to the bud union. Long canes are likely to die over winter anyway, so it can be wise to remove them in fall. Many rose growers cut canes back to 45 to 60 centimetres (18 to 24 inches) and then mulch the plants to the top to protect the canes.

- ✔ **Mulch the plant.** After most tree leaves have fallen, and when frost is visiting regularly at night, mound soil from another part of the garden over the rosebush to a height of 30 to 45 centimetres (12 to 18 inches). Wait until the ground has frozen, and then cover the soil mound with about 30 centimetres (1 foot) of straw, leaves, or compost.

  If your winters are really harsh, wrap a cylinder of chicken wire around the entire plant and then dump in soil, which is one of the best insulating materials. You may even want to tie the canes together to help prevent wind damage. Tying the canes together also makes them more compact and easier to protect with mounded soil. Don't uncover the plant until you're sure spring has truly arrived, and then do so gradually. Scoop off or hose off the mulch over a period of several days or a week.

  Even in Zone 7 or warmer, keep soil or mulch mounded over the bud union of a grafted plant to protect it.

- ✔ **Give climbers and hybrid teas extra TLC.** These taller rose types are more exposed and need more protection. In areas colder than Zone 5, it's a good idea to lower climbers off their supports and then bury them in an adjacent trench 30 centimetres (1 foot) deep. Tree roses can be entirely dug up, potted, and kept indoors or in a shed. Or, in marginally hardy areas, they can be tipped over, with half their roots brought above the ground. Then cover the whole plant, exposed roots and all, with a 60-centimetre (2-foot) layer of soil and mulch.

**WARNING!**

Avoid those Styrofoam rose cones for winter protection; they can heat the plants too much during January thaw and other unexpected rises in temperature.

# *War of the roses: Tackling rose pests*

We're not going to lie — other creatures as well as humans adore roses. But here's the good news: Many modern roses have been bred for resistance to common rose pests and diseases. More improvements show up every year, so roses are definitely a case of where newer is often better.

Just as with humans, if the rose plant is in good health, it's far less vulnerable. So review and apply the care advice in the previous sections. That said, forewarned is forearmed, so here's some straight talk about the most common potential foes. Take a look at the list of least-wanted insects:

- **Aphids:** These critters are tiny, pear-shaped sucking insects that especially relish new growth. They excrete honeydew, a sticky, sweet substance that can turn black as sooty mould grows on it. (Ants may appear to eat the honeydew, but they don't harm your rosebush otherwise.) Knock aphids off with a stiff blast from the hose, or spray with insecticidal soap. Never spray when the temperature is above 27°C (80°F).

- **Japanese beetles:** These metallic-looking copper and green bugs are really creepy, especially when they appear in great numbers. In small infestations, you can bravely pick them off and drown them in soapy water (don't squish them — you'll just release pheromones that will attract more bugs!). Japanese beetles are late risers, so if you go out early in the morning, you can shake the sleepy critters into a plastic baggie. Insecticidal soap with *pyrethrin* (a natural insecticide produced by certain species of the chrysanthemum plant) is an effective spray for adult beetles. Use *parasitic nematodes* (small roundworms that kill insects but are harmless to other organisms), sold at most nurseries, for the grubs; apply them to the soil at the base of the rosebushes in spring.

- **Thrips:** Thrips are tiny yellow or brown bugs that lead to misshapen leaves, deformed buds, and discoloured flowers (with brown spots). They especially love light-coloured roses and are most common in early summer. You can spray with insecticidal soap or neem oil.

Roses are also vulnerable to some pretty unpleasant fungi. Check it out:

- **Black spot:** Rose leaves can develop small black spots with fringed edges. The fungus that causes black spot is worse in hot, humid weather.

  To treat, remove and destroy affected leaves (don't add them to the compost pile). Prune the plant to improve air circulation, and water in the morning. Some sprays that fight this disease include a dormant spray with sulphur, summer oil (a light horticultural oil), neem oil, a baking soda solution, and strong chemicals — ask at your local garden centre.

✔ **Powdery mildew:** This fungus appears in dry weather, creating a white powdery residue, especially on the leaves. You can spray with summer oil, a baking-soda solution, an anti-transpirant (which prevents drying out), or a sulphur-based fungicide.

✔ **Rust:** This fungal disease is most common in dry weather. Get rid of affected leaves, and water carefully only at ground level. Spray options include dormant oil, lime-sulphur fungicide, or rusticide (again, check with your garden centre and follow label directions exactly).

# Part III
# Stretching Your Garden Beyond Its Boundaries: The Permanent Landscape

The 5th Wave     By Rich Tennant

"Those aren't actually mole hills — the entire lawn is made up of over 900 chia pets."

# In this part . . .

Gardening is more than planting flowers and vegetables in a garden bed — it actually encompasses your entire yard, including the trees and hedges that enclose your space, the groundcovers that define and outline your garden beds, and your neatly trimmed lawn. Gardening isn't just about making a beautiful space — it means making a space that welcomes visitors and makes you feel comfortable, too. Sure, much of the work you do to achieve this serene backdrop falls under the category of landscaping (covered in greater detail in *Landscaping For Dummies*). But if you garden with all the elements described in this part in mind, you can look on not only your flower and plant beds but also your entire growing space as your garden — and an extension of your home.

# Chapter 10

# Growing a Perfect Lawn

● ● ● ● ● ● ● ● ● ● ● ● ● ● ● ● ● ● ● ● ● ● ● ● ● ● ● ● ● ● ● ● ● ● ● ● ● ● ● ● ● ● ● ● ● ● ● ● ●

● ● ● ● ● ● ● ● ● ● ● ● ● ● ● ● ● ● ● ● ● ● ● ● ● ● ● ● ● ● ● ● ● ● ● ● ● ● ● ● ● ● ● ● ● ● ● ● ●

*A*h, to run and play, or nap, or wiggle your bare toes on a lush and perfect greensward — it may seem like an unattainable dream, but there's good news! A fine-looking lawn is perfectly doable and within your reach if you approach the project gradually, doing the right things month to month and year to year.

Lawns consist of many different small plants, often different varieties of grasses — almost like a miniature stand of corn (they are related!). So growing grass is like raising a crop or a specialty garden of turf grass.

Extensive lawn care is beyond the scope of this book, so if you want more information than what we present here, we highly recommend picking up *Lawn Care For Dummies* by Lance Walheim and the U.S. National Gardening Association (Wiley). It's worth it to put a lot of effort into your lawn, because a good lawn makes everything else look good, and a gorgeous, well-kept lawn sets the tone for an entire yard. You know that old saying about how a rising tide raises all the boats in the harbour? The purpose of this chapter is to demystify the basics. Find out what to do, when, and how, and then you're in business.

# In the Beginning: Getting Ready to Make a Lawn from Scratch

Chances are if you're a homeowner, you already have a lawn of some kind. But if you're a new homeowner or have bravely decided to remove your old lawn and start over with a clean slate, you may envy those neighbours who have lush, established lawns. Well, they should envy *you*. You have a fabulous chance to get off on the right foot. If you plan it carefully and maintain it right, your new lawn can be a showpiece. This section shows you what a new lawn needs and how you can provide it.

## Preparing your yard for a lawn

Before you do anything, you need to rid your property of all those things you don't want in your lawn: No weeds, no horrible old remnants of a failed lawn, no rocks, no construction debris, no toxic waste, no junk, no cars you plan to fix up, no dead and dying plants, no roots from long-gone plants. Scrape, dig, haul away — do what you must.

In most provinces, you're legally required to check for utility lines before digging. So call the gas company, phone company, cable company, and water company if you have to dig. They're only too happy to come out, check, and flag the stay-away and don't-dig areas for you.

After you've cleared the space for your lawn, make sure you follow the advice in the next few sections.

### Start with weed prevention

The minute you clear an area, weeds rush in to fill the void. Unless you're prepared to forge ahead quickly, these eager settlers are a problem. But they don't have to be. If you treat the area properly to kill the weeds now, before putting in the new lawn, you can be sure they won't be there when the lawn goes in. Talk about a fresh start! You can kill weeds and weed seeds on-site in lots of ways.

Cultivating or tilling the area, although it makes you feel like a gardener, is perhaps the worst thing you can do if you want a weed-free lawn. You're sure to dredge up all sorts of long-dormant weed seeds and bits that can regenerate. Instead, if the area isn't too big, cover it with black plastic or organic mulch (rather thickly — 15 centimetres [6 inches] isn't overkill). Any inexpensive, lightweight mulch that's readily available is a good choice — try pine needles or even a layer of chopped or ground-up leaves. Straw is a better choice than hay, which usually contains weed seeds.

The object of covering the ground is to keep out light and water, and, thus, smother any ideas that lingering weeds may have of germinating. If possible, keep this barrier in place for a month or even a full season. After the grass starts to sprout, don't be concerned with removing the mulch. Just let the small seedlings grow through the barrier; it'll eventually decompose and enrich the soil. Raking it up can dislodge and damage the young grass plants.

For more information about dealing with weeds, see the "Warring with Weeds" section later in the chapter.

### Improve soil quality

You rarely think of your lawn as a garden, yet it is — a garden of grass. Putting in a new lawn is your chance to provide it with that fertile, well-drained earth that all gardens love so well. Lay down plenty of organic matter, such as compost, *leaf mould* (composted tree and shrub leaves), or well-rotted manure. Add topsoil, too, but only if you can get a weed-free batch. You can mix these goodies with the native soil if it's not dreadful. Otherwise, provide at least 15 to 20 centimetres (6 to 8 inches) of the good stuff, the depth to which grass roots generally grow.

### Grade the yard

Lawns grow well and look splendid on fairly level ground. Seeing to the gradient before planting, of course, is best. You want your lawn to slope slightly, away from your house. Otherwise, both rainfall and zealous watering can lead to a wet basement and a weakened foundation. Work when the ground is moist (dry soil resists grading) and use a shovel, a rake, and even a carpenter's level. The slope doesn't have to be perfect, but do the best job you can.

If the grading process daunts you — and it should if your yard's terrain is full of hills and dales or you know darn well the land slopes toward your foundation — by all means, hire a contractor. Refer to Chapter 2 for more information on getting some help.

### Check the drainage

Make sure your soil drains well. If the lay of your land or the soggy or clay-laden quality of your soil is cause for concern about drainage, do get help. Gravel-filled trenches, French drains, underground pipes, and so forth are all remedies, but installing them isn't for the amateur or the faint hearted! Refer to Chapter 4 for more tips on dealing with drainage.

## Designing the lawn

After you have your ground prepared, you're ready to contemplate actual lawn size and shape. Some of the improvements you may consider adding are borders along the pathways or flower beds. You want to allow space for these features and for edgings such as boxwood hedges. Eventually, you may decide to place a tree or two in the middle of the yard. Design is really up to personal preference, and you can apply some of the tips for designing a garden to lawns as well (refer to Chapter 2). But for now, make sure your lawn has the following qualities:

- ✔ It's out in the open — plentiful sunshine is a recipe for lawn success.

- ✔ It's not in a spot people constantly walk through to get to a door or patio, for example. In these areas, installing a paved walk or gravelled path is more practical. Installing walkways before you start your lawn usually works best.

- ✔ It's not too big; it's in scale with your house and the rest of your property.

- ✔ Its shape is compatible with the surroundings. A strict, straight-edged, geometric lawn looks formal — is your house's architecture formal, too? Perhaps softer, less-rigid boundaries work better in your yard.

# Seeding and Sodding: Adding the Grass

Whether you're starting with a new lawn or trying to improve an already existing lawn, the grass is the real point and makes all the difference in the world. Unfortunately, having great grass isn't simply a matter of going to the store and buying grass seed.

You can choose from many types of grass seed, and the type you need depends on the climate you live in, the amount of light your yard receives, and whether you have any texture, colour, and height preferences for your lawn. Some people like slow-growing grasses so they don't have to mow quite as often. Other people insist on having Kentucky bluegrass in their yards — even though they don't actually live in Kentucky. We cover many of the options available to you in the next few sections.

Some people even choose to have a lawn without grass. You can avoid grass entirely by planting clover (yes, clover!) or using low-growing groundcovers like thyme, ivy, or, in shady areas, moss. They're terrific alternatives that don't require a lot of mowing or extra care. For more information on groundcovers, hop on over to Chapter 12.

## Determining the kind of grass you want or need

If you're shopping and you don't yet know what you want to plant in your lawn, browse the grasses available, looking for one that appeals to you and seems like a match for your growing conditions. If you're really at sea, call a landscaper or lawn-service company and have a professional come over to view the intended site and discuss your options.

If you don't know what type of grass you have in your existing lawn and you want the new grass to blend in properly, do this simple step: In late spring or early summer, when the grass is thriving, dig up a representative chunk and take it to your local garden centre, a good landscaper, or even a lawn-service company representative. These professionals know or can point you to someone who can identify the grass.

Please note that grass comes in many varieties and related varieties — hundreds, in some cases. The differences among grasses may be pretty subtle. Don't worry, though. Some grass varieties perform better than others in a given area, and the way to find out which type is best for your yard is to ask someone knowledgeable, such as a staffer at your local nursery, a landscaper, or a lawn-service person. Don't forget your provincial ministry of agriculture if there's an office nearby. (We're assuming that the people who order grass seed and sod for your local retail stores know what they're doing and order only what prospers in the area.)

## Planting the right grass

Cool-season grasses are the grasses we grow in Canada — where summers, although warm and sometimes humid, are short and where winters are cold and usually snowy. These grasses grow actively in spring and fall, slow down a bit in summer, and then start to go dormant in the winter. Just so you know, these grasses do best at temperatures between 16°C and 27°C (60°F and 80°F) and survive freezing winter temperatures; they can't tolerate truly hot weather without going dormant. Favourite cool-season grasses include Kentucky bluegrass, fescue (fine and tall), bent grass, and perennial ryegrass.

Warm-season grasses, which you can see in the southern U.S., have broad leaf blades and grow vigorously above 27°C (80°F). These grasses aren't grown here, even in the warmest parts of British Columbia, where mixtures of fine and tall fescues are favoured.

For details on cool-season grasses, including info on appearance, descriptions, and care instructions, see Table 10-1.

***Note:*** Check out "Mowing the Lawn, Cutting the Grass, and Otherwise Giving the Yard a Shave," later in this chapter, for more information on mowers.

| Table 10-1 | Cool-Season, Northern Grasses | | |
|---|---|---|---|
| **Type** | **Appearance** | **Ideal Mow-to Height** | **Description and Care** |
| Kentucky bluegrass | Blades are fine to medium textured, canoe shaped, and a dark blue-green colour. | 6 to 8 cm (2½ to 3 in.) | Hardy but not very drought-tolerant (goes dormant when it's too hot and dry); water generously! Good disease resistance; requires more fertilizer than other varieties; doesn't tolerate heavy foot traffic; has relatively shallow roots — makes a good showpiece lawn rather than one that's trod upon a lot. |
| Fescues, fine and tall | Texture is very fine, and bristle leaved; colour is medium green. Tall fescue has a wide blade similar to Kentucky bluegrass but not as dark in colour. Good for coastal areas. | 6 to 8 cm (2½ to 3 in.) | Doesn't like to be soaked or soggy; water deeply and infrequently. Shade-tolerant. Tall fescue is the favoured grass type for sports fields, so you know it tolerates foot traffic! Some varieties perform well on poor soil and in some shade. Fescues are often mixed with other grasses or with each other. |
| Bent grass | Very fine textured; at a couple of centimetres (about an inch) tall, a blade begins to bend, hence the name. | 3 to 4 cm (1 to 1½ in.) | A thirsty grass — give it plenty of water, as often as weekly during the height of the growing season. The stems (technically *stolons*) are wiry and form thick mats, so don't let this grass get too tall or unkempt, or you'll soon have a major thatch problem. That said, bent grass is a popular grass for golf courses, putting greens, and grass tennis courts. Use a mower with very sharp blades. |

| Type | Appearance | Ideal Mow-to Height | Description and Care |
|---|---|---|---|
| Perennial ryegrass | Fine textured; glossy, dark green blades. | 6 to 8 cm (2½ to 3 in.) | Likes consistent, regular water; has shallow roots. Fine textured; disease-resistant; tolerates foot traffic well. Nice in full sun or shade, but not reliably hardy even in Zone 6. Often used in blends because it germinates and grows quickly. |

## Growing lawns from seed

Growing a lawn from seed is cheaper than installing sod; it's also satisfying, and it feels like actual gardening. The disadvantages are that the grass takes longer to become a lawn, you have to protect the baby lawn from birds and pedestrians, and watering just right is tricky but critical.

When sowing a new lawn — or when doing patch repairs with seed — make sure you start at the right time. In Canada, the ideal time for planting our cool-season grasses is in the late summer or early fall. The ground is still warm, and fall rains may help with the watering. Early spring is a second choice, as long as the new lawn has a chance to get up and running before really hot weather hits.

To prepare the soil, follow the instructions we set out earlier in this chapter (refer to "Preparing your yard for a lawn"). Basically, you want to clear out an open area of weeds and obstructions, add some organic matter, and rake it neat and level. Before planting is also the perfect time to put in sprinklers or a more-elaborate, in-ground watering system. Chapter 4 gives more details on this kind of equipment.

Buy good-quality seed. Except for Kentucky bluegrass, seed is not generally sold for home use in bags of only one variety. (Commercial mixes contain more varieties.) Check the label to see what you're buying — it might be only one cultivar of Kentucky bluegrass or it may contain several, and be forewarned that it may be a grab bag of older varieties. Better to get a bag that touts its contents in loving detail, naming the names of the varieties it includes.

A *mixture* of seeds may contain a combination of, for instance, Kentucky bluegrass mixed with fine fescue and perennial ryegrass, which is fast growing and puts out a green cover in as little as a week. (See Table 10.2 for days to germination for various grass seeds.) Make sure your mixture isn't loaded with cheaper, coarser grass varieties — read the label carefully! The better mixtures have a low percentage of "other ingredients" and no annual ryegrass.

You can even find disease-resistant varieties or grasses with some pest-destroying extras. If you're at a loss as to what grass to choose, get some professional advice.

### How much seed to use

As with calculating the amount of fertilizer to spread (see "Knowing your serving sizes: How much fertilizer is enough?"), you need to know the area of your lawn to know how much seed to use.

So spend some time measuring your lawn to figure out its *area* — you know, length × width, or if your lawn's round shaped, the radius squared × *pi* (3.14). If you can't remember this elementary-school math, get a smart kid to help you — bill it as a practical lesson! By the way, if you already know your yard's size in acres, there's no need to measure: 1 acre = 4,047 square metres (43,560 square feet).

Consult your bag of seed to find out how much seed is recommended per square metre of lawn (you use more seed to plant a new lawn than you use to overseed an existing lawn. But here's a rough guideline: 1 Kg (2.2 lbs.) of grass seed mixture covers between 63 and 82 square metres (735.29 square feet), depending on the mixture purchased. Don't overdo it — excessive seed only makes a weaker lawn: The seedlings are all fighting for limited soil space, nutrients, and light.

| Table 10-2 | Grass Seed Time till Germination |
|------------|----------------------------------|
| *Type* | *Days to Germination* |
| Bent grass | 13 to 15 |
| Fine fescue | 13 to 15 |
| Tall fescue | 13 to 15 |
| Kentucky bluegrass | 21 |
| Perennial ryegrass | 4 to 6 |

### How to spread seed

You need the help of some sort of tool so the seeds spread as evenly as possible. Buy this tool at a home-and-garden supply store; for bigger jobs, you may prefer simply to rent the necessary equipment or hire someone else to do the job. Generally, though, here are your choices (see Figure 10-1):

✔ **Cyclone spreader:** This hand seeder is relatively cheap and easy to use. Dump in the seed and then trot along the seedbed, turning the handle as you go. The seed sprays out in a semicircular pattern. Obviously, this method isn't very practical for large lawns, but it's just fine for modest-size ones.

✔ **Rotary spreader:** A wheeled or hand-held spinning spreader (also known as a *broadcast* or *centrifugal spreader*) is perfect for bigger lawns. You just fill it up and walk along slowly, pushing it at an even pace.

✔ **Hydroseeding:** This technique involves spraying the yard with a mixture of grass seed, water, fertilizer, and mulch. Most people hire someone to do the work for them. Hydroseeding is usually less expensive than laying sod but costs more than regular seeding. Many times, people lay biodegradable netting on steeply sloped areas before they're hydroseeded to prevent erosion. This technique is usually very successful as long as you keep the seeded area damp.

No matter how you spread the seed, start by applying two side-by-side header strips at the bottom and top of the lawn to provide turning space (see Figure 10-2). Run the header strips along the short edges of a rectangular lawn. If your lawn is round, oval, or irregular in shape, just do the perimeter (see Figure 10-3).

Go back and forth the longest way until you've finished applying seed. Shut off the spreader occasionally to prevent double applications. For instance, shut it off in the header areas, when approaching and leaving a tree, when backing, when turning around, and any time you come to a complete stop.

**Figure 10-1:**
Spreading seed with cyclone-type and rotary spreaders.

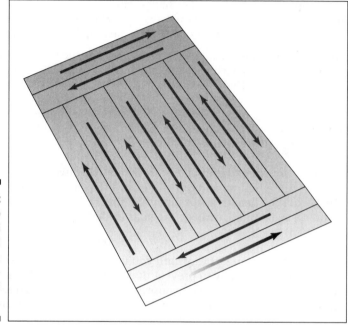

**Figure 10-2:**
How to spread grass seed in a rectangular-shaped lawn.

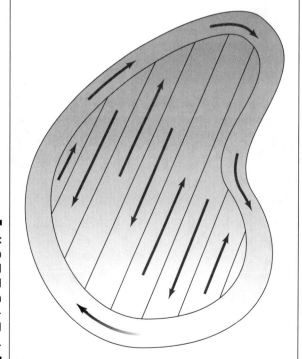

**Figure 10-3:**
How to spread grass seed in an irregular-shaped lawn.

# *Your own turf: Growing lawns from sod*

The real advantage to using sod is that it's fast! It also smothers weed seeds. After being laid down, it's not as vulnerable to birds, foot traffic, or drying out. It's also easier for getting a lawn going in shade or on a slope. However, sod is much more expensive than sowing seeds, and for some gardeners, it feels like cheating!

You can lay sod just about any time, so long as the ground isn't frozen. However, the best time is right before the grass is about to surge into its peak growth period. As with seeding, this means it's best to lay sod in late summer or early fall; your second choice is early spring. If rain is in the forecast for *tomorrow,* plant sod *today!*

When laying sod, have bare ground ready to go. Moist ground receives sod best — too dry is unwelcoming, and too soggy or muddy is no good, either. Use a good, sturdy, steel rake to give the ground one last neat levelling before you begin.

Check with your local suppliers for the best deal on the best type of sod for your area, and buy the sod as close as possible to the time you want to use it. Sprinkle the sod with water to keep it moist and cool, but don't make it drippy and soggy (it'll just tear if you do that). Never let it sit around for more than a day if you can help it! Ideally, pick it up the night before and plant it the very next morning.

Here are some recommended tools for laying sod — also see Figure 10-4:

- ✔ Strong, sturdy, steel rake
- ✔ Sharp knife, for cutting pieces and patches
- ✔ Board to kneel on so you don't squash the sod with your knees
- ✔ Hose and sprayer, to keep the sod moist as you work
- ✔ Wheelbarrow, to transport sod
- ✔ Water-filled roller, to smooth the lawn at the end of the job

To lay the sod, rolling out the green carpet isn't necessarily hard or complicated work, but you do have to work fast so the sod doesn't dry out. And if your lawn is big, the sod rolls can be heavy and unwieldy. Line up some helpers.

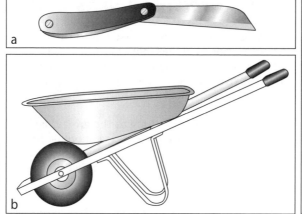

**Figure 10-4:**
Sod-laying
equipment.

Here are some tips for sod-laying success:

- ✔ Keep things damp! Don't allow the sod to dry out at any time in the process — and when it's finally down, soak the daylights out of the new lawn!

- ✔ Place edges tightly against boundaries and edges.

- ✔ Stagger the ends of the sod pieces, as if you were laying brick.

- ✔ Keep levelling the area with the rake as you go.

- ✔ Water *every day* (or more often if the weather turns hot) — frequent light waterings help the sod establish itself.

If all goes well, the roots start growing into the new soil in about a week.

# *Watering a Thirsty Lawn*

Watering is the *most* misunderstood aspect of lawn care, so pay attention, folks! Lawn grasses are *not* notoriously resilient or deep rooted, so you can't neglect them in this department. Of course you have to water them often when they're first installed and are getting established — up to twice a week, depending on the type of grass and your climate. Established lawns need water whenever they get dry, which likewise depends on temperature, humidity, amount of sunlight, wind, and soil type. The following sections give you some more information on how to water well.

Whenever possible, water your lawn in the morning hours, certainly before lunch. At this time, you probably have residual moisture or dew from overnight, and water soaks in better on slightly damp ground. Also, this timing gives the lawn a chance to absorb the drink in the warmth of the sunny day (a drenched lawn at night, especially a humid night, is an invitation to disease). Also — as you may remember from long-ago science class — water and sunlight work together to fuel photosynthesis and subsequent plant growth. Help your lawn do what it needs to do: grow.

## Getting the water balance right

Figuring out the details about when and how much to water can be like a juggling act, but you can at least avoid the extremes. Gardeners know of some classic, telltale signs that an established lawn is crying out for water. Don't let it get to the point of a crisis. Here are the signs that indicate your lawn is a bit parched:

- ✔ When you walk on it or somebody rides a bike over it, the lawn grass shows the marks — that is, the blades don't bounce back.

- ✔ The lawn's colour changes. Formerly shiny green, the blades now look rather dull; they may even take on a smoky, grey-blue colour. Yikes!

- ✔ You plunge in a stick, screwdriver, or soil-moisture sensor to a depth of at least 15 centimetres (6 inches) and two things happen: The tester doesn't go in easily, and it comes up dry.

Grass certainly needs regular waterings (whether from you or from Mother Nature), but on the other hand, overwatering can be dangerous because it

- ✔ Deprives the roots of needed oxygen

- ✔ Causes wasteful runoff, sometimes carrying soil and fertilizer with it

- ✔ Destroys soil structure

- ✔ Encourages disease activity

When you do water, how much water to use is something you figure out on the job. There's no universal advice here, because so much depends on the type of grass, the setting, the type of soil, and your climate (including how often it rains). However, a general rule is between 3 and 4 centimetres (1 and 1½ inches) per week. Water more when the weather's hot, and less when it's cool. The object is to wet the entire root zone but not saturate it. This concept is especially true on heavy clay or *loamy soil* (rich soil with mixed particles).

After you successfully wet the entire root zone, observe how fast the lawn absorbs the water so you know how often to water. Generally, you want to let the soil dry out between waterings. Shallow-rooted grasses, naturally, get thirsty again sooner than deep-rooted ones. It's in your best interest (less work for you plus a healthier lawn — *win-win,* as lawyers are fond of saying!) to encourage deeper root growth by watering deeply. Once or twice a week does the trick.

Frequently cut, shorter grasses dry out faster than ones that you let grow a little taller between mowings.

## Boosting watering efficiency

Here are a few ideas to help you get the most out of your lawn watering, reducing waste and saving on your water bill:

✔ Watch — don't walk away or leave on errands! If the lawn gets soaked and runoff starts, you can intervene right away. Keep busy in other parts of your yard and check back for runoff every 15 minutes or so.

✔ Water slowly. Water runs off if you put it on too fast, especially on parched ground.

 If runoff starts and you turn off the hose and check saturation depth only to find that the water hasn't soaked in deeply enough, don't worry. Try the 15 minutes on, 15 minutes off method until you can verify that the water has succeeded in reaching at least 15 centimetres (6 inches) down.

✔ Yank out weeds and other encroaching plants. Weeds suck water away from the lawn.

✔ Mulch any adjacent bare or open areas of soil to reduce evaporation.

✔ Make sure you don't have any leaks at hose connections, including at the originating faucet and along the line(s).

# Feeding and Fertilizing

A lawn is actually a dense gathering of many plants, clamouring for nutrition. Even if your yard is blessed with wonderful, organically rich soil (you've put in a lawn over a former farm field or barnyard, say), over time, it won't be enough. The lawn will grow thinner with each passing year.

A well-fed lawn grows densely and is healthy. And a healthy lawn, like a healthy person or a healthy pet, is strong enough to resist disease and pests as well as environmental stresses. If you don't want your lawn to cause you trouble, don't neglect fertilizer. Fertilizing your lawn is pretty straightforward, really, and the following sections explain how to do it.

Never apply fertilizer without water. Water dilutes fertilizer appropriately and helps deliver it to the roots, where the grass can put it to good use.

Many common weeds adore infertile soil. Indeed, that preference lends itself to a good definition of *weed:* an opportunistic plant that grabs and dominates a niche. If you underfertilize your lawn, the secret will get out, and weeds will run right over the top of the lawn to colonize the area.

## What's your type? Deciding on the kind of fertilizer

As you may know, fertilizer contains three main elements (nutrients) critical for good plant growth — nitrogen (N), phosphorus (P), and potassium (K). *Nitrogen* is the element that enhances foliage and stem growth. That's why nitrogen dominates lawn fertilizers. Common formulations include 22-3-7 and 21-0-0. Chapter 4 covers garden fertilizer in some detail, but here we discuss fertilizer that's strictly for lawn use.

When you go shopping for lawn fertilizer, read the labels very carefully (see Figure 10-5). You'll probably find three types:

- ✔ **Quick-release lawn fertilizer:** With this fertilizer, you get a gratifyingly quick response; the lawn greens right up after application. However, because the lawn consumes it quickly, you have to apply frequent subsequent doses.

- ✔ **Slow-release lawn fertilizer:** This plant food supplies the same nutritive benefits as quick-release fertilizer but not as quickly. You can expect consistent, sustained growth, and you don't need to apply it as often.

- ✔ **Mixture of both:** A mixture of quick-release and slow-release fertilizers lets you have the best of both worlds.

Most commercial lawn fertilizers are inorganic (synthetic); but as far as the plants are concerned, the nutrients are the same. Yes, inorganic fertilizers are manufactured chemically; they come in granules, powders, and liquids and are fairly inexpensive. And yes, people worry that they damage — or at least don't enhance — soil biology. But especially for lawns, constant renewal of the organic content isn't so easy (you're not digging it up every spring like in the vegetable garden). Synthetic fertilizers are easy to get and use, and they may turn out to be your choice out of sheer convenience.

Figure 10-5:
A typical
lawn
fertilizer
label. This
fertilizer has
a 22-3-7
balance,
which is
representa-
tive of ratios
used by
many
companies.

Guaranteed Analysis:

Total Nitrogen (N)......................................................................... 22%
    4.5% ammoniacal nitrogen
    13.5% uria nitrogen
    4.0% water insoluble nitrogen
Available Phosphoric
Acid ($P_2O_5$)................................................................................ 3%
Soluble Potash ($K_2O$) ................................................................. 7%
Primary nutrients from urea,
Ureaform, Ammonium Phosphate, and Muriate of Potash

Organic fertilizers include things like fish emulsion and manure, which you dilute and spray on the lawn or apply and water in. Sometimes they're a bit smelly, at least immediately, but they're not something any red-blooded gardener would recoil from. Natural fertilizers often contain trace amounts of other elements, but these elements aren't desperately needed in most garden soils. At any rate, the advantages of organic fertilizers are clear: the improvement of soil texture and slower, more measured action.

Assuage your guilt, if any, over choosing the inorganic lawn fertilizer by using it properly and responsibly. And realize that the abuse of organic ones can cause serious problems in the environment, too. Here are some of the problems excess fertilizer can cause:

✔ **Damage to the lawn itself:** There *can* be too much of a good thing. Excessive nitrogen burns your lawn (the grass looks literally torched). Or the fertilizer may inspire overly lush growth, which is an open invitation to lawn diseases and hungry lawn pests. Fast, lush growth has another downside — you have to mow a lot more often!

✔ **Damage to the environment/watershed:** Please, don't be wasteful! Water runoff carrying nitrogen-laden fertilizer pollutes groundwater, streams, lakes, rivers, and marshes — even estuaries and the ocean if you're in range. Blooms of algae can occur, water plants can be damaged or have their growth habits altered, and the changes can adversely affect animals that live in these places and depend on these foods. And don't forget — to make water safe for drinking, water treatment facilities have to deal with any contaminants that end up in your rivers, reservoirs, lakes, and streams.

Sandy soil alert: Nitrogen travels quickly through lighter, quick-draining soils and then leaches away. You don't have to forgo feeding your lawn, but be careful. Try applying half as much, twice as often, or use only slow-release lawn food.

## Knowing your serving sizes: How much fertilizer is enough?

To determine how much fertilizer to use, you have to read the label on the bag or container and then follow the application directions *to the letter*. All recommendations are based on 93 square metres (1,000 square feet) of lawn (go out and measure and then refer to "Growing lawns from seed" to figure out your lawn's area). Generally speaking, the typical dose never exceeds 450 grams per 93 square metres (1 pound per 1,000 square feet) of lawn. Like aspirin, more fertilizer is *not* better — for the lawn or the environment!

## Checking out the feeding schedule

First, you need to know when not to fertilize your lawn. Don't feed your lawn in winter or when the grass goes dormant in high summer — let a sleeping (or dormant) lawn lie. And don't feed on especially hot days, whether in spring, summer, or fall. Grass plants respond to the stress of blazingly hot days by slowing down their growth, and a jolt of fertilizer during this time isn't a good thing. That pretty much leaves moderate days in spring and fall as your best times to fertilize grass. Here's a feeding schedule:

- **The minimum:** Once in the fall; this schedule keeps the grass plants growing longer, encouraging root growth and thus providing the reserves the grass needs for quick green-up when spring rolls around again. Late fall is fine too — the grass may not use the food right away, but it will get a head start in spring before you may be ready to spread the fertilizer.

- **A little better:** Once in the fall and again in early spring; the spring feeding jumpstarts the new season (don't go too early — you'll get overly lush top growth at the expense of root growth, plus you may inadvertently fuel a burst of young weeds).

- **Pampering:** Start in late spring and repeat at regular intervals into fall, perhaps every six to eight weeks during active growth; hold off in midsummer if the weather's really hot and the lawn is taking a nap (you know the lawn's dormant when it loses some colour or even turns a shade of buff).

# Mowing the Lawn, Cutting the Grass, and Otherwise Giving the Yard a Shave

Mowing the lawn may be the job you love to hate, or you may relish the sweet scent of freshly mown grass. But no matter how you feel about it, it has to be done. Everyone can agree that a mown lawn looks better than the alternative — a rangy, overgrown neglected patch.

Mowing also has a purely practical side: It maintains your lawn's health. Mowing regularly

- **Helps fight weeds:** Mowing helps prevent weeds from germinating and invading. How? Mowed at the right height, lawn grass shades out both weed seeds and seedlings. If weeds begin to grow, mowing chops off their heads, thwarting their drive to grow, mature, and spread.

- **Makes the grass grow more densely:** Well, you know how when you pinch off the tip of a plant, it reacts by producing more-lush growth lower down on the plant? The same principle is at work when you mow and remove a grass blade's growing tip — the plant is inspired to spread out.

Basically, mowing turns grass into a lawn (and not, say, a wildlife preserve for ticks). Read on for some advice about mowing and the basic mowing equipment.

How often you should mow depends — surprise, surprise — on how fast your grass grows. You'll be busy in the height of the growing season, to be sure. Three key factors affect growth rate:

- **Time of year:** Cool-season grasses motor during spring and fall, but summer's heat slows them down.

- **Amount of water:** More water equals more grass equals more mowing. If you're sick of mowing, cut back on watering. But be careful; if you cut back too much, your lawn may show signs of distress or go brown and dormant (see "Getting the water balance right," earlier in this chapter).

- **Amount of fertilizer:** More nitrogen and more lawn food equal more grass and more mowing.

Don't mow when the grass is wet. This advice holds even if you don't have an electric mower (and especially if you do). Wet grass is tough to mow; it mats and mushes and cuts unevenly. The clippings settle in damp globs, smothering the grass. It also rots with a rank smell! Later, when things are dry, you find out your hard work resulted in what looks like a very bad haircut. Also, cutting wet grass promotes the growth and spread of lawn-disease organisms. Not worth the trouble, not worth the risk!

How high to mow varies by grass type. In general, though, you cut grasses with an upright growth habit — which account for virtually all the grasses we grow in Canada — relatively high, to 6 to 8 centimetres (2½ to 3 inches). Check out Figure 10-6 to see how to adjust your mower, but don't sweat about getting your mower blade to exactly the right height. The ideal mow-to height is just that: ideal. (For a general list of ideal mow-to heights, refer to Table 10-1.) Do the best you can, and of course, watch how your particular lawn responds to your regimen. You'll get into a groove.

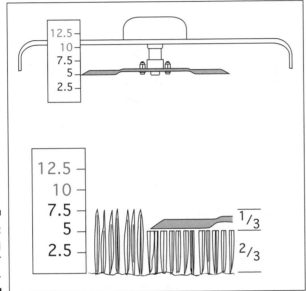

**Figure 10-6:**
Setting
mower
height.

Adjust your mowing height according to the weather. If temperatures are really high, let the grass be taller; short haircuts are for cooler weather. Longer grass is better able to cope with the stress of drought and heat.

Suppose heavy rains inspire a burst of growth, or you go away on vacation and the lawn gets a little out of control. It happens. Don't fret. Respond with a two-part attack. For the first mowing, set the blade higher than usual and go to it, mowing only some of what you really need to (and you may need to do some raking after). Follow up a few days later with a second mowing at the proper or usual height.

For information on types of lawnmowers and their maintenance, please see *Lawn Care For Dummies* (Wiley).

# Warring with Weeds

The reason weeds grow in and around your lawn is the same reason your lawn grows there — it's open and it's sunny. Even if you're a wonderful lawn steward, totally eradicating these pesky invaders is nearly impossible. But as in other parts of your yard and gardens, you can work things out so you still enjoy and feel proud of the plants you planted.

The main thing to understand about weeds is that although lawn grasses are perennials, many lawn weeds aren't — they're annuals. This information can colour your battle; forewarned is forearmed!

Common lawn weeds include crabgrass, chickweed, dandelion, dock, English daisy (although many people like English daisies sprinkled throughout their lawns, considering them weeds only when they become invasive), ground ivy, moss, oxalis, and plantain. We do suggest growing ivies and mosses as lawn alternatives, but they're less desirable when they invade your grass and try to outgrow it.

## Preventing lawn weeds

Good news — in point of fact, ideal lawn conditions and ideal weed conditions aren't exactly the same. So to try to get the upper hand, follow these tips:

- **Provide and then nurture good ground.** Grass likes fertile, loose, middle-of-the-road soil, and many weeds don't. Weeds like poor, compacted soil. Some like it soggy; some like it parched. Any way you can nudge your lawn area toward good and moderate can help.

- **Mow often.** This move chops off the weeds at the knees. In particular, you want to thwart the development of flowers (and definitely the seeds or seed heads that follow — that's how weeds love to reproduce).

- **Mow at the right height.** If you scalp your lawn grass too short, weed seeds and seedlings suddenly get the light they need to grow. Longer is better, in this case. The grass shades them out.

## Treating already-weedy lawns

Having too many weeds in a lawn is more than a call to arms; it's a wake-up call. Something isn't right if they're winning. On the other hand, you can and will, frankly, have to live with a few. To get rid of the weeds you already have, follow these tips:

✔ **Assess and correct.** If your lawn was healthy, you wouldn't have so many weeds, and that's the truth. So what's wrong? Are you not watering or feeding enough, which stresses the grass and eventually leads to sparser growth and areas where weeds can sneak in? Are you mowing too low, which allows weeds to germinate? Refer to the earlier parts of this chapter to read the basic care sections on watering, fertilizer, and mowing to see what you can figure out.

✔ **Hand-pull.** Yank out weeds one by one each time you pass by — be sure to get all of the root system — or try an all-day assault. If you get the kids to do it ("What'll you pay me?"), teach them the importance of getting out the entire root system. To dig out pesky dandelions or other long, tap-rooted weeds, purchase a tool with a long blade and a *V* cutout at the end; it allows you to cut and lift out the root of the invader in its entirety.

✔ **Consider weed killers.** But don't take herbicides lightly, no matter how frustrated and annoyed you are. You have to examine environmental and toxicity and safety issues, and you need to check your municipal government's Web site to see if herbicide use is restricted in your area. You don't want to harm your lawn or other garden plants in the process (or people and pets who may wander out there). Getting the right weed killer for the job and applying it properly and especially *at the right time* are key. (*Pre-emergent* herbicides, which are somewhat less toxic, are used early in the year, before the weed seeds germinate; *post-emergent* ones damage and kill growing weeds, some through the leaves, some all the way down through the root system. Corn gluten, an organic pre-emergent, is applied in the fall.) Get your enemy weeds properly identified, read labels, ask questions, and be careful if you decide to go ahead.

✔ **Get professional help.** Consult a lawn-care company to see what the workers say. A reputable company won't put a bandage on the problem by applying a herbicide without talking to you first about the conditions that allowed weeds to prosper.

✔ **Renovate.** Now may be the time to take out that sorry lawn and start over. Check out the info in the section "In the Beginning: Getting Ready to Make a Lawn from Scratch," earlier in this chapter.

Or rather than try to get rid of the weeds, you can learn to live with them. Who is your lawn's worst critic? Why, you are, of course. Stand back — across the street, or over in the driveway, say — and look at the lawn. Is it generally thick and green at this vantage? You don't want to surrender (you can still hand-pull whenever you have the time and inclination), but perhaps you can reach a truce and even start to appreciate some of the diversity in your yard. Some people consider clover to be a weed, but it adds nitrogen to the soil, feeding the grass; besides, you may get lucky and find a four-leaf clover!

# Chapter 11

# Reaching New Heights with Trees and Shrubs

*T*rees and shrubs are important because the point of gardening is the cultivation of plants — and woody plants are a significant presence in any garden. Trees are normally the biggest and longest-lived plants on a property, with shrubs not far behind, which is why giving serious thought to their selection and placement is so crucial. A mistake costs a lot of time, not to mention money. Conversely, a correct choice adds immeasurably to the good looks of your home, to your comfort, and ultimately, to the value of your property.

Shrubs are usually less than 4.5 to 6 metres (15 to 20 feet tall), and trees tend to grow taller than that. But you can find small-size trees and large-size shrubs — plants that blur the line. Your real object is to pick out something that fits into the location you have in mind, so what the plant is called may not really matter. And yet classification can have some bearing, because trees and shrubs have somewhat different growth habits that have less to do with how tall they get and more to do with how wide they get or how much space they take up.

Here's the scoop: Ideally, a *tree* has a single main stem, and the branches appear up higher and spread outward. Generally, shrubs don't grow like that — not without pruning help, anyway. Most *shrubs* are multistemmed, and over time form a barrier or thicket (which is why they make good hedges or property-line plants). So think about what you want the plant to do for you. Plan the look you want. Stand and ponder the appointed spot in your yard.

For tree and evergreen types, shopping tips, and advice on planting and care, read on. We take a look at trees first in this chapter, and shrubs follow. For specific information on the planting and care of fruit- and nut-bearing trees, though, please see Chapter 15.

# Knowing Your Trees

If you're shopping for a tree or just trying to figure out what to do with one you've inherited in your yard, a basic understanding of its characteristics can help you out. The object is for the tree to enhance your property, so you really need to know your options, which we cover in the next few sections.

## Exploring evergreen trees

People often refer to all evergreens, including Christmas trees, as "pines," but of course, the truth is that they're so much more than pines. The term *pines* frequently refers to trees with needles — but this isn't always the case (see "Broadleaf evergreens," coming up). Calling them *conifers* (cone bearing) covers much of what the experts classify as evergreens, but again, not all.

In botany, *evergreens* are plants that don't lose their leaves or needles all at once on a yearly basis like deciduous trees do in autumn. By this definition, most tropical plants are evergreens, and some conifers, like the larch and the bald cypress, are deciduous because they shed their needles each year. Small wonder that this term is confusing!

Always find out what the mature height and girth of an evergreen is before you commit yourself. Even if the tree grows slowly, say, only a few centimetres per year, you may find in time that the plant is wedged too close to the house or is banging its head on an overhanging eave. You can slow down an evergreen's growth rate somewhat by not pampering it (reducing water and fertilizer) or by placing it in a less-than-ideal spot, but why stress the tree? You're better off making a match between site and plant.

### Needled evergreens

Good landscape trees in the needled group include pines, spruces, cedar, arborvitae, larch, fir, Douglas fir, dawn redwood, juniper, and yew. (**Note:** Larch trees and dawn redwoods are unique — their needles yellow and drop in the fall, and the trees generate fresh ones every spring.)

Within these groups, a gardener can choose from many attractive variations, as you can see if you visit a good nursery. You have no need to get the plain old (species) forest tree when you can get a descendant or variety — also called a *cultivar,* short for "cultivated variety" — that grows shorter and neater, or has handsome, distinctive bluish or golden needles, or bears shorter or longer needles.

Regular shearing (which we mention in the "Shearing hedges" sidebar at the end of this chapter) can, within reason, keep a needled evergreen at the size and shape you want. However, picking a tree that will fit your chosen spot at maturity saves you a lot of maintenance.

### Dwarf needled evergreens

You can look into a whole class of evergreens called *dwarf evergreens* or *dwarf conifers* that are worth considering, especially if your yard is small. These trees can range from tiny 15-centimetre (6-inch) tufts to knee-high miniature trees. If you have the space and the inclination, a grouping of dwarf evergreens, perhaps coupled with some judiciously placed rocks, makes a splendid display. Dwarf evergreens also make attractive hedges, boundary plantings, foundation plantings, and path side edgings.

***Note:*** *Dwarf* can also mean small in relation to the regular tree of its type. For example, a dwarf white pine (depending on the variety) may grow to 4.5 metres (15 feet) tall, which is, in fact, dwarfed by a regular-size white pine, which can grow 24 to 30 metres (80 to 100 feet) tall! That 4.5-metre tree may not be quite what you have in mind when you see a cute dwarf plant in a 4-litre pot. Read the label to find out the plant's mature size.

### Broadleaf evergreens

*Broadleaf evergreen* trees (ones that hold their leaves over the winter) aren't common in Canada except on the West Coast, where tall rhododendrons and hollies are an outstanding presence. Other good landscape trees in the broadleaf group that grow in warmer parts of British Columbia include bay laurel and arbutus (or Pacific madrone, also sometimes called strawberry tree). Many shrubs and vines hold their leaves over winter, however. For suggestions, see "Knowing Your Shrubs," later in this chapter, and check out the information on evergreen vines in Chapter 12.

Read descriptions carefully: Even in mild areas, the leaves of plants labelled as "semi-evergreen" may fall, curl, or become discoloured until spring, when fresh reinforcements are generated.

Unlike their needled counterparts, many broadleaf evergreens sport attractive flowers, so you may get some spring or summer glory. Arbutus, for example, has white flowers in May and red-orange fruit in fall. With spring-flowering shrubs like rhododendrons, make sure late frosts don't damage the buds (pick a variety touted as cold hardy in your area). Also, ensure that you don't inadvertently prune off the show before it begins (see the later section called "Life and limb: Pruning judiciously"). Some evergreen shrubs and vines, such as cotoneaster and firethorn, show off bright red berries in fall that stay on the branches into winter.

Broadleaf evergreen trees and shrubs do best in soil that's slightly acidic. If you're not sure whether your yard offers the right growing conditions, get a soil test and amend the soil as recommended beforehand. An acidic mulch, such as chopped-up dried fall leaves from oaks or pine needles, also helps. (Refer to Chapter 4 for more info on soil preparation.)

# Falling for deciduous trees

The definition of a *deciduous* tree is simply one that sheds its leaves every fall and generates new ones the following spring. Good landscape trees in this group include maple, dogwood, beech, gingko, cherry, katsura, birch, linden, oak, tulip tree, buckeye, ash, sweet gum, aspen, and redbud. Consider all your options! Each of these trees comes in many different forms or varieties. A well-stocked nursery offers many options.

Deciduous trees keep life interesting. They have a different appearance in every season — fresh new leaves in spring; often flowers in spring or summer; possibly a fall leaf-colour change; and finally, a stark, architectural profile and perhaps interesting bark in the winter months. Many of these trees also bear fruit or nuts — see Chapter 15 for information on these types of trees.

Many deciduous trees end the gardening year in a blaze of glory. Because you generally purchase young trees in the springtime, you may forget about fall colour. But if autumn colour is desirable, find out whether your chosen tree is known to put on a show. Some Japanese maples, for instance, are pretty, but have plain green leaves all season until fall creates an astounding and spectacular change to crimson, orange, burgundy, or cherry red.

Favourite trees for spectacular fall colour include maples (especially Japanese and sugar maples), gingko, sweet gum, katsura, hawthorn, red oak, some varieties of pear and cherry, sourwood, and mountain ash.

By and large, deciduous trees tend to grow faster than evergreens, making them good choices where you want faster gratification, faster results. Within the different kinds, or species, the speed of growth varies considerably — ask when you buy. Growing conditions are also a factor. If your site is stressful for a tree (poor soil, not enough light, windy, and so on), it won't perform as expected. Fast growers include willow, tulip tree, poplar, and paper, grey, or yellow birch.

### Deciduous shade trees

One of the primary reasons for choosing a tree is shade. A shade tree's cooling shelter is something to look forward to, and the dappled light under its arching branches is something to savour on hot summer days. In time, placing a seat, bench, or table underneath the tree may be in order. Sited near the south-facing side of your house, a shade tree can help cool the house in summer, saving you money on air conditioning. Choose wisely so your vision can come true.

Get information on the ultimate mature size of any tree before you buy. If the one you thought you wanted is predicted to be too big for the spot, don't despair — ask about smaller-size options within the group or opt for a reasonable substitute. If the nursery staff's answers don't satisfy you, do a little research on your own.

The best shade trees are those with a single, thick main trunk. Discover whether this growth habit is natural for the tree you have in mind; if it isn't, you can cut off side trunks while the plant is still young.

Consider what you want to grow under your shade tree. You can place the tree in the middle of your lawn when you first bring it home, but as it grows, you may find that the grass below becomes thin and scraggly — or dies back altogether — due to the lack of sunlight as well as nutrients and moisture, caused by the greediness of the tree's roots. Down the line, then, prepare to underplant your shade tree with shade-tolerant grass or a shade-loving, drought-tolerant groundcover. Or if you plan seating under the tree's shelter, consider placing nothing but mulched ground around the tree's base.

Trees with weeping habits aren't ideal shade trees because their downward-swooping branches don't allow people to stand under them comfortably, never mind underplanting or placing seating in their shade. Classic examples are weeping birches, beeches, and willows. These trees are lovely in their own right and still deserve to be grown, but grow them in some spot where using their shade isn't important to you.

### Flowering deciduous trees

Get double the pleasure from a landscape tree when you choose one that flowers. Generally, the show is early in the gardening year, and, generally, it doesn't last long. But that brevity doesn't mean you can't revel in its beauty. Favourite flowering trees include crabapple, dogwood, Japanese tree lilac (otherwise known as ivory silk tree), ornamental pear, flowering cherry, golden chain tree, chestnut, redbud, and fringe tree.

Depending on what's going on nearby or in the rest of your garden, the flower colour of your flowering tree may or may not be a part of a larger display. An easy way to avoid a clash is to plant a white-flowered tree — or conversely, to favour white-flowered spring bulbs, perennials, and shrubs in the vicinity. But if you're daring, beholding some red tulips at the foot of a red-flowered dogwood or a redbud tree — or the Easter-egg hues of pink and purple hyacinths skirting a cherry tree — can be a real thrill.

For best results, observe your new tree's flower colour — and blooming duration — for one spring or two. That way, you can decide whether the tree's existing companions please you or whether you want to install some complementary ones for *next* year.

# Choosing the Right Tree for Where You Live

A classic mistake that eager homeowners make is choosing a tree based on looks alone. A tree is a significant, long-term investment, so make your selection carefully.

Native trees are often a smart choice; they're already adapted to local weather and soil, and they're probably resistant to common pests or diseases in your area. If which trees are native and which aren't isn't obvious to you when you go shopping, ask. Or better still, first visit a nearby park, botanical garden, or arboretum where trees are mature *and* labelled.

Horticulturists breed or select cultivars of native trees, and these cultivated varieties are seen as variations or improvements on their wild forebears. Where available, they may be your best bet of all because they build from natural adaptations.

Otherwise, just make a smart match: If your soil is naturally dry, sandy, or quick draining, don't choose a thirsty tree like a birch or a willow. Keeping the tree healthy and looking good would only become a major, and perhaps frustrating, project. Shop close to home — reputable local nurseries have plenty of stock that ought to thrive for you. If your chosen site has any special or unique conditions (boggy soil, say), tell the salesperson so he or she can assist you in making an appropriate choice.

Beware of shedders: Trees that dump leaves, seedpods, catkins, fruit, or nuts end up being a lot of extra work unless you're prepared to handle it. Examples of shedders include poplar, mulberry, willow, sweet gum, eucalyptus, horse chestnut, and black walnut.

Consider shade density. If you prefer dappled shade (and hope to grow lawn underneath the tree), choose a tree with a lighter canopy. Examples include ash, birch, honey locust, and linden. If you want dense shade, go for an oak or maple.

If your summers are long and hot, you don't want a new young tree to just dry out and die, even despite extra water and attention from you. Your ideal tree has small, rather than large, leaves (this includes needles!). Leaves with less surface area conserve moisture better. Also, pick a tree that has deep roots that can travel to where sustaining moisture is. Good drought-resilient trees include Eastern red cedar, hickory, Kentucky coffee tree, honey locust, bur oak, pin oak, gingko, laurel, some pines, blue Atlas cedar (hardy only in Zones 7 to 9), and Colorado blue spruce.

# Getting Treed! Planting Trees

Trees take up space. Okay, maybe the sky's the limit with vertical space, but you have to account for the horizontal space — how big around, how broad, how spreading — that a tree requires. A tree in a crowded or cramped setting, or one that has outgrown its spot, runs the risk of becoming not only unhealthy and a hazard but also a sorry sight. A poorly planted tree is also a big pain in the neck to chop back or remove, if it comes down to that. So plan ahead!

## Deciding when to plant your tree

The best time to plant trees is spring. New, young plants are surging into growth and — assuming you plant your new tree or trees in a good spot and with care — are full of energy for the months ahead. In other words, spring planting corresponds favourably to a tree's metabolic cycle. Roots are ready to grow, and the tree has time to settle in. A tree's a big plant, after all, and it needs all the time it can get to adjust to its new home.

Fall planting is your second choice. Tree Canada advises that you can plant deciduous trees — except poplars, willows, ash, elms, and birches, which should be planted in spring — from after they've dropped their leaves until freeze-up. You can plant evergreens from about the first week of August to the end of October. Whether you plant after leaf drop or just before frost hits, be sure to water the tree in well at planting time and keep the soil moist until winter arrives.

## Finding a suitable location

When trying to decide where to put a tree, first find out your chosen tree's mature size. Figure out the standard dimensions of the exact variety you've chosen. Varieties vary. For example, the handsome English oak (Quercus robur) in its "plain old species" form can reach more than 30 metres (100 feet) tall, whereas a cultivar of it called 'Westminster Globe' gets to only about 14 metres (45 feet). Here's a less-dramatic example: The native red maple (Acer saccharum), noted for its spectacular fall colour, can grow to 20 metres (65 feet) tall. But 'Green Mountain', a cultivar of A. saccharum with scorch-resistant, leathery leaves, reaches a maximum height of 15 metres (50 feet), which may make it more appropriate for your yard.

You can find the information you need about a tree's mature size on the tag or on a sticker on the pot, or it's available from the garden centre's inventory list (flag down a staffer). Or you can consult reference books or nursery catalogues, or do a little Internet research.

Now, assume the tree *will* grow to its maximum mature size, even though research has suggested that tree-dimension results vary from place to place, from garden to garden, and from setting to setting (garden settings versus park or wooded settings). Better to overestimate than underestimate! Read on for info on how best to place your tree.

### Avoiding trouble spots

A tree is a long-term investment, and you're best off when you find it a good home in the first place. Put some thought into the place that's most likely to make your relationship with your tree a comfortable one.

Bring the info on the tree's mature size, and march out boldly into your yard or garden with your tape measure and some means of marking the tree's estimated *canopy* — that is, an outline on the ground of how far the branches will extend into your space (a length of garden hose or heavy-duty electrical extension cord will do). Mark the spot, making a big outline. It doesn't have to be precise or perfect — this outline is for the purposes of eyeballing the tree's potential and making sure you don't plant it too close to your house or the neighbour's fence. Information about the mature width of the tree should be on the plant's label; if it isn't, be sure to ask the grower or nursery owner.

Consider the following factors when you situate your tree:

- **Initial dig:** Assess your desired location to see whether digging there is possible and practical. Call your utility companies to have them mark where your phone, electric, gas, and sewer lines are before you make any decisions.

- **Root-system potential:** *Where will the roots end up?* is a very good question, and tracking down the answer isn't always easy. But you're safe in assuming they'll eventually extend farther than the reach of the tree's branches (the *drip line,* landscapers call this).

  Some trees, such as willows, seek water, and they tend to thrive right by the septic system (where they can cause expensive damage). Keep trees away from septic fields. Other trees are shallow rooted and may uproot the surface of a driveway or sidewalk if you plant them too close.

- **Canopy encroachment and leafy obstructions:** Know the ultimate height of the trees you're buying before planting them under utility lines. And remember that planting trees and shrubs close to the road can be hazardous! When placing these plants, provide yourself and visitors with adequate lines of sight for safely pulling in and out of your driveway.

Now is the time to discover whether your tree's going to collide with your garage or shrub border or driveway, or encroach on your neighbour's property, as it grows — and to adjust your plans accordingly, either by scooting the projected site over by a few metres or by switching your plans to a smaller tree. Mark the middle of the estimated canopy, because this place, of course, is where you'll dig your tree's hole.

When planning where to plant a tree, figure out whether you'll want to do other substantial digging nearby. Having a strong, well-developed root system is critical to the health of a tree. Roots anchor the tree in the ground and are its lifeline in obtaining the huge quantities of water and nutrients that it needs from the soil (see Figure 11-1). Amazingly, most tree roots grow in only the top 45 centimetres (18 inches) or so of the soil! This fact illustrates why you have to be careful not to damage trees' vital and vulnerable roots when digging nearby.

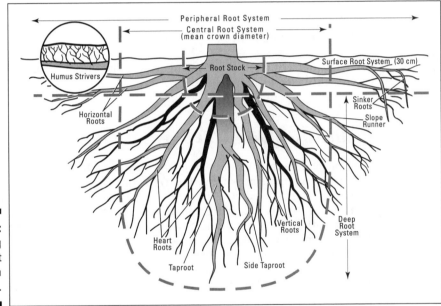

**Figure 11-1:**
Examining the root system of a typical tree.

### Designing to conserve energy and block the wind

Sometimes the addition of a tree, or trees, is practical as well as decorative. Not only do trees look attractive and provide a suitable support for your hammock, but they also filter pollutants from rainwater, reduce the amount of water that ends up in storm drains, decrease surface ozone, and put out a supply of free oxygen. Not too shabby! Trees can also help you to conserve energy by shading your house in the summer, letting sunlight in during winter months, and blocking the wind. Depending on what you want the tree to do, some trees are better candidates than others.

To shade your house in the summer, plant deciduous trees where you get southern or western exposure. If possible, try to shade the air conditioning unit. After the trees shed their leaves in the fall, they'll let the winter sun warm your house.

Evergreens often serve as windbreaks to protect gardens, homes, and other structures. Ideally, a windbreak tree has certain useful qualities:

- ✔ It grows fast.
- ✔ Its branches and twigs aren't brittle.
- ✔ Its foliage is naturally thick.
- ✔ It develops deep roots or a taproot to help it remain anchored.
- ✔ It tolerates drought (because winds dry it out).
- ✔ In groups, it grows densely.
- ✔ It bends before it breaks.

Use a row of trees to block prevailing winds. Planting a double row of evergreens is sometimes more effective.

## *Planting your tree*

Planting involves a point of debate. You may know that welcoming other new plants (say, a perennial or a rosebush) to your yard with amended soil is a good idea. The usual advice is to dig the hole and mix some of the native soil with some good organic matter, on the grounds that few of us have fabulous, perfect, native soil in our yards. Should you follow this procedure for an incoming tree as well? Actually, no — but not because digging a tree-size hole is a lot of work. And not because anyone assumes that your yard has fabulous, perfect, native soil. A tree's roots are eventually going to expand well beyond the planting hole you make for them. They need to go deep and wide over time.

If you make the initial hole full of wonderful, organically rich soil, tree roots may never journey beyond the bounds of your planting hole. And journey beyond it they must, if the tree is to grow and eventually reach its mature size. So do the roots of your new tree a favour and don't coddle them with amended, improved soil in their youth. They have to adapt to their lot in life!

If you're installing a tree on a lot that was recently built upon, improving the soil *is* necessary. You can pretty safely assume that the soil is not only compacted (from all the construction equipment running over and over it) but also of poor quality. In fact, the topsoil may have been scraped off long ago, when the site was being prepared. That leaves subsoil, which is often lousy and poorly draining and may be full of rocks. Therefore, make all planting holes as big as you can (bigger than you would otherwise), remove all rocks and debris, and then backfill with a combination of that subsoil and some good organic matter such as topsoil, loam, compost, and/or dehydrated manure.

In the next few sections, we give you details on how to handle trees depending on how they come to you: as a container tree, a bareroot tree, or a balled-and-burlapped tree. For now, though, here's the basic information you need on how to plant a tree. Just follow these steps:

1. **Lay a tarp on the ground (or position a wheelbarrow) near the planting site.**

   You can shovel or scoop planting-hole soil on and off the tarp as you work, thus preventing making a mess of your lawn or planting area.

2. **Dig a substantial hole, twice as wide as, but only a few centimetres deeper than, the root ball.**

   Rough up the sides of the hole with a shovel or garden fork. Make sure you have a mound of loose soil in the bottom of the hole as you set the tree in to allow the roots to grow easily into the area.

3. **Set the tree in the ground at the level it was growing previously.**

   Look for a soil line where the roots meet the main trunk.

4. **Hold the tree erect and in place as you backfill the soil.**

   If you can't do both at once, get a helper to do one of these activities while you do the other.

5. **Water well to eliminate air pockets, which can cause some settling; then add more soil as needed.**

6. **Create a basin of mulch or soil around the edge of the planting hole to catch rain and future waterings.**

   The size of the basin depends on the size of the tree, though it's generally 60 to 90 centimetres (2 to 3 feet) in diameter.

7. **Mulch the area well to help keep the soil from drying out and to keep weeds or encroaching lawn grass at bay.**

   Keep mulch a couple of centimetres away from the trunk of the tree.

8. **Add a stake (or two or three if the tree is wobbly) to encourage straight growth.**

   This stake also helps the tree withstand wind until it's established and well anchored in its new home. But don't stake too firmly; you want the tree to be able to move with the wind without whipping back and forth, which can cause root damage.

### Container trees

Even though Canada is a metric nation, most nurseries still sell large plants like young trees in 5-, 10-, and 20-gallon and larger pots. A few nurseries convert these measurements to litres — 22, 44, and 88 litres, respectively. The newly purchased trees need to get out of these containers soon! Otherwise, they run the risk of becoming rootbound. You can check a tree's root condition at the nursery before buying; simply tip the pot to the side to see whether the roots are in a dense tangle or whether some roots are questing out of the drainage holes in the bottom — both signs of a rootbound plant.

Buying a slightly rootbound seedling tree is okay. When you get the tree home and are about to transfer it to the planting hole, you can score the sides of the root ball vertically with a sharp knife (a mere 6-millimetre, or ¼-inch, slice). Rather than harming the root ball, this act forces the roots to generate fresh, new, feeder roots at the incision.

### Bareroot trees

Bareroot trees are dormant, but they won't be for long if spring is in the air. However, you can buy them earlier in the season than you can potted trees, and, therefore, plant them earlier, without fear of transplant shock. When in the ground, they emerge from dormancy and start growing at a gradual rate.

Regardless of whether you buy a bareroot tree at a nursery or order one via mail order, do check it over for quality and health. The roots should be crisp and white or brown. A few bedraggled or blackened limp ones can be clipped off, but if you notice a lot of these, you have an unhealthy specimen.

You may observe that the tree has little or no signs of green leaves or buds. For a novice gardener, buying one of these is indeed an act of faith. But it will come to life; it will!

Here's a special tip for bareroot trees: If you have a mere slip of a young tree, consisting only of one main stem and no limbs as yet, cut it back by about a third prior to planting. Yes, this trim sets back upward growth for a while, but it also allows the young tree to direct more energy into root growth, which is so important at first.

### Balled-and-burlapped trees

Balled and burlapped is a time-honoured way to sell a tree; it indicates that the plant was recently dug out of the ground. The burlap and twine is there to hold the root ball together, usually along with some soil. This state of affairs is meant to be temporary; the wrapping is just to make transporting the tree easier and neater.

If for some reason you can't plant your "b&b" tree right away, it can keep for a few days or a week if you stash it in a shady, sheltered spot and keep the burlap dampened.

Make sure you remove every bit of the burlap covering and all the twine or string from your balled-and-burlapped tree on planting day. Arborists used to advise that you tear open only the bottom of the burlap and let the rest rot in the planting hole over time, but this idea has been discredited. Also, some modern burlap and string have plastic woven in, which never breaks down and can constrict the roots' growth.

# Taking Care of Your Tree

Trees, sadly, are often cared for only when first planted, and then they're left to fend for themselves in landscapes after they've matured. People usually end this isolation only if the trees become diseased or damaged. Yes, you should take special care of your tree when it's newly planted to help it get established, but you should also make a habit of caring for it season by season, year by year, as it matures and grows. A healthy tree is a happy tree, and trees reflect the care you put into them in their beauty. Healthy trees often make the most beautiful trees, after all.

## Giving trees a tall drink of water

The most important times to water a tree are when it's newly planted — indeed, throughout its first year — and during dry spells. Deep, soaking waterings are ideal. If you've made a basin around the tree on planting day (as we advise in the "Planting your tree" section), the water goes where needed instead of dribbling away.

Lay a hose at the base of the tree and run it on a slow trickle. Check back at intervals to make sure the water's soaking in. If it starts to run off, stop for a spell, let the water soak in, and then resume.

If you're wondering whether the water you supply is actually reaching the roots, dig about 30 centimetres (1 foot) down with a trowel to find out. You may be surprised to discover that you have to water for much longer than you thought. Trees are heavy drinkers!

Soak new, young trees twice a week during their first year. Mature trees, of course, can go longer. How long depends on the type of tree, your soil, and the weather. When in doubt, water mature trees about once or twice a month during the height of summer.

In a drought, don't wait until a tree is shedding leaves or wilting to apply supplemental water (assuming your municipality doesn't forbid watering) — withholding water is very stressful for an already weakened plant.

Water bags are very handy for watering recently planted trees. Simply place these clever devices around a tree at ground level and fill them with water. They're designed to slowly release water so that it gently saturates the soil around the tree roots without running off. See Figure 11-2.

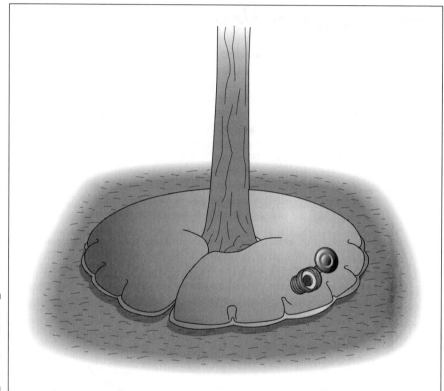

**Figure 11-2:**
Water bags give trees a long, slow drink.

## *Fertilizing trees*

Whether to fertilize a tree is strictly your call. If you know your garden soil isn't very fertile or you want to pamper a new, young tree, you may fertilize monthly or even more often during the growing season. Check at a nursery or garden centre for tree fertilizer, and apply or dilute according to the label directions.

Stop fertilizing as fall approaches! Plant food inspires fresh bursts of growth, which cold weather or an early frost can damage. Fall is the time when your tree is slowing down in preparation for the coming winter, anyway.

# Life and limb: Pruning judiciously

Pruning a tree and pruning a bush are really quite similar processes. You can really prune trees any time. Prune to remove obviously dead or damaged growth, to keep the tree healthy and your landscape beautiful, and to remove potentially dangerous branches that may fall and create a lot of damage.

Use sharp tools so you don't mash or rip your tree's growth, and use the right tool for the job — if hand-held clippers struggle to make the cuts you want, graduate to loppers or a saw (refer to Chapter 5 for info on tools). Figure 11-3 shows you the basics of pruning trees and bushes. More-detailed information on pruning bushes is located later in the chapter in "Pruning for shape and rejuvenation."

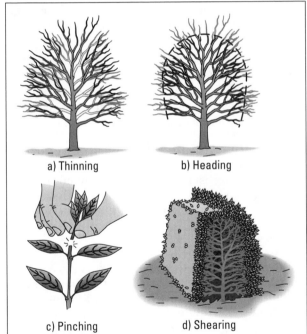

**Figure 11-3:** Four common ways to prune trees and shrubs.

a) Thinning

b) Heading

c) Pinching

d) Shearing

In the spring, you can also remove suckers and watersprouts right at the base, whenever they appear, to help keep your tree well groomed. *Suckers* are shoots that originate underground from the roots; *watersprouts* are the usually fast-growing vertical shoots that sprout along a branch or the trunk of the tree.

Winter is the best time to do maintenance pruning. The tree's profile is easier to see and assess, and the tree can recover from your cuts. Thin out tangled growth or a crowded interior and generally shape the crown. Remove branches that are crossing one another or are in danger of rubbing against each other.

### Training and pruning young trees

If you can get 'em while they're young — that is, prune a tree wisely and properly while it's still small — chances are that you'll have little more to do when it's older. Also, such cuts are smaller and consequently heal faster. But what you cut depends on what your goals are. Perhaps you want a single trunk. If so, watch and pick a trunk, and remove the competing leader or leaders.

Because distance from the ground never changes, and distance between branches never changes, make your pruning cuts only after careful observation of the entire tree. You want evenly spaced branches going up in a spiral so the mature tree will be attractive and full from all angles. Pick your keepers and remove all others.

### Maintenance pruning of mature trees

Sometimes a branch, or more than one, needs to be removed from a large tree. Perhaps the branch was damaged by some sort of accident or a storm, or perhaps it's threatening a roof or power line.

Big limbs are best removed in a three-cut approach (see Figure 11-4) so you can lower them in pieces to the ground without damaging anything or hurting anyone. This approach also ensures that the limb's removal doesn't involve ripping or twisting, which mars the tree itself. You may have to tie a rope securely to the branch's end so you, or a helper, can control its fall.

Here's how the cuts work:

1. **Make an undercut about 10 to 12 centimetres (4 to 5½ inches) out from where the branch attaches to a larger limb or the trunk, about halfway through. On a very thick branch, you might have to make these measurements farther out.**

2. **Make the second cut from the top of the branch about 5 centimetres (2 inches) farther out.**

   As a result, the branch breaks off cleanly.

3. **Remove the stub flush against the main branch or trunk, thus finishing the job neatly.**

   Don't bother with glue or tree paint. The wound will heal itself.

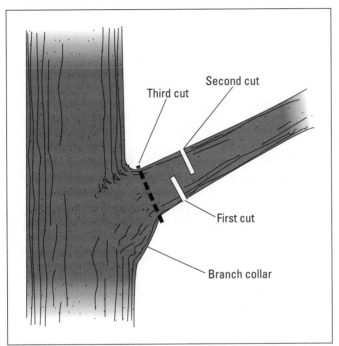

**Figure 11-4:**
Removing a
large limb in
three steps.

If the branch is heavy, up high in the tree, or seems to warrant the use of a chainsaw rather than a handsaw, this is a job for a professional arborist. For branches that are threatening a power line, notify your power company of the problem, but do be aware that they often just lop off a tree to prevent it from hitting the wires. If they don't take care of it, or if the tree is a well-shaped one and you don't want to risk having it deformed, consult a professional arborist who's experienced in working around power lines.

Ask at a local garden centre, ask neighbours who have had tree work done, or look in the Yellow Pages to find a licensed, certified arborist. Then have the arborist over to look at the job and give you a written estimate. At this time, your instincts can tell you whether the arborist seems confident and compe-tent. But still find out whether he or she is insured and has the right creden-tials, and get the phone number of at least one other customer as a reference. You don't want to hire an amateur and incur damage or have an accident on your property for which you may be liable. If you can, ask to see the arborist's work. Steer clear of those who *top* trees (lop off the ends of terminal limbs), which some untrained tree pruners may do even if the limbs aren't in the way of power lines. This mutilation results in an unsightly, stubby-looking tree with large wounded limbs that are susceptible to disease and insect infestations.

*Candle growth* is the tender new growth (before the needles have expanded) of conifers. You can cut or "pinch" these growths when they're young to encourage branching (see Figure 11-5).

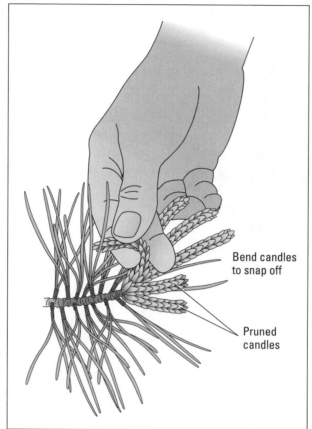

Bend candles
to snap off

Pruned
candles

**Figure 11-5:**
Pruning
candle
growth on
evergreens.

# Raising the stakes: Offering some support

Staking is usually warranted only when a tree's trunk is frail or exposed to strong winds. Wood stakes or metal, it doesn't especially matter, so long as the stakes are quite long, strong, and sturdy.

Stakes work best when they're sunk deep into the ground — another reason to stake when the tree's young (with a larger tree, you may find the roots obstructing the way or you may harm the roots as you plunge in the stake). Unlike staking, say, a top-heavy dahlia, tree stakes are *not* placed right close to the stem they're meant to support. Tree stakes are much more effective when you put them a distance away (just beyond the watering basin is good — refer to the "Planting your tree" section) and connect them with string, wire, or cloth to the tree. See Figure 11-6.

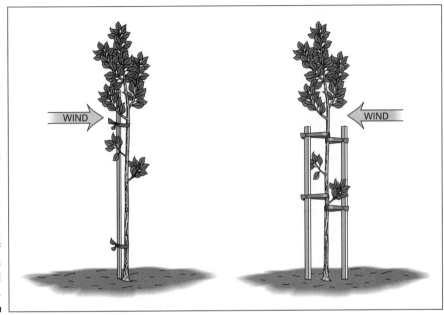

**Figure 11-6:**
Two
different
ways to
stake a tree.
Use the
method on
the left if
wind comes
from one
direction;
use the
method on
the right if
wind comes
from several
directions.

To prevent laceration of the tree trunk or branches from staking a tree, protect wire or twine with plastic or a length of hose, or use a softer material such as cloth strips.

If you drive two stakes into the ground on opposite sides of a small tree and connect each one to the trunk, the result is quite stable; using three stakes balances the tree even better, especially when you have prevailing strong winds. You can probably remove the stakes after the first year — their work is done, and the youngster is ready to stand on its own.

# Knowing Your Shrubs

Shrubs are the real workhorses of the home landscape. For all intents and purposes, regard them as permanent or long-term fixtures. They're something to see and appreciate in all seasons, bringing heft and stability to your yard. And after they reach mature size, you can maintain them that way with little trouble. So it behooves you to choose wisely, matching your yard's growing conditions and planning the look you want. In the following sections, we cover the different types of shrubs.

Consult your local garden centre or your provincial ministry of agriculture to find out which cultivars are best suited to, and hardy in, your area — and also to know which shrubs are invasive and potentially illegal to grow where you live.

# Nonflowering shrubs

Just like trees, shrubs may be deciduous or evergreen, needled or broadleaf (refer to the earlier "Knowing Your Trees" section). Here are some of your best bets for nonflowering shrubs (check with your local garden centre to see which specific varieties of these trees and shrubs are best suited to your area):

- ✔ **Evergreen needled:** Some ideal needled shrubs include Japanese yews, mugo pine, junipers, boxwood, dwarf conifer, and arborvitae.

  Some herbs also fit this category, such as sage, lavender, oregano, thyme, and rosemary. See Chapter 14 for information on herbs.

- ✔ **Evergreen broadleaf:** Broadleaf shrubs that keep their leaves year-round include Japanese pieris, mountain laurels, boxwood, rhododendron and azalea ('P.J.M.' is said to be the hardiest of all rhodos — it's hardy to Zone 4 and is a reliable bloomer in Zone 4b but not 4a; in ten years it can reach more than a metre, or 39 inches, tall), cotoneaster, wintergreen, barberry, mahonia, euonymus, and various hollies.

- ✔ **Deciduous:** If you want shrubs that drop their leaves every year, consider privet, beautyberry and snowberry (both retain their berries for winter), alpine currant, spirea, and various willows.

  Some deciduous shrubs can give you a fantastic show before shedding their leaves. Favourite shrubs for spectacular fall colour include barberry, aronia, winged euonymus (burning bush), blueberry, viburnum, sumac cultivars, dwarf fothergilla, some hydrangeas, cotoneaster, and smoke bush.

# Flowering shrubs

Flowering shrubs give you the most bang for your buck. You get the benefit of their foliage all season long, so they're a substantial presence in your yard while other flowers — annuals and perennials — come and go at their feet. But these shrubs also contribute pretty flowers. Some shrubs flower in spring, summer, and even the fall, but spring-flowering shrubs are the most common.

Spring-flowering shrubs come in many hues, and matches are fun to make when you're viewing the yard as a whole. Bloom times may or may not match up, though. (If only bridal-veil spirea, frothing with lacy white flowers, bloomed at the same time as the white magnolia!) Of course, in different parts of the country, spring may be extended so that you don't get much overlap, whereas in colder areas, such as in the Prairies, the same spring bloom is compressed into a much shorter time, so you see much more overlap.

From time to time, you need to prune flowering shrubs, mainly to shape them. The right timing is important, or you may accidentally cut off the buds before they have a chance to flower! Consult "Pruning for shape and rejuvenation," later in this chapter, for details.

Some flowering shrubs are deciduous and some aren't. Deciduous azaleas are, of course, deciduous, whereas evergreen azaleas and rhododendrons are not.

Favourite spring bloomers include lilac, spirea, forsythia, daphne, ceanothus (California lilac, West Coast only), rhododendron and azalea, heather, winter jasmine (hardy to Zone 7, occasionally to Zone 6), mock orange, viburnum, serviceberry, and fothergilla. If you want to look into obtaining bushes that sometimes bloom in summer or early fall, look into roses (refer to Chapter 9), broom, hydrangea, clethra, potentilla, rose-of-Sharon, butterfly bush, glossy abelia, abutilon (flowering maple), and golden rain tree.

# Planning Practical Uses for Bushes

Sometimes gardeners grow shrubs in groups, rows, or masses — for purely practical reasons, not just for their beauty. Of course, their beauty is a nice plus! For best results, plant the young shrubs close together but not so close that they soon crowd one another (which leads to misshapen growth and poor health). Finding out and planning for their mature size can help you space them appropriately.

Here are some possible uses and recommendations for shrubs:

✔ **Visual screens and sound barriers:** A boundary of shrubs around a patio or deck or along a property line does more than screen out a view of the outside world (your neighbour's house, driveway, or trash bins or a busy street). A boundary creates a sense of enclosure and intimacy, and it may also cut down on noise — a nice plus. Some good choices include holly, rhododendron and azalea, hydrangea, privet, red twig dogwood, and rose. For year-round privacy, be sure to choose evergreen plants such as nest spruce, evergreen types of euonymus, mugo pine, columnar cedars, junipers, and hollies.

✔ **Hedge or fence:** Closely planted shrubs, shoulder to shoulder, can act as a living fence along a property line or anywhere you need to put up a barrier. People and animals are discouraged from crossing, and the hedge looks a lot nicer and softer than many fences may look. Some good choices include mountain laurel, holly, caragana, chokeberry, yew, abelia, columnar cedars, and privet.

✔ **Foundation:** A traditional use of shrubs is to hide a home's concrete or stone foundation from view. As side benefits, foundation shrubs help integrate your home into your landscape and may help hold in warmth in winter and coolness in summer. Some good deciduous choices include spirea, forsythia, elderberry, bluebeard, dwarf fothergilla, flowering quince, and hydrangea; good evergreen choices include aucuba, nandina (also called heavenly bamboo), holly, cotoneaster, firethorn, daphne, rhododendron, spruce, and yew.

# Planting Shrubs

A shrub needs elbow room. Eventually, it'll reach its mature size, and growth will slow and stabilize. At that point, the shrub shouldn't be crowding other plants, including other shrubs and your flower garden, nor should it be encroaching on areas where you need to walk or keep things, including garden furniture. The ultimate height and width of the plants are things you need to plan for even before you buy your shrubs.

Know the limits; find out the projected mature size of the shrubs you want ahead of time. This information ought to be on the nursery tag or on a label on the pot; otherwise, someone on the nursery staff can tell you, or you can look it up. Read on for some planting info.

## Deciding when to plant your shrubs

As with trees, plant in the spring! This timing gives young plants an opportunity to establish themselves in your yard — a few months in which to develop roots that both anchor and fuel the show this year and for years to come. Local nurseries have the best and broadest selection waiting for you in spring.

Fall planting is also possible, right after summer's heat begins to dissipate and well before a frost is expected — four to six weeks before frost is a good time frame. Gardeners in mild-winter climates tend to have better luck because of the longer spell of hospitable weather. Either way, though, don't expect significant above-ground growth (new leaves or flower buds); some root development at this point can give new shrubs a jumpstart on next spring. To help the plants prepare for dormancy, don't fertilize fall-planted shrubs.

Avoid summer plantings, even if the shrubs are on sale! Summer heat and sun are stressful for newly planted shrubs, and they may struggle, dropping leaves and buds. If you simply must, coddle the youngsters by rigging up some temporary shade (a burlap enclosure, for example) and giving them plentiful water.

## Situating your shrubs

Where to plant your shrubs has as much to do with the ground quality as with the location. A single shrub, sited solo and out in the open, is what landscapers call a *specimen plant*. People view it from all angles. So attend to the ground below (is it good soil, or soil that can be improved, and free of obstructions, including tree roots and utility lines?), and attend to the space around (will it have enough space to grow and reach its full potential?).

Shrubs are great in rows or sweeps; as screens, barriers, or hedges; and as foundation plants. For best results, clear the area in advance and make sure the shrub isn't too close to a building, fence, or other obstruction that may inhibit or halt its growth. Depending on how many shrubs you're installing, either dig a line of individual planting holes or make a big, long trench.

The concept of planting shrub borders isn't new, but it goes in and out of garden fashion. The idea is to plant a group or row of shrubs that are different sorts, weaving together a compatible, textured show. It can have an informal or wild look, or it can be an artful tapestry. Because the different plants have different growth habits or profiles, you may need to intervene from time to time with your clippers or loppers to keep the look you want and to discourage more aggressive growers from dominating.

Pay attention to your lines of sight if you're planting in the front yard. A shrub set too close to the road can make pulling out of the driveway a harrowing experience.

## Perfecting your shrub-planting skills

Amending the planting hole is usually a good, practical idea. If you know your yard's soil isn't that great, or if your new shrub has a particular soil requirement (for instance, rhododendrons prefer acidic soil), by all means, make soil adjustments. The general rule is half native soil and half organically rich amendments (which can be any or all of the following: topsoil, compost, dehydrated manure, loam, or slightly moistened peat moss). Chapter 4 has more info on soil amendments.

For the shrub to receive the maximum benefits of the improved soil, make the planting hole as big as you figure the root ball will become over time (the rule here is that the root ball ultimately will become as deep and wide as the plant above is tall and wide).

In the next few sections, we give you a few more details on how to plant your bushes based on the form they're in when you buy them, whether as container plants, bareroot plants, or balled and burlapped plants. For a general approach to planting bushes, no matter what form they arrive in, apply the info in the earlier section "Planting your tree." (Follow all the instructions save for the last one, on staking.)

### Container shrubs

Suppliers commonly sell shrubs in pots. Your main concern is that the plant not be too terribly rootbound. Tilt the pot and nudge out the root system for a look, if possible. The roots should fill the pot but not be an impenetrable mass; some roots may be questing out the bottom drainage holes. (If the root system seems small for the pot or dirt spills out all around, the shrub is not well rooted; bypass the plant in favour of a better specimen.)

When you're ready to plant back at your house and you coax the root ball out of the pot for the last time, you can help encourage new growth. Using your fingers, tease tight roots loose, especially on the bottom. If the side roots are fairly tight and resistant, you may score them very lightly with a sharp knife 6 millimetres (¼ inch) deep on four sides to inspire fresh root growth when the plant's in the ground.

### Bareroot shrubs

Occasionally, shrubs are available earlier in the season or via mail order as bareroot plants. These plants are dormant plants and, truthfully, don't look too promising, but don't be fooled. You should see no evidence of green growth on the top part. The root system should look healthy, though, with crisp white or brownish roots. If you have wiry, black, or limp roots — only a few — clip them off; if you see a lot of these, the plant is in rough shape — reject it.

Bareroot shrubs can go into the ground earlier in the spring, because they're still dormant and won't be traumatized by the cooler soil and air. Properly planted, they come to life gradually along with the rest of nature.

### Balled-and-burlapped bushes

Larger shrubs and field-dug ones are often sold balled and burlapped later in spring, when freezing weather is past in cold-winter climates, and sometimes fall through spring in mild-winter climates. The root system is wrapped up in a protective cover of burlap that's laced securely in place. This wrapping allows you to get the plant from nursery to home without making a mess.

Eyeballing this mass can give you an idea of how big a hole you need to dig — aim for at least several centimetres deeper and wider than the root ball. A hole the size of the mature plant, partially filled with a mix of native and amended soil, may be even better.

Prior to planting a balled-and-burlapped shrub, remove or cut off all the burlap and twine. In the past, some landscapers and gardeners simply opened up the bottom of the bundle and put the plant in the hole, leaving the remaining burlap and string to rot over time in the hole. But this tack is no longer advisable — today's burlap and twine may contain plastic, which doesn't biodegrade. Take it all off!

# Caring for Your Shrubs

A well-cared-for shrub is beautiful and healthy, and it remains so. Frequent attention to the plant's needs is crucial for the first year or two, less so as the years go by and the plant becomes an established part of your yard. The following sections give you the basic information that you need to take very good care of your bushes.

## Watering your shrubs

When first planted, and indeed throughout the entire first growing season, water your new shrubs deeply and often. Deliver the water directly to the root area (a hose trickling slowly into the basin you created on planting day is perfect). Twice-a-week watering may be necessary through the spring and summer months — slow down and stop at the beginning of fall, sending the plants into winter with one last good soaking.

A young shrub can't tolerate dry spells and drought because its roots are still developing and may not dive very deep into the ground. An older, established plant can withstand drought better but shows signs of distress by dropping petals or having unopened buds and dried, curled, or yellowing leaves — don't let the situation come to that. (Dramatic cycles of soaking and drying out are also stressful for a plant and weaken it, making the shrub more vulnerable to pests and disease. Neglect becomes a downward spiral.)

Lay down a layer of mulch, at least 2 to 5 centimetres (1 or 2 inches) thick, in spring or summer, all across the shrub's root zone. This mulch helps retain soil moisture. It also keeps encroaching weeds or lawn grass, competitors for soil moisture, at bay. Keep mulch a couple of centimetres away from stems.

## Fertilizing your shrubs

For newly planted shrubs, some people have found starter solutions useful. These solutions consist of water-soluble fertilizers (usually high in phosphorous) and vitamins and hormones that stimulate new root growth. Regular fertilizing can begin in the second year to

✔ Boost overall plant health and vigour

✔ Help green up the leaves and encourage thicker foliage

✔ Promote more buds and, thus, more flowers

Apply a general-purpose garden fertilizer, diluted according to the label directions. For best results, feed every two weeks or monthly throughout the growing season.

If your yard's soil is good or the plants seem fine without fertilizer, of course, leave well enough alone.

## Pruning for shape and rejuvenation

Most shrubs require at least some pruning to control growth and to shape the plants. Always use sharp, clean tools; try clippers for the smaller branches and loppers for the larger ones. Electric hedge trimmers can be useful when shearing hedges (see the sidebar "Shearing hedges") but aren't recommended for other pruning. Hand tools do the job more precisely with cleaner cuts (refer to Chapter 5 for info on tools).

Generally, late winter or early spring is the best time to work on your shrubs because that's when they're dormant (but see the following info about spring-flowering shrubs and shrubs that grow fruit). Also, if the shrubs are deciduous, they aren't cloaked in foliage at these times and you're better able to see and assess the branches' forms and condition and the plant's overall profile.

Shrubs grown for their flowers that bloom in spring and early summer are the exception to the spring-pruning rule. If you cut them in early spring, you remove the coming season's show. Wait until just after blooming is finished. The shrub gets time to recover and to generate new flower buds for the coming year's blossoms before winter comes.

Knowing when to prune shrubs that you enjoy for both fruits and flowers (such as viburnum and rose) is hard because you're forced to sacrifice either some of the flowers or some of the berries or hips. Your best bet is to split the difference: Do some trimming right after the bloom, and then cut the plant a bit more in the fall (in the case of viburnums, you can call the fall pruning *berry harvesting* — the berries are very decorative, perfect for holiday swags and wreaths).

Getting an overgrown shrub — one that's too big, too wide, or growing thick and wild — back into shape takes time and patience, but it's possible, and you'll be so proud of the results. This pruning isn't hard work, but it does take several years. Follow these steps and the illustration in Figure 11-7:

1. **Remove all nonnegotiable growth.**

   Cut out all dead, diseased, broken, or damaged wood. Cut this growth right down to the ground and get it out of there. The shrub looks better immediately!

# Shearing hedges

*Shearing* is a term used to describe the pruning method used most frequently to create or shape hedges. Instead of hand pruners, you use hedge shears, the hand or electric type, to do the job.

When pruning shrubs, try to maintain the natural shape of the plants. A common mistake is to shape shrubs with a wide top and narrow base. A lack of sunlight shades out lower interior growth, resulting in a leafless, woody base.

Unfortunately, many gardeners use or misuse the shearing technique to shape shrubs into balls or other geometric shapes. Your shrubs beg you not to do this — it results in a yard full of shrub lollipops! The shapes look very artificial, and after you start this process, you're forced to keep it up every year. Save yourself work and your shrubs embarrassment by pruning them to their natural form.

2. **Take out a few of the older stems.**

   Don't remove all of them — not more than about a third for starters. Let the plant recover for a year before you decide to remove even more.

3. **Shorten the remaining stems late the next winter or in early spring to just a bit lower than the height you want the shrub to be.**

   Then let the shrub grow — the wounds will soon be hidden from view, and in ensuing years, you can maintain the plant at the size you want.

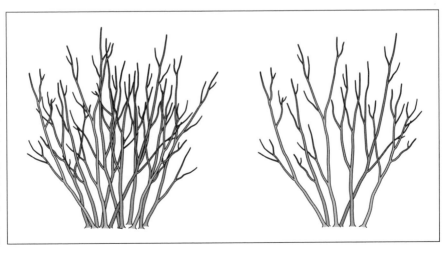

**Figure 11-7:** Rejuvenation pruning, or thinning, for shrubs. Left is the bush before pruning, and right is the bush after pruning.

# Chapter 12

# Climbers and Crawlers: Growing Vines and Groundcovers

. . . . . . . . . . . . . . . . . . . . . . . . . . . . . . . . . . . . . . . .

. . . . . . . . . . . . . . . . . . . . . . . . . . . . . . . . . . . . . . . .

**P**eople give so much attention to flowers, both annual and perennial (refer to Chapters 6 and 7, respectively), that they sometimes forget the rest of the story — or rather, they forget that gardeners have other important possibilities for their gardens.

When you include vines, you decorate the vertical plane of a fence, wall, or trellis. When you add some groundcovers, the horizontal plane of the yard gains a living carpet, an attractive alternative to a span of cement or gravel or lawn grass. Some plants, notably English ivy and wintercreeper, can fill either role.

Vines and groundcovers are very important in gardening because they embrace and effectively soften the floor, walls, and ceiling of your garden. Properly planted and, in the case of vines, supported, these versatile plants are both easy to grow and essential. Use vines and groundcovers to make the most of limited space or to make a sprawling area more intimate. This chapter gives you the information you need to get started.

## Looking at How Vines Hold On

Vines are interesting plants. Consider this: Vines have evolved to seize and enjoy a niche in the crowded world of plants, opportunistically going wherever the available space and adequate sunlight are. If their roots are secure and nurtured in the soil below, the top growth of vines is amazingly flexible. A vine can clamber through other plants, up or sideways as needed, and navigate tight spots until it arrives where it can bask and thrive. Pretty impressive!

Vines have adaptations that help them in their journeys. Or to be more specific, vines have their ways of hanging on as they climb. Some twine, using a stem, leaf, or tendril to do so, and need a support to cling to or wrap around; others adhere on their own to a vertical surface using rootlike growths along their stems (sometimes called holdfasts) or suction cups at the ends of small, modified tendrils; still others are not vines in the true sense because they don't grow any kind of twining or clinging parts, but they have long, flexible stems that can be trained as vines. This information is important to know because it affects the area or support structure you choose for your vine — you don't want damage to the structure or support, and you want the going to be easy. The following sections give you an overview of climbing methods, also illustrated in Figure 12-1.

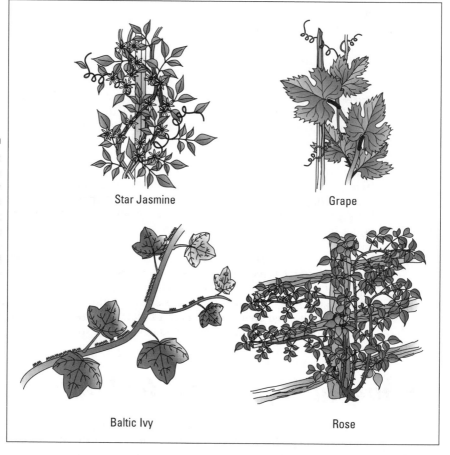

**Figure 12-1:**
Star jasmine climbs by twining its stems; grapes climb with tendrils; Baltic ivy climbs via holdfasts; and climbing roses tend to sprawl and need a support such as a fence.

Star Jasmine

Grape

Baltic Ivy

Rose

# Twining

Twining is the simplest means for a vine to climb onward and upward. In *twining,* a vine's stems spiral around a support on their own and are thus anchored. Interestingly, some vines prefer to ascend clockwise, others counterclockwise. You can peer closely at your vine to discover which it is. Or you can try this fun backyard experiment: Find a stray stem and wind it around the support. If the stem stays in place an hour or half a day later, you guessed correctly; if it stubbornly unwinds and slings itself back into the open air, you guessed wrong.

The key to a successful display is to provide ample support, or supplementary support (such as strings attached to a wooden trellis), to guide growth in the direction you want. Favourite twining vines include morning glory, star jasmine, moonflower, and wisteria.

# Tendrils

*Tendrils* aren't the vine's stems, but thin, short appendages on the vine that do the grabbing and attaching work. Technically, tendrils may be modified branches or leaves. Though small, vine tendrils are often quite tough and resilient, hanging on even in high winds or blustery storms or when pushed about by passing people or animals.

The key to a successful display is matching the thickness of the support or parts of the support to the tendrils' size, so they can grab on and wind around more than once for extra stability. Generally, thinner is better; if you still need sturdiness due to the plant's overall weight, try steel, cast iron, or stout plastic. Plastic netting stapled to a lattice fence works well for vines with thin stems and delicate tendrils or twining leaves. Favourite tendrilled vines include sweet pea, grape, clematis, and gourds.

# Adhesive discs and holdfasts

*Adhesive discs* are actually small, modified tendrils, with the same toughness and resilience as tendrils but with an extra boost: Each tendril has a disc-like suction cup at the end. These amazing structures afford a vine great adaptability — the vine can grab on to many kinds of supports, especially relatively smooth walls.

Though adhesive discs thrive with a smooth wall, they don't do as well on rougher textures, such as brick or stone, although they will adhere. A favourite adhesive-disc vine is Virginia creeper.

Some vines, like climbing hydrangea, Baltic ivy, wintercreeper, and trumpet vine, attach themselves with small, rootlike structures, along their stems, sometimes called holdfasts. These vines thrive growing up slightly rough surfaces like bricks, or stone. They will also grow over and through structures: Over several seasons you can hide unsightly chain-link fences with a combination of ivy or wintercreeper (both are evergreen, so they look nice in winter) and trumpet vine (for colour and attracting hummingbirds in summer).

Vines with adhesive discs or holdfasts can wend their way into porous surfaces like the mortar between bricks, eventually breaking down the mortar.

## Sprawling

Vines in the sprawling group don't have the advantages of the others. All they really have going for them is long, pliable stems that adapt and look good when encouraged to grow upward. Yep, *encouraged.* You have to help by hooking or tying them along their lengths so they can scramble in the right direction and stay on their supports.

The key to encouraging a successful display of sprawling vines is to start tying or otherwise attaching the stems to the support early and often. Use wire, wire hooks, twist ties from the kitchen, string, twine, yarn, or rags. If you're worried about abrading the stems, opt for the softer material. Loop the tie once around the stem and once around the support instead of tying the plant and support directly to one another. If you don't want the ties to show, use thin ones or green ones that the vine's foliage can hide.

Favourite sprawling vines include climbing roses (if thorny, the thorns may prove nominally helpful in grabbing and staying on the support) and sweet potato vine. Cherry tomatoes fit this category, too.

# Choosing the Right Vines for Your Garden

Ask yourself what you want from a vine. Do you have a good spot, or can you create one? Some vines are big, rambling plants; others can fill and remain in their allotted spaces. Some vines offer temporary coverage, and others are long lasting. Figure out whether you want flowers or fruit and whether you want the vine for part of the growing season or all of it.

The following sections cover the kinds of vines available and how you can match a vine to your wants and needs and the environment you can offer. (***Note:*** You may want to choose the support before choosing the vine. If so, see the later section called "Planting and Supporting Vines.")

# Considering your basic options

Like other plants, vines fall into annual and perennial categories. Read on for info on which kind of vine may be a good fit for your garden.

## Annuals and tender perennials

If you want quick gratification, annuals and tender perennials are for you. The vines grow quickly. If they're genuine annuals, they're capable of growing from seed to plant to flowering-and-fruiting plant over the course of one growing season. If they're tender perennials, they can accomplish much the same thing but benefit from a head start indoors (because they can't go outside until all danger of frost is past).

Annuals can't survive a typical Canadian winter with freezing temperatures, so you have to replace these vines each year. As for tender perennials, unless you live in the warmest parts of British Columbia, your best bet is to consider a tender vine an annual. Yank it out in the fall, after cold weather withers its growth (or let winter kill it if you're feeling lazy), and then buy a new one or try something else next year. Favourite tender perennials include black-eyed Susan vine, cup-and-saucer vine, mandevilla, jasmine, and passionflower; favourite annual vines include moonflower, morning glory, climbing nasturtium, and annual sweet pea.

Can you cheat? Of course! Accomplished gardeners consider it a badge of honour to succeed in growing something that's considered not hardy in their area. If you're really fond of a tender vine, cut it back, dig up as much of the root ball as possible, pot it, and keep it inside during the cold months. Put it in a nonfreezing place and water sparingly so its growth slows down, yet not so little that the plant dries out and perishes.

## Hardy perennials

For a longer-term, dependable investment in your garden, perennial vines are practical choices. Much like the perennials in your flower beds, perennial vines typically spend their first season getting established. An old gardener's saying describes the growth pattern of most perennial vines well: "The first year, they sleep; the second year, they creep; and the third year, they leap!"

*Hardy* really means cold hardy, and it indicates a plant that can survive weather that goes down to freezing — 0°C (32°F) or below. The plant's foliage may fall off, but its roots remain safely viable under the cold soil and snow and ice. Just as with other perennial plants, hardy vines benefit from a little extra protection over the winter months; namely, several centimetres of mulch over the root area.

In ensuing seasons, these vines return reliably and put on a good show year after glorious year. Please note that over time their growth may get woody and some pruning may be necessary. Some favourite perennial vines include Baltic ivy, American bittersweet, Dutchman's pipe, clematis, climbing hydrangea, akebia (also called chocolate vine), honeysuckle, hardy kiwi, silver lace vine, trumpet creeper, Virginia creeper, and wintercreeper.

Perennial vines can differ in their foliage:

- ✔ **Deciduous:** The definition of a *deciduous* vine is one that sheds its foliage at the end of the growing season (just like a deciduous tree — refer to Chapter 11). And just like a deciduous tree, the vine may treat you to a colourful fall foliage display first. Winter is a dormant period, and then the vine revives the following spring. Favourites include Virginia creeper, clematis (the fluffy fall seed heads are an attraction), roses, silver lace vine (a mass of late-summer flowers), trumpet vine, hardy kiwi, and climbing hydrangea (when the leaves fall off, you can admire the handsome, shedding red bark).

- ✔ **Evergreen:** Evergreen vines keep their foliage over the winter months (individual leaves do get replaced over time, but you don't run into wholesale or dramatic shedding time). In colder areas, the leaves may look rather freeze-dried, but they hang on, and many hold their berries for at least part of the winter, until the birds eat them. No matter where you live, if you don't want a barren-looking winter in your yard, evergreen vines are worthwhile. Favourites include various kinds of ivy, winter-creeper, and firethorn.

If a vine is *marginally hardy,* meaning only a zone away from yours, it may survive a mild winter in your garden. Or you can increase its odds of survival by growing it in the warmest spot in your garden (in a warm microclimate — for more info on this concept and how to exploit it, refer to Chapter 3) and mulching it well when winter approaches. Be prepared to lose the top growth (everything above ground); the aim is to keep the roots alive so they can regenerate next spring.

## Sizing up your vines

Keep your head when vine shopping. Although the flowers or foliage of a certain vine may win your heart, you need to find out about its growth habit and pace before you commit yourself. Some very pretty vines are — to use the wry term of an experienced landscaper — house eaters. Wisteria branches have been known to separate gutters and support beams from a house. Hop vines grow very fast, and if they run out of space, they may send tendrils out to grasp at passersby.

To avoid scenarios of an out-of-control vine, spend a few minutes assessing the spot where you want to place a vine. *How high is it?* For upward growth, you can be fairly indulgent, though you probably don't want something that'll overgrow the house. *How broad is it?* is the more pressing question. Keep these general dimensions in mind when you go vine shopping.

So how do you find out whether your vine will politely stay within the confines of your arbour or attempt a hostile takeover of the Maritime provinces? Mature vine size is usually expressed as a range — for instance, "2.5 to 3 metres (8 to 10 feet) tall and up to 1.5 metres (5 feet) wide" — because, of course, dimensions vary according to the plant's health as well as the growing conditions and care you provide. Check the nursery label, catalogue description, or a reference book for a good idea of a vine's potential size.

Make sure you allow elbow room. If a vine's appointed spot is too narrow, you'll be trimming and shaping constantly. Poor air circulation in a tight spot can lead to fungal diseases that mar the plant's appearance. Count on planting most vines at least 30 centimetres (a foot) away from their supports, for starters. A spot that's too confining is, frankly, a darn shame; vines are at their best when allowed to be their exuberant selves.

## Examining site considerations for vines

You can find a vine for almost every part of the garden. The idea is to make a match so the plant thrives. Examine your gardening site carefully and watch out for the following variables when deciding on the vines you want.

### Amount of sunlight

How much sun reaches a vine can have a big effect on the plant's quality of life. Check out the following sun conditions:

- ✔ **Sun:** Lots of vines like full sun, growing lustily in its warmth and producing plenty of foliage, flowers, and fruit or seed heads. But vigorous growth requires energy to fuel it, and plentiful sun alone isn't enough. Make sure your sun-loving vine has fertile soil and ample water. Favourite sun-loving vines include ornamental grape, hops, black-eyed Susan vine, climbing nasturtium, morning glory, and trumpet vine.

- ✔ **Partial shade:** Plenty of vines prosper in part-day sun, filtered sun, and eastern- or northeastern-facing exposures. Indeed, some cooling shade keeps the plant looking lush, and its flowers and fruit are less prone to fading or falling off prematurely. Favourite partial-shade vines include Baltic ivy, variegated porcelain vine, and climbing hydrangea.

✔ **Shade:** Yes, some vines do just fine in shady spots, some even tolerating life on the north side of your house or under the shelter of tall trees. Not surprisingly, their main attraction tends to be their leaves. Use these plants to create a cool, soothing oasis from the blazing heat of summer. Favourite shade vines include ivies, akebia, and wintercreeper.

## Soil quality

The majority of vines prefer fertile soil that's neither soggy nor dry. Obviously, prepared ground is important so that the roots can establish themselves and expand without running into obstructions, so it's always wise to prepare the spot ahead of time: Dig down about 30 centimetres (1 foot) and mix in some compost, humus, or rotted manure.

Some vines, such as hardy kiwi, do better when the soil is slightly acidic; others, such as the clematis, like it slightly *sweeter* (more alkaline), so add some lime to the planting area if necessary. (Test your soil first; refer to Chapter 4 for info on soil tests.) But most vines are happy with average soil — which is what most people have, anyway.

## Weather exposure

The majority of vines appreciate a little shelter, which can come from their support, a wall or fence, or even just the nearby plants of your garden. If you grow a vine out in the open, winds can dry it out and may tear it off its support. (In other words, vines are team players, not solo performers. But isn't that why you want to invite some into your garden?)

## The choosy clematis: Water, water, and more water

It used to be a maxim of gardening that clematises liked to have their roots cool and shaded and their foliage in warm sun, but now it's thought that what clematises really wanted all along was lots and lots to drink. Cool, shaded roots help hold water in the soil.

The clematis vine is one thirsty plant. Expert clematis growers tell us the plant needs at least 10 litres (2½ gallons) of water each and every week, and after it's had a good drink, you can almost see it stretch out and start to grow. In fact,

we're told a clematis can benefit from as much as 20 litres (5 gallons) a week.

Direct a gentle spray of water on the roots, being careful not to dislodge the soil. The best method is to place the hose nozzle or a soaker hose on the soil beside the plant and then let the water drizzle in slowly. Add a thick layer of mulch to hold moisture in the earth. Feed your clematis well and water it generously during its first two years of growth, and it'll do you proud.

# Planting and Supporting Vines

Planting a vine is really no different from planting either an annual or a perennial (refer to Chapters 6 and 7). What really matters with a vine is how you plan to support it. Whatever you choose for supporting and displaying your vines, be sure it's equal to the job. It's a pain in the neck to have to keep pruning back a heavy plant, a disappointment to witness a rampant vine knock down a support or cause it to lean, and a hassle to have to constantly intervene to send growth in what you consider the correct direction. Head off these problems at the pass.

In fact, your best bet is to *first* decide on, and find a place in your garden for, a support; then choose an appropriate vine. But if you choose the vine first, at least do smart, practical matchmaking with the support.

## Giving vines a little backup: Trellises, fences, and arbours

You may buy trellises, fences, and arbours fully or partially assembled, or as kits, from a variety of sources — home and garden centres, hardware stores, and specialty catalogues. Figure 12-2 shows you a sampling of the types of supports available.

Shop around not only for the best price but also for the best quality. A support structure isn't the place to cut corners. Some shopping considerations follow.

### Evaluating materials and construction

Supports generally come in wood (cedar or redwood are best), metal, or plastic. Consider the support's construction: Examine the width of the individual slats or pieces, of course, but also inspect the intersections and joints. Are they strong and secure? Braces may be optional or necessary, and so may hooks that help hold the item in place (to attach a trellis securely to a wall, for instance; some supports just can't stand upright alone).

Knowing how the vine clings to the support can give you some hints about ideal support shape or materials. See "Looking at How Vines Hold On," earlier in this chapter, for details.

### Staying grounded: Anchorage

Remember that in order to be securely anchored in your landscape, the support has to be pushed well into the ground — 30 centimetres (a foot) deep is not too much, depending, of course, on the weight of the mature plant that it'll bear. Factor in that reduction in height when looking at the support when you're buying it, as well as when envisioning it plant-draped in your garden.

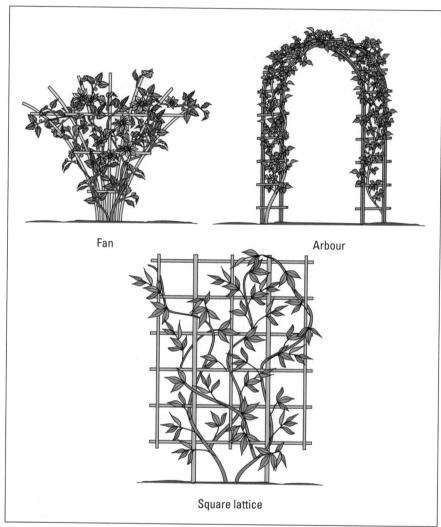

Fan

Arbour

Square lattice

**Figure 12-2:**
Typical
store-
bought
supports for
vines — a
fan trellis,
an arbour,
and a
lattice.

# Using trees and shrubs as living supports

Yes, a vine can twine and climb another plant, particularly a tree or shrub. It happens all the time in nature; walk through any woodland, and you can see plenty of examples. But you may be worried that the vine will steal the show. Or smother the living support. Legitimate concerns! Of course, you want to make a match. Don't pair a heavy, aggressive vine with a young dogwood tree, for example. More-mature trees are more welcoming and less daunted. Avoid vigorous twiners like honeysuckle and wisteria, which can literally strangle and squeeze the life out of a tree or shrub over time.

The match should also be aesthetically successful. Trees or shrubs that either don't flower or have only a fleeting display are best, because you don't want a clash or competition in the colour department. Evergreen trees, shrubs, and hedge plants are more accommodating this way.

One practical concern is soil. Both the vine and its host need everything the soil has to offer — physical support for their root systems, nutrients, and water. One way around this potential conflict is to start the vine growing farther away and train it toward its tree or shrub, which it'll eventually ascend. Or you may be able to place a potted vine at the base of the host plant — you just have to remember to stop by often to feed and water the vine (Chapter 16 can tell you about container gardening). In any event, ideally the soil is as good as possible for both plants so that they can both be healthy and happy.

Sometimes an old tree dies or has to be cut back to a bare trunk or stump. A vine turned loose over such a relic can turn a potential eyesore into a garden highlight.

# Maintaining Perennial Vines through Pruning

You may have an idealized vision of a vine in your garden, draped lushly over a trellis, a pergola, or even a gazebo, alive with beautiful flowers. Just realize that to get from here to there, you have to do some work. Vines don't grow quickly and to exactly the right height before stopping to coast on their loveliness.

Perennial vines look their best when you cut them properly. Pruning can and does help a reluctant vine bloom. But first, make sure you've attended to the more obvious requirements:

- **Sufficient sunlight:** If the plants don't receive enough sunlight, removing some crowding stems helps.

- **Regular watering and fertilizing:** A thirsty, undernourished vine jettisons expendable growth — namely buds and flowers — in favour of the survival of its leaves.

If the sunlight, water, and fertilizer check out, some judicious pruning can jump-start flowering. Thin out old, unproductive wood in the hopes that new growth will fare better. Never cut back severely. Many perennial vines bloom on *old wood* — wood that grew the previous year. That's why you don't want to chop out all of it. *New wood* simply means this year's new stems. These newcomers may yet be productive if they have room to grow and you meet their needs.

One thing to try is *root pruning,* or cutting back some of the root system without digging up the entire plant. This technique can jolt a plant into fresh productivity.

Pruning, of course, is essential for maintaining the shape of the plant, and the growing season is the time to trim your vine to stay within its limits. No trauma or harm to the plant will result. In early spring, remove dead and damaged growth, and thin out old wood while you're at it. If you act before the vine leafs out, the wood and stems are easier to see and work with. Also, cuts don't bother a dormant plant — the coming spring growth surge will allow it to recover and replace stems.

Always take off dead and wayward branches at the base of the vine, or as near as you can get. Sharp clippers or loppers make the work so much easier (refer to Chapter 5 for info on the tools of the trade)! Remove dead branches any time you see them — winter, spring, summer, or fall. They're not going to come back to life, so timing is not an issue! Still, the best time to remove wayward branches is spring, before the plant is fully clothed in leaves and buds. Take out branches that are turning back toward the plant's centre, rubbing against others, or heading off in the wrong direction.

Don't be afraid to cut back stems that are going the wrong way or refusing to remain on the support. Keep after your vine as it grows, editing out wayward stems as you spot them and training and tying the rest in the way you want. This practice is especially important while the plant is still young. Older vines get obstinate.

# Looking at Groundcovers, a Living Carpet

By definition, a *groundcover* is a low-growing plant that naturally forms a colony or mat, making a living carpet in your garden. Groundcovers can be real problem solvers, growing where nothing else will (including lawn grass) and sprucing up otherwise undistinguished or difficult-to-landscape areas. Height is generally under 30 centimetres (a foot) or so, and often much lower, but more important to you is whether the plant can do the job you ask: provide good-looking coverage of its appointed spot.

In any event, the more you know about groundcovers, the more you may be sold on them. They're some of the most useful, easy-to-care-for plants you can have.

## Examining groundcover varieties

Gardeners can take advantage of various types of groundcovers — almost a staggering variety — so a good way to start is to make your choice based on the growing conditions already present in your yard. You still may have to make a few improvements prior to planting, such as cutting back encroaching or overhanging branches or making soil amendments, but the idea is to match the plant to the site. That way, the groundcover can prosper, and you can congratulate yourself on your gardening savvy.

Here's a sampling of the various groundcover forms and functions that may be available in your area:

- Sunlight

    - **Full sun:** Cheddar pinks, candytuft, blue rug juniper, potentilla, prairie smoke, creeping thyme, and sempervivums

    - **Partial shade:** Epimedium, bearberry, plumbago, cotoneaster, wintercreeper, Aaron's-beard (also known as creeping St.-John's-wort), lilyturf, sedum, and creeping phlox

    - **Full shade:** Bugleweed, European wild ginger, ivy, lily-of-the-valley, pachysandra, periwinkle, and sweet woodruff

- Drainage

    - **Dry or well-drained soil:** Sedum, prickly pear, pachysandra, ajuga, creeping thyme, and bush cinquefoil

    - **Moist ground:** Plumbago, lilyturf, epimedium, creeping phlox, European wild ginger, and lily-of-the-valley

- Basic appearance

    - **Shrubby looking:** Barberry, cotoneaster, bush cinquefoil, and juniper

    - **Delicate looking:** Epimedium, prairie smoke, creeping phlox, and sweet woodruff

    - **Evergreen:** Ivy, pachysandra, creeping juniper, bergenia, periwinkle, sweet box, skimmia, and wintercreeper

- Accessories and features

    - **Edible parts:** Cheddar pinks (flowers), sweet woodruff (leaves and flowers), thyme (leaves and flowers), and creeping rosemary (leaves and flowers)

    - **Inedible berries:** Cotoneaster, bearberry, sweet box, skimmia

    - **Attractive or showy flowers:** Candytuft, creeping phlox, epimedium, periwinkle, sweet box (fragrant), skimmia, and lily-of-the-valley

    - **Handsome foliage:** Epimedium, bugleweed, bergenia, lilyturf, ivy, pachysandra, dwarf hostas, and wintercreeper

### Enjoying flowering groundcovers

Like other perennial plants, many groundcovers bloom — some just for a week or two, others on and off for many weeks. A low-growing but flower-studded display adds a lot of charm to a garden. Just make sure the colour fits in with its surroundings.

Oh, yes: Be patient — let the groundcover get established for a year or two before expecting a good flower display. Favourite flowering groundcovers include cheddar pinks, candytuft, potentilla, plumbago, Aaron's-beard (also known as creeping St.-John's-wort), creeping phlox, lily-of-the-valley, and periwinkle.

Good growing conditions (especially fertile soil and ample sunshine) and consistent water inspire the best flowering performance.

### Taking foliage colour into consideration

A lot of garden colour flows from nature's bounty of green, so sophisticated garden designs often rely on green's infinite variety — from rich mint green to apple green to chartreuse and every shade in between. Mix and match various greens within a groundcover display, and you can enjoy a rich tapestry:

- **Variegated leaves:** Particularly in shade, leaves that are dappled, spotted, striped, or rimmed in white or gold really stand out and add welcome sparkle. Try lamium, dwarf hostas, or wintercreeper.

- **Purple, red, or burgundy leaves:** These colours have the effect of anchoring and giving solidity to groundcover displays because they look rich and substantial. Try heuchera or bugleweed.

- **Fall colour:** Like trees and shrubs, some groundcovers have good-looking foliage when the weather starts to turn cold. Try bearberry, cotoneaster, low-bush blueberry, or sedum, which has interesting flowers.

## Reaching out: How the groundcover spreads

A good groundcover is one that gets right to work, growing ever-outward and filling its assigned area. The right growing conditions, including decent soil and adequate water, certainly help this process along. But take a closer look at the groundcover you're considering. Its means of spreading is worth knowing so you can encourage it (and, should it become too eager or rampant in time, so you can manage it or rein it in). The following sections tell you a bit about how groundcovers reach out.

### Branching out from the crown

A groundcover that expands outward from the crown sends out stems that get ever-longer over time, but you can trace one stem all the way back to the centre of the original plant. Such groundcovers may need to be anchored or pegged in place at intervals to keep them where you want them or to guide them (see "Keeping groundcovers in shape: Pruning and pegging," later in this chapter). Examples of plants that branch out from the crown include creeping thyme, cotoneaster, and periwinkle.

### Sending out new roots

If the groundcover sends out roots along the stem or at nodes as the plant stems travel along the ground, new roots may drop down opportunistically into the soil at intervals. These new roots generate a new young plant. You can separate these young plants from the originating stem and even move them if you want; just be sure to treat them as gently and indulgently as any seedling. Of course, this ability can become a liability over time as the plant makes inroads into places where you didn't want it to go; in such a case, cutting back the advancing edge, especially early in the growing season, is often necessary. Examples of plants that shoot out new roots include ivy, wintercreeper, bugleweed, and pachysandra.

### Self-seeding

If a groundcover flowers and develops seeds at the season's end, the plant's natural inclination is to drop them in the vicinity. This practice means a new crop of seedlings will appear by next spring — and thus you have a self-seeding groundcover. Assuming you can count on this ability, you can get away with planting fewer individual plants at the outset. Examples of plants that usually propagate by seed include epimedium and bearberry.

Setting groundcover seedlings out in neat rows makes your display look more like a crop or vegetable-garden plan than the carpet you seek. For a more natural look, stagger the rows and make sure all plants are equidistant from one another in all directions. Instead of a large square or rectangle, grow groundcovers in a natural-looking swath. And try mixing two or three kinds of plants in largish patches to get what gardeners like to call a "tapestry" of plants.

Not all groundcovers are friendly characters. Some are greedy for space and like to take over, growing farther than you'd planned and edging out other plants. Examples include goutweed, which comes with all-green foliage or green-and-white variegated leaves, and snow-in-summer, which has small, downy grey leaves and abundant white flowers in summer. Both are attractive enough, but they're thugs in most gardens and should usually be avoided at all costs. But like all plants, sometimes they do have a place: They can be useful on large slopes or otherwise difficult-to-plant areas in a large country garden.

## Spacing out: Considering the room the groundcover takes up

Because the size definition of a groundcover is pretty loose, you're free to choose whatever appeals to you. But of course, try to pick a plant that fits whatever you want to get out of the site. Mature-plant dimensions are, or should be, on the plant's tag or container or included in a catalogue's plant description. Otherwise, you can certainly look the information up in a reference book or online. *Note:* Different cultivars of the same type of plant aren't always created equal. For instance, although some cotoneasters lie low and sprawl, others are practically bushes.

Here are your size options and what they can do for you:

✔ **Tall groundcovers:** Ground-covering plants that grow up to 30 centimetres (1 foot) or more in height have the advantage of creating a barrier. Pedestrians, kids on bikes, and pets are less apt to pass through. So use such plants at property lines or in an unfenced front yard, or even to landscape a curb strip. Examples include candytuft, creeping juniper, potentilla, bearberry, plumbago, Aaron's-beard (creeping St.-John's-wort), and some varieties of lilyturf.

✔ **Intermediate groundcovers:** These groundcovers are of moderate height, say, 20 to 30 centimetres (8 to 12 inches) high at most. These plants are ideal for creating low-maintenance sweeps and swathes, in shade or out in the open. You can place taller plants, including perennials and shrubs, beyond or among them — effectively, intermediate groundcovers simply set the stage. Examples include some varieties of lilyturf, epimedium, lily-of-the-valley, creeping phlox, and candytuft.

✔ **Low-growing groundcovers:** True carpeters — under 15 centimetres (6 inches) high or even less — are better in broader, more irregular-shaped settings such as under a shade tree, in a side yard, or flanking a walkway or entrance area. Low-growers can create a transition from hard surfaces to garden. When established, some withstand foot traffic, some do not. Examples include creeping thyme, cheddar pinks, sedums and sempervivums, bugleweed, prairie smoke, and sweet woodruff.

In terms of spreading, knowing the ultimate reach of a single groundcover plant is worthwhile simply so you know how many you need to plant. The goal is for them to mix and interlink and overlap so that, ultimately, you can't distinguish individual plants. If you overplant, you can yank out surplus plants. If you underplant, on purpose or not, fill in the open areas with weed-suppressing mulch until the plants reach their mature size and inhibit invading weeds on their own.

You can buy fewer plants and space them 30 centimetres (a foot) or more apart and then wait for them to fill in whatever way they will (which, depending on the plant, its growth rate, and the hospitality of the site, can take one or more seasons). If you're impatient or in a hurry, you can get more plants and space them closely so the carpet fills in well in the first year.

## *Exploring site considerations for groundcovers*

Some groundcovers are well adapted to challenging growing conditions. So rather than struggle to change or improve that troublesome spot in your yard, why not turn it over to a groundcover that's likely to thrive? Here's what to look for in the site you have in mind:

✔ **In the shade:** The quality of life in shady areas varies: Soil may be thin or poor or it may be organically rich; the area may have some sun; tree roots may hog all the water and nutrients; or the area may be naturally damp. So choose your groundcover also based on what kind of growing conditions are available in addition to the reduced light. Try bugleweed, European wild ginger, ivy, lily-of-the-valley, pachysandra, periwinkle, or sweet woodruff. Make sure the area is cleared of competing weeds and the soil is organically rich.

✔ **In dry soil:** Sandy or gravelly soil may be your lot, or hot sun may bake the ground even if it isn't of poor quality. Periods of drought may be a factor. Luckily, some plants stand up to such difficulties in style. Try sedum and sempervivum, pussy-toes, potentilla, or bearberry. Make sure the area is cleared of competing weeds and that you water the young plants until they're established, at which time they'll be drought tolerant.

✔ **In poor soil:** Ground that's perpetually infertile (and that's a nuisance or too much work to improve) can still host certain groundcovers. These plants hail from poor-soil areas in the wild and adapt to similar conditions in a garden setting. Try creeping thyme, sempervivum, wintercreeper, or pachysandra. Clear the area of obstructing and competing weeds first, and water the young plants regularly until they're established.

✔ **On a slope:** Notoriously difficult to landscape, a slope allows water to run over and through it, no doubt carrying away both valuable moisture and nutrients that may have otherwise sustained some plants. Don't despair. A few groundcovers don't mind life on a slope; these stalwarts grab on and stay, beautifying the area even as they prevent future erosion. Try juniper, periwinkle, bearberry, or cotoneaster. Either terrace the slope or erect some soil berms to help the plants retain water while they're getting established.

When planting a groundcover on a slope that already has existing vegetation, don't dig up the whole slope. Just do individual planting holes. When the newcomers start to spread, gradually yank out adjoining plants to make way for them.

For additional colour, you can interplant spring-blooming bulbs with an evergreen groundcover. The groundcover will hide wilting leaves as the bulb display fades. Refer to Chapter 8 for more info on bulbs.

# Planting and Maintaining Groundcovers

Planting groundcovers is like planting annuals and perennials (refer to Chapters 6 and 7, respectively), though you want to pay careful attention to how much the mature groundcover is expected to spread so you can gauge how close or far apart to plant the individual plants. When they're in the ground, though, the truth is that groundcovers actually don't need much care — which is a big reason why people grow them. But a little attention every now and then, and especially at planting time, goes a long way toward having a handsome display. Read on. (And refer to Chapter 4 for some general info on watering, fertilizing, and mulching.)

## Watering

Although most groundcovers are pretty resilient characters, no seedling can gain a foothold and thrive if you allow it to dry out. Regular, consistent watering, especially in the early days, is essential.

A good, gentle, deep soaking — as from a soaker hose or a sprinkler — is better than frequent but shallow watering. You want your groundcover roots to go deep, not just to anchor themselves in place but also to be able to tolerate the heat of summer and periods of drought.

## Fertilizing

Feeding groundcovers isn't required. The majority of groundcovers emerge as tough, vigorous plants without any extra help. However, if growth seems thin, leaf colour is pale, and flower production is disappointing, you can dose them every now and then with a general, all-purpose garden fertilizer, such as a 30-30-30, to boost performance. Always follow the label directions regarding dilution and timing.

# Mulching

Mulching on planting day is important! Without a doubt, mulching is the single most valuable and helpful thing you can do for your groundcover display. Lay mulch down on planting day around the seedlings to keep encroaching weeds at bay and to help retain soil moisture.

If you've spaced the young plants widely and are banking on their filling in the open areas in time, mulching is also key. Weeds love open space and tend to take advantage faster than you may believe. So cover the exposed areas in your display with 2.5 to 5 centimetres (1 to 2 inches), or more, of mulch. Replenish as needed. In time, your plants will indeed fill in the space and the mulch will simply break down and contribute texture and perhaps organic matter to the area's soil — which is a good thing.

# Keeping groundcovers in shape: Pruning and pegging

Plants bounce back from cuts better when they're growing strongly, so it stands to reason that the best time to prune (or, where warranted, mow) a rampant grower is at the height of the growing season — summer, in other words. Don't, however, make the cut on a blazingly hot day or during a prolonged dry spell, or the surviving plant parts may suffer.

Groundcovers that exceed their allotted boundaries can and should be sheared back as often as necessary. Start early in the gardening year and keep after them with regular haircuts; if you wait till late summer or fall, you may have a major hacking job on your hands.

If your groundcover spreads by branching out from the crown (see "Reaching out: How the groundcover spreads"), you may want to peg the vine in place. Simply arch a piece of the long stem and pin it to the ground with *soil staples,* which are just U-shaped pieces of metal that you can buy or make from pieces of metal coat hangers. After a month or so of this, the stem that touches the ground will sprout roots and become its own plant.

# Getting weeds out (and keeping them out)

Most weeds are sun lovers, and the good news is that — depending on its eventual mature height — your groundcover can defend itself, at least somewhat, by shading out weeds. The ultimate defence against weeds in a groundcover display is thick growth. Eventually, your plants will dominate.

However, unless your groundcover is a naturally thick, dense grower, weeds can and often do insinuate themselves into the display. Weedy invasion isn't just unattractive. Those weeds are competitive thugs that grab the soil nutrients and moisture that your plants need and even shade out necessary sunshine.

There's only one remedy: Yank out the interlopers. You can't use a herbicide because you'd endanger the desirable plants (on top of the fact that herbicides are restricted in many municipalities, anyway). No, you have to wade in and pull out the weeds. Weed after a rain or after a good, soaking watering, and the invaders come out of the ground more easily. Then get rid of them. Young weeds are easier to pull out, but you have other practical reasons for an early assault: Young weeds hopefully haven't yet started to reproduce, whether by runners or seed. Get them out of there before they can increase their numbers!

# Part IV
# Producing Your Own Produce

The 5th Wave                    By Rich Tennant

That's very nice of you, dear. But I really don't think just one beetle in the garden will do much damage.

# In this part . . .

For many gardeners, veggies, fruit, and herbs are what gardening is really all about — the satisfaction and pure culinary joy of growing your own food, perhaps even growing better produce than what you can find at your local grocery store. The chapters in Part IV show you how to get started doing just that. Whether your preference is tomatoes plucked straight from the vine, berries harvested from their bushes, or herbs like mint and rosemary arriving as fresh as possible in your kitchen, you can enjoy produce grown all by your lonesome — with a little help from Mother Nature, of course.

# Chapter 13

# Food, Glorious Food! Growing Your Own Veggies

. . . . . . . . . . . . . . . . . . . . . . . . . . . . . . . . . . . . . . . . . . . .

### In This Chapter

▶ Looking at veggies and vegetable-garden fruits

▶ Getting seeds and transplants

▶ Designing your garden and preparing the site

▶ Sowing seeds and planting transplants

▶ Making safe compost for edibles

▶ Feeding your food with fertilizer

▶ Supporting vegetable plants

▶ Keeping pests away

. . . . . . . . . . . . . . . . . . . . . . . . . . . . . . . . . . . . . . . . . . . .

*F*or the cost of a packet of seeds, you can have your own, homegrown produce. The requirements are simple: good soil, moisture, and full sun. This type of gardening is usually called *vegetable gardening,* even though it also involves growing items that are technically fruit, such as tomatoes and melons (Chapter 15 can fill you in on growing traditional fruits and berries). Growing your own produce — or vegetables, as it were — can be fun and fairly easy for the beginner gardener. This chapter gives you the basics.

If you're new to vegetable gardening, you may have a vague sense that it's complicated — seeds to start indoors and other things to sow outside or plant right into the ground; garden layouts that deliver the best results somehow; weird insect pests; and the mysteries of harvesting — When? How? Should you freeze or otherwise preserve the harvest? Relax. Start small, taste success, and let your knowledge and triumphs grow from one year to the next.

Growing your own veggies really isn't and shouldn't be about saving money — though you may, even after factoring in your labour. It's about freshness (and thus nutrition; freshly harvested vegetables are always nutritionally superior to anything you buy at a supermarket — or even at your local farmer's market). And it's about flavour — oh boy, is it about flavour!

# Varieties of Veggies

Lots of wonderful and worthwhile types of vegetables are available — too many to list, really, but they're fun to explore. Read this section with the goal of figuring out what you may want to grow where you live. Favour vegetables that are too expensive at the store or never available locally. Treat yourself to new foods or enticing variations on old standbys.

Vegetable varieties vary in many ways. That's what makes vegetable gardening possible for everyone and keeps it so interesting. You could garden all your life and still not get around to growing all the tempting choices that would prosper in your particular region!

*Days to maturity* refers to the time elapsed between sowing a seed and picking the harvest for those veggies that are directly sown. Something like a radish or mesclun salad mix can accomplish this in 30 days or less. For plants that are normally grown from transplants, like peppers and tomatoes, the maturity time dates from when the small plants are planted in the ground until they bear.

Generally speaking, varieties of the same vegetable are ready at around the same time, give or take a few days. If you have a big gap, there's an explanation. For instance, 'Easter Egg' radish is ready in 28 days, but 'Summer Cross' takes 55 to 60 days because it's one of those giant white Oriental daikon types.

Please note that the days-to-maturity figure is relative — it's a prediction. Results vary according to your climate and the conditions in your garden. So consider it a ballpark figure or a way to roughly plan how fast some veggies are ready to eat relative to others.

## Growing vegetables by seasons

Matching your vegetables to your season length is sensible advice. If your growing season is approximately 90 days, growing anything billed as maturing in that amount of time or less ought to be easy. If you push the envelope, be prepared to help that variety with an early start indoors or some extra coddling in the fall. With experience, you can find out what you can and are willing to do.

First, though, get an idea of the growing seasons that you have to contend with (for info on growing seasons, refer to the frost zone info in Chapter 3). Typically, the vegetable-gardening season is summer, bookended by late spring and early fall. Gardeners mark the start of the season by the last spring frost date, and the finish by the first fall frost date (although some crops, like parsnips and kale, can stay out in the cold a bit longer and even gain improved flavour).

Your local weather forecaster may announce the frost date each spring (last frost) and fall (first frost), or you can call your local garden centre or the nearest provincial ministry of agriculture office to ask. The dates vary somewhat from one year to the next.

If your growing season is long and warm, you can get started earlier and may even plant two or three rounds of crops. You may, however, have to contend with hot, dry weather at the height of summer, which is stressful for some vegetable crops (so mulch them and supply extra water).

If your growing season is short, you can still have a very bountiful vegetable garden. Choose vegetables that mature faster, and try some season-extending tricks. Here are two favourites:

✔ Start seeds early indoors or in an outdoor cold frame, which is basically a box made of such materials as wood or concrete blocks covered with a glass or plastic sash that protects smaller plants from extreme cold and wind. Raising the plants to seedling size until putting them out in the ground is safe. (See the section "Starting your own seeds indoors," later in this chapter.)

✔ Use plastic coverings (from row-cover sheeting or tunnels to cones to recycled milk jugs to "water wall" wraps) to keep a plant and its immediate soil safely warm. See Figure 13-1.

**Figure 13-1:**
A "water wall," consisting of plastic sleeves filled with water, offers cold protection.

You can grow some vegetables during the winter. Yes. Really! In the milder parts of Canada — such as the Zone 7b and 8a parts of British Columbia — you can enjoy kale, carrots, broccoli, Brussels sprouts, and leeks, and some greens like radicchio, cress, and corn salad, for a long period from late fall into early winter. You may have to mulch them and then poke under to harvest, but hey, it's worth it! In really mild areas, like the southern part of Vancouver Island, you can even sow salad greens in October and then harvest them extra-early in spring. Mmm. If you have an adventurous soul, you might want to try October planting in southwestern Ontario, too.

Table 13-1 gives an overview of which vegetables tend to do better during which seasons.

| Table 13-1 | Ideal Seasons for Growing Vegetables | |
|---|---|---|
| *Type* | *Description* | *Examples* |
| Cool-season vegetables | These plants tolerate some frost and temperatures between 13°C and 21°C (55°F and 70°F). As such, they're fine choices for most Canadian gardeners. | Asparagus, beets, broccoli, Brussels sprouts, cabbage, carrot, cauliflower, collard, endive, kale, kohlrabi, lettuce, onion, Oriental greens, parsnip, peas, potato, radish, Swiss chard, spinach, turnip, and turnip greens |
| Warm-season vegetables | These plants are readily harmed by frost; they also fare poorly in cold soil. Grow these plants in temperatures ranging from 18°C to 27°C (65°F to 80°F) in areas where the season is long enough to allow them to reach maturity. In short-season areas, be sure to choose varieties that mature early, or grow them with protection, such as in a small greenhouse. | Beans, corn, cucumber, eggplant, melons (muskmelon/cantaloupe, watermelon), pepper, sweet potato, pumpkin, squash, sweet corn, and tomato |
| Perennials | These edible plants live from one year to the next, typically producing good crops in their second or third seasons and thereafter. You can grow them in most climates, providing a protective winter mulch if warranted. | Asparagus and rhubarb |

When planning a veggie garden, think ahead to what your favourite vegetables are and how you can make use of them. Focus on those delectables that you use a lot or that you like but are expensive or difficult to find in your local market. Maybe you like ethnic vegetables, or ones that are particularly ornamental.

For example, if having a fresh tasty salad is one of your summer pleasures, try lettuce and greens of all colours and textures to give you variety (see Figure 13-2). Consider growing gourmet cucumbers or carrots to go in your salad. Sweet cherry tomatoes are another tasty addition you'll want to add.

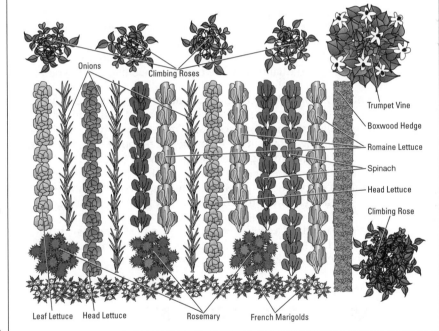

**Figure 13-2:**
A decorative yet practical garden plan for salad lovers.

# *Defining hybrids*

You may see the term *hybrid* on seed packets and in seed catalogues. All it means is that the vegetable variety in question is a result of a cross (through pollination) between two parent plants of the same species but different subspecies or varieties.

Generally speaking, crossing two different plants — plants of different kinds or species or families or orders — doesn't work (you can't cross a carrot with a tomato without splicing some genes). No seed is produced, or the seed that's produced is infertile and doesn't germinate. This setup is nature's way of keeping species unique and the plant kingdom somewhat orderly. But an early-ripening tomato crossed with an especially juicy and tasty one — now we're talkin'!

An *F1 hybrid* (first filial hybrid) is the first generation resulting from a cross between two parent plants; *F2* and *F3 hybrids,* then, are the results of subsequent crosses of the crosses. Complicated! Often experimental, too. (Austrian monk Gregor Mendel actually laid out the basics of heredity for us in the 1800s with his experiments with garden peas.) Don't fret. Seed companies do this work under highly controlled conditions, winnowing out the duds and making sure the plants can replicate desirable results with precision. All you have to do is buy the good seeds.

Uniformity, predictability, and disease resistance are the results of combining the genetic traits of two good parents and repeating the same cross. Hybrid offspring are often more robust and productive than either parent. Something called *hybrid vigour* often appears, a healthy exuberance that seems to result from the good qualities of one parent cancelling out the bad of the other.

What's the catch? Actually, we can name two. Producing hybrid seed requires the seed company to maintain the two parent lines and often to laboriously hand-pollinate, so hybrid seeds are more expensive than the alternative (see "Appreciating heirlooms"). Also, there's no point in saving seed from a hybrid you like and replanting it next year — it won't "come true," as they say — that is, it won't be the same and indeed may exhibit various mongrel qualities from either of its parents. So you're bound to purchase fresh new hybrid seeds each year if you want to grow a hybrid variety that you like.

Favourite hybrid vegetables include 'Big Boy' beefsteak tomato, 'Blushing Beauty' bell peppers, 'Nantes' carrot, 'Salad Bowl' leaf lettuce, 'Silver Queen' sweet corn, and 'Earlidew' honeydew melon.

## *Appreciating heirlooms*

*Heirloom vegetables* are vegetable varieties that people save and pass on for more-practical, home-gardener virtues such as excellent flavour and a prolonged harvest period. Commercial seed companies, on the other hand, breed for uniformity as well as good shipability (thicker, tougher skins on tomatoes and squash, for instance) and for vegetables that ripen all at once (for harvesting convenience). You may prefer heirlooms.

When a variety is called *open pollinated,* it means the seeds are the result of natural pollination by insects or wind. With veggies that have open-pollinated seeds (nonhybrid varieties), you can save the seeds and plant them again next year; they'll be the same. Heirloom varieties are simply those that have been passed down through generations of gardeners, like any other family heirloom. Realize that older varieties that are still in circulation have obviously stood the test of time and are therefore worth your while.

# Genetically engineered plants: A miracle or a monster?

Boy, is this an emotionally charged issue! Most people are either strongly for or against genetically engineered plants, but there are few fence sitters.

Here are the common points made by those who support genetic engineering:

✔ It can lead to higher yields and less pesticide use.

✔ It's merely an extension of traditional breeding.

And here are the common points made by those who are against genetic engineering:

✔ As with all new technology, it may lead to unknown side effects to the environment and to humans.

✔ It uses artificial techniques, and it dangerously alters genetic material.

So, you choose sides.

So far, only large-scale agronomic crops like corn, wheat, rice, and soybeans are being genetically altered, mostly because that's where the big money is and the engineering process is very expensive.

Specialty seed catalogues have wonderful selections (do an Internet search, or comb the ads or editorial catalogue lists in gardening magazines and send for the catalogues). Many mainstream catalogues are offering more and more heirloom vegetables in response to popular demand. You can also nose around your neighbourhood gardens, community gardens, or farmer's markets to meet other like-minded gardeners who can share their seeds and knowledge.

Whether it's a charming tradition, a survival skill, or a way to honour gardeners of the past, saving seeds from your favourite vegetable varieties is an enjoyable and rewarding skill. Depending on what else you grow in your garden, cross-pollination can interfere and must be prevented — either by covering flowering crops (to keep insects and bees from tampering or the wind from contaminating) or staggering planting dates. At season's end, you have to harvest ripe seed, extract it from its fruit, dry it, and then store it in a cool, dry place until you need it next year. If you'd like to give seed saving a try, start with squash or pumpkins — they're easy. For details on techniques as well as much more fascinating and useful information on heirloom vegetables, check out Seeds of Diversity (www.seeds.ca).

What's the catch with heirlooms? Well, they're not as perfect or as uniform in their growth. Because heirlooms aren't commercially bred, they may be more colourful and more variable in size and shape than their hybrid counterparts. Also, their skins may be thinner, so you get great flavour, but they don't travel well and may be vulnerable to bruising — or they may have lots of seeds inside (as in certain squashes and pumpkins), causing you a bit of extra work to separate the edible parts.

Favourite heirloom vegetable varieties include 'Moon and Stars' watermelon, 'Tom Thumb' baby butterhead lettuce, 'Gold Nugget' winter squash, 'Ragged Jack' kale, 'Super Italian Paste' tomato, 'Henderson's Bush' lima bean, and 'French Breakfast' spring radish.

# Designing for Dining and Getting Your Vegetable Garden Ready

Most produce is, of course, grown in a vegetable garden, and it's always best to get your garden started before acquiring your plants. Before you plant, you also have to dig the soil and work in organic matter. The first step, however, is designing your garden.

## Sketching out your plan

The best planning advice is simple: Start small. Just be sure you locate the vegetable garden in a spot where expansion is possible, in case you'll want to make a bigger garden in ensuing years. As for actual size, it depends on what you want to grow. Just to give you a general idea, here's what you can put in the following standard-size gardens:

- A 1.8-x-2.4-metre (6-x-8-foot) plot can support a couple of tomato plants, maybe some bush beans, and some lettuce.

- A 3-x-5.5-metre (10-x-18-foot) plot can hold all that, plus a couple of space-consuming squash plants and cucumbers, and maybe some carrots or beets.

- A 6-x-7.3-metre (20-x-24-foot) plot can hold all the aforementioned plants, plus peppers, leeks, broccoli, turnips, and maybe some herbs as well.

- A 12-x-18-metre (40-x-60-foot) plot allows you more of everything, plus some bigger items such as corn and asparagus or rhubarb. But let's face it: Corn isn't worth growing unless you can have a dozen or more plants; otherwise, they don't pollinate, or don't pollinate completely, and you end up harvesting gap-toothed ears.

Sketch out your vegetable garden plan on paper ahead of time. Figure out how much space to allot to individual plants — and don't forget to allow for space between the rows, or paths, so you can tend the plants. (Mature sizes of various vegetable varieties are noted on seed packets and often in catalogue descriptions.)

You may want to try *succession planting:* If a vegetable is harvested early in the summer, lettuce, say, or peas, you can then free up that space for another crop, such as carrots. Succession planting is a good trick, but to pull it off, you may need to do some research as well as some trial and error — and be willing to invest the time and effort. See Figure 13-3 for a plan that may work for you.

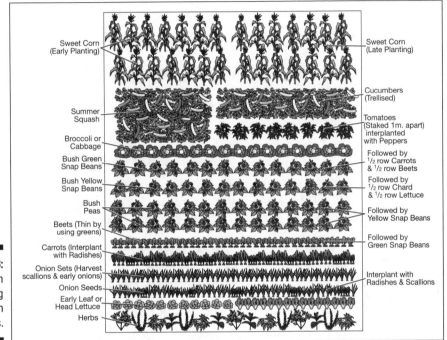

**Figure 13-3:** Garden plan showing succession plantings.

*Intercropping,* also called interplanting, is really very simple. Just have two different plants share the same part of the garden in an alternating or checker-board pattern. This setup can look rather nifty, but it has practical advantages as well. Smaller, faster-maturing plants can grow with larger, slower-growing ones so you always have something to harvest. And plants that appreciate a little shade can grow in the shelter of taller ones (have pole beans next to lettuce or spinach, for example). See Figure 13-4 for an example.

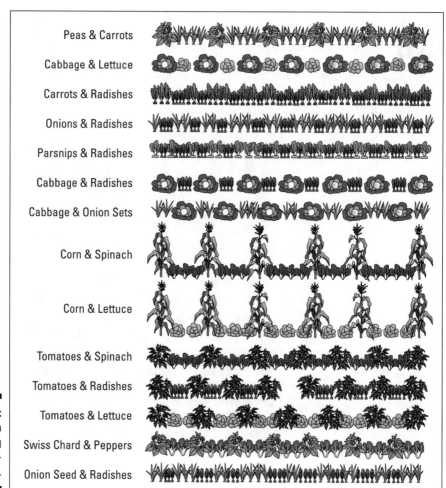

Peas & Carrots

Cabbage & Lettuce

Carrots & Radishes

Onions & Radishes

Parsnips & Radishes

Cabbage & Radishes

Cabbage & Onion Sets

Corn & Spinach

Corn & Lettuce

Tomatoes & Spinach

Tomatoes & Radishes

Tomatoes & Lettuce

Swiss Chard & Peppers

Onion Seed & Radishes

**Figure 13-4:**
Garden plan
showing
inter-
cropping.

# *Working with the sun: Where to plant vegetables*

Most fruiting vegetables like the environment sunny and open — the soil is warm, light is plentiful, and they grow easily, developing and ripening their fruit with minimal stress or impediments. (If conditions aren't ideal, they make less fruit and take longer to ripen — also, the plants may lean or grow toward the light source in a bid to get as much as they can.) Examples of sun-loving vegetables include tomatoes, peppers, squash, beans, okra, eggplant, and corn.

To maximize needed sun, site your vegetable garden in a south-facing spot; plant taller plants to the north end so they don't cast shade over their shorter fellows.

Some vegetables are less dependent on full sun, which can fade or dry out their foliage or slow their growth. Or the plants may just like cooler temperatures. Vegetables that gardeners grow for their leaves fall into this group, as do ones with edible roots. Examples include lettuce, mixed greens (mesclun), chard, potatoes, carrots, and turnips.

To maximize sheltering shade, grow these vegetables in an east- or west-facing garden; site taller plants and objects (including trellises, teepees, and caged or staked tomatoes) in front and to the south of these shade lovers. Or grow shade-loving plants earlier in spring or in midsummer — assuming you have enough time to ripen them before winter comes, that is — when the sun is lower in the sky.

## Using planting patterns and systems

As much as you may like to toss a packet of seeds into a pile of dirt and let the plants grow where they fall, you're better off working with some kind of system. The following sections provide info on how you can design around a natural garden, raised beds, or existing landscaping.

### Natural garden beds

Natural garden beds can be in-ground or mounded up, without wooden sides. Either way, work the soil between 20 and 30 centimetres (8 and 12 inches) deep to accommodate the roots of most vegetables.

Natural beds don't need any kind of edging, but you do need to remove the sod if you're turning part of your lawn into a garden. Removing the sod with a sod knife (a special tool that can be rented) or a spade is best. For larger jobs, you can rent a sod cutter, which is a machine that penetrates the soil about 8 centimetres (3 inches) deep and cuts off the roots of the sod. It can then be rolled up and removed. For smaller jobs, you can rent a manual sod cutter or you can use a spade. (See Figure 13-5 for how to make a natural, mounded-up bed.)

Removing the sod and then rototilling the soil is important. Don't try to rototill over the grass. First of all, only larger rototillers are capable of doing this, and secondly, if you till in the grass, it'll be impossible to completely remove it and it'll constantly resprout — a real pain!

As far as weeds go, remove as many as you can before you till or work up the soil. Then when new weeds sprout, remove them as soon as possible — when they're young and before they go to seed (and produce more weeds!).

More-ambitious vegetable gardens need plenty of paths and rows to allow access — for you, for a hose, for a wheelbarrow. Ideally, you want access from all four sides of a particular bed. Build pathways into your master plan when you're first sketching out the layout. Then, to clarify where the paths are and also to prevent weeds from seizing the open space, "pave" the paths with a layer of straw (not hay), dried grass clippings, or gravel.

### Raised garden beds

Using raised garden beds is a very practical way to construct a good vegetable garden. Raised beds have good drainage; their soil warms up quickly in the spring; they're easy to weed (because they're higher than ground level); and you're less likely to step on and compact the soil (roots grow better in looser, well-aerated ground). To make a raised bed with wooden sides, follow these steps:

1. **Choose a sunny, flat area for your garden.**

2. **Remove the sod in the garden area (refer to the preceding section, "Natural garden beds").**

3. **Make a bottomless wooden box between 20 and 30 centimetres (8 and 12 inches) deep, the same size as your garden area. Place the wooden box over it.**

4. **Fill the box with good soil.**

   Native soil can be used if it's of good quality; otherwise, half-native and half-added purchased soil works fine.

5. **Plant your veggie seeds or transplants.**

See Figure 13-5 for a finished raised bed in a wooden frame. If you use more than one raised bed, space them so you can walk between them or bring a wheelbarrow down the row. Construction tip: Brace each corner with a corner post for extra stability.

If tunnelling rodents are an issue where you garden, keep them out of your raised bed by lining the bottom with a layer of chicken wire (remove the sod, lay down the wire, and then build the soil up over top). Use a slightly-too-big piece so you can pull it partway up the sides of the bed and tack or staple it in place.

Use untreated lumber for wooden vegetable-garden frames. Treated wood may leach harmful preservatives, which isn't a risk you want to take when raising edibles. Rot-resistant redwood or cedar is great; other softwoods, including pine, will also do, but they tend to rot away after a few years and need replacing. You can certainly use plastic, cinder blocks, and even bales of hay to establish a box. Just be sure the walls are securely in place before adding soil to the interior.

**Figure 13-5:**
Images A and B show how to make a natural mounded-up bed. First build up the earth for planting (A). Then plant your garden (B). Image C shows a similar bed with wooden walls.

# Prepping your soil

The biggest mistake beginning vegetable gardeners make is using lousy or too-thin soil. Gardening isn't rocket science, folks (even if NASA *is* working on growing vegetables in space). Please, before a single vegetable begins its hopeful, potential-filled life in your yard, give it a very good home! This prep work can save you untold disappointment and, perhaps more than any other factor, assure a bountiful and delicious harvest.

If you're working with a brand-new vegetable garden (or one that fell fallow and you're bringing it back to life), we suggest you stake it out and get it ready the autumn before you plan to plant. This act gives the soil and the amendments you've added time to settle and meld. It also means you have less work to do next spring.

If a fall start isn't possible or practical, go ahead and prepare the ground in spring — but don't start too early. If the ground is still semifrozen or soggy, digging in the soil can compact it and harm its structure. How do you tell whether it's ready to be worked in? Grab a handful and squeeze — it should fall apart, not form a mud ball.

Follow these steps when preparing your soil:

1. **Dig deep.**

   Most vegetables are content with 15 to 20 centimetres (6 to 8 inches) of good earth for their roots to grow in. If you're planning to grow substantial root crops (potatoes, say, or carrots), go deeper still — up to 30 centimetres (1 foot) or more (yes, you can use a technique called *hilling*, where you mound up good soil around crops like potatoes, but this method doesn't excuse you from digging deep to amend the soil).

2. **Fill 'er up.**

   Add lots and lots of organic matter! Try compost (make your own — see "Composting for Vegetable Gardens" later on), dehydrated cow manure, shredded leaves, well-rotted horse manure (call nearby stables), or a mixture thereof. If your yard happens to be blessed with fertile soil, adding organic matter is less crucial, but most soils can stand the improvement. Mix it with the native soil, 50-50, or even more liberally.

Here's a word about difficult soils: Maybe your area's soil is notoriously acidic, or very sandy, or quite obviously lousy for plant growth. The good news is that organic matter can be like a magic bullet in that it helps improve whatever you add it to. You have to replenish the organic matter at the start of every growing season or maybe even more often. (If the soil stubbornly resists improvement, resort to setting raised beds atop it and filling these bottomless boxes with excellent, organically rich soil.)

# Finding Your Vegetables

Generally, most gardeners buy their vegetables as seed packets or as young transplants or container plants. People often purchase plants and seeds in the spring from a variety of places, including markets, home stores, and nurseries. Racks of veggies sprout up everywhere in the springtime! You'll notice different brands and companies, but, quite frankly, not huge differences in price.

Whether you choose to grow plants from seed or buy started plants may depend on cost, the kind of selection you want, when you want to begin, and the type of plant. Read on for the basics of how these beginnings vary.

## Buying seeds

Seed packets are particularly popular because they help save money and provide a broader, more interesting selection. Upon purchase, or certainly upon opening a new seed packet, you quickly notice an awful lot of little seeds in there! The reasons are many: The seed company wants to make you feel as though you're getting something substantial for your money, and when you sow, some won't sprout or will be thinned out later.

Furthermore, you get enough for successive sowings or to save for next year (note that little seeds, like lettuce seeds, tend to dry out if stored for a year, whereas big seeds, like bean seeds, can keep for several years). Keep seeds in a dry, cool (nonfreezing) place until you're ready to sow them.

Certain seeds can, and should, be started indoors, well before the garden outside is awake yet — so read the labels to see whether indoor starting or *direct sowing* (sowing outside, when the soil and weather are warm enough) is recommended for the area where you live.

## Buying nursery transplants

You can purchase transplants, container plants, or seedlings locally — at a garden centre, home store, farmer's market, or spring fair, or from roadside entrepreneurs — or from mail-order companies. Someone else has done the seed-starting work for you; all you have to do is choose, take 'em home, and care for them. If you can't get the plants into the ground right away, set them in a sheltered spot out of the hot sun and wind, and water them often (small pots dry out alarmingly fast, and young plants can't tolerate neglect).

Transplants are the way to go if you can't or don't want to bother with seed starting, or if you wait till the last minute to decide what you're growing this year. They're worth the cost for the convenience.

Just as with seed shopping, you can shop for different varieties (buy three different kinds of tomatoes, for example). Again, though, the selection may not be too exciting comparatively.

Plants to buy prestarted include tomatoes, peppers, and eggplants. Certain vegetables simply don't transplant well from a wee pot to the garden, such as direct-sow plants like corn, carrots, and potatoes.

Of course, you can also create your own transplants from your own seeds. For how to do it, see "Starting your own seeds indoors," later in this chapter.

# Planting Your Vegetables

When getting ready to plant, the first rule is to pay attention to which items are cool-season vegetables and which are warm-season vegetables (refer to the earlier section on "Growing vegetables by seasons").

Start some warm-season veggies, such as tomatoes and peppers, indoors; they benefit from an early start, because they take many weeks of growth to bear ripe fruit. But don't bother to start corn, carrots, or potatoes indoors; they grow fairly quickly and sometimes don't like to be transplanted. Put the transplants of warm-season vegetables outdoors only after all danger of frost is past.

If you decide to start cool-season veggies such as broccoli, cabbage, or Brussels sprouts indoors, remember that you can move the little seedlings outdoors earlier than tomatoes or peppers because they're more cold tolerant (some can even go outdoors before the last frost). And some cool-season vegetables, like lettuces and spinach, can be sown from seed right in the garden in spring, as soon as you can work the ground — in fact, they prefer cool weather for germination and quick early growth.

After you figure out which veggies are which in your planting plans, you're ready to determine when to start planting. (For info on location, please refer to "Working with the sun: Where to plant vegetables.") And then, of course, you're ready to plant!

## Deciding when to plant your veggies

Determining the date of the last frost is your green-light date, the date when you're now free to plant vegetable seedlings or direct-sow vegetable seeds in the garden. The last frost date is in late spring, but the date varies from year to year and from zone to zone. You can find out down at the local garden centre or from the nearest provincial ministry of agriculture's office.

### When to plant transplants

If you have seedlings ready to go into the garden after the soil is ready and sufficiently warmed up — seedlings of your own or ones you've bought — your garden can get off to an earlier start. This timing puts fresh food on the table sooner. In the final analysis, your garden will be more productive this year! Vegetables that you can and probably should start early indoors include cabbage, tomatoes, peppers, and eggplant.

Remember, if you start too early, your seedlings may be too big too early, making them a little hard to accommodate and care for — you may even have to start over. Here's a general list to get you started; you can tinker as you get more experience raising various sorts of seeds. Yep, get out your calendar — some counting backward is in order:

- **Onions:** 12 to 14 weeks before the safe planting-out day (which, in the case of onions, is 4 to 6 weeks before the last frost)

- **Broccoli, collards, and cabbage:** 5 to 6 weeks before the safe planting-out date (which is after the danger of snow and ice is past, but while nights are still chilly)

- **Lettuce:** 5 to 6 weeks before the safe planting-out day (which is 4 to 5 weeks before the last frost)

- **Peppers:** 8 to 12 weeks before the last frost

- **Tomatoes and eggplant:** 6 to 8 weeks before the last frost

- **Cucumbers and melons:** 2 to 4 weeks before the last frost

### When to sow seeds directly

Gardeners generally sow seeds directly in the garden after the last frost, after the soil has warmed up and the weather seems to have settled into an early-summer groove. Direct sowing in cold and/or soggy soil is a bad idea — it's muddy work for you, and the seeds usually sprout poorly or rot; then you have to start over. Best to wait for the right time.

Though you can buy tools and gadgets to help you with this work, there remains something so primal and satisfying about going out with a seed packet and digging in the dirt with your hands.

Vegetables that you can direct-sow include lettuce, onions, peas, radishes, turnips, beets, carrots, beans, corn, parsnips, and cucumber.

# Sowing and planting your veggies

How to plant vegetables really depends on the form in which you've acquired them. Do you want to plant seeds, or do you want to plant transplants that you've acquired? Or do you want to combine both approaches and create your own transplants from seeds? Here's some information on all three approaches, starting with creating your own transplants from seeds.

## Starting your own seeds indoors

A sure way to banish the winter blues, as well as get a jump-start on your vegetable garden, is to start some seeds indoors early. To find out how early, consult the back of the seed packet; you want to time it so you have several seedlings that are a couple of centimetres (about an inch) high in late spring, after the danger of frost in your area has passed. See Figure 13-6 and follow these steps:

1. **Select a good spot.**

   In milder climates, gardeners can sow seeds early in a cold frame or greenhouse, if they have one. Everyone else has to make do indoors. The best spot is an area out of the path of household traffic. You don't want people bumping into your tender sprouts, or curious pets coming around. Pick a spot that's also warm and out of drafts. A basement, sun porch, and spare room are all good options. Some people even raise seeds on the tops of dressers, cabinets, or refrigerators!

2. **Provide light.**

   Some seeds germinate under a thin layer of soil mix and some are pressed lightly on top, but in all cases, the seedlings that sprout need between 12 and 16 hours of light per day — that's a lot.

   Sunlight from a window is not at all ideal. It's pale and limited in late winter and early spring. To make your seedlings work, you need artificial light. Fluorescent is best, and a timer at the outlet can help you regulate the hours it's shining on your baby plants. See Figure 13-7 for a good light setup.

3. **Prepare pots or flats (which need drainage holes).**

   Begin with a sterile seed-starting mix. (This mix is available in bags wherever gardening supplies are sold. It looks like very fine potting mix.) Fill the containers about three-quarters full with dampened, not drenched, mix (see Figure 13-6). Tamp the surface flat and level with the flat of your hand or a small piece of wood before sowing.

4. **Okay, sow!**

   The back of the seed packet can tell you how deep and whether you should cover the seeds with mix. The packet can also tell you how far apart to place the seeds. Sow carefully by hand — a pencil tip is a useful tool when placing small seeds (see Figure 13-6, image B).

TIP

Don't sow too many seeds! Overplanting can lead to a forest of seedlings, growing too thickly for you to thin them without damaging some.

If you're sowing into a flat, make little furrows with the pencil tip or a finger and then space the seeds up to 2.5 centimetres (1 inch) apart (see Figure 13-6, image C).

5. **Cover.**

Cover the container the very day you plant. Plastic wrap is great, but depending on the size of your starting containers, you can instead use a plastic bag (Figure 13-6, image D). This covering holds in warmth and humidity, giving the seeds the best chance of absorbing moisture and getting going. Don't seal too tightly, though. A tight seal causes condensed water to drip back down into the mix, making things too soggy.

6. **Check back daily.**

Don't let the planting mix dry out, or the seeds' growth will come to a halt. Open the bag a couple hours every few days to let the soil breathe some fresh air. Then close it back up. The best way to keep developing seedlings evenly and consistently moist is with bottom watering. Just set the container into a few centimetres of water (in the sink or a tray) and let it wick up the water it needs before returning the container to its spot.

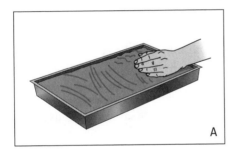

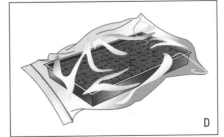

**Figure 13-6:** Seed-starting trays.

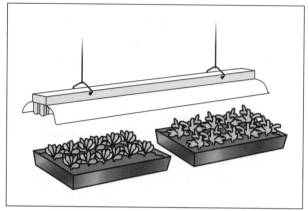

Figure 13-7:
Seedlings
growing
under
fluorescent
lights.

The first little seeds usually take a week or two to poke up their heads. But what a thrill! Here's what to do now to ensure that they survive and thrive:

✓ **Snip away extras.** Use tiny scissors (fingernail or beard-clipping ones work well) to gently cut weaker seedlings away at soil level. Pulling, rather than cutting off, can damage the roots of the surrounding seedlings. The properly spaced survivors gain better air circulation, which is important for their health, and their developing roots don't have to compete for precious resources.

✓ **Water from above with a fine spray.** As the seedlings grow bigger, bottom watering may no longer be practical. You can shift the flat's plastic covering on and off for ventilation — after a while, the young plants become too tall, and you have to remove it completely.

✓ **Start fertilizing.** A diluted, half-strength, flowering-houseplant fertilizer delivered with a regular watering is just fine. Fertilize about every two weeks.

✓ **Check that the seedlings are well rooted when they're several centimetres high.** Never tug on the stem! Gently tug on the true leaves (not the first, or *cotyledon,* leaves that come up — the second set to appear are the true leaves). If the seedlings hang on and otherwise look husky, they're ready to be hardened off (see the next section).

### *Planting transplants in the garden*

Regardless of whether you grow your transplants yourself or purchase them from a supplier, the first step toward getting them into the ground is the hardening-off process. This interim step in the life of your precious baby seedlings is a way to ease them from their plush indoor life to the realities of life in the real world — outdoors in the garden.

After the threat of frost has passed, move your seedlings outside to a place that's sheltered from sun and wind. Start with leaving them outside for an hour a day, and gradually work it up to 24 hours over a two-week period. (Bring the seedlings indoors or cover them on chilly nights or if frost threatens.) Stop fertilizing them. If you bought your transplants from somewhere else, you may be able to shorten this process by asking the seller whether they were hardened off (or if they were displayed for sale outdoors, you can pretty well assume that they were).

When the seedlings are hardened off, you need to plant them properly to get them off to a good start. Ideally, work on an overcast day (or plant late in the day), when the hot sun won't stress them or you. Here's what to do:

1. **Water the seedlings well the morning you plan to plant.**

2. **Dig individual holes.**

   Make the holes at least as deep and wide as the pots the seedlings come in. How far apart to dig depends on the plant; the tag that comes with it should have this information, but when in doubt, allow more elbow room rather than less. Seedlings may look puny, but if you give them a good home, they'll soon take off like gangbusters.

3. **Pop each plant out of its pot carefully, handling the seedlings by gently gripping the leaves.**

   Tease apart the roots on the sides and bottom so they'll be more inclined to enter the surrounding soil in their new home. Place the roots gently in their hole, and tamp the soil in around them firmly to eliminate air pockets.

   You can plant tomato seedlings deeper than they were growing in their pot. In other words, you can bury much of the stem with no harm done; just keep one or two sets of leaves above ground and gently remove the lower ones. Not only does this planting depth lead to better stability in the hole, but it also makes the stem respond by producing more roots along the buried part.

4. **Water; then mulch.**

   Gently soak each seedling quite well, using a wand attachment on your hose or a watering can. Then lay down a layer of mulch 2.5 to 5 centimetres (1 to 2 inches) deep and a couple of centimetres (about an inch) away from the base of each seedling, spreading it outward about the same distance. The mulch conserves soil moisture as well as thwarts sprouting weeds. Don't let the mulch touch the stem, or you risk insect and pest problems later on.

After planting transplants in your garden, offer them a little protection. Sudden exposure to sun and wind can stress out little plants. Get them through the first few days by setting some boxes or boards nearby to create a barrier — or set a few lawn chairs out in the garden over the seedlings. It helps.

### Sowing seeds directly into the garden

All danger of frost is past, the air and soil have warmed up, and the ground is slightly damp or even somewhat dry. In other words, it's late spring or early summer and you're ready to sow your seeds. In the case of lettuce or spinach, there may even be a wee nip in the air: You can plant some vegetables while the weather is still quite cool.

Assuming that the garden area is prepared and ready to go, head outdoors one fine day with seed packets, a trowel, a planting dibble or hoe (depending on the size of the project), and something to sit on. Be prepared to get a bit dirty and sweaty and to feel the warm sun beam down on your head and shoulders as you work. Don't rush — putting seeds in this good Earth gives you a wonderful, soothing, productive feeling!

Follow these steps:

1. **Make planting holes or furrows.**

   Recommended planting distances are noted on the seed packets.

2. **Follow the "three friends" rule — plant three seeds per hole.**

   At least one will likely sprout well. If all three do, you can thin out two of them later to favour the most robust one.

3. **Cover each hole as you go, tamping down the soil to eliminate air pockets.**

4. **Label.**

   The now-empty seed packet, stapled to a small stick, is a long-time labelling favourite. But you can simply write the name of the vegetable (and the variety, if you're growing more than one of the same kind) as well as the date on a stick with a marker and then plunge it in at the head of the row.

5. **Water well with a soft spray so you don't dislodge the seeds.**

   A wand hose attachment is good, as is a watering can with a rose head. If your vegetable garden is fairly big, use a sprinkler.

6. **Mulch.**

   Lay down 2.5 to 5 centimetres (1 to 2 inches) of mulch after watering over the entire bed; keep the mulch a couple of centimetres away from your new planting so that the seeds don't have to try to get through the barrier. Mulching conserves soil moisture and discourages sprouting weeds.

# Composting for Vegetable Gardens

Perhaps you've been wondering why so many vegetable gardeners have compost piles. The short answer is that it's downright sensible. Compost is a bountiful and free source of organic matter, which vegetables adore and consume like crazy. To have it always handy when you need it is unbeatable. Compost is a pile of organic waste that breaks down into rich, dark, crumbly material that jubilant gardeners call black gold! It's an excellent way to add humus to your garden, and it also acts as a natural, slow-release fertilizer. You also get to feel virtuous and efficient because you're not sending perfectly useful materials away with the household garbage.

Store-bought compost, bag for bag, may not strike you as terribly expensive, but it really starts to add up when you're starting or maintaining a vegetable garden. You're better off making your own. And hey, it's easy.

Okay, here's the short course on creating compost for your vegetable garden. If you have need of mountains of compost or really get into composting, you can try out some more-sophisticated methods and rigs. For now, though, follow these steps:

1. **Pick a good spot.**

   Look for a location that's level and out of the way of foot traffic but not far from your vegetable garden. A sunny spot is better than a shady one, because warm sunshine helps the pile warm up so the contents break down faster.

2. **Erect, on this spot, a cage, square or circular.**

   The cage needs to measure at least 90 x 90 centimetres (3 x 3 feet) to be effective. Commercially available bins of tough plastic with a lid on top and a hatch or hatches in the bottom ("Darth Vader" bins) are this size, or you can make your own out of chicken wire, concrete blocks, wooden pallets, lumber, or even piled-up hay bales.

3. **Create a base.**

   Set or scoop in a layer (10 to 30 centimetres, or several inches to a foot thick) of thin branches, chopped-up corn stalks, or something along those lines.

4. **Layer away!**

   A proper compost pile, if viewed in cutaway, resembles a layer cake. Make each layer about 10 to 20 centimetres (a few inches) thick. Alternate green (grass clippings, young pulled weeds) and brown (ground dried leaves, shredded bark) layers. Organic material that is softer (green) decomposes more quickly.

   Smaller or shredded bits break down faster than big chunks. If you're adding dry stuff, soak the pile with the hose or a watering can right after adding to moisten it. (See the upcoming lists of acceptable and unacceptable materials.) Maintain your compost pile at about the moisture level of a wrung-out sponge.

5. **Check on your pile, and turn it every few days or whenever you add more material.**

   A good mix heats up to between 38°C and 49°C (100°F and 120°F) — on warm summer days, you may see the pile steaming. Turn it (with a stick, shovel, or pitchfork — whatever works) to keep it working. Your compost is ready to use when it fails to heat up again after turning. Refer to Chapter 4 for more information on composting.

Here's what should go into a vegetable compost pile:

- ✔ Coffee grounds and tea leaves (even tea bags; just remove the staple)
- ✔ Crushed eggshells
- ✔ Corncobs (chop or grind them up first)
- ✔ Vegetable and fruit peelings and leftovers
- ✔ Shredded leaves
- ✔ Shredded newspaper (just the black-and-white pages)
- ✔ Straw (not hay — it contains weed seeds)
- ✔ Prunings from your yard (chopped small)
- ✔ Lawn clippings

Here's what shouldn't go into a vegetable compost pile:

- ✔ Big chunks of yard debris
- ✔ Plants that are diseased or full of insect pests
- ✔ Weeds
- ✔ Plant debris that's been treated with weed killer or pesticides
- ✔ Any meat product (bones, grease, and fat included)
- ✔ Fruit pits and seeds (they don't break down well and attract rodents)
- ✔ Cat, dog, or other pet waste (which may contain meat products or parasites)

When in doubt as to what should and shouldn't go into your compost pile for your vegetable garden, you can set up a rule for yourself. The rule isn't foolproof, but it can definitely give you peace of mind: Remember that the veggie plants soak up the materials that come out of the compost. If you wouldn't put it or part of it in your mouth, then don't put it on your compost pile!

If your compost pile seems to be breaking down too slowly, you can add these jump-start materials in moderation to boost things a bit: commercially available compost booster (beneficial microorganisms), blood meal, bone meal, or dried manure (from vegetarian animals only).

# *Fertilizing Your Vegetable Garden*

If your vegetable garden has fertile soil enhanced by compost and other organic materials, fertilizing may not be urgently necessary. Still, vegetables are a hungry group, and feeding them can certainly speed growth and improve your harvest.

The main nutrients are nitrogen (N), phosphorus (P), and potassium (K), which is why the labels of general-purpose fertilizers have three numbers. A fertilizer such as 10-10-10 is a *balanced* fertilizer because it contains equal proportions of all three nutrients, whereas a 15-0-0 is obviously nitrogen-heavy. Other elements are necessary for plant growth, but plants need them in much smaller amounts, and they're often already present in the soil (also, many commercial fertilizers include them).

Nitrogen enhances the growth of leaves and stems; phosphorus helps flower, fruit, seed, and root production; and potassium ensures general vigour and increases your plants' resistance to disease. So for most vegetable crops, your best bet is a balanced fertilizer.

*Fertilizer* is anything, organic or inorganic, that provides nutrients for growing vegetable plants. (*Soil conditioner,* on the other hand, is material that improves your soil structure.) Just to give you some context, here are different ways to nurture your crops:

- ✔ **Side dressing:** This term means sprinkling some fertilizer beside the plant, rather than on the plant itself. Dry fertilizer can be scratched into the soil with your fingers or an implement such as a trowel or fork. See Figure 13-8.

- ✔ **Foliar feeding:** You add foliar fertilizer to water (diluted according to label directions, of course) and then spray it right onto the leaves.

- ✔ **Top dressing:** Top dressing is when you apply fertilizer over the surface of the garden.

Always follow label directions regarding how much to apply. Too much isn't good — you can overdose or burn your plants. Good timing is also important. Usually, you're advised to feed the plants at planting time to get them off to an early and vigorous start. A second, midseason application is worthwhile if you're growing a succession of crops in the same row or if you're intercropping (see "Sketching out your plan," earlier in this chapter, for info on these growing methods).

Liquid fertilizers are concentrated, so you have to dilute them in water according to label directions; do two half-strength doses rather than one full-strength, if you like. Liquid fertilizers are mostly used for foliar feeding. Dry ones, on the other hand, come as powder or granules and need to be watered in.

**Figure 13-8:**
Side-
dressing
fertilizers.

Dry fertilizer that remains dry never does any plant any good. Dampen the garden before and after watering so the fertilizer can get into the soil and down to the roots, where it's needed.

For information on how to decide between organic and inorganic fertilizers, please refer to Chapter 4.

# Using Frames, Supports, and Structures for Veggies

Oh, those little seedlings — how fast and tall some of them grow! Midway through the summer, they're big; by August, they're out of control. You compromise the health as well as the manageability of certain crops, not to mention their productivity, if you don't step in with some kind of support. And the time to do so is well before the plant becomes unwieldy. (Support is also important if your vegetable garden is out in the open and is occasionally subject to blustery winds.)

The time to get started on support is when a plant is a few centimetres high. The support is so much easier to position then, plus — and this idea's important — when you plunge a support into the ground near a seedling, you don't harm it or its root system. Procrastinate, and you may.

Your support options include:

- **Wooden, metal, or plastic stake:** Plunge this support deep (30 centimetres [a foot] or more) into the ground near the plant so the support will be stable when it's weighted down with foliage and veggies. Site the stake near the main stem (not right on top of it! — a few centimetres away), and secure the plant loosely with soft ties as it grows; as the plant fills out, it'll eventually hide these ties from view.

- **Trellis:** Don't use the sort of trellis you train a climbing rose or clematis on but rather something broader and less decorative, something with plenty of horizontal wires or slats for tying onto.

- **Teepee:** A teepee is a good choice for climbing plants that can get rather tall, such as pole beans or miniature pumpkins and squash. You can buy a wooden, plastic, or metal teepee, or rig one out of branches and twigs pruned from your yard. (See Chapter 19 for info on using a teepee as a place for children to play.)

- **Fence:** A climber or tall-growing veggie can lean on a fence if you site the plant near it, but you may have to help guide it and anchor it with string and/or the occasional tie.

- **Cage:** Wire cages are sold specifically for supporting tomatoes, but they turn out to be useful for other vegetable crops as well, such as sugar-snap peas, cucumbers, and smaller melons. Get the tallest cages you can, or put one atop another, because many tomatoes can grow to 1.8 metres (6 feet) or taller, easily toppling shorter cages. See Figures 13-9 and 13-10.

**Figure 13-9:** Supporting melons.

**Figure 13-10:**
Two
different
types of
tomato
cages.

TIP

To secure the veggies to the support, don't use material that abrades or cuts into a plant, such as wire or twist ties; use something soft, like lengths of cloth (rip up old T-shirts or pillow cases) or plastic tape. Also, when you tie, loop one end around the support first, and then pull the tie over to the plant and make a loop there as well — like a figure-eight. Do this tying loosely. This way, the plant won't be harmed and can also move a bit, safely, in a breeze.

Vegetables that need or benefit from support include peas, pole beans, tomatoes, cucumbers, small squash and zucchini, mini pumpkins, and melons.

Row covers (Figure 13-11) are usually made of plastic or spun synthetic fabric. These covers serve as miniature greenhouses, holding in heat, protecting the plants against wind, and in some cases, shading the plants and reducing the plants' exposure to insects.

**Figure 13-11:**
Row covers.

# Dealing with Vegetable Pests

If you build it, they will come, sorry to say. Because you're growing edible plants, be very reluctant to throw chemical remedies at pest problems in your vegetable garden. Fortunately, you can choose from plenty of proactive, less-risky strategies and deterrents.

Of course, as with so much of gardening, a plot in good health — with good soil, ample fertilizer and water, and elbow room for good air circulation — resists such problems better than an unkempt or crowded one. Also, always

- ✔ Select disease-resistant varieties.
- ✔ Clean up garden debris promptly.
- ✔ Keep after and yank out all weeds, which harbour and feed various pests.

Rotate crops: Don't plant the same veggies in the same place year after year. Always make sure you know what or who is attacking a crop — watch at odd hours, such as in the morning or evening, set a trap, or creep in close to the affected plants and look under leaves and in nodes (where leaf stalks meet the stem). Telltale signs also include nibbled leaves and collapsing stems — here again, a little poking around should reveal the culprit. If it's an icky bug, capture a few, stick 'em in a baggie, and show them to someone who can help you identify them.

There isn't much that home gardeners can safely do if their vegetables have fungal disease. The best thing is to purchase disease-resistant varieties and grow them under good conditions (sufficient air flow, fertilizing, and watering). If disease is suspected, it's usually best to uproot the plant and discard it in the trash, not the compost pile.

Garden dusters (Figure 13-12) are used to apply a very fine coat of powdered insecticide or fungicide to the surfaces of leaves. Dusters are most effective when used early in the morning when there's no breeze and the leaves have dew on them so the dust can better adhere to the plants.

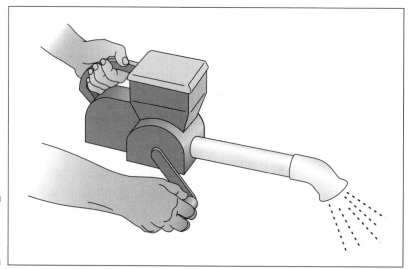

**Figure 13-12:**
Garden
duster.

# Rodents, rabbits, and other miscreants

Mice, shrews, moles, voles, gophers, and other little rodents often burrow in mulch, either to nest or to root around for seeds to eat. Replace the mulch with gravel. Or reduce it, or at least scrape it away from the bases of your plants. A cage or barrier of chicken wire or poultry netting under or around the perimeter of the garden can also discourage the rodents, provided the holes are too small for them to squeeze through. You can also try trapping them or flooding their holes/tunnels with the hose. Enlisting the help of a cat who's a good mouser is the best bet.

Rabbits, groundhogs, raccoons? These brazen marauders may make you homicidal enough to reach for a gun, hand grenade, or poison-baited trap, but you can choose from some less drastic (and more humane) tacks. The best defence, quite honestly, is a good garden fence (include a gate, of course, so *you* can get in and out). Select one that's tall enough to discourage climbing over, but also sink it several centimetres into the ground to discourage digging under. Other remedies that are said to work include hot sauce, commercial repellents, bags of human hair (collected from a salon), a noisy radio, water-gun repellents, and owning an alert dog.

# Deer

First of all, let's be completely frank here: Gardening in deer country is a challenge. Modern-day deer are overpopulated because of having fewer natural predators and because their natural habitats are shrinking due to development. And when they're hungry, they'll eat almost anything, including the contents of your vegetable garden.

The best defence is a good garden fence. But because deer are good leapers, it needs to be quite tall — 2.5 metres (8 feet) or so. A lower fence may work if you set it at a 45-degree angle, or even lay it on the ground on the theory that deer don't like to get their hooves snagged. For extra insurance or if the deer are really hungry and persistent, you need an electric fence (hardware, home, and farm-supply stores sell them) or a double fence — two 3-metre (10-foot) fences, 1.8 metres (6 feet) apart.

# Birds

Birds are mainly a threat to newly planted seeds and ripening fruit (especially berries — see Chapter 15). Cover the seeds with soil and/or netting to discourage birds; then cover plants with netting until the fruit is ripe and you're able to pick the harvest.

# Bugs

Correct identification is key. Capture a few and show them to someone who knows (a garden-centre staffer, a landscaper, or another, more-experienced vegetable gardener), or look the bugs up. If you can't find the pest, a sample of typical damage should help your expert identify the culprit.

As you can see in the upcoming culprits' table, we're not hastening to recommend spraying chemicals in a vegetable garden (and you may not be able to use chemicals in your area, anyway). Try other tactics first.

If you catch the problem early, it's not unrealistic to manage by picking off offending bugs and drowning them in soapy water (not a coffee can of gasoline — this method makes a disgusting and toxic brew that's hard to dispose of) or putting the bugs in a zipper-type plastic bag. Or shower the plants with water. Often, a good spray with the hose can drown and knock off offending pests.

Spray with pesticides only as a last resort, because you can harm unintended targets (plant and animal) or taint your garden soil. (Check with your municipal government to see which pesticides have been approved for use in your area.) To be on the cautious side, you also want to thoroughly wash your harvest before eating or cooking. Always get the right product for the targeted pest and follow the directions on the label to the letter. Note that most sprays are most effective when used in the early stages of a pest's development. Examples of sprays that you can use include insecticidal soap, neem oil, horticultural oils, and garlic or pepper spray.

Table 13-2 lists the common culprits.

| Table 13-2 | Vegetarian Bugs, Grubs, Slugs, and Other Critters | | |
|---|---|---|---|
| *Type* | *Description* | *Favourite Targets* | *First Control* |
| Aphids | These tiny, plant-sucking insects are usually green but may be red, brown, grey, or black. They stunt and distort plant growth and spread disease. | Broccoli, cauliflower, kale, cabbage, and Brussels sprouts | Knock them off with a stiff blast from the hose. |
| Beetles | Identification is important because some beetles are perfectly harmless. The main vegetable-garden villains are cucumber beetles, Colorado potato beetles, and little flea beetles. | Cucumbers, squash, pumpkins, melons, and potatoes (above-ground growth) | Hand-pick them off or use row covers or other physical barriers to keep them away from their favourite plants. |

| Type | Description | Favourite Targets | First Control |
|---|---|---|---|
| Caterpillars | Not all caterpillars are harmful, so be careful when identifying them. Some are large, some are small, some are colourful, and some are spiny or hairy. | The leaves of any vegetable plant | Hand-pick them off. |
| Cutworms | These little larval fellows relish young seedlings, which they neatly chop off at the soil line. | Beans, corn, pepper, tomato, and cabbage | Because cutworms don't like to climb, putting a collar around the vulnerable plant keeps them out (make it from a can or stiff cardboard). |
| Leafhoppers | These very small flying pests pierce and suck the life out of plant parts, especially foliage (though they love bean blossoms). | Beans, lettuce, potatoes, tomatoes, and squash | A collar of aluminum foil around the base of a plant can deter them. |
| Leaf miners | These tiny insect larvae travel within leaf tissue, leaving meandering trails. These paths weaken a plant and consequently reduce its harvest. | Cucumbers, peppers, squash, melons, and tomatoes | Pick off and dispose of affected leaves. |
| Root maggots | These critters are most active in spring as little egg-laying flies. | Cabbage, broccoli, cauliflower, Brussels sprouts, kale, radish, and onion | Sprinkle coffee grounds or fireplace (wood) ashes around vulnerable plants. Fine-mesh screen cages may also deter them. |

*(continued)*

**Table 13-2** *(continued)*

| Type | Description | Favourite Targets | First Control |
|------|-------------|-------------------|---------------|
| Snails and slugs | Crowded, damp conditions prove irresistible to these slimy nibblers. They're most active at night. | Any vegetable plant! | Erect copper barriers around vulnerable plants (these give them an unpleasant "electric shock"); trap them with pie tins of beer; spread diatomaceous earth on the ground (it feels like flour but is full of sharp particles that irritate their skin). Cocoa hull mulch deters them, while some bark or wood mulches have pieces that are large enough for these slimy nocturnal critters to sleep under. Put out a single board in the garden, and the snails and slugs will use it for shelter during the day. Lift it up and scrape them off. |
| "Worms" (moth larvae) | Cabbage loopers and corn earworms are the worst vegetable-garden pests. | The part you like — the fruit of cabbage-family crops, corn ears, and ripening tomatoes | Protect your plants with row covers. Also, because the worms can overwinter in garden soil, turn over the soil in late fall to expose them to freezing temperatures — and rotate your crops. |

# Chapter 14

# Adding Spice to Your Garden: Growing Herbs

· · · · · · · · · · · · · · · · · · · · · · · · · · · · · · · · · · · · · · · ·

*In This Chapter*
▶ Growing and cultivating herbs
▶ Caring for your herb harvest

· · · · · · · · · · · · · · · · · · · · · · · · · · · · · · · · · · · · · · · ·

*I*f you suspect that the definition of *herb* is a bit loose — it includes rosemary but also nasturtiums — you're right. Defining a *herb* is easier said than done, but the important thing to keep in mind is that herbs are plants that not only have ornamental merits but also are useful in some way. Just to complicate things, some plants called herbs are fast-growing annuals (refer to Chapter 6), and others are long-lived perennials (Chapter 7).

Gardeners grow many herbs for their foliage, which is often deliciously scented; people value others for their edible flowers, seeds, or roots. A lot of herbs are boons in the kitchen, adding exciting new dimensions to all sorts of recipes. Still others are reputed to have healthful or healing properties. The uses of the various herbs are too many and too detailed for the scope of this book.

Even with their broad definition, the majority of herbs have common growing conditions and harvesting techniques. Herbs are usually very easy to find — look for them where you buy your annuals and perennials; or perhaps you have some friends, relatives, or neighbours who won't mind your taking some herbs from their gardens and planting them in your own. And here's some good news: Herbs are among the easiest and most rewarding of all plants to raise. This chapter fills you in on how to grow and care for herbs.

## Planting Herbs: A Lesson in Adaptation

When you're planting your herbs, there are no hard or fast rules, folks! Herbs are wonderfully versatile and flexible, and as we mention at the beginning of this chapter, herbs come in a huge variety of annual and perennial types of plants.

The main thing to do is to pay attention to the type of herb you're trying to plant: Is it an annual? A perennial? Fast growing? Slow growing? Is it an invasive plant, like mint, or does it get along well with other plants? These considerations are important before you start adding herbs to your garden — and probably even before you acquire the herbs themselves! Do your research beforehand: Ask your gardening friends or the staff at the local nursery to find out more about the growing habits of certain herbs.

## Getting the timing right

When you plant your herbs really depends on the plant, but you can't go wrong planting herbs the same way you plant vegetable seedlings; that is, plant them out in the garden after all danger of frost is past (refer to Chapter 13 for info on vegetable gardening). The reason this strategy works for most herbs is that a lot of them aren't especially cold tolerant. This technique also gets herbs in the ground under encouraging conditions: warm soil, warm air, and a good summer stretching out ahead of them — they'll surge right into robust growth.

Of course, many herbs are perennials and can be planted whenever you put perennials in your garden, in April and early May in most parts of the country. Examples of perennial herbs are sage, tarragon, lavender, oregano, and culinary thyme, although not all of them are dependably hardy in all parts of Canada.

Avoid planting herbs — even if you spot plants for sale somewhere at a bargain price — in the heat of summer. Planting then stresses out even dryland natives like oregano and lavender. Also, obviously, late fall isn't a desirable planting time. If you want to enjoy some herbs during the winter months, you're better off growing them in pots that you can bring indoors to a sunny windowsill. See Chapter 16 for details on container gardening, or check out the upcoming section titled "Potting your herbs."

## Helping herbs find their place in the world

When you're deciding where to plant your herbs, just remember that most of them like plentiful sunshine and appreciate well-draining ground (as opposed to very dry or very soggy sites). Read on for your placement options.

### Inviting herbs into your current garden

If you're considering planting your herbs in an existing garden, here are two options:

✔ **Herbs growing by vegetables:** Adding edible herbs to your vegetable garden is a good idea. Vegetables and herbs like the same growing conditions of fertile soil and full sun, and when you're in the mood for a spontaneous summer meal, everything you need is right at hand. Some favourite choices include basil, dill, parsley, cilantro, fennel, thyme, and chives. Refer to Chapter 13 for info on vegetable gardening.

✔ **Herbs mingling with flowers:** This type of planting works best for herbs with pretty flowers of their own, as well as ones that can contribute attractive foliage. Imagine not just how pretty the flower bed will be but also the intriguing homegrown bouquets you can assemble if you widen your palette to include some herbs. Favourite choices include sage (including the kinds with colourful or variegated leaves), dill, mint, basil (especially the purple-leaved kind), artemisia, and borage. For info on growing annuals, refer to Chapter 6; Chapter 7 discusses perennials.

### Creating a herb garden

For many gardeners, the best solution for growing herbs is to put them all in their own garden. Follow the usual rule for flower gardens; namely, place taller herbs to the back or in the middle of a bed, with shorter ones at their feet, so you can see, appreciate, and have easy access to everything for care and harvesting. Give every plant ample room to spread — if some herbs emerge as thugs over time, stealing the stage from less aggressive growers, just chop them back or take them out of the display altogether (see the sidebar called "Going solo").

You can choose from many types of herb gardens, but generally they're either formal or informal. You'd be wise to plan a formal garden ahead of time on paper, making a geometric design (perhaps composed of squares, or like slices of a pie) to your liking — take a look at Figure 14-1, or refer to Chapter 2 for advice on designing a garden. Install the layout first, with edgings and pathways in place; for paths, use bricks, rocks, gravel, or even grass. Edging plants such as small boxwood plants, germander, or a sheared low hedge of lavender or dusty miller also work but require more care.

## Going solo

Some herbs that are tall or hog horizontal space are meant to be alone. They monopolize the garden's resources — soil nutrients and water — or have a tendency to grow rampantly. In other words, they're not good team players. If you really want them, why not segregate them in their own area, bed, or pot? Plants that do better solo include mint, oregano, and marjoram.

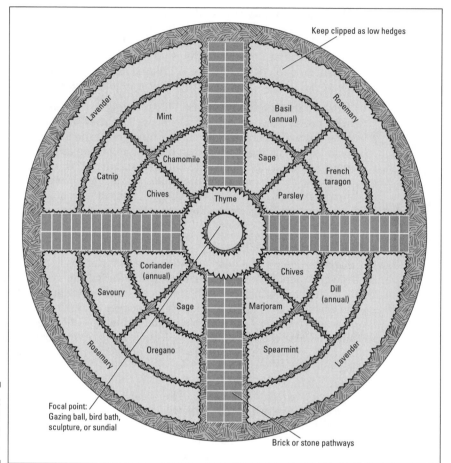

**Figure 14-1:**
A formal
herb garden
plan.

If you prefer informal herb gardens, take note: A casual bed devoted to all herbs can look delightfully cottage-gardeny, or it can look like a jumble. (A jumble is bad: It's hard to care for and harvest from, and crowded plants become more vulnerable to pests and diseases.) So make a plan on paper for this sort of garden, too — set it up like your vegetable garden or your favourite flower garden — and then see what happens, making alterations as you see fit. Aim for a harmonious mix of foliage colours and types, with the occasional flowering herb as an exclamation point.

### Potting your herbs

A lot of people like to grow herbs in pots: A pot contains a plant's growth, and it can be placed near the kitchen door. Container gardening is a terrific way to raise edible herbs that you use often in your kitchen.

The most important thing to do for potted herbs is keep them watered; potted plants dry out notoriously fast, and cycles of soaking and drying out aren't good for a plant's health, even a tough little herb plant. (***Note:*** The Mediterranean herbs — such as thyme, rosemary, lavender, sage, and oregano — prefer poor, almost sandy soil; they'll rot if they're too wet. Use a sand or pebble mulch around them.) So site potted herbs where you won't forget about them, such as right outside the back door or on the patio in full sight of the kitchen window. A window box (see Figure 14-2) is a particularly effective and practical way to grow herbs in a container. See Chapter 16 for more information on container gardening.

**Figure 14-2:**
A window
box of
herbs.

Some herbs, such as mints, lemon balm, and lemon verbena, can become garden thugs. They're very invasive, so containers are perfect for keeping them where you want them and preventing them from wandering and taking over. (Check for square stems on plants — these traits can indicate you're dealing with thugs.)

Mixed displays can look great. Fill larger pots with several different herbs, or assemble a gathering of individual pots and array them on a deck or patio. You can even tuck a potted herb into your garden proper as an accent, shifting it around as you see fit. If colour or interest seems to be lacking, just choose especially decorative or colourful pots — they make a dramatic difference and add to the fun.

Frequent harvesting from potted herbs has an important benefit, by the way. When you snip off the tips, the remaining plant is inspired to grow more thickly and compactly — which looks better in a pot.

## Putting herbs in their place: How to plant

Planting herbs is as easy as 1-2-3, and really isn't much different from planting an annual or perennial. When planting a new herb in a garden, just follow these basic steps (if you need tips on preparing the garden beforehand, refer to Chapter 4):

1. **Use a trowel to dig a hole in a sunny spot with well-drained soil.**

   Make the hole slightly deeper and wider than the pot the herb is currently in. Add a little compost or other organic material to the bottom of the hole for the roots to grow into.

2. **Pop the plant out of its pot.**

   If tugging is necessary, handle the plant by its stem, never by its leaves. Using your fingers, gently push up on the roots at the hole on the bottom of the pot. Hold your hand over the surface of the plant, with your fingers separated to accommodate the main stem, and then turn the pot upside down in your hand. Alternatively, you can run a dull knife around the edge of the pot, as if you were removing a cake from a pan.

3. **Scrape the sides of the root ball to loosen the root system.**

   Loosening the root system encourages it to grow beyond its current size.

4. **Plant the herb at the same depth it was growing in the pot (if you're not sure, look closely on the stem for a soil line).**

   Backfill soil in and around the hole, and firm everything into place with your hands to eliminate air pockets. Soak thoroughly.

When choosing a planting spot, be sure to find out and take into account your herb's expected mature size. You don't want it to be crowded or cramped; it won't be as healthy or productive.

Planting herbs in a container is a bit different from planting them in a garden. Follow these steps:

1. **Choose an ample-sized pot and be sure it has a drainage hole in the bottom.**

   Most herbs can't tolerate wet feet.

2. **Fill the pot with damp potting soil mix.**

   Premoistening the mix makes the job soooo much easier!

3. **Eject the herb seedling from the pot you bought it in, place it in the soil, and water it.**

Containers, particularly clay pots, tend to dry out quickly, especially when placed in the sunny spots herbs like. Although many herbs are tough customers and drought tolerant, subjecting them to extreme cycles of drought and drenching causes stress. Don't neglect your potted herbs! Place them in plain sight or in an area you pass by often so you don't forget them.

## Raising herbs from seed

The majority of herbs are easy to grow from seed. Also, some types of herbs — interesting or offbeat or rare varieties — are often for sale only in seed form. Here's the good news: Unlike some flower and vegetable seeds, you don't have a long wait from sowing to having a productive plant.

To plant your herb seeds, follow these steps:

1. **Prepare a flat of sterile soil mix or the pot in which you plan to keep the herb(s).**

   Be sure the flat or pot contains drainage holes to prevent the possibility of rot.

2. **Sow the seeds on top of the mix or under a thin layer of mix, whichever the seed packet recommends.**

   The packet also advises you on how far apart to sow the seeds.

3. **Care for the seeds for a few weeks or until the seedlings are several centimetres high and ready to be transplanted.**

   Bottom watering is advisable, as is warm and indirect light — again, the necessary details are on the seed packet. To bottom water the seeds, place the container in a tub or sink. Gradually add warm water (which penetrates the soil quicker than cold water) so that it reaches a depth of about half the height of the container in which the seeds are sown. Let the container sit in this warm water until the surface of the soil in the container is wet (the soil takes on a darker colour). This may take an hour or so. Then either remove the seed container from the tub or let the water out of the sink and allow the excess water to drain from the container.

Many herb seeds are quite small, and seed companies give you much more than you need in a single packet (for example, a typical packet of basil seeds can have 250 individual seeds in it!). Don't use them all at once.

The biggest mistake beginning herb gardeners make when sowing seeds is sowing too thickly. The result is a forest of small plants! Be conservative when sowing, and even so, you may still have to thin. (Wait till the seedlings have at least a second set of leaves before thinning; then carefully, carefully, cut out the weaker plants with tiny scissors.)

# Taking Care of Your Herbs

Caring for herbs isn't much different from watching out for your other annuals and perennials, but herbs may have a few special requests. The following sections tell you how to make sure your herbs have what they need to succeed, including protection from the baddies of the insect (and mite, snail, and slug) world.

## Providing a herb's basic needs

Although each type of herb has its own growing requirements, it's pretty safe to say that most herbs are unfussy plants. Most prefer full sun. Most prosper in good, moderately fertile soil. And most require that the soil be well drained so they get the moisture they need to grow but don't suffer from wet feet. If your chosen site is lacking in any of these requirements, take steps to improve it. Clip back overhanging trees and shrubs. Dig in organic matter such as compost and/or dampened peat moss, as well as some sand, to poor soil to improve its texture. (Refer to Chapter 4 for more information on improving soil conditions.)

Herbs rarely need fertilizer! In fact, excess fertilizer may lead to lax, floppy growth that's unattractive and vulnerable to diseases and pests; it may also inhibit flowering.

## Caring for potted herbs indoors

Herbs are easy and fun to grow inside, which also extends the harvest into our cold, Canadian winters. Herbs are best kept on a kitchen windowsill, provided it gets plenty of sun. That way, they're handy when you need them for a recipe; plus, the sight of them certainly adds character and a pleasant fragrance to your kitchen. Here are couple other tips:

✓ **Turn herbs occasionally so they're healthier and look fuller/balanced.** Potted herb plants naturally grow toward the source of sunlight, and they may start to lean or look one-sided unless you give them a quarter-turn every few days.

✓ **Trim or harvest often.** Life in a pot is pretty confining for most herbs, and you don't want them to outgrow their space or start getting floppy or lanky. So cut off tips often; this trimming inspires the plant to branch and to grow more densely and compactly.

After a while, the herbs may naturally peter out and need to be replaced. So enjoy them to the fullest while they're in their prime!

Some herbs like "sweeter" soil (soil with a higher pH, or alkaline soil — refer to Chapter 4). If your garden's soil tends toward the acidic side, a sprinkling of lime powder or chips at the herb's base at planting time may be in order. Examples of herbs that like this treatment include lavender and echinacea.

Make sure you water in your herb plants on planting day. Then water the plants often in the following days and weeks until they become well established. Well-established herbs may be fairly drought tolerant, but that doesn't excuse you from getting them off to a good start while they're young.

Some herbs really prefer soggy ground. The drawback is that if you put them in such a spot, they may grow too rampantly; be willing to let them do as they will. If that's not practical, simply raise them in a pot and keep the pot well watered, and/or set them in a saucer of water so the growing mix is perpetually damp. Examples of herbs like this include mints, bee balm, cardamom, chervil, goldenseal, and sorrel.

## *Dealing with herb pests*

Believe it or not, many herbs are pest free, which is one of the many reasons gardeners find these plants so easy and fun to grow. Some herbs even *repel* pests from themselves as well as adjacent plants. However, you may meet a handful of pests. If you do, act quickly to rescue your harvest, either by treating the plant or by tearing it out and getting rid of it before the problem can spread. Check out Table 14-1 for a rap sheet of the major troublemakers.

| Table 14-1 | | Pests and the Herbs They Dine On | |
|---|---|---|---|
| *Pest* | *Appearance* | *Effect on Plant* | *Food Preference* |
| Aphids | Tiny, sucking insects that congregate in groups; they may be white, greenish, or black | A severely infested plant turns yellow and dies. | Caraway, lovage, nasturtium, and oregano |
| Carrot weevils | Tiny, hard-shelled brownish bugs | Carrot weevils attack the root as well as the top of the plant. | Parsley |
| Japanese beetles | Green-and-copper-coloured bugs that are about 1 cm (½ in.) long | These bugs are voracious foliage eaters. | Basil and echinacea |
| Leaf miners | Bugs that start as tiny, yellowish larvae and then turn into small, black flies with yellow stripes | Affected leaves have meandering tunnels and blotches. | Lovage, oregano, and sorrel |
| Scales | Bugs that look like small waxy or cottony bumps | Scales feed by sucking sap, and they leave behind telltale honeydew (which, in turn, attracts ants and sooty mould). | Bay, myrtle, and rosemary |
| Slugs and snails | You know these slimy characters! But you may not always see them — they're most active at night | Slugs and snails devour foliage. | Basil, calendula, and sorrel |
| Spider mites | Wee relatives of the spider | Spider mites suck plant juices, leaving telltale pinprick spots and puckering. | Angelica, germander, lemon verbena, mint, oregano, rosemary, sage, and thyme |

The pests that go after herbs may seem as varied as the herbs themselves, but here are a few defensive strategies you can take to protect your herbs:

- ✔ Make sure your herbs are in good health, well watered, and, in particular, have sufficient elbow room.

- ✔ Remove affected leaves; pull out severely infested plants and throw them away before the problem spreads.

- ✔ Dislodge small infestations with a spray from the hose; larger insect pests may be hand-picked and destroyed.

- ✔ Try insecticidal soap, which is nontoxic, if you have to spray. Make sure the pest you're targeting is listed on the label, and then carefully follow the directions regarding how and when to apply.

- ✔ Combat certain pests with beneficial insects (such as ladybugs or lacewings). Look for more information — as well as help in attracting or acquiring the right helper — from a good garden centre or from your provincial ministry of agriculture, or do an online search.

If you succeed in beating back a herb pest and later want to use the herb in your kitchen, be sure to wash it thoroughly first!

# Chapter 15

# Sweet and Crunchy: Growing Fruits, Berries, and Nuts

Homegrown fruit, berries, and nuts take more time and care than some other plants you may grow in your garden. Although soft fruits like strawberries, grapes, and raspberries yield delicious results within a few months or less, tree fruits and nuts require more patience and can take several years to be productive. Fruit and nut trees also require a different sort of preparation than other trees and bushes. But at harvest time, the work is all worth it! In almost every region of Canada, you can find a type of fruit or nut (or variety of fruit or nut) that's well adapted and fairly easy to grow.

*Note:* Many gardeners collectively group fruits, berries, and nuts together as a topic because the cultivating methods are similar for all of them. So for the sake of making the descriptions in this chapter simple, when we mention fruit, we mean fruit, berries, and nuts unless we state otherwise. Also, all of the fruit-bearing plants in this chapter, except strawberries, are woody. Strawberries die back to the ground and only their crowns and roots overwinter, so in that way, they're much like most herbaceous perennials. All the fruits in this chapter are considered "perennial" in that they come up every year and are winter hardy.

For now, though, let your imagination savour the aroma of sun-warmed fruit, picked fresh in your own garden. Then read on as we help you make that vision a reality.

When is a veggie a fruit? Yes, this is a bit of garden trivia, but a *fruit* is defined as a ripened ovary. You can think of a fruit as a pregnant flower. Using this definition, many plants that are known as veggies, like squash, cucumbers, tomatoes, and peppers, are actually fruits — but even though they are technically fruits, they're considered veggies by gardeners.

# Fruit Basics: Knowing and Choosing the Right Fruits for Your Garden

Realistically choosing the type of fruit you can support and grow is important, making the difference between easy success and frustration or failure. Before you get your heart set on a certain kind of fruit you want to grow, do a little research.

Now, you know that fruits come later in a plant's seasonal cycle, right? First, the flowers bloom, and then the petals fall as the fruit starts to swell (pollination from the same plant or an adjacent one may be necessary — bees often help out). At first small, hard, and green, a fruit expands in size and changes colour on the way to becoming juicy and ripe. The seeds or pits are nestled within (strawberries are an exception to the rule), and the flesh of the fruit is actually meant to protect and nourish the seeds, which is why small plants may eventually sprout and grow where unharvested ripe fruit falls to the ground.

Why not just produce seeds? Why go to all the effort to make fruit? The probable answer is that fruit-producing plants adapted themselves so that birds and animals would eat the fruit and therefore distribute the seeds far and wide. Back in the mists of history, food gatherers discovered that the flesh of fruit can also nourish people. The art and science of cultivation led to better fruit size, quality, and flavour. Modern-day fruit varieties are much improved over their wild forebears but require care to achieve a good harvest.

## Examining the types of fruits

Not all types of fruit are suitable or easy for home gardens, owing to their size or growth and maintenance requirements. Peach trees, for example, can be large, demanding trees, but they're worth the effort if you have the interest and time to grow them. And many tree fruits aren't hardy in the coldest parts of Canada, although some varieties of apples and plums can grow in Zone 2, and some apricots and peaches have been developed to survive short growing seasons and very cold winters. When it comes down to it, home gardeners do have a wide range of choices available. Here are some examples:

✔ **Tree fruits:** Apple, apricot, cherry, crabapple, pear, peach, nectarine, plum, quince, pawpaw, and persimmon (Yes, pawpaw and persimmon trees can be grown in some parts of Canada — pawpaw to Zone 5 and persimmon to Zone 6 — with winter protection for the first two or three years until they're established.)

All nuts are technically "seeded fruits," including peanuts!

✔ **Vine fruits:** Grape and kiwi

✔ **Shrub fruits:** Blackberry, saskatoon berry, elderberry, raspberry, gooseberry, currant, and blueberry

✔ **Ground-covering fruits:** Strawberry and melon (for info on growing melons, which aren't woody fruits but annuals, refer to Chapter 13 on vegetable gardening)

✔ **Nut trees:** Walnut, pecan, butternut, and hazelnut

Another thing you may want to consider when looking at types of fruit is how long you have to wait before getting a yield. For instance, strawberries bear fruit in their first year. Raspberry canes, however, bear fruit during their second year, and then they die back to allow the younger, second-year canes to prosper and produce fruit. (But be warned: Raspberry canes have a tendency to march through your garden as they grow, unless you're vigilant about holding them within bounds.) Most shrub fruits, such as gooseberries and saskatoons, take two to four years to yield substantial amounts of fruit. Fruit trees take a few to several years to bear, depending on variety and the type of rootstock they're on. Dwarf fruit trees tend to bear sooner, within three years, while trees on standard rootstocks can take four or more years.

Most woody fruits can last many years. Some apple orchards and vineyards are generations old. In general, when fruits start losing their productivity, it's time to replace them with newer stock.

## *Putting a nut tree in your future*

Most Canadian gardeners consider growing a backyard nut tree to be an exotic pastime suitable only for more southerly gardeners, but actually, we can grow many of the tasty delicacies in various parts of this country. And in fact, we already grow many nut trees (such as ginkgo, oak, and black walnut) simply because they're fine landscape and shade trees. Nut trees have a long history of value to humans: to produce food, to make dyes and high-quality furniture, or simply to supply materials for use as tools — some sculptors and stoneworkers still use the shells of walnuts as an abrasive to fine-tune the finish of their works.

Many nut trees — the Persian walnut and northern pecan, for example — can be grown to bear fruit successfully in Zone 5. Butternut, the hardiest of the walnuts, is hardy to Zone 3. Buartnut, a cross between heartnut and butternut, is a vigorous, disease-resistant tree that's hardy to Zone 4 on its own roots; grafted trees are reliable only to Zone 5. Even the pine nut, used in pesto and salad, is hardy to Zone 4 and is borne by an attractive tree to boot. Hazelnuts have been bred for hardiness in Zone 5, and the Manitoba-bred 'Skinner' hazelnut survives in areas much colder.

While discussing roses in Chapter 9, we raise the subject of *grafting;* that is, splicing the top part of one plant to the rootstock of another. Experts tell us that grafted trees generally bear fruit earlier than own-root, or seedling, trees — sometimes within two or three years — and are chosen from top-quality, high-producing stock that has superior kernel flavour and cracking quality. Seedling trees can take four to eight years to bear.

Nut trees require similar planting and growing conditions as do fruit trees (see "Planting Your Fruit," later in this chapter). Plant them in spring in a well-drained site with the *root collar* — the place where the stem and roots meet — just below the surface and the graft above the ground. Don't plant too deeply — it may kill the tree. As with other trees, dig good soil into the excavation before planting. Water the tree well after planting and prune the top back by about a fifth to promote new growth. Keep an area about 2 metres (6½ feet) wide around the tree weed free until the tree is mature — weeds compete too much for the nutrients the tree requires.

Two different cultivars of the same tree are generally needed for nut production (for more information on cross-pollination, see "Going solo or in pairs: Looking at pollination," later in this chapter). Check with the nursery or catalogue where you buy your nut trees to see how far apart you should plant them.

## *Studying your size accommodations*

Adding fruit plants of some kind to your home landscape isn't just about harvesting delicious fruit. The size of the plant is important, as is the relative beauty of its flowers and foliage. Ideally, the plant fits in and enhances the attractiveness of your yard even when it's not producing fruit.

Pick a plant that fits into its allotted space in your home landscape. Be realistic, because fruit-bearing plants already require consistent maintenance without you also having to constantly cut them back in an effort to get them to fit in a too-small area.

To find out the predicted mature size of a specific cultivar, look on the label, ask a nursery staffer, or look up the plant in a reference book or nursery catalogue or on the Internet. If your space is limited, go looking for a *dwarf cultivar* or one explicitly billed as having a *compact growth habit.* First, be aware that except for apples, few dwarf fruit trees are hardy in areas colder than Zone 5b. But do check out the Colonnade series of apple trees: They have a single main trunk and a tapered habit suitable for small spaces and usually grow to 3 metres (10 feet) tall. Other dwarf varieties that reach about 3 metres but grow wider than Colonnade types include 'Braeburn' and 'Gala'.

Remember that apples, in general, require careful pruning to keep them in good condition for bearing. Don't consign yourself to a career of shaping and pruning unless you have the time and inclination! On the other hand, don't overprune in an effort to keep an eager tree in bounds so it'll fit in your garden — you run the risk of reducing your potential harvest, not to mention making the plant look awkward or unattractive.

Access may also be a consideration for you. If you dream of simply strolling out with a basket and gathering up fresh fruit, choose a fruit that doesn't require a ladder to care for and harvest from. Examples of favourite, more-compact growers include currant, gooseberry, blueberry (both high-bush and low-bush), strawberry, and some blackberry, raspberry, and grape cultivars. Figure 15-1 shows a typical strawberry garden plan that's set up for easy harvesting.

Generally, two kinds of fruit trees are suitable for a home garden: regular and dwarf or semidwarf. The latter type is best if your space is limited, of course. Caring for and harvesting from fruit trees often requires a longer reach; namely, the use of a ladder and pole saw or long-reach pruners. Examples of favourite taller or larger fruit plants include kiwi vines and apple, pear, peach, apricot, and plum trees.

Here are a few more ideas to consider as you explore how to fit fruits into your garden:

- Use a line of berry plants as a property boundary.
- Put single berry plants at the corners of your vegetable garden.
- Use a shrub or small tree fruit in your foundation planting.
- Plant a fruit tree in your entryway garden (so long as it gets enough sun).
- Create a small orchard in your back forty.
- Expand your vegetable garden to include a strawberry or melon patch.
- Add a berry bush or two to an informal shrub border.
- Plant berry bushes at the base of a gazebo (without blocking the way in).
- Site one or more fruit trees in an informal lawn, on a slight slope, or in other open areas.
- Plant fruit trees in your streetside curb strip.
- Plant a fruiting vine so it grows over a pergola or archway, creating shade below.

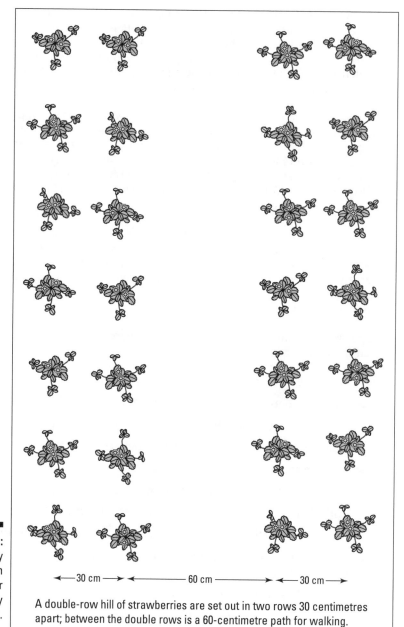

← 30 cm → ← 60 cm → ← 30 cm →

**Figure 15-1:** Strawberry garden plan aligned for easy harvesting.

A double-row hill of strawberries are set out in two rows 30 centimetres apart; between the double rows is a 60-centimetre path for walking.

If you have the room, install a full-blown fruit garden, like the one in Figure 15-2.

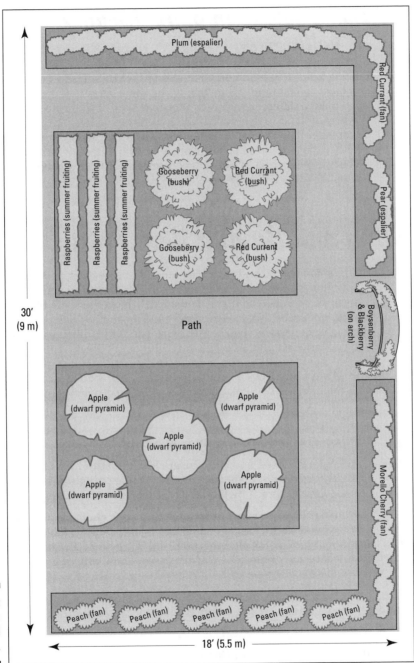

**Figure 15-2:**
Plan for a good-sized fruit garden.

Because some plants can't pollinate themselves, you may have to allow room for two or more plants. See the following section for details.

## *Going solo or in pairs: Looking at pollination*

Certain fruits require cross-pollination to set their fruits. Sometimes it's sufficient to plant more than one of the same variety, and other times you must plant a different variety of the same type of fruit to get the best results. It's very difficult to generalize which fruits are which. The best approach is to carefully read the catalogue or ask the salesperson you're buying from whether the plant is self-fruitful or requires different or additional pollinators. If your supplier can't answer this question, buy from someone else. You need a supplier who knows for sure.

# *Finding and Buying Your Fruit Bearers*

Unlike some annual and perennial flowers and veggies, fruit-bearers aren't plants you want to try raising from seed — it takes forever! Not only that, but many fruit bearers also don't "come true" (have the traits of their parent plants) from seed. No, for the fastest and most gratifying results, buy plants. Here's our general advice, before delving into the different forms in which you can buy fruit plants:

- **Always buy from a reputable source.** Ask around, nose around, and examine the source's guarantee and refund policy. Your provincial ministry of agriculture's office may be able to point you toward good nearby sources.

- **Don't bother with bargain hunting.** You get what you pay for.

- **Require a label and/or accurate identification.** This label includes not only the type of plant (for example, apple or highbush blueberry) but also the cultivar ('McIntosh' or 'Bluecrop', respectively).

- **Ask or look for some assurance that your choice is "certified" or "virus tested."** Virus-infected plants don't always look diseased, at least not at first. If you skip this step and bring home an infected plant, it'll decline over time, and you may never know why or may think you did something wrong.

- **Check visually for plant health.** Make sure both the top growth and the root system are intact and in good condition, showing no signs of damage, rot, galls, or pests.

At local nurseries, buy the largest fruit plants you can find and afford so you can get off to a faster start. Confirm that the plant's well rooted by poking into the soil mix and/or tipping the pot and sliding it out to see for yourself. Choose plants with buds over ones that are already flowering — the trip home or the transition from pot to garden soil is likely to make them jettison blooms early in favour of establishing their roots in their new home. New buds, flowers, and eventually, fruit will come along in due course!

You can also get fruits bareroot. Although a bareroot fruit tree may look like nothing more than a slender branch (a *whip*) with some roots, you're still concerned with the quality of the root system in particular. Many broken or dried-out roots aren't a good sign. You may end up trimming either the top growth or the roots prior to planting (see "Bareroot plants" in the upcoming planting section), but you want to head into the project with a good plant.

With mail order, though, our central advice is to shop with a specialist. Avoid nurseries where the plants aren't clearly or fully identified. Steer clear of nurseries that offer fruit plants only as a sideline. You want people who propagate and ship the plants themselves; they know what they're doing, and this streamlined system also keeps the quality higher and the costs down. Find such companies in the ads in gardening magazines (particularly in the classified ads in the back or on their online catalogue listings), in the appendix in this book, or online.

# *Planting Your Fruit*

When you think you're ready to plant, the first thing to do, probably even before you acquire your plants, is prepare the soil. It is a far, far better thing to deal with the soil before you plant than after — a berry bush, fruit tree, or strawberry patch is a major landscape investment, and there's no sense in cutting corners from the get-go.

Good-quality soil is especially important when raising edibles. You want your crop to be both safe and tasty. Do a soil test on the intended spot (buy a kit, follow the directions, mail the sample into a lab, and await recommendations — for more information, refer to Chapter 4).

Because you remember to name on the form the sort of fruit you intend to raise (hint, hint), the recommendations for soil improvement that come back from the lab are tailored to that crop. For example, blueberry bushes prefer a lower pH, so the lab may suggest that you add some sulphur to make your soil more acidic; peach trees and certain European grape cultivars like conditions a bit more alkaline, so some supplemental lime may be in order. Note that these amendments take time to move through the soil, so try to add them the fall prior to spring planting.

Organically rich soil, not surprisingly, is ideal. It offers a slow-release reservoir of nutrients that your fruit-bearing plants need and relish. Dig some organic matter into your soil ahead of time, and replenish it at least annually. It lightens heavy clay soil and improves sandy soil, making the entire area more hospitable to plant roots. Good choices include compost, well-rotted manure, rotted sawdust, chopped-up leaves, and spent mushroom soil. Yes, adding periodic doses of fertilizer can also help your crop along, but you need to create an initial foundation.

## Making the prepared soil deep and wide enough

As with so many other plants in your garden, fruit-bearing plants need ample space for their roots to develop. Sufficient soil both nourishes and anchors plants. Take measure of how extensive the root system is on planting day, and then go farther to allow for future growth.

For example, because strawberry plants generally send their roots 15 to 30 centimetres (6 to 12 inches) down, provide them with prepared soil that's at least that deep, with several more centimetres to spare. An apple or plum tree, on the other hand, may send roots many metres deep into the ground over the course of its career. You're not likely to be willing or able to excavate a major hole and have to count on the chosen spot having decent soil, so just give a young root ball ample space. Usually, a hole 30 to 45 centimetres (12 to 18 inches) deep and wide does the trick. Remember to scrape the sides of the hole with your shovel or trowel to loosen the soil and thus help the roots expand beyond its bounds.

As for width, accommodate the root ball and then some. For a fruit tree, although you may not dig a hole that extends as far as the branches and roots may someday extend, you can spread amendments out that direction, mix them in, and then leave them to work their way down gradually.

## Choosing the best time to plant fruits

Here's the basic principle about timing, folks: Plant to allow maximum time for the fruit plant to get growing before the most stressful conditions of the year occur. In colder climates, get the plants in the ground as soon as you can in the springtime so they can enjoy a nice, long summer before cold weather arrives in the fall. But at the same time, be sure to wait till all danger of frost is past so young buds aren't harmed or killed. Plant bareroot plants as soon as you can work the ground in spring.

In the milder fruit-growing areas of the country, you can also plant in late summer or early fall. This timing can allow young stock to establish root systems before being called upon to produce new spring growth. Still-warm soil and drenching fall rains welcome the new arrivals and hasten this process along.

# Deciding where to plant your fruits

Gardeners talk about three main factors to consider when finding a home in your landscape for fruit, nut, and berry plants. Ideally, you want to satisfy all these conditions so your crop doesn't struggle:

- **Sun:** Plentiful sun is a requirement — this means at least six to eight hours a day, or even more. Fruit simply doesn't develop or prosper in shady conditions (even plant foliage may suffer or be sparse). So choose a south-facing spot, or in a pinch, an east- or west-facing location. (Morning sun — an east-facing exposure — is better because it dries morning dew; morning dew that hangs around too long can cause fruit to rot.)

- **Elbow room:** Pick a site out in the open, well away from the shade cast by a house, other building, fence, or other obstruction. Prune back any nearby shrub or tree branches that may be encroaching.

  Planting distances vary according to the type of fruit and the rootstock it's on. Read the planting-distance guidelines in the catalogue or on the plant label.

- **Drainage:** You want a spot with decent soil and good drainage. No berry-producing plants or fruit trees like wet feet (naturally damp spots or places that hold rainwater for more than 12 hours). This waterlogging deprives the roots of needed oxygen and may actually inhibit the uptake of some soil nutrients.

If drainage is iffy in your yard, favour an upland spot or slope. In any event, planting fruits in the lowest part is never advisable. Heavy clay soil is a problem — though improving drainage by digging in lots of organic matter is possible. If your soil is poorly drained, definitely consider a raised bed for strawberries — they require good drainage. Make it at least 30 centimetres (1 foot) high.

If you're space challenged but still want to experience the sweet flavour of homegrown strawberries, plant up a strawberry jar. It's a tallish container with "pockets" on the sides to hold the trailing plants. We recommend that you select the ever-bearing or day-neutral varieties so you can enjoy the fruits throughout the growing season. For more information on container gardening, see Chapter 16.

Here's where *not* to plant fruits, and why:

- **Low, boggy areas:** These spots have poor drainage.
- **Steep slopes:** Slopes are hard to plant, and the plants are hard to care for.
- **Shade:** Fruit doesn't develop without days in the sun.
- **Lousy soil:** Plants struggle in poor soil.

✔ **Middle of a pampered lawn:** Lawn fertilizer is too nitrogen-heavy for fruit plants to tolerate, and mowers and string trimmers can be a hazard.

✔ **Against a wall or fence:** Barriers crowd a plant, and poor air circulation isn't good for its health (the exception is an espaliered fruit tree — see the upcoming section titled "Supporting and training your fruit").

## Getting your fruit in the ground

How to plant fruit depends very much on the type of fruit you want to plant and what form it comes in. The following sections cover some pointers on planting according to whether your fruit is initially available to you in a container, as a bareroot plant, or as a balled-and-burlapped tree. Then we advise you on how to plant a berry patch, because you handle growing berry patches slightly differently from growing other fruit.

### Container plants

Container plants are the form in which you commonly buy berry bushes and some small fruit trees. Assuming you have an appropriate spot ready, the planting process is simple and logical if you follow these steps:

1. **Choose a good day.**

   All danger of frost is past, but the weather is overcast or drizzly. A hot, sunny day is too stressful. If the weather is clear, at least plant late in the day.

2. **Prepare the plant first.**

   Water it well and let the excess drain away. Groom it lightly, trimming away damaged branches and leaves. Pinch off buds, if any (most, not all); this encourages the plant to redirect its energies toward root development. After the plant establishes itself, it'll surely generate new buds, anyway.

3. **Pop the root system out of the pot.**

   If the root system is thick and dense, sliding a butter knife or stick around the perimeter should dislodge it, or perhaps you can cut the container away with tin snips. Tease the roots loose on the bottom and a bit on the sides — this act encourages the plant to venture out into its new home in your garden soil. If the plant is rootbound, score the sides at four or so even intervals with a sharp knife, slicing only a couple of centimetres (about an inch) in toward the centre — this scoring severs girdling roots and inspires new feeder roots to start growing. If there are significant roots girdling the exterior of the root ball, gently tease them loose and spread them out, away from the root ball.

4. **Put the plant in the ground at the same level it was growing in the pot, and then water it.**

   Backfill soil into the hole and lightly firm it in place to eliminate air pockets. Water well, let the ground settle, and add more soil as needed.

## Bareroot plants

Many fruit trees, and sometimes berry-producing shrubs, are sold as bareroot plants; strawberry plants are commonly sold in small bareroot bundles. These plants are dormant, which means you can buy and plant them earlier in the gardening year — as soon as the soil is dry enough to crumble easily in your hand. If you can't plant right away, store bareroot plants in a cool, shaded spot and keep them moist.

On planting day, here are the steps to follow:

1. **Prep the plant first.**

   Unwrap the plant, and if the roots are more than about 30 centimetres (a foot) long or look damaged or frayed, trim them back with clean, sharp clippers. Then soak the roots and stem in a bucket of tepid, muddy water (add a handful of soil) for a few hours or overnight to rehydrate them. As for the top growth, if the plant has branches, shorten them a few centimetres (cutting to just above an outward-facing bud); this trim inspires vigorous, spreading growth. If the tree or shrub is a mere whip (single stem), cut it back to 60 to 90 centimetres (2 or 3 feet) tall if the grower hasn't already done so.

2. **Make a mound inside the hole.**

   Use the excavated soil (or a mixture of it and some organic matter) to make a mound in the hole; you'll set the plant here and spread the roots over it, so make the mound tall. To allow for some settling, adjust the height of the mound so the plant stands about 5 centimetres (2 inches) higher than it stood in the soil at the nursery. (How do you know that? Look for the telltale soil line low on the trunk.)

3. **Add the plant and position it.**

   Place the tree or shrub atop the mound and spread the roots out evenly on all sides. Be careful not to bend or break them, and don't crowd them either. If the tree is branched, orient it with the lowest branch facing southwest — this positioning will eventually help shade the trunk and lessen the chance of sunscald. If the site, being out in the open, is windy, lean the tree ever so slightly into the direction of the prevailing winds.

4. **Backfill.**

   Hold the plant steady (or get a helper to do so) and scoop soil back into the hole. You may have to bounce the plant up and down slightly as you work to settle the soil among the roots. When it stands on its own, add more soil, tamping it down gently with your hands as you work to prevent air pockets.

5. **Create a basin.**

   Make a basin about 30 to 60 centimetres (a foot or two) out from the trunk, mounding up soil on the outer edge to several centimetres high. Fill it partway with compost or other organic material, which will nourish the new young feeder roots that are developing. Top it off with some weed-inhibiting mulch.

6. **Water.**

   Finally, soak slowly and thoroughly today and at least once a week for the rest of the season, unless you get good rainfall. The best way to water is to leave a hose inside the basin area overnight, leaking a slow trickle of water. A young fruit tree or berry bush is a thirsty plant.

### Balled-and-burlapped plants

Fruit trees and larger berry-producing shrubs may be available in balled-and-burlapped form, which indicates that the plant was recently field-dug. The purpose of the burlap or other cloth and trusses is to hold the soil protectively in place around the root ball. Here are the steps to follow to return the plant to the ground in your own yard:

1. **Get the hole ready.**

   The size of the root ball in this case is perfectly obvious, which is nice. Make the hole slightly bigger, both for manoeuvrability and also to encourage the roots to move outward in their new home. Assuming the plant is not too big, you can check your work by temporarily holding the trussed plant in the hole.

2. **Double-check depth.**

   Set the trussed root ball in the hole, and then place a piece of lumber or a rod of some kind across the top of the hole. The top of the root mass should meet the lumber. If not, you know what to do — dig the hole deeper or backfill a bit, depending on whether it's too deep or too shallow.

3. **Unwrap the plant.**

   Do this unpacking outside of, but right beside, the hole. Cut off or unwind all rope, twine, string, or whatever is holding the burlap or cloth in place. Be especially careful to get off any material binding the trunk. Modern burlap may contain synthetic (plastic) material that practically never decays, so don't leave the burlap on. Some root balls are also enveloped in a planting bag or wire basket — whatever you have, remove it.

4. **Plant.**

   Set or wiggle the root ball into the prepared hole, making sure the roots are loosened and spread out, and backfill thoroughly to eliminate air pockets. If the tree is branched, orient it with the lowest branch facing southwest to eventually help shade the trunk and lessen the chance of sunscald. If the site is windy, lean the tree slightly into the direction of the prevailing winds.

**5. Create a basin and then water.**

Make the basin 30 to 60 centimetres (a foot or two) out from the trunk, mounding up soil to several centimetres high. Fill the basin partway with compost or other organic material, and top it off with some weed-inhibiting mulch. Soak slowly and thoroughly at planting and at least weekly till the end of the season (unless you get good rainfall). To be sure the water doesn't wash away the soil, leave a hose emitting water slowly inside the basin area overnight or for several hours. Watering is particularly critical because the root ball may have dried out while it was out of the ground, despite its protective wrapping.

## A berry patch

Want to grow raspberries or blackberries? Planting a patch of these berry canes is a little different than growing an orchard of trees or a low-growing strawberry patch, because you have to install a support, or trellis, to contain the canes. The trellis keeps your plants upright (rather than in a slumping tangle) and also keeps them drier and thus less prone to disease. And it's much easier to harvest the fruit when the canes are growing upright. We advise starting with a single row of plants.

Don't grow cultivated raspberries or blackberries anywhere near wild brambles or near an area where you grow or have recently grown eggplants, peppers, tomatoes, potatoes, or strawberries — all these plants can host diseases that are harmful to cultivated berries.

Here are the steps to follow when creating your berry patch:

**1. Make the row.**

Clear out an area of all weeds, grass, and physical obstructions. Make the area about 60 centimetres (2 feet) wide and as long as you want.

**2. Create a planting trench.**

The roots of berry bushes are likely to grow down to about 30 centimetres (a foot) deep, so excavate to at least that depth. Improve the soil with organic matter and with amendments that adjust the pH, if recommended by a soil test. For example, raspberries like a pH level of 5.6 to 6.2.

**3. Erect a support.**

The object is to keep the canes off the ground and not to crowd them. You want good air circulation, which lessens the chance of disease. Use wooden posts (rot-resistant wood, like cedar) or metal posts, plunge them deeply into the ground, add braces if warranted, and then run strong wire between them to support and confine the plants on each side of the row. Your support setup options include

- Posts at the four corners of a berry patch with only a couple of rows

- V-shaped posts set at about a 30-degree angle at each end of a row

- Single posts with T-shaped crosspieces at each end of a row

The standard advice is to set your posts in the ground so they're about a metre (just over 3 feet) tall above ground and to run two or three wires from end to end down the supports to encase the canes.

4. **Plant.**

Space the canes at even intervals, 60 to 90 centimetres (2 or 3 feet) apart, down the row and under the lowest wire so the wire will support the canes as they grow. Follow the previous planting directions in "Container plants," including giving each plant a good soaking.

5. **Cut back.**

After planting and watering is complete, tiptoe into the patch with your clippers and cut the plants off at ground level. Yikes, this shearing sounds drastic, but one of its goals is to eliminate canes that harbour diseases. (The space and good air circulation provided by frequent pruning is also crucial for established raspberry canes to inhibit disease and encourage a good crop.) Plus, you don't want the plants to charge into early growth and fruiting. Instead, this step forces your new berry plants to focus on establishing and expanding their root systems. New canes will appear soon enough.

# Taking Care of Fruits

Modern fruit cultivars are bred to be productive and deliver a bountiful harvest. This trend is all well and good, but there are downsides. The sheer volume and weight of lots of fruit can cause a plant to slump, slouch, bow down, or trail fruiting branches on the ground. Also, humans aren't the only critters who like to eat fruits and nuts, and keeping these crops protected well enough so you can have something to show for all your hard work can be a challenge. In this section, we give you the pointers you need to keep your fruit healthy, happy, and plentiful enough to enjoy!

## Watering

Although too much water or poor drainage can drown a plant or encourage disease, fruit plants still need moisture. Shallow-rooted crops, like blueberries and strawberries, especially need ample water. Even if your climate provides lots of natural rainfall, you may still have to supplement it. The most critical periods are at planting time and during fruit swell.

We recommend trickle irrigation for watering berry-producing plants, either with a soaker hose, a regular hose set to a mere trickle, or an in-ground system with emitters especially designed for this purpose (refer to Chapter 4). These methods allow the water to reach the roots evenly and gradually and yet avoid wetting the fruit (wet fruit is susceptible to rot, a particular concern for raspberries, blueberries, and strawberries).

## Fertilizing

Unlike, say, vegetable crops, the majority of fruit-bearing plants aren't heavy feeders. If your soil is fertile or you've improved soil fertility prior to planting, feeding isn't a big part of maintenance. (Sure, commercial orchards dose their trees and bushes on a regular basis, but they're aiming for maximum yields; home growers can afford to be less indulgent.)

In any event, before you decide to go to the trouble of applying fertilizer, check your soil's pH level by having a test done (see the appendix for sources). A pH level that's too high or too low hinders plants from taking up the nutrients they need, making your adding fertilizer a waste of time and money.

There's mixed advice about fertilizing fruit trees. Some experts say that fruit trees don't require fertilizer until they're of fruit-bearing age, at which time you should use a 10-10-10 balanced formula — but never apply it after July 15. Using fertilizer after this date can encourage fresh new growth that may not have time to harden before cold weather sets in and potentially damages tender shoots. Environment Canada advises fertilizing with compost or fish emulsion. The University of Saskatchewan says to fertilize fruit trees only if they show pale leaves and weak growth, and to use 16-20-0; their experts also say you should never fertilize young trees because they'll take longer to mature and bear fruit. And the University of British Columbia never fertilizes its fruit trees. If you do decide to use fertilizer, apply it at the rates described on the label. More is not better!

Some fertilizers can be spread over the soil surface and then scratched into the top couple of centimetres or so of the soil (this method is called *top dressing*). Fertilizer spikes are poked into the ground at intervals around the tree and above the root system. The nutrients get to the plant roots only when watered in. In fact, you're best off watering before and after feeding the trees, no matter what fertilizer you use.

No particular type of fertilizer can compel your fruit plant to bear at an earlier age. The age of bearing is mainly influenced by the variety, how and when you prune, and by certain rootstocks, in the case of grafted fruit trees.

## Cutting back on mulch

We know, we know; you're always being told to mulch garden plants to keep weeds at bay and conserve soil moisture. But mulching isn't as critical with many fruit plants because the trees tend to cast shade over their bases, which helps with such matters. Mulch can even be a detriment in a berry patch or small orchard because it can harbour pests — hungry little rodents or voracious slugs.

## Supporting and training your fruit

To keep your harvest off the dirt and in the air where it's able to develop freely and enjoy good air circulation and plentiful sunshine, supports may be in order. A wide variety is available, depending on the fruit you want to grow. Figure 15-3 shows two different ways to train grapes with supports, though there are several methods of training grapes.

Supports also help keep a developing harvest visible and train the fruit in a certain way to make it easily accessible; they also ensure a larger harvest. The supports may consist of anything from bracing boards under a heavy branch to a sturdy trellis to rigs of posts and wire. Figure this need for support into your plans when selecting both a spot and a cultivar.

All of the systems have one thing in common: They're designed to keep the vines off the ground so the fruit has good air circulation and exposure to sunlight and is easier to harvest. If your vines don't end up looking just like a book drawing, don't worry — it isn't critical.

Fruit tree training systems, on the other hand, are designed to expose the fruit to good air flow (to reduce disease) and to bright sunlight (to ripen the fruit), and to encourage a tree structure that's strong and will promote more fruit production. The training systems in Figure 15-4 are fairly easy to follow, but other methods may be equally as successful.

*Espalier trees* are trained to grow in one dimension or plane (again, see Figure 15-4). They're commonly used against fences or buildings. Their shapes can be quite artistic and ornamental. In addition to being aesthetically pleasing, they also result in high-quality fruit that's easy to tend and harvest.

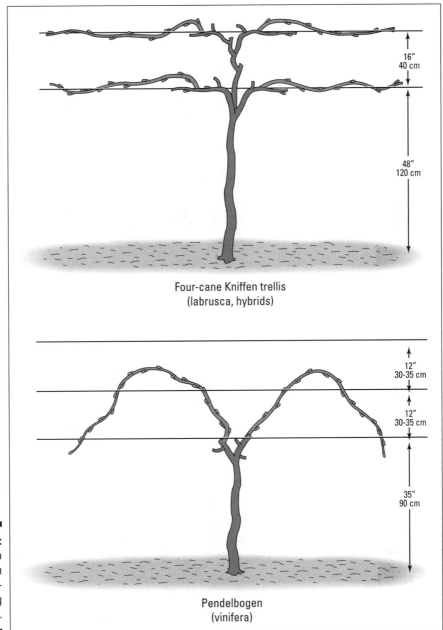

Four-cane Kniffen trellis
(labrusca, hybrids)

Pendelbogen
(vinifera)

**Figure 15-3:**
Two
common
grape-
training
systems.

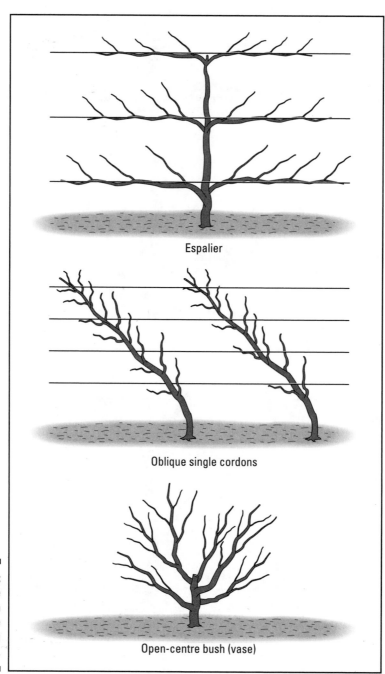

Espalier

Oblique single cordons

Open-centre bush (vase)

**Figure 15-4:**
Three
common
fruit tree
training
methods.

'Morden Blush' (below) is a hardy Canadian-bred, low-growing rose that blooms all season after putting forth a heavy flush of flowers in June. The flowers are light pink in cool weather or pale pink to almost white when it's hot. The striped and very fragrant Rosa gallica 'Versicolor' (left), also called "Rosa mundi" for a mistress of Henry II, dates back to the 16th century. The rose blooms only once each year, in early summer. (Chapter 9)

Roses are the country's favourite plants. Both 'John Cabot' (above left), a climbing Explorer rose, and 'The Fairy' (left), a sprawling groundcover polyantha rose, are hardy in most parts of Canada. (Chapter 9)

Ground-covering plants grow low and create a mat in your garden. They're useful on slopes, narrow entranceways, or other areas that are difficult to landscape. Low-growing moss phlox (above left) is a mass of cerise, pink, red, or mauve flowers in spring. The heather (above right) has rosy pink flowers in late summer and a twiggy growth. (Chapter 12)

Thyme is more than a culinary herb; it's also a versatile groundcover with many cultivars and types to choose from. This thyme plant is 'Bressingham'. (Chapter 12)

Sweet woodruff, a lacy ground-cover that thrives in shade, has star-like white flowers in spring and a fresh, hay-like scent. (Chapter 12)

The tasty produce in a vegetable garden can be pretty as well as practical. For example, check out the two-tone flowers and slender pods of 'Painted Lady' runner bean (left) and the colourful and delicious 'Bright Lights' Swiss chard (below). (Chapter 13)

Smooth, frilly, or lacy, veggies have a variety of textures to add character to your garden. 'Cupid' cherry tomato (left) is smooth, bright, and sweetly delicious. 'Cololsa' cabbage (below) has a layered structure and strong presence, and 'Fern Leaf' dill (bottom) has an airy feeling as well as bright colour and zesty taste. (Chapter 13)

Basil is a natural with tomatoes, both in the garden and on a plate. The variety above is 'Lettuce Leaf'. (Chapter 13)

Many herbs, such as the lush basil on the left, grow well in containers. Keep your herbs well watered and move the pots around to follow the sun. (Chapter 16)

One glorious planter filled with hydrangea, tulips, pansies, and hyacinths, and accented with twigs and ivy, adds colour and drama to an entranceway. Change the planter's look as the flowers fade by adding new pots of started plants. (Chapter 16)

A pale pink beautybush sprawls over a fence, joined by 'The President' clematis. To get this effect, choose varieties of plants that bloom at the same time. (Chapters 11 and 12)

A wide windowsill is an obvious place for a window box — giant tuberous begonias grow in the boxes at left — but a fence is a less-likely location. Brace the planters well on the inside of the fence and then fill them with annuals like the 'Purple Wave' petunias, yellow bidens, and blue scaevolas shown below. (Chapter 16)

Water adds atmosphere to a garden, and the sound of water is soothing. Hollowed-out bamboo makes a unique spout; the one to the left, called a deer-scarer, fills with water slowly and then empties, creating a pattern of sound. (Chapter 17)

Children love to help with garden chores and raise a few of their very own veggies. A teepee of runner beans adds height to the garden and has bright flowers that grow magically into tender green pods. (Chapter 20)

Butterfly weed is a magnet for the monarch butterfly. (Chapter 20)

# Pruning

Fruit-bearing plants need regular pruning. It keeps the plants in bounds, attractive, and healthy, and — perhaps most important — it helps them be more productive.

Always use clean, sharp tools when you prune. *Clean,* because you don't want to spread disease, and *sharp,* because blunt cutters mash and crush stems and branches. And always use the right tool for the job; applying a hand-held clipper to a thick branch is frustrating and foolish (Chapter 5 can fill you in on tools).

Finally, if any pruning maintenance is too difficult, too dangerous, or too time consuming, consider scaling back your plans or hiring qualified help. Whatever you do, don't let the problem go. A neglected fruit tree or berry patch is a sorry sight, not to mention hard work to reclaim.

Here's the general rule: Prune fruit plants when they're dormant, in late winter. You're better able to see what you're doing without a lot of foliage and so forth in the way, both in terms of shaping the plant and making sure you cut right above a bud. You also get little or no sap bleeding. And when growth starts up, the plant will grow as you plan and direct.

## Tree fruits

A crop of tree fruits can be heavy, so shape a tree from an early age so that it has a strong framework that can bear the weight. That said, do no more pruning on a young tree than is totally necessary, or you risk delaying its first crop.

*Scaffold limbs* are supporting limbs that are evenly spaced, come out from the main trunk at wide angles, and over time, have a spiral arrangement around the trunk. To achieve strong scaffolding limbs, prune out branches that crowd, cross, or shade others, and remove them at the trunk (leave no stubs, in other words).

In later years, do an annual pruning to maintain this early form. Cut to reduce the fruit load and stimulate new shoot growth. How much should you cut? It depends on the size and heft of the particular fruit and the bearing habit of the tree. So read up in more detail on your particular tree or get the advice of a more experienced fruit grower.

Apples, pears, and other tree fruit often have *June drop,* in which immature fruit falls from the tree. This natural fruit loss is a reminder to thin the fruit. Too many fruits clustered too closely together don't ripen well, nor do they reach their ideal size. Thin so you have 15 centimetres (6 inches) between fruits. Remember that pruning and thinning are harder on you than on the plant.

A grafted fruit tree is one where the top part of the tree (called the *scion*) is grafted or joined to the rooting portion of the plant (called a stock, or rootstock). The rootstock of the tree determines its vigour and growth habit (full-sized or dwarf), while the scion determines its flowering and fruiting characteristics. By grafting, horticulturists are able to combine the positive characteristics of two trees to get a desired result — like a dwarf tree with a strong, vigorous root system that bears large, flavourful fruit.

### Shrub fruits

Fruits that grow on bushes need to be prevented from becoming crowded; a tangle is difficult to prune, tricky to harvest from, and more prone to diseases and pests. You don't have to do much during the first season or two, but in subsequent years, you have to make an annual habit of thinning out the older wood (older branches, older canes). This pruning makes way for the new shoots, which, honestly, are *always* coming on. If you see a lot of new shoots, you may even have to thin out some of them. Figure 15-5 shows how to prune raspberry bushes; you can apply this method to most other shrub fruits.

Some berry plants produce fruit on first-year canes, and some on second-year canes, so be careful that you don't cut out all the productive canes in your zeal to control the patch. You can find out which kind your berry bushes are either by simply observing or by asking when you purchase the plants.

The normal bramble life cycle of many shrub fruits is to produce a vegetative cane *(primocane)* in their first year; the cane overwinters, becomes a fruit-producing cane *(floricane)* the following year, and then dies. So your training becomes a cyclical matter of supporting these stems, encouraging them to stand up and trail outward along the wire, and then removing them at ground level when they're through at the end of their second year. You can use cloth ties or just guide the fast-growing, lax, thorny stems.

### Vine fruits

How you prune grapes, hardy kiwi, and other vine fruits depends on the sort of support you've chosen for them and how much space you allow them to fill. At the outset (the year you plant), cut the plant back rather drastically to a few buds. This trim channels energy into the growth of one or two main stems, or "trunks."

Subsequent side branches, evenly spaced off the main trunk, are called *cordons* and are considered more or less permanent. Often, the more of these branches, the better — they make for a fuller and more productive vine in the long run. So give the plant good care (regular water, fertilizer, and so on) in its first season or two so you can encourage plenty of cordons. Off these side branches grow the third tier of branches, known as *fruiting arms.* These structures get a season to produce fruit, and then you cut them back somewhat, or all the way back, to the originating cordon in order to stimulate new growth and a fresh crop. That's it. Not as hard or complex as you thought, eh?

**Figure 15-5:**
Prune raspberries so that they don't grow together too densely. Dense bushes produce less fruit.

Prune old shoots to 6 in. (15 cm)

If you don't prune a vine fruit each year, it can soon grow longer and higher until the fruit you want is far out of reach. To bring it back down into range, all you need to do is identify, and then cut back to, a main trunk and some evenly spaced cordons. Cut back while the plant is dormant.

## Dealing with fruit pests

Homegrown fruits are so delicious that we aren't the only ones who like to eat 'em. If a certain kind of pest or disease is a common problem in your area, choose a variety that's billed as resistant. Your provincial ministry of agriculture may be able to help you with this selection.

And, of course, a healthy plant is a more-resistant one. So take good care of your fruit plants, making sure they have the sun, space, air circulation, water, and food they need to thrive. In particular, water at the base of the plants so the foliage or fruit doesn't become wet; this method heads off at the pass all sorts of fungal problems.

In case these preventive measures fail, the following sections outline some tactics for warding off the competition.

### Targeting birds, bugs, and beasties

No matter how healthy your plant is, you may still end up doing battle with the animal kingdom:

- **Birds:** These flying scavengers adore berries and strike with precise timing, at the peak of ripe perfection. Don't allow this pilfering! Cover the plants after flowering is over (so you don't thwart pollination) but before green fruit begins to ripen. Use plastic netting, cheesecloth, or anything that covers the plants but still lets in light, air, and water (see Figure 15-6). For larger berry patches, some gardeners rig a wooden framework over them and drape the protective cloth over this; then they can just lift one end to harvest, like raising a flap to enter a tent.

  Covering the trees with netting may or may not be practical, depending on their size. At the least, you can try draping netting over the lower branches and letting the birds have the higher-up fruit, which is harder for you to harvest, anyway. Hanging bright and noisy objects from the branches, such as pie tins, sometimes works.

- **Rodents:** Gnawing critters can do extensive damage to fruit trees. Wrapping the trees with a protective covering sometimes helps. Also, be sure not to pile mulch up against the trunk of the trees over winter. Doing so can provide a cozy hiding place for these creatures that may make a meal of the tree bark during the freezing weather.

- **Bugs and other creepy crawlers:** Sorry to say, but you're up against all sorts of buggy threats, like ravenous caterpillars (apple trees), fruitworms (cherry trees), codling moths (apple, pear, and crabapple trees), peach tree borers (apricot, cherry, chokecherry, nectarine, peach, and plum trees), and many more! It seems so unjust when you're already growing an allegedly resistant variety and you're genuinely giving your plants good growing conditions and good care. What can you do? You're not out of the fight yet:

  - **Practise good sanitation.** Remove all plant debris at the base of the plants and groom the plants often to get rid of any growth or fruits in poor condition or already affected. Get rid of all of this material — send it away with the household garbage!

  - **Identify the culprit.** You can't truly fight back until you know thy enemy. If you need help with identification, take an affected plant part and/or the suspect to your local nursery or a knowledgeable landscaper.

- **Try nontoxic weapons first.** If practical, knock off pests with a blast from the hose, or hand-pick the offenders. Spray with insecticidal soap (or a fungicide that's approved for use in your area, if the problem is a disease and not a pest). Introduce beneficial insects that target your particular pest.

- **Spray pesticides only as a last resort and with a government-approved, appropriate product for the problem.** Always follow label instructions to the letter regarding dose and timing, and protect yourself with full-body clothing and goggles.

- **Inspect and wash off all fruit before eating or cooking it.** You may come to tolerate small imperfections rather than declare an all-out war.

**Figure 15-6:**
A fruit tree or shrub covered with netting keeps the birds at bay.

### The blanket effect: Spraying fruit trees

Well, it's a cold, hard fact, folks: Unless you don't mind finding tunnels in your ripe fruit, biting into a fat worm, or having to discard the crop you worked so hard to grow, you have to do at least some spraying. The spraying is preventive. Spraying controls both bugs and diseases that can harm your crop.

Organic or synthetic, the product you want for this job is an all-purpose mixture of fungicide and insecticide that's approved by your municipal government and labelled for orchard use, or a dormant oil. Buy these products at any nursery or garden centre in the springtime. Follow the label instructions to the letter regarding application and timing, and be sure to wear protective clothing and to use a clean, well-functioning sprayer.

Halt spraying two or more weeks before harvest, and always wash your fruit before eating or cooking it.

Here's a typical spraying schedule:

- ✔ **Early spring, when the tips of the buds are swelling and showing green:** This spraying combats late scab, brown rot, and other common woes. The first spray of the season is the most important and is meant to head off at the pass numerous potential pest problems. It controls scab (an early-spring problem, technically a fungus) and early flying insects, such as coddling moths.

- ✔ **A few weeks later, when leaf buds (not flower buds — leaf buds are thin and pointed) are just unfurling:** Like the first spraying, round two fights late scab and brown rot.

- ✔ **At blossoming, when the fat, coloured blossom buds (white or pink, usually) are almost ready to burst open:** This spraying prevents the diseases that attack these young flowers and eventually infect the developing fruit.

- ✔ **At petal fall, when nearly all petals are off the tree:** Insects are beginning to hatch just now, so this spray is especially critical.

- ✔ **Later sprays — every week or two, as needed:** These sprays control mites, sawflies, curculios, and apple maggots as well as summer diseases like scab and brown rot.

# Part V
# Designing Special and Fun Gardens

"Well, Roger wanted to design the garden, and of course I <u>knew</u> he was a paleontologist, but I had no idea..."

# In this part . . .

Of course, all gardens are special and fun, but the ones we cover in Part V are truly, well, special and fun. They're a little bit different from what most people think of as gardens. Do you live in an apartment or have no yard to speak of but want a garden anyway? Or can you spend hours watching goldfish in outdoor ponds, dreaming of having a garden pond of your own? Fear not — you can create these slightly unconventional gardens with the information in these chapters. Just read on!

# Chapter 16

# Mini Gardens and Microcosms: Gardening in Containers

*R*aising plants in containers is quite possibly one of the most satisfying and enjoyable types of gardening. It's so easy — all you do is supply the right soil and water and then fertilize as needed. And the show is perfectly versatile and portable! You can move pots around to capture more sun, to join a grouped display, or to decorate front steps, a back patio, or a tabletop. You can even use potted plants to inject colour or interest in your in-ground displays. With a variety of containers, some attractive and colourful plants, and a dash of creativity, you can really boost your home and garden's interest and appeal.

The basics of container gardening are covered in this chapter. If you want more details about container gardening, we recommend *Container Gardening For Dummies* by Bill Marken and the editors of the National Gardening Association (Wiley).

## Exploring Different Kinds of Containers

Container gardening is all about growing plants in containers of all kinds. Going hunting for pots and other potential containers can be a lot of fun. Often, you put the horse before the cart — in other words, you choose the pot first and the plants second. This order isn't mandatory, of course, but it has the advantage of letting you picture and plan the look you want.

Before you impulsively start collecting all sorts of pots, remember three key practical concerns when picking out a container:

- **Drainage:** Most potted plants don't like to sit in soggy soil, so having some kind of drainage hole is critical. Turn over every pot or potential container to see whether it has drainage holes. If not, perhaps you can add a hole with an awl or high-speed electric drill/masonry bit. You can grow plants in pots without drainage holes, but doing so requires a lot of care to make sure the roots of the plants aren't sitting in water. *Note:* If you don't want water getting on the patio, deck, or entranceway where you have the pot displayed, you need to include a saucer. Lots of pots are sold as pot-and-saucer sets.

 *Tip:* Don't risk breaking an expensive or unique pot by trying to make a drainage hole. Instead, use the container as a *cachepot,* a decorative pot that hides another container: Fill the bottom 5 centimetres (2 inches) of the cachepot with pea gravel, and then put the plant into a smaller plastic pot that fits inside the ornamental one.

- **Colour:** A neutral hue (white, tan, brown, or plain green) lets the plant be the star. On the other hand, a brightly patterned container adds drama and excitement to an otherwise ordinary plant display. You can also look into matching a colour on the container to a flower or foliage colour. Done well, this effect can be quite fabulous.

- **Longevity:** Think about whether you want to use the container for just one summer or keep it as a long-term feature of your garden. And decide whether you want to leave the pot exposed to the elements all winter. Inexpensive pots, of course, tend to be less durable, to break or crack or fade when left out for a long time in the sun and weather. Thicker, heavier pots and some of the new (and lighter) fibreglass, polyresin, and fibrestone containers are usually winter worthy but much more of an investment.

The following sections give you a rundown of container sizes, shapes, materials, and other trappings that help you hold things together.

## *Examining standard container materials*

What a container is made of is actually very important, and it's something to be aware of when searching for the perfect container. For example, you want a container that

- Is nontoxic to plants
- Doesn't overheat quickly in the hot summer sun
- Is durable enough so it can continue to serve and support its contents and look good on display

Here are the container material options you're likely to encounter:

- **Plastic, polypropylene, fibrestone, and resin:** Lots of containers are made of plastic, from flimsy to substantial. It's a very practical material, inexpensive and versatile. However, it tends to hold in moisture and not breathe well, which may or may not be a problem for your chosen plants.

  If you go with plastic, have fun — don't limit yourself to the ubiquitous white and green plastic pots when, with a little searching, you can find other colours and sometimes patterned ones. Some of the better faux terra cotta plastic pots are really quite attractive and are great light-weight alternatives to pottery or real terra cotta.

  Polypropylene, fibrestone, and resin pots are the relatively new kids on the block, and although they tend to cost more than plastic, they come in many classic (and classy) styles — many are made to look like aged clay pots. These pots are also light and durable, and probably worth the investment.

  Self-watering containers are getting a lot of attention these days because they make watering a snap and are perfect for vacationing gardeners who have to leave their thirsty plants unattended for several days at a time. These containers are considered to be self-watering because they have reservoirs that hold runoff and then, as the soil dries out, release the moisture by means of a wick or a column of soil.

- **Terra cotta:** Technically, terra cotta is unglazed pottery; it's a garden classic and looks handsome in so many situations. This material is generally affordable, except for very large pots or for those with elaborate patterns. Drawbacks? Well, terra cotta wicks moisture away from plant root systems, and over time, it tends to develop cracks or to flake. Because terra cotta absorbs water, which expands when it freezes, the container will likely crack and break if you leave it outdoors during winter, especially if you leave the soil in the pot. Soil also expands and contracts and applies pressure to the walls of the pot. Always remove the soil, even if you store your pots in a reasonably protected place like a shed or garage.

- **Glazed pottery:** With glazed earthenware, you get to enjoy the greater heft of clay but have more colour options and usually a measure of elegance as well. These containers are fairly durable, though they, too, can crack in winter if any small portion isn't glazed.

- **Wood:** Containers of wood, especially softwoods like pine and fir, sop up moisture and eventually rot or fall apart. Yet there's no denying their wonderful rustic look. The solution may be to nest a plastic pot inside a wooden container. Otherwise, you may get more use out of a container constructed from rot-resistant wood such as cedar.

- **Metal:** You can press metal containers into plant-holding service. Remember the need for a drainage hole, and beware of displaying the container in full sun, which will cause it and its contents to really heat up. Some possibilities include old olive-oil containers, buckets, and cast-iron kettles.

✔ **Concrete:** When you want a tough, long-lasting, cold-resistant container, concrete is a fine choice, whether as an urn or as a planter box. It can be pretty heavy and hard to manoeuvre, though. Therefore, it's often wise to place a concrete container on your chosen spot before filling it with potting soil and plants.

## Thinking outside the pot: Alternative choices and offbeat containers

More-unusual containers can be a lot of fun and add unexpected pleasure or whimsy to your displays. If the item isn't entirely suitable (an odd shape, or one that's not conducive to providing good drainage), simply nest a plastic pot inside it — the developing plants will hide the inner container from view over time. Check out these options:

✔ **Hanging baskets:** With a hanging basket, always make sure that you account for drainage and that the resulting display is adequately supported by wires, chain, string, rope, or what have you, because a full hanging basket can be quite heavy. If taking the display down to water it is a hassle, try using a watering wand. Some possibilities include plastic, clay, wood, and coconut- or moss-lined wire rigs. See Figure 16-1.

✔ **Wall containers:** A wall garden is a clever and often quite charming way to display container-grown plants. You fasten wall containers to a fence, courtyard wall, or other vertical surface (or a trellis against one), preferably at eye level so you can readily appreciate them.

Many containers intended for this use have one flat side so they can go flush against the wall (these containers are sometimes called *half pots*); though this feature isn't a requirement, it does look better and allows the plants within to grow upright. Obviously, the supporting wire, brackets, or hooks have to be equal to the job, and that means holding the weight of a *filled and watered* container. Although you can rig something yourself, well-stocked garden supply stores often have a selection of these containers, and they come with whatever support is necessary.

✔ **Old shoes and boots, tea kettles, wicker baskets, cookie tins, old tires, wagons and wheelbarrows, and more:** You can recycle all sorts of wacky and whimsical objects to hold and display potted plants — just use your imagination! Browse garage sales, thrift shops, junk piles, or even your own garage, basement, or attic. Any vessel of weather-resistant material can be a candidate. Avoid containers, like oil barrels, that at one time held toxic chemicals and also those constructed of wood products that contained harmful preservatives, like creosote.

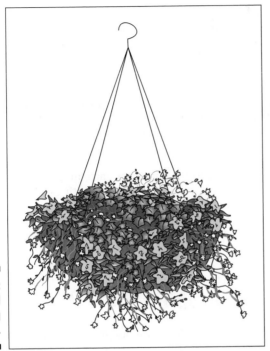

**Figure 16-1:**
Typical
hanging
basket.

Oddball container choices work best when the plants within don't over-whelm them or spill over the sides and hide them from view, so choose small plants or slow-growing ones. Also, ensure that plants have drainage.

---

# A barrel of fun: Whisky barrel gardens

The word *whisky* comes from a Gaelic phrase for "water of life," and a plant can certainly live a happy, well-watered life in a (whisky-free) whisky barrel. Half whisky barrels are popular choices for containing many plants or large plants, including small trees or even water lilies and other aquatics (in a plastic-lined miniature pond — see Chapter 17 for details on water gardens).

Line a barrel with plastic or use a plastic insert made for this purpose before planting; this liner helps to prevent rot and helps stays and slats stay secure. A liner also protects the soil and, thus, the plants from absorbing any leached tar or creosote that may be lingering on the slats. And don't forget that one of these barrels filled with anything is mighty heavy, so move it to its intended site before filling it.

Whisky barrels are pretty standard at garden and home supply centres.

# The Inside Track: Getting the Container Soil Right

Because a container-grown plant is confined to its space, its roots can find nourishment and anchoring only in whatever soil you provide. So soil isn't the place to cut corners — take a moment to provide a welcoming environment. The following sections give you info on choosing a potting soil or making your own.

Don't use regular old garden dirt for container gardening; it's often too heavy or dense, plus it may not drain well in a container setting. When wet, it tends to stay soggy too long — and then it dries into hard mud. It may even contain weed seeds, unwelcome guests you may not discover until it's too late. No, you definitely want to use those bags of soil mix you buy at the garden centre or home-supply store.

## Purchasing a soil mix

A container garden is a good case for store-bought soil mix, which is *not* heavy and dense. Potting soil contains and holds nutrients your plants can use, and it drains well. It can contain all or part of the following ingredients:

- ✔ **Organic matter:** The organic matter in potting mix is typically some or all of the following: dried manure, compost, peat moss, and finely ground bark. Organic matter adds nutrients to the soil.

- ✔ **Perlite:** Perlite appears as little crunchy white "pebbles" (they're actually smaller than most pebbles); interestingly, perlite is a natural volcanic ash that's been superheated and fluffed up, like popcorn. This substance increases the flow of air while helping the soil hold water.

- ✔ **Vermiculite:** This mineral has been heated and fluffed up, though its form is flat and flaky. It increases airflow, retains moisture, and helps make minerals accessible.

- ✔ **Coarse, or "sharp," sand:** The sand in soil mixes isn't beach sand, which is too salty, or river sand, which is too fine. Coarse sand helps with drainage.

- ✔ **Moisture-retaining gels:** When they come into contact with water, these gels swell up and then slowly release the moisture back into the mix over time.

✔ **Fertilizer beads:** These fertilizer sources usually look like tiny yellow or brownish BB pellets.

✔ **Charcoal:** Manufacturers include a bit of charcoal mainly to absorb odours and gases from the natural decomposition process of the other ingredients.

To be honest, the majority of potted plants are perfectly happy with a general, all-purpose potting soil mix. You may want to buy a more-specialized one if you're growing something with special needs — for instance, potted azaleas like a mix that's more acidic, and cacti, of course, like one that has a higher sand content.

Of course, if you're aware of a certain plant's special requirements, nothing's wrong with buying regular, general potting soil and then mixing in whatever else the plant needs — sand, lime, moisture-retaining gels (see "Whipping up your own soil mix"), whatever.

You may see *sterile* potting mix touted on the bags and bins. All the term means is that the mix has been treated to kill possible pests, diseases, and weed seeds. That's a good thing!

You get what you pay for. Cheap potting soils seem to have too much peat moss or poorly shredded bark, or they lack perlite or vermiculite. You can't always rip open a bag in the store and shove your hand in it to check it out (though some places have a display of samples to help you choose). So read the bag with care — not the claims about how terrific the contents are but rather the list of ingredients and their various percentages.

## Whipping up your own soil mix

Yes, you can create your own soil mix, but it's not really a matter of saving money, because you have to purchase individual ingredients separately and then mix them. It's certainly not a matter of saving time, either. What it is, our friend, is a matter of control. When you make your own mix, you can make sure every bit of it is of good and consistent quality. Best of all, you can customize: If the store-bought mix seems too heavy, you can easily lighten it by stirring in some more perlite or some finely ground bark. And of course, you can make a blend that's more acidic or more alkaline as need be. The most commonly available bark is composted, hardwood, fir, or pine bark — any are fine to use.

Here, then, are some recipes to follow when stirring up a batch of your own mix:

- ✔ **Standard mix (also sometimes called *houseplant thirds* because it's suitable for the majority of common houseplants):** One part packaged soil, one part peat moss, and one part perlite or sand.

- ✔ **Light mix, for plants that like good drainage:** Two parts peat moss, one part sand, one part perlite, and maybe a dash of powdered lime (the mineral, of course).

- ✔ **Heavy mix, for plants that like their soil more moisture retentive:** One part peat moss, two parts bark, one part sand, and maybe a dash of powdered lime.

- ✔ **Tree and shrub mix:** One part sterilized topsoil, one part peat moss, two parts bark, one part sand, and maybe a dash of powdered lime.

Using moisture-retaining *soil polymer gels* is a good idea if your pots dry out really fast, if you're going on vacation, or if you're simply not the sort of person to water diligently. These gels naturally absorb moisture when you water the plant, swell up with it, and then gradually release it to the roots for them to use between waterings. They come in crystal form, and you mix them into the soil prior to planting. Follow package instructions; even a little too much makes your soil mix's texture a bit slimy, but that *eeew* factor may be a small price to pay for the convenience.

# Planting in a Container

After you choose your container, pick your plant (see the upcoming section "Picking the Best Plants for Your Containers"), and purchase or create your potting soil mix, it's time to get planting. To properly plant a container, see Figure 16-2 and follow these steps:

1. **Knock the plant out of its pot by holding the pot upside down and tapping its rim on a hard surface, or thumping the bottom of the pot with your fist.**

2. **Pry the roots loose with your fingers or cut through them shallowly (vertically) with a sharp knife if they're wound around the bottom sides of the pot.**

3. **Put enough of your chosen soil mix in the bottom of the container to bring the crown of the plant (the spot where the roots join the stem, or, if you can't see the roots, the top of the root ball) at least 2.5 centimetres (an inch) below the rim of the container.**

4. **Place the plant in the container and spread out the roots.**

5. **Fill the potting soil in and around the root ball, making sure you press it in firmly, to eliminate any air pockets.**

6. **Water the plant deeply with a slow stream of water.**

   If the soil around the root ball settles, fill in the depression with more soil.

7. **Cover the soil with a layer of mulch (shredded bark, compost, or wood chips, for example).**

   Mulch keeps the soil moist and cool, allowing the plant to become established.

Many gardeners put pebbles in the bottoms of their containers, which isn't really necessary in a pot that has a drainage hole, especially with today's well-draining potting materials.

**Figure 16-2:**
A cross-section of a container, ready for planting.

# Picking the Best Plants for Your Containers

So you're ready to start choosing plants. We know what you're thinking: small ones! Well, of course, but size doesn't have to be a limiting factor. Almost any sort of plant can adapt to life in a container. For instance, you can try a small herb plant or a wee bonsai-size Japanese maple in a small ceramic pot. Or you can grow a wide array of herbs or flowers (or both — why not?), or a dwarf edition of any number of popular trees, in a big planter box or tub (although trees or shrubs aren't hardy in all winter conditions). Look through the plant chapters in this book for ideas. You can even grow bulbs in containers — forcing bulbs indoors is a popular practice among container gardeners (refer to Chapter 8 for details).

A container display looks best and serves its residents best when the plant and pot are in proportion to one another. You don't want a little plant to get lost in a big pot, nor is it practical or attractive to allow a larger plant to teeter or look top heavy in a too-small pot. Plus, the roots need to fit without being crammed in there. So make a match. (Think ahead to a plant's potential size, not the youngster you first install.)

Consider what you want your display to do for you. Then read on for some advice on how to pull it off.

## Up-close-and-personal displays

If you like to have potted plants where you're nose to nose with them almost daily, such as on a deck or patio (or indoors, for that matter), choose plants with interesting details. We're talking pretty or very colourful flowers, fragrant flowers, fragrant foliage, unusually shaped or coloured leaves, or edible parts. Avoid plants that attract bees, that don't smell too good, that have prickly parts or thorns, or that have rambling, unruly growth habits (unless you want plants that fall over the sides of the container, such as sweet potato vine).

Many container gardens exist indoors or in shady areas like porches and patios. If you want your close-up container garden to look its best in a shady location, be sure to pick out plants that grow well in shade. See Figure 16-3 for an example of a container garden you can design for the shade.

**Figure 16-3:**
A container planting for the shade can be just as full and vibrant as one for the sun.

## Tucked-in attention grabbers

For pots that you strategically position to draw interest to their part of the yard or to their garden companions, you want lush, dramatic leaves, big flowers, and attention-grabbing colours — anything that causes you and your garden visitors to trot over for a visit and a closer look. So avoid plants with fine or wispy-textured leaves and stems, ones with small or fleeting flowers, and ones with dark colours (which recede into the shadows).

## Containers of mixed company

There's no rule that says a container should hold only a single plant, and in fact, most containers look better filled to overflowing with plants. So feel free to tuck in several types, in effect making a mini garden. Remember, when planting, don't crowd — the plants will fill in the space and grow upward and outward, and you want the show to last a while and not require constant editing. (In other words, you want to avoid a lot of pruning and trimming, and even the necessity of taking out an entire plant that becomes constricted.) Here are a few guidelines to get you started:

- ✔ Combine plants of similar needs.

- ✔ Include both foliage and flowering plants.

- ✔ Include plants of different forms: spiky or strappy leaved, rounded or mounded, and low or trailing. This sort of variety works well out in the regular garden and translates easily to container compositions, just on a smaller scale.

- ✔ Position taller plants in the middle (or to the back if you plan to display the container against a vertical surface so people can't view the plants from behind); put shorter plants at the taller plants' feet.

- ✔ Place plants with trailing or cascading stems at the very edge so they can get where they want to go unimpeded.

Mixing colours in a containerized display is an art, and done well, it makes a wonderful impression — something you're really proud of and delighted with. Remember, the colour can come from foliage as well as flowers, and often the colourful foliage delivers a longer-lasting show. Here are some colour combinations you can try:

- ✔ **Bold, primary colours:** Mix one or two plants each of blue, yellow, and red. Look for ones of similar "strength" or intensity.

- ✔ **Compatible combos:** Colours that fall between the primary colours (called secondary colours) tend to be harmonious companions. Try yellowish orange with violet-blue, or reddish orange with bluish green.

- ✔ **Pastel hues:** Stick to selections of softer hues (pink, pale yellow, soft blue, light purple, cream rather than white, and so on). If you're including foliage plants, complement with gentler ones such as those with grey, silver, or sage-green leaves.

- ✔ **Single-colour shows:** Combine several different plants that share the same flower colour. Sure, you may end up with slight variations in tone, but you actually want that; it makes a more diverse and interesting display (perfect colour matches, or using only one type of plant, can end up looking like a dense colour blob).

- ✔ **Opposites attract:** Contrasting colours always look fabulous together, particularly if they're of similar strength or intensity. Try blue with orange, or purple with yellow.

- ✔ **Colour boosts:** Favour one hue, say, purple, and then tuck in a close hue for subtle contrast, such as a blue companion. Try an all-red show with a dash of orange or yellow, or an all-pink display with a jolt of red, and so on — you get the idea!

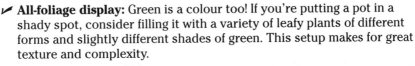

✔ **All-foliage display:** Green is a colour too! If you're putting a pot in a shady spot, consider filling it with a variety of leafy plants of different forms and slightly different shades of green. This setup makes for great texture and complexity.

Gardeners grow plenty of plants mainly for their colourful or patterned leaves. Examples include hostas, coleus, ferns, ornamental grasses, cannas, and all sorts of houseplants, just to name a few.

# Arranging Containers for a Container Garden

Just because plants are in different pots doesn't mean they can't be neighbours. Setting up containers in small or large gatherings has practical advantages: You're more likely to remember them and water and fertilize them at the same time, keeping the entire display looking good. Groups also tend to raise the plants' local humidity and to moderate the effects of hot sun, which can be a good thing, depending on what you're growing.

Groupings can also be wonderfully attractive and appealing if artfully arranged. We can offer a few suggestions, but make sure you also experiment and vary the show from time to time. That's one of the many beauties of raising plants in containers — you can cycle plants in and out of the show as you see fit (taking away a plant that's struggling or no longer blooming, for example, and replacing it with something similar or completely different).

Here are some container grouping ideas:

✔ **Group various-sized containers.** Put tall containers to the back and shorter ones at their feet so you don't block any one display from view. Try not to group containers of widely varying sizes, though — tiny pots at the feet of big tubs just go unnoticed. Mix and match complementary pot colours, materials, and forms until you get a look that pleases you. Or create a gathering of all the same type of pot but with a variety of sizes, forms, and contents (plants).

✔ **Display containers on a tiered stand.** Tiered stands are practical because, ideally, they allow room for each pot of plants to distinguish itself from its fellows; they also permit good air circulation. Keep the entire thing as sturdy as possible by leaning or even securing it to a wall or other backdrop support, if warranted. Don't put heavy or top-heavy plants on upper or rickety shelves — instead, set these containers lower down and reserve the narrow and upper shelves for smaller containers. For a more interesting look, intermix types: Don't put all only-foliage plants together and all flowering ones on a separate shelf. And you don't need to purchase plant stands — we've seen ladders, benches, and old garden chairs used as plant stands.

✔ **Tuck in nonplant extras.** Some gardeners have a lot of fun boosting the interest, whimsy, and/or colourfulness of potted plants by adding some décor. These accents can be anything from a small ceramic turtle or bird, to a whirligig, to a decorative birdhouse on a stick or even a faux flower.

# Taking Care of Your Container Plants

Container plants require the same care as do plants in a garden, with one important difference: A plant growing in a container can't do what regular, in-ground plants do, which is send roots off far or deep in a wider area in search of moisture, nutrients, and such. And potted plants grown indoors can't rely on rain. When you live in a pot, it's a small world, after all.

Container-grown plants that endure drastic cycles where they dry out and then get drenched are generally unhappy customers. The extremes stress out the plants. And of course, if you rush in to rehydrate a plant wilting in distress and you're too late, it drops all its leaves, swoons, and dies. Be consistent! The most vulnerable container plants are these:

✔ **Newly potted or exposed plants:** These babies need the help of regular water to establish themselves and to send their roots out into their new home — in other words, to get their legs under them. Plants grown in full sun or windy, exposed locations are vulnerable, too, because they dry out so fast.

✔ **Plants grown in dark-coloured pots:** Dark colours absorb more heat. Plants in light-coloured containers have a slightly easier time of it because the pot reflects light and, therefore, heat.

✔ **Plants with large, thin leaves:** Plants whose leaves have a lot of surface area really rely on water to remain hydrated and plump as can be. Plants with small leaves, succulent leaves, or needlelike foliage are better able to cope with dry times.

✔ **Plants in lighter soil mixes:** Light soil mixes drain moisture away faster.

✔ **Plants that are rootbound:** Plants whose roots take up most of the pot don't have enough soil to hold moisture for them to use as needed, so they need to be transplanted. To know when to transplant, turn the container upside down and knock the plant out of the container by thumping the bottom. Examine the roots. If the roots have hit the outside of the pot and are starting to mat together, it's a good time to transplant. Don't wait until the roots start to circle the inside of the pot. Here's another telltale sign: roots shooting up at the surface or out of the bottom of the pot.

# *Gauging your container garden's water needs*

The top few centimetres of the soil mix in any given pot is sure to dry out faster than the soil below, so don't trust your eyes to tell you whether the pot is thirsty. Plunge in your thumb or a finger to a depth of at least 2.5 centimetres (1 inch) and as much as 7.5 centimetres (3 inches) to find out whether there's moisture at that level before concluding that the mix is dangerously dry. (Okay, you can also buy a product called a *moisture meter* and insert its long, needlelike probe into your pots to get a fairly accurate reading. If you like gadgets, go for it. But keep in mind that you're sacrificing a prime opportunity to play in the dirt.)

Watch for drooping or wilting, or a tired or off-colour overall look to the plants. Also, if you can pick up the container, you may notice that it feels too light.

To water your plants properly, you have a variety of options; use whatever's convenient for you and for the potted plants. Look into using the hose with a hand attachment to deliver the water softly; a watering can, perhaps with a long neck and with or without a "rose" shower attachment; drip emitters; or a plastic watering tube inserted into the middle of the container. In some cases, *bottom watering* (setting the pot on a saucer or tray of water and letting it soak up what it needs from below) works quite well. Recently, there's been a lot of innovation with self-watering pots, and you may want to invest in one of those.

No matter how you water your container garden, be gentle. A jolt or direct hit can splash soil out of the pot and maybe even dislodge your plants. Also, sloppy watering tends to wet plant foliage, which is wasteful and can lead to fungal diseases.

Here are a few moisture-conserving tricks for plants that dry out too fast:

- ✔ Spread a very thin layer of mulch on the surface of the potting mix.
- ✔ Move pots into the shade for part of the day.
- ✔ Sink a pot partially or fully into the ground in your garden.
- ✔ Nest a small potted plant in a larger container that can "take the heat" for it.
- ✔ Yank out any weeds that appear in your containers — weeds are notorious water hogs!

Many tropical plants, tropical houseplants, and large-leaved plants appreciate a little extra humidity — a little more than what's available naturally in the air. Here are a few good ways to help them:

- ✔ Set the pot on a tray or dish of pebbles, where excess water from above can sit and then gradually evaporate, which effectively raises the local humidity.

 ✔ Get in the habit of misting such plants regularly. In fact, keeping a water-filled mister nearby is a good way to remind yourself to do this.

 ✔ Clustering or grouping such plants is always a fine idea — there's strength in numbers. The close proximity encourages a damper micro-climate and reduces sunlight on the sides of the pots, because some of them will block, or partially block, one another. (Plus, keeping the plants in a group can look quite splendid.)

## Fertilizing your container plants

Life in a pot is finite. A newly potted plant may be able to subsist on the nutrition inherent in the potting mix. But after a time, that food source becomes depleted. You can repot, of course, but it's far easier to get in the habit of feeding your potted plants regularly.

Potted plants grown for their flowers or fruit especially benefit from fertilizer, because producing these things requires so much energy.

How often you fertilize depends on the plant and the pot size. However, generally speaking, the rule for the garden at large still applies: Feed at the start of the growing season to get the plants off to a roaring start, feed at regular intervals during the height of the growing season, slow down near the end of the season, and then stop in the fall when the show is over. If you have a large container filled to overflowing with many plants grouped tightly, feed the plants at least once a week with a water-soluble fertilizer — some avid gardeners fertilize every few days, giving the plants a mixture diluted to half strength. If the plants are annuals, you can fertilize them right up until Jack Frost claims them.

Fertilizer leaches out or washes away with every watering, so you need to keep it up. Also, the limited amount of soil in a pot limits the amount of nutrients it can hoard and supply to the plants. Especially with smaller pots, or containers filled with many plants, feeding twice as often at half the strength is a good idea.

Unless you're growing something fussy or offbeat, or something with special requirements, a general all-purpose garden fertilizer is perfectly fine for almost all potted plants. All-purpose fertilizer comes in different forms, so experiment to discover what you and your plants prefer. Options include liquid fertilizers, dry or granular fertilizers, fertilizer beads, and fertilizer sticks. Whatever you decide, always follow the label directions on how and when to apply to the letter — like aspirin, more isn't better!

# Chapter 17

# Taking the Plunge: Gardening with Ponds and Fish

*W*ater doesn't just add life to a garden; it adds atmosphere as well. Whether you're talking about a barrel or a tub with a few plants or an in-ground, natural-looking pond, gardeners often cite water features as the elements that truly complete a garden.

Truly, water brings magic. Maybe it's the reflections of passing clouds; maybe it's the soothing sound of a trickling or splashing fountain; maybe it's your gasp of awe when your first water lily blossom bursts open; maybe it's a child's excited shout when a dragonfly or small frog visits. The magic is all this and more. Go ahead: Read this chapter and take the plunge, because — good news — water gardening is easier and more affordable than ever before.

## Planning Your Water Garden

The main thing you need to know about planning a water garden is that almost all the effort and expense are at the outset. After a water garden, large or small, is up and running, it's surprisingly easy to maintain. You have to ensure that you can meet the important needs of the plants and the fish before you even acquire them, and you do that through careful planning. The following sections run you through some planning considerations.

Your pond's size, the elements you add, and other factors can affect its cost and maintenance. Make sure you take a realistic look at your budget and the time you're willing to invest in your water garden. "Picking Out Your Water Garden Parts and Supplies" gives some details on cost. For information on upkeep, see "Maintaining Your Water Garden," later in this chapter. And if you need basic planning advice, including tips on defining what you want, gathering ideas, and putting the plan in action, refer to Chapter 2.

## *Looking at location*

You can find the answers to many of your questions about garden type when you know *where* you want your garden to be, and that's why picking a good spot is the first order of business. Even before you go shopping, you need to evaluate the area where you're thinking of putting a water garden and determine its basic requirements:

- **Sunlight:** Most water garden plants adore full sun and bloom with gusto as a result — specifically, six or more hours per day is great. Any spot where you can put a sunny flower bed or a vegetable garden can also host a water garden.

- **Openness of the area:** You want ample elbow room, not just so the plants have the space they need but also to allow you access to them and, well, give you room to appreciate them. Perhaps you want to put in a bench or dining set nearby. Sufficient air circulation is also good for the health of the plants and any fish in the pond.

- **Proximity of current large vegetation:** Trees and shrubs interfere with roots from below, and these big plants shed leaves, twigs, petals, and fruit from above, which can encourage algae to grow. Avoid putting your water garden under or too close to trees and shrubs.

- **Levelness of the land:** Levelness is important because water always responds to gravity — you don't want runoff or spillovers. Granted, few spots are *perfectly* level, but you can always make the necessary minor adjustments during installation.

- **Location of utility lines:** Digging into power lines, gas lines, fibre optic cables, phone lines, pipes, and other such things can be expensive and incredibly unpleasant. Call your utility companies to have these lines marked — most do so for free. Also, consider the location of your power outlets before planning to use a pump.

✔ **Available room:** If you aren't sure you want a large water garden, start small with one or more container displays, even if you have room for more. However, if you have the space and the dream of a big, beautiful pool of water, go for it! Realize that you're unlikely to do it over, and install a pond that's as big as or slightly bigger than what you want. (Heed the words of at least one of the landscape contractors we know: "None of my clients have ever complained their water garden was too big!") A water garden appears to shrink in size when filled with water and plants. Make sure you have enough room for the kind of water garden you want.

✔ **Desire for fish:** Not all water gardens have fish or are even appropriate for fish, so it's best to start off by assuming you won't have fish. You can add fish later, after your water garden is established and healthy and you've had a chance to evaluate its capacity to maintain them.

To overwinter fish, you need a pond that has a place where the water is at least 1 metre (about 3 feet) deep so it won't freeze all the way to the bottom. If you're concerned about freezing even with this allowance, you can also add a floating de-icer heater especially developed for this purpose. See your local pond supplier for details.

Instead of having an elaborate water garden, you can certainly put a small tub display or little pool with a running fountain in a shady nook. Just heed all the rest of the requirements on the preceding list. And if you add plants in a shaded pond, don't expect flowers; pick plants based on their handsome foliage.

A child or pet can drown even in a few centimetres of water. You never want to risk that. For this reason, some municipalities don't allow water gardens (particularly in-ground ponds) in front yards. But front yard or back, a water garden needs to be watched, so site it where you can see it from elsewhere in the yard and also, ideally, from a window inside the house. Caution children and supervise them. Erect an encircling low or high fence (with a gate, of course) if required or warranted — better safe than sorry. Poolside edgings, judiciously placed, can also restrict or inhibit access — we mean hard edgings like rocks, as well as lush plants. Even adjacent seating can help because it provides a safe and relaxing viewing opportunity.

## On the level: Deciding between above-ground and in-ground gardens

If you know where you want your water garden, you can begin to explore the physical form that it will take. Water gardens generally are either above ground in a container of some sort or set into the ground as a pond. Read on for some points to consider when deciding which type to go with.

### Above-ground water gardens

Consider where you've decided to locate your pond. An above-ground water garden is a commanding presence in a landscape. For this reason, gardeners generally site them where people can enjoy them up close, such as on a patio or deck, or next to one, or against a wall or fence, where blocking things from view or obstructing foot traffic isn't an issue. Figure 17-1 shows a typical *containerized,* or above-ground, water garden.

Above-ground displays involve an important practical concern, too. They're substantial and heavy. You want to make sure you can find a container, tub, or liner that can support the weight of the water without buckling or bursting. One way around this issue is to erect a support around the container, insulated if you like. Use stones, bricks, or timber.

Last but not least, a broad lip or edge allows you to sit beside the display to admire and care for the fish and plants within. Above-ground tubs and water gardens, therefore, are good choices for anyone who can't or prefers not to do a lot of bending and stooping.

**Figure 17-1:**
A con-
tainerized
water
garden,
ideal for
porches,
patios, and
balconies.

## In-ground water gardens

In-ground water gardens, of course, look more natural and thus are the best choice when you want to integrate a water garden into a lawn or garden. After the liner of your choice is in the ground, you can attractively edge it in stone or brick and some landscaping (picture some lush hostas or irises, or even simply some drooping ferns). The end result becomes an enchanting garden focal point or destination, and it can look like it has always been there! See Figure 17-2 for an attractive plan for an in-ground water garden.

In addition to accommodating the site issues we describe in "Looking at location," you also have to deal with the issue of the potential runoff or seepage of water and dirt (or mud!). Never fill an in-ground pond so that the water is flush with the surrounding terrain. Here are two ways to handle this issue:

- ✔ **Allow for a raised lip.** Seat the lip a couple of centimetres or more above the ground. Don't worry that it looks unnatural; edging materials and pondside landscaping can hide the edge from view.

- ✔ **Grade the land away from the pond's edges.** This grade encourages runoff to travel away from rather than into your display. If your site has a slight slope to it, a berm or retaining wall may be necessary, and making a drainage trench on the uphill side is wise. Creating planting ledges within your pond, as shown in Figure 17-3, can also help.

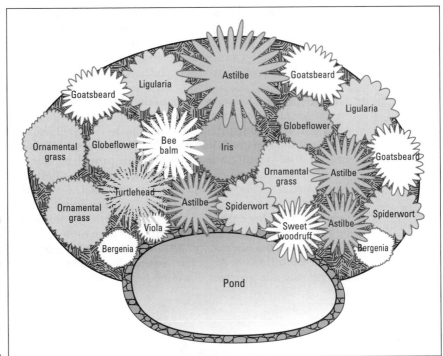

**Figure 17-2:** A garden plan for an in-ground pond featuring a garden "backdrop."

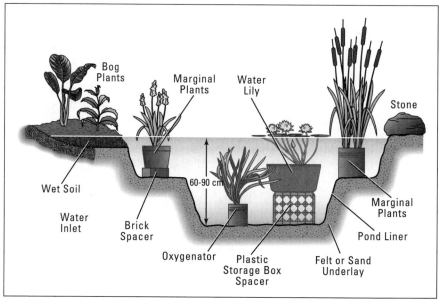

**Figure 17-3:**
A cross-
section of a
pond plan
showing
critical
depths and
planting
ledges.

## Choosing the best lining

When you know the type of water garden you want, you have to take the garden's lining into consideration. Most soil is porous, so without a water-proof liner, the water will eventually leak out. Also, water gardens being what they are, leakage can be a serious problem if you don't line them properly. Liners generally consist of two types: flexible liners and hard shells.

✔ **Flexible liners:** This term refers to the big sheet that you lay in a hole, mould to shape, and then trim to fit. Polyvinyl chloride (also known as *PVC*) is a reasonably priced material that's UV-stabilized and lasts about ten years but can crack in very cold climates. A synthetic rubber liner called *EPDM* — which stands for ethylene propylene diene monomer, folks (we can't imagine why you'd prefer it to the initialism!) — is used more often now. The advantage of using a flexible liner is that the size and shape of the pond is *your* choice. Also, the edges are easier to con-ceal from view because they aren't rigid. Metre for metre, medium and large ponds lined with EPDM are cheaper than preformed shell liners. However, flexible liners don't last as long as hard shells do, and they puncture more easily. Also, the installation is trickier because you're dealing with a large sheet of a fairly heavy, bulky product.

✔ **Hard-shell liners:** These preformed liners come in fibreglass and poly-ethylene, almost universally in black, and in a variety of shapes and sizes. Fibreglass is a stronger product than polyethylene, with a longer life expectancy — probably longer than you'll be around in your garden — and it can also be used above ground. The most popular shape of liner is kidney, but you can get amoeba and muffin shapes, or simple ovals and circles. Some hard-shell liners come with side shelves, and some offer the option of a spillway slot so you can connect two ponds or add a stream or waterfall to your display. In any event, the standard depth is 30 to 46 centimetres (12 to 18 inches), but some of the big ones are deeper. The trick to installing these liners is getting them level and making sure the bottom comes into contact with the soil over its whole area.

# Picking Out Your Water Garden Parts and Supplies

Unless you're especially handy, buying and installing some of the stuff you want for your water garden can be daunting. But you *still* want or need the stuff, right? No problem! Start by getting some good advice. Talk with a specialist or landscaper who installs water features, or call a mail-order supplier, and discuss your options. Their expertise can be invaluable. Even if you end up hiring someone to help you, it's still good to be an educated consumer.

As with any form of gardening, the cheapest road toward installing your water garden is to do all of it yourself, and many home and garden centres stock everything you need to bring your garden plans to life. If you don't have a water garden supplier near you, numerous mail-order houses can help and offer impressive, wide-ranging selections to boot.

Going with the cheapest versions of things isn't always wise — you get what you pay for. Buy supplies for your water garden from a reputable source, and be sure you understand the return, refund, or replacement policy, just in case.

Here's a list of the things you're most likely to need and what they'll probably cost you:

✔ **The pool itself:** The container or liner is probably your biggest expense. Tubs and other suitable smaller containers (including handsome ceramic pots without drainage holes, which make good water gardens) range from about $30 to $100 or more. Specially formed plastic liners can run as low as $25 for one that fits in a half whisky barrel to as high as hundreds of dollars for a substantial, shaped, in-ground form. Flexible liners can also cost several hundred dollars, depending on the quality you buy and the size of your pool. You can use flexible liners to line small containers used as water gardens, although fitting one in smoothly and hiding its top edge can take some time and dexterity. If you haven't yet decided what kind of pond you want, review the previous sections.

With flexible liners, you also need to use an underlay, which protects the liner from damage from pebbles and stones in the soil as well as from waterfall or edging rocks. You can use thick pads of newspaper, but the best product is a synthetic fabric underlay called *geothermal textile,* or *geotex.*

✔ **The inner workings — pipes, tubes, valves, filters, fountains, fittings, pads, screens, holding tubs, and more:** Yep, these interlocking and sometimes complex pieces of hardware are part of the show behind the scenes. These parts may be under the water or they may run behind or next to your display, or both. Match the item to your display's size and water volume; the vendor can help you with this. See Figure 17-4.

When all is said and done — that is, when these fixtures are installed and doing their jobs — your job becomes twofold: Keep them clean and in good repair, and hide these manmade items from sight behind or below lush plants or rocks so the natural look prevails. Some of these items are covered in more detail later in the chapter.

Water and electricity can be a dicey combination. And yet, it's often necessary, if not simply decorative, to have items that run on electricity associated with your display, such as a pump-driven fountain or waterfall, a filter, or atmospheric lighting. Here's our main advice to you on this issue:

- Hire help. Unless you're a licensed electrician, don't mess with installing and hooking up wiring around a water feature. Get it done right by someone experienced. This person can also help you with hiding the lines from view.

- *GFCIs* (ground-fault circuit interrupters), or *GFIs* (ground-fault interrupters), are musts on every electrical item associated with a water garden. These extension-cord-style devices automatically and instantly shut off power when they detect a leak in the electrical current (thus preventing shock).

✔ **Edging material (brick, rocks, flagstone, wood, whatever):** These items are purely the gardener's choice, and the cost and amount needed depend entirely on your plans.

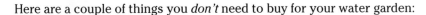

✔ **Plants:** Water lilies and lotuses can run from about $25 up to $50 or more, per plant. Other water plants — from water hyacinths to irises to cannas to floating hearts to underwater/oxygenating plants — are often much less. See "Choosing Plants for Water Gardens," later in this chapter, for more information.

As for pondside landscaping, that of course varies depending on your taste and the style of the display.

✔ **Fish:** Goldfish and their near relatives are pretty cheap; the big koi can be very pricey. We're talking fish as cheap as a buck versus thoroughbreds that run hundreds of dollars apiece. And don't forget the filter and the fish food they'll need. Again, we cover fish in more detail later in this chapter in "Adding Fish to Your Water Garden."

Before you commit yourself to adding fish, get your water garden set up *first;* then do your research into the types and number of fish your water garden can support — it may be less than you think (note that fish overcrowding is bad for fish health as well as water quality).

Here are a couple of things you *don't* need to buy for your water garden:

✔ **Potting soil:** It's a water-gardening no-no (it's too light, so it floats away; it's also too rich and can contribute to the development of algae). Use heavy garden soil from your own yard — some of the soil from the pond excavation works just fine. For more details on planting water plants, consult "Choosing Plants for Water Gardens."

✔ **Creatures:** If you build it, they will come! Aside from fish, your display may support dragonflies, frogs, turtles, and birds. Some visitors are obviously welcome; others, such as mosquitoes, which thrive in still water, turn out to be pests.

## Pumps

A pump's job is to recirculate water in your water garden or to power a filter, fountain, stream, or waterfall. Make sure the equipment is a match for the job, or you'll burn out the motor or won't have enough power to do the job — again, seek expert advice here. Estimate the pump's capabilities conservatively. That way, your pump can manage the job without being maxed out. Pumps are essential to produce waterfalls and send water up into fountains, and they're useful to circulate water and thus oxygenate it for the fish. If there are no fish or water features, pumps aren't needed.

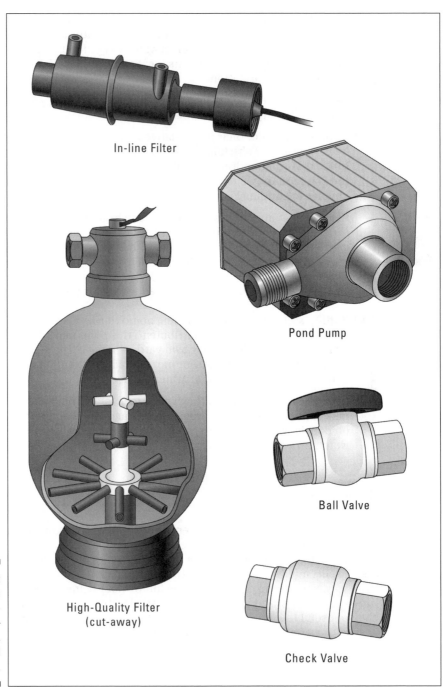

In-line Filter

Pond Pump

Ball Valve

High-Quality Filter
(cut-away)

Check Valve

**Figure 17-4:**
Common
pond equip-
ment —
pumps,
filters, and
valves.

Package, catalogue, and Web site descriptions can give you performance charts, if you want to study them. The basic gist is how many gallons per hour they can handle. *Head* or *lift* refers to the various heights above the pump that it can raise water. Just remember that 0.03 cubic metres (one cubic foot) in your pond holds 28.3 litres (7½ gallons) of water! Here are two types of pumps for water gardens:

- ✔ **Submersible:** These pumps are sunken out of sight in the bottom of a water garden (or raised up a bit on a cinder block or other support while still underwater), quietly keeping the water moving through your water bubbler or up to your waterfall. These pumps are fine for small to medium ponds. Some water gardeners stash them in a mesh laundry basket, which makes hauling them out, when necessary, a bit easier.

- ✔ **External:** Site this larger, noisier pump close to your pond (hide it from view behind a plant or other barrier). It can power big jobs — large water gardens, a series of ponds, or displays that include a stream or waterfall.

## Bubblers and fountains

For many people, a fountain or a bubbler is an essential part of a water garden. These items work like this: A small, submerged pump circulates water up through plastic tubing and into the fountain or bubbler, which returns it either to a catch basin or back into the pond. From there, the water's routed and pumped back up through the tubing.

A fountain, of course, sprays water up into the air, whereas bubblers cause water to simply gurgle out, not spray up. Bubblers create a sound like a stream and don't generally need as powerful a pump as do fountains, because the water isn't lifted as high. Water garden suppliers, home and garden centres, and mail-order suppliers offer an amazing array of choices. For perhaps more stylish or customized fountains, search on the Internet or prowl arts and crafts shows. The pump and tubing generally come with the fountain, so you don't have to bother with power and capacity calculations.

For fountains, height and shape (from a gentle, misty fan to a towering spurt) are determined not only by the power of the pump but also by the nozzle on the fountain's head. Often the same fountain can be fitted with a variety of nozzles, so examine your options carefully.

# Filters

Using mesh or foam screens, a mechanical filter traps algae and larger pond debris, thus keeping your pond water cleaner. Not surprisingly, you have to rinse out the filter often and replace it periodically. A pump attached to a filter protects the pump and keeps the water moving through it: dirty in, cleaner out. Match your filter to your water garden (or run the risk of ruining the pump by burning it out — or at least causing yourself too-frequent rinsings). If your water has a lot of algae and fine particles, you don't want an extremely fine mesh, obviously.

Biological filters are larger, more-expensive pondside contraptions, recommended for pools with lots of fish or many large fish such as koi. The water is cleansed with gravel and beneficial bacteria; fish waste is converted from ammonia into nitrate, boosting water health for the fish as well as the plants. See Figure 17-5.

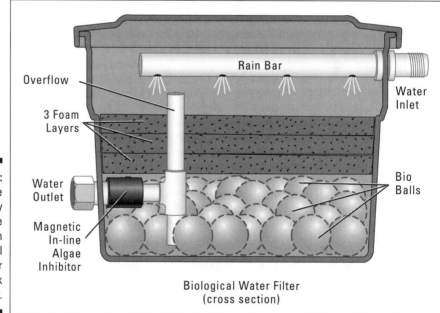

**Figure 17-5:**
Make sure to properly align the elements in a biological filter for it to work correctly.

Overflow

Rain Bar

Water Inlet

3 Foam Layers

Bio Balls

Water Outlet

Magnetic In-line Algae Inhibitor

Biological Water Filter
(cross section)

# Installing and Filling Your Pond

Here are some steps to take when building a simple in-ground pond, without all the bells and whistles of bottom drains and fancy filtration systems. If you want a more-advanced pond system, talk with a water garden specialist or a contractor.

1. **Plan where you're going to put the soil you remove before beginning to dig your pond.**

   You can add the soil to raised beds in your vegetable garden, or use it to add height to a waterfall.

2. **Dig with whatever shovel you're comfortable using (and remember to shape earthen shelves for your water plants, if desired).**

   A long-handled model is easier on your back. If the job is a large one, consider hiring a contractor with a backhoe to do the heavy work.

3. **Put down a layer of about 5 centimetres (2 inches) of sand, and then add the underlay of geotex or a thick layer of newspaper.**

   As we mention in "Picking Out Your Water Garden Parts and Supplies," this underlay serves as protection for the liner from rocks or roots that may be jutting up. The sand further protects the underlay and liner from punctures.

4. **Lay down the liner.**

   You may need a few people to help you with this step because liners of any size are quite heavy. Pleat the material into the corners, and make sure to allow it to lap over the edge of the hole by about 30 centimetres (1 foot).

5. **Secure the edges of the liner with rocks or bricks, and begin filling the pond with a hose.**

   If it's a very large pond, you may have to call a company that specializes in providing large quantities of water for swimming pools.

6. **Trim off the excess liner with a sharp knife after the pond is filled.**

7. **Use flat stones to create an edge or coping around the pond.**

8. **Let the water settle for few days, and then put in your plants.**

   Try not to step into the pond, but if you have to, do it wearing only socks on your feet so you don't damage the liner.

# Choosing Plants for Water Gardens

Stocking a pond is such fun. Water plants, especially the ones that bloom, are so gorgeous. They're not at all hard to grow, and you can purchase many of them from retail or mail-order garden suppliers. When your water garden is set up, the plants' main need — water — is already fulfilled. Before you start looking for water plants, here are a few tips for success:

- ✔ Always keep water plants in pots while they're in your water garden (except for floaters). This move controls their growth and makes maintenance easier. If you use tap water and plan to add fish, wait 48 hours before adding the fish, to allow chlorine in the water to dissipate. The chlorine won't hurt your plants.

- ✔ Use heavy garden soil in your water garden, never bagged potting soil mix, which is far too light and drifts off to make a mess. To keep the heavy garden soil from getting away and muddying the pool, top off each pot with a couple of centimetres (an inch) or so of pea gravel.

- ✔ Use plant tubs or pots with no drainage holes. These containers ensure that the heavy garden soil doesn't get loose in your water garden. You can also buy special mesh pots made for growing plants underwater.

- ✔ Proper planting depth is usually 2.5 to 15 centimetres (1 to 6 inches) below the water's surface. So elevate the pots on blocks, bricks, or overturned pots, or on the shelves (many hard shell liners come with shelves already built in, or you can build shelves into the sides of your in-ground pond — refer to "Installing and Filling Your Pond").

- ✔ Buy and pot water plants in late spring, lowering them carefully into warmed-up water. Hardy water plants can go in water that has reached 10°C (50°F); tropical ones have to wait for at least 21°C (70°F) water. Some plants, such as native water lilies and water irises can winter over in the pond, as long as it's deep enough that the water doesn't completely freeze.

- ✔ Don't overplant your water garden, or your plants will crowd one another and require constant pruning or even eviction (packed-in water lilies do a desperate and unattractive thing called *pyramiding*, where their leaves rear up into the air). Your goal is two-thirds coverage of the water surface — this amount looks attractive, prevents algae growth, and still allows some open water for reflections.

## Water lilies

Two basic kinds of water lily, hardy and tropical, are available. To the uninitiated, the two types seem much the same, but these plants have significant differences. Provided you attend to the water-temperature requirements, you can grow either or both kinds in most parts of the country. However, you have to bring the tropicals inside for the winter or treat them as annuals and plant new ones each summer (for more information, see the upcoming section about lotuses). Here are descriptions of some water lily varieties you're likely to encounter:

- **Hardy water lilies:** Hardies are generally smaller (flowers *and* plants) than tropical water lilies, and the hardy flowers usually float on the surface of the water among the leaves. Popular varieties include bright yellow 'Joey Tomocik', ruby red 'James Brydon', hot pink 'Mayla', pastel pink 'Lilypons', and pristine white 'Virginalis'.

- **Tropical water lilies:** Tropicals have larger flowers than hardies do and are often more-sprawling plants. They proudly hold their flowers above their leaves. Common varieties are sunset-hued 'Albert Greenberg', lavender-pink 'General Pershing', royal purple 'Panama Pacific', and raspberry pink 'Miami Rose'.

As for colour, water lilies come in shades of white, cream, bright and soft yellows, red, pink, and salmon. The tropicals extend the range into some gorgeous hues of blue and purple. Water lily blossoms' centres are usually yellow (sometimes with the *stamens* — stalks with pollen sacs — tipped in a petal-matching colour). The contrast between the bright centre and petals can be quite stunning. As a bonus, some water lilies are sweetly fragrant, especially the tropicals.

## Lotuses

As a symbol of creation, the lotus stakes its place as a sacred flower in Buddhism and Hinduism. To be sure, the lotus is one of the most exotic and beautiful creatures in the plant kingdom: The big, dramatically stalked leaves are attractive, and they shed droplets of water like quicksilver — gorgeous! The buds and blossoms are utterly magnificent, and the large, unusual seedpods are decorative in their own right.

Despite their big size, lotuses grow from a surprisingly delicate, banana-shaped rootstock. Get one in spring and handle it exceedingly gently, especially when potting it. Favourite lotus varieties include ivory-white-with-hot-pink-margins 'Chawan Basu', yellow-to-cream 'Perry's Giant Sunburst', and rosy pink 'Momo Batan'. Here are the growing requirements:

- **A big, big planting tub, full of heavy garden soil (and no drainage holes):** A tub that measures about 60 x 23 centimetres (24 x 9 inches), such as a laundry tub, is reasonable.

✔ **Enough space:** Not every water garden can hold a lotus. Some varieties can spread 3 or 4 metres (10 or 12 feet) or more, with those leaves rearing up on 2-metre (7-foot) stalks. Submerge the potted lotus in 2.5 centimetres (1 inch) of water to start; then move it to 10 centimetres (4 inches) or more over time — less is better, though.

✔ **Sun:** Lotuses need at least six to eight hours of sunlight a day. (A lotus can tolerate some shade if the air temperatures are warm and if you aren't banking on getting it to bloom.)

✔ **Plenty of food:** Poke fertilizer into the pot often, and carefully, to prevent disturbing that fragile rootstock. Four to six water lily–fertilizer tablets monthly is a typical dose, but get exact information from the place where you buy your lotus.

✔ **A long growing season, if you want the flowers and pods that follow:** A short summer won't do — lotuses really need two or even three consecutive months of temperatures over 27°C (80°F).

✔ **Patience:** A lotus often spends its first season just getting used to life in its tub and in your water garden. Lush growth and — maybe, just maybe — those sensational flowers usually happen in the second season. Some lotuses are hardy to Zone 6, especially if planted in a deep pond. If your climate is colder than Zone 6 (or if it's on the border line), don't take a chance: Lift the lotus out of the water in its container before freeze-up, remove its foliage, and store it in a cool cellar or garage with a temperature of 5°C to 10°C (41°F to 50°F). Don't allow the rootstock to dry out.

## So-called marginal plants

*Marginal plants* are the plants that supply height in a water garden (or "vertical interest," as landscapers say). Though you may have seen them in containers or growing on land in damp ground, they're well able to grow in a pot that's immersed in a couple of centimetres or more of water. Other names nurseries use for this sort of plant include *bog plants, emergent plants, pondside plants,* and *moisture-loving plants.* Marginals grown for attractive foliage include canna, mosaic plant, papyrus, various irises, arrowhead, spike rush, umbrella palm, and elephant's ear. If you want beautiful flowers from your marginals, check out canna, golden club, various irises, pickerel weed, and lizard's tail.

Like water lilies, some of these plants are winter hardy; others are tropical. The tropicals can't go in the water till the weather has warmed up to at least 21°C (70°F) and must come out when the water and weather begin to cool down in the fall (either to be discarded as annuals or overwintered indoors — see "Winterizing your plants and fish" for more information). Hardy marginals are fine in 10°C (50°F) or warmer water.

Water gardeners can grow either tropicals or hardies or both kinds almost anywhere in North America. Mix and match them for a more interesting, textured display. Favourite hardy marginals include arrowhead, cattail, golden club, various irises, lizard's tail, pickerel weed, and spike rush. Favourite tropical marginals include canna and water canna, papyrus, mosaic plant, umbrella palm, and elephant's ear.

## Floaters and submerged plants

Though not as flashy as some of the others, floaters and submerged plants are important to having a successful water garden. Floaters are welcome because they help fulfill that two-thirds-coverage requirement for the water garden's surface. They also provide shelter for fish and use nutrients that may otherwise feed unwanted amounts of algae. Favourite floaters and submerged plants include eelgrass, fairy moss, parrot's feather, water hyacinth, water lettuce, and hornwort.

Submerged plants can fill a similar role as floaters do, or they can just hang out under the water. Occasionally, you'll see submerged plants billed as *oxygenating plants,* though the oxygenation doesn't occur constantly — they generate oxygen underwater only during the daylight hours. If you peer into the water, you may see tiny bubbles percolating from their foliage into the surrounding water.

Many popular floaters and submerged plants are problems in the wild. They multiply amazingly fast, clogging waterways and upsetting the balance of nature, so it's now illegal to sell or transport some of them. So don't cheat — buy floaters or submerged plants only from a reputable nursery, make sure they go straight into your water garden, and *never, ever,* improperly discard any part of them. That means don't toss or dump them into wild or manmade waterways, or even in your back forty or compost pile. Play it safe and bag up unwanted plants and plant parts, and then send them away with your household garbage. See Chapter 21 for more information on invasive plants.

# Adding Fish to Your Water Garden

One of the main reasons many people want a water garden in the first place is so they can have fish. Fish make the whole scene come alive! Caring for pond fish is very similar to caring for aquarium fish, except you have to deal with the issues related to keeping fish outdoors. You have plenty to discover about the selection and care of pond fish. Get help and information from wherever fish are sold.

Two types of fish are commonly kept in water gardens: common goldfish and koi, or Japanese carp (see Figure 17-6). For common goldfish, keep 2.5 centimetres (1 inch) of fish per 19 litres (5 gallons) of water. Koi, because they're so big, need a bigger pond and a rate of 2.5 centimetres (1 inch) per 38 litres (10 gallons) of water (and Koi more than 15 centimetres require even more space to roam). For advice on helping your fish survive the winter, see "Winterizing your plants and fish." For more information on keeping koi, read *Koi For Dummies* by R. D. Bartlett and Patricia Bartlett (Wiley).

Koi can be very destructive to plants: They like to eat 'em! So protect your plant roots or, better yet, stick with goldfish, which cause much less plant havoc.

Adding game fish is practical only with large ponds, 0.2 hectares (a half acre) in size or more. Those kinds of ponds are beyond the scope of this book. Native fish can be stocked, but most people opt for ornamental, cold-loving fish like goldfish. Most garden centres and pet stores stock fish that are appropriate for ornamental ponds.

A common beginner's mistake is adding too many fish to a pond; it's bad for the fish and bad for your water garden. Results of overcrowding include excessive fish waste (which can smell bad and fuel algae bloom — check out "A sea of green: Controlling algae in troubled waters") and poor fish health — *ick*. Be conservative and don't add too many fish, especially to smaller water gardens and container displays.

Here are the basics of adding fish to your water garden:

- **Don't use chlorine or chloramines!** If you fill your water garden with municipal tap water, it's been treated with either or both of these chemicals. Although these chemicals kill bacteria and make for safe drinking water, it's harmful to fish. Luckily, if you let the water sit for a few days, the chlorine dissipates. As for chloramines, they have to be neutralized — ask your water department for help.

- **Let the water warm up before adding fish.** Allow the water to warm while you're waiting for water-treatment chemicals to subside. The fish will appreciate that (hose water is chilly).

    A well-planted pond provides lots of hiding places to protect your fish from predators. Also, to keep predators like raccoons and herons out, make sure the edge of the pond abruptly falls off by 60 to 90 centimetres (2 to 3 feet) deep so these creatures can't wade in to get the fish. (This deep edge can conflict with the shelves you may want to build into the sides of the pond to hold plants, however.) Some people buy heron decoys or movement-activated water sprays to put at the edge of the pond to frighten off raccoons and other predators.

- **Add the fish gradually.** Fish are cold blooded, and they need time to adjust to the temperature of their new environment. The best method is to float the fish in the water-filled baggie they came in on the surface of the water for a few hours before you release them.

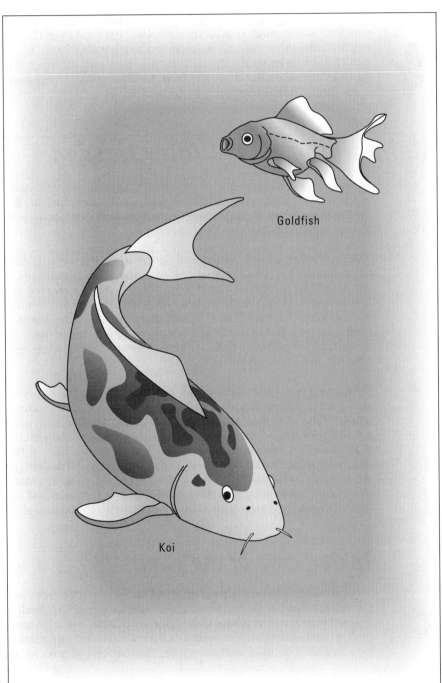

Goldfish

Koi

**Figure 17-6:**
Koi (bottom)
and goldfish
(top).

Don't overfeed your fish! The general rule is that however much food they consume in five minutes is all they get. Uneaten food fouls the water. Overfed fish are unhealthy and also generate too much waste. Truth is, you really don't *have* to feed your fish at all, because they can survive on the natural foods in the water. But it's fun to feed the fish, so if you want to, do it sparingly. Once a day is plenty.

# Maintaining Your Water Garden

As we hint in this chapter's introduction, taking care of an installed and stocked water garden is pretty easy. You're out there admiring it and monitoring the progress of water lily buds and other bloomers anyway, so just turn those frequent visits into a brief checkup.

The main water-garden water issue occurs when the water level drops. On hot summer days, you can lose a bit to evaporation. Top off the water garden with the hose; just make sure the end of the hose is immersed and that the flow of water doesn't dislodge a pot or plant. (Yes, we do caution you about the dangers of chlorine and chloramines in municipal tap water in the preceding section, but that info's for when you're pouring in many litres for the initial filling. A little bit of those chemicals entering the water now won't do your fish or plants any harm.)

If you come out some morning and the water level has dropped dramatically, your liner is damaged and leaking. Siphon off water until you find the problem spot and then stop and patch it (patch kits are available wherever liners are sold). To siphon, insert a garden hose so that one end is submerged. Place the other end of the hose outside the pond so it's below the level of the end in the pond. Inhale once to start the suction, and this gets the water flowing. If the pond is lower than the ground surrounding it, this manual suction won't work, so get a submersible pump. Put it in the pond and attach tubing to the output end of the pump. Turn it on, and it rapidly drains the pond.

## Taking care of the plants

Because water garden plants are potted, sooner or later they run out of food, even though you've potted them in the right kind of heavy garden soil. Your best bet is to feed the plants with water lily tablets, available wherever water garden plants are sold. These tablets have a balanced formulation that's ideal for water lilies, lotuses, and marginals. They're easy to poke in (use a finger, dibble, or even a broom handle), and they break down gradually while nourishing the root system.

Feed your water plants on planting day and then monthly thereafter throughout the growing season. Slow down and stop as fall approaches so the plants can enter their normal dormancy.

As the summer progresses, water plants can exceed their bounds and grow a little too lustily. Always remove stems and leaf stalks right at the base (where the pea-gravel layer begins in the pot) so nothing is left to rot and foul the water. Cut or twist the pieces off; never yank, or the whole plant may come out in your fist!

Don't toss pieces of pruned or removed water plants back in the water where they can break down and foul the water! Add them to the compost pile or dig them straight into a vegetable garden's soil. For potentially invasive floaters and submerged plants, play it safe and add them and their prunings to the household garbage (for details on invasive species, see Chapter 21).

## Winterizing your plants and fish

As fall approaches, the water temperature cools down, you cease fertilizing, and the plants begin to go dormant. Lower the water level by a few centimetres, and float a ball or block of wood on the surface to prevent a total freeze-over. (A complete coating of ice is bad because it prevents the exchange of oxygen and allows toxic gases to build up. Fish and plants below, even when dormant, can perish.)

Haul tropical plants out of the pond and toss them onto the compost pile. Or if you want to overwinter them indoors, refer to the advice about overwintering in the "Lotuses" section, get the details from wherever you bought the plants, or try to find a more-experienced water gardener to help you. Some tropicals can stay in heated aquariums; you can strip others of all growth and store their little tubers or rhizomes in damp sand.

Hardy plants need to be hauled out, too, and given a haircut, leaving only a stub of foliage. If your winters aren't too severe (Zone 7 or warmer), you can return the plants to the deepest parts of the water garden (no elevating supports now) for the coming months. Otherwise, hardies can come indoors to a nonfreezing place and be heaped with straw or another blanketing of mulch until spring returns.

Many pond fish can remain outside during the winter if the water is deep enough (it cannot freeze right to the bottom), but it really depends on where you live and on the type of water garden you have. Depending on these conditions, you may have to set up an aquarium inside your home and transfer your pond fish there over the winter season. Again, get help and information from wherever you buy your fish.

Fish that remain in the pond slow down and go dormant in cold weather, just like hardy plants. Reduce feeding in the fall. Eventually, the fish retreat to the deepest part of the pool, perhaps burrowing into some muck there. To ensure their survival, be sure to keep an air hole open. If the water freezes over despite the block of wood you're floating on the surface, don't break it with an instrument — the pressure of the sound wave may kill the fish. Instead, pour some boiling water over the ice until a section melts. But don't fool around with the fish's lives — if you fear for their survival in a very cold climate, net them and keep them in an aquarium for the winter.

## A sea of green: Controlling algae in troubled waters

If your water turns a murky green, the first thing to remember is, *don't panic!* The second thing to know is that no garden pool is ever completely clear and algae free. Indeed, algae growth is part of the ecological balance. A small amount of algae — visible as a slightly green (or bronze) cast to the water, or as a coating that forms on the sides — is both normal and healthy. That said, algae can get out of hand at times.

In the early days of a new water garden's life, there's inevitably a flush of algae growth, called a *bloom*. This bloom occurs because plenty of light is available, not to mention dissolved nutrients to nourish it. Small or shallow water gardens are the most vulnerable because they heat up faster, and algae love very warm water. Wait it out. As your water lilies spread their pads and other plants grow and contribute to the desirable two-thirds coverage that we mention several times in this chapter, the algae will subside.

If a smelly pea soup prevails, you do have a problem, but you also have options. Diagnose the cause, and then take steps to treat it:

✔ **High water temperature:** Algae prospers with warmth. Add more plants, particularly floating plants, which can outcompete the algae for minerals dissolved in the water. Provide extra, cooling shade, such as a large beach umbrella overhead in the hottest part of the day.

- ✔ **Excessive fish food:** The food the fish don't get around to eating breaks down in the water, adding to the organic broth. Fish waste and its byproduct ammonia also encourage algae growth. Try feeding fish less (only as much as they can consume in five minutes is the rule) and/or take out some fish. Install a filter to help remove fish waste. Treat the water with a liquid ammonia remover (such as Ammo-Lock); follow label directions with great care.

- ✔ **Excessive nutrients:** The source may be runoff from your adjacent garden or lawn, or perhaps you're overfertilizing your water garden plants. Cut back on the fertilizer and/or create diversion and drainage channels to keep runoff away. Keep yellowing and fading plant parts trimmed off (don't let them break down in the water). Also, make sure leaves and other lawn debris don't end up in the water.

- ✔ **Improper water pH level:** Buy a simple kit and test the water (first thing in the morning is the best time to check). You want it to be between 6.5 and 8.5, ideally around 7.0. Adjust with water garden chemicals as necessary (get the products and advice from wherever you got the test kit).

You can use your bare hands to remove algae, but understand that hauling out algae is a temporary solution — it can make your display look better for a while, but if you don't address the cause, more algae soon replace the algae you remove.

# Part VI

# The Part of Tens

The 5th Wave                    By Rich Tennant

"The seeds fell out of Walt's pocket six years ago and since then every August we just sit somewhere else."

# In this part . . .

*H*ere's where you pick up some quick-and-dirty
information (well, if you're gardening, dirt's probably
involved, right?) about a variety of topics that may interest
you as a gardener. Find out what most people ask about
gardening when first starting out — chances are, you've
asked a question or two from the list. Get information on
enjoyable garden projects for yourself and your kids. And
if you're eco-conscious — and most gardeners are — the
last chapter gives you ten tips on how you can be a Good
Garden Citizen.

# Chapter 18

# Ten Common Questions from (And Ten Common Answers for) Gardening Beginners

• • • • • • • • • • • • • • • • • • • • • • • • • • • • • • • • • • • • • • • • •

## In This Chapter

▶ Identifying plants and problems

▶ Investigating plant health

▶ Special growing conditions: Knowing what to plant where

▶ Fighting deer, weeds, and erosion

• • • • • • • • • • • • • • • • • • • • • • • • • • • • • • • • • • • • • • • • •

*T*here are just as many different questions as there are different gardeners, but some questions seem to pop up more than others. Those questions are the ones we address here. And don't think that only beginners ask about gardening — the pros often have questions, too. In fact, some old hands may find some of the information here useful as well. So read on!

# What's the Difference between an Annual and a Perennial?

Plant classification is something that often confuses new gardeners, so here are the short-and-sweet answers: An *annual* lives for only one growing season; a *perennial* slows down or dies back in the winter months but comes back bigger and better the next year, and the one after, and so on. Whether a plant is an annual or perennial may depend on the climate where you live.

So you have to buy and plant new annuals every year, while perennials are long-term investments. You can refer to Chapter 6 for the lowdown on annuals and Chapter 7 for info on perennials.

# *What's Organic Matter?*

When plants and animals die, bacteria and fungi and other critters move in and break down the dead material into simpler substances. The end product is a smorgasbord of nutrients for your plants.

*Organic matter* is any material that originates from a living (well, once-living) creature; you can dig this matter into your soil, and as the material decays, it improves the soil's condition. Examples of organic matter include compost, dehydrated manure (never fresh, which "burns" the plants), chopped-up fall leaves, peat moss (which is most effective when predampened), ground-up bark, and so on. You may have some of this stuff on hand, or you can certainly buy it bagged. Refer to Chapter 4 for more information.

# *Why Does Everything I Plant in My Flower Bed Die?*

If you have an epidemic of sick or dying plants, you probably aren't cursed. Your problems may be due to one of many not-so-supernatural reasons, and you can take some steps to narrow down the possible culprits — like poor soil, soil that's too acidic or too alkaline (its pH level is too low or too high), or a lack of sunlight or water. Improve or modify these items one by one until the health of your plants improves. For more information on evaluating these factors and maintaining the proper conditions in plant beds, refer to Chapter 4.

# *How Do I Prepare the Ground for a Brand-New Bed?*

Completely clear the ground you want to use of weeds, rocks, roots, and other debris. Make the bed deep enough for the roots of the plants you want to put in there; about 15 to 20 centimetres (6 to 8 inches) suffices for the majority of choices. You can borrow or rent a rototiller or use a simple shovel, depending on the size of your growing area and your own strength and inclination. Then improve the soil by adding organic material. Almost any soil benefits from the introduction of some good organic matter. Refer to Chapter 4 for more information.

Call your electric, telephone, cable, and gas companies to verify the locations of underground utilities in your yard before you start digging. Hitting one of these wires or pipes with a tool can cause you serious harm through electric shock, or at the very least, damage the utilities in your house.

# Do I Have to Spray Chemicals on My Rosebushes?

You don't have to spray chemicals on your roses — if you choose the right rosebush in the first place. Find out the main problem in your area: Rust? Mildew? Insect pests? Jealous, scheming neighbours? Then get good advice on resistant rose varieties. Rose breeders have been answering the call for tougher plants, so often some of the brand-new ones are good choices. Oldies but goodies, especially naturally durable shrub roses, are also worth looking into. Refer to Chapter 9 for more-detailed information, or look for the information on these Web sites: www.organicrosegardening.com/index.html or www.canadianrosesociety.org.

# Do Any Vegetables Grow in the Shade?

Well, tomatoes won't do too well in shade, but you can certainly grow a fine crop of lettuces and mixed greens, as well as kale and collard greens. Peas, broccoli, and cabbage can get by with less than full sun. Some root crops such as onions, radishes, and turnips also manage in somewhat shady growing conditions. For more on vegetable gardening, flip to Chapter 13.

# It's Hot and Dry Here in Summer. What Are My Options?

Your best bet is to take a look at native, or *indigenous,* plants — the ones that are adapted to your local growing conditions. View indigenous plants in other people's gardens or public/botanic gardens in your community. Find them for sale at garden centres that specialize in native plants, at large general-purpose nurseries (often off in their own section), or at botanic-garden plant sales. Check out the appendix for sources, and be amazed at the diverse and beautiful native plants that are available. You may even discover a variety of cactus that's native to your area, and we all know they thrive in hot, dry summers — the hotter and drier, the better!

# What Can I Plant on a Steep Bank to Prevent Erosion?

To keep "steep" dirt from washing away, you want a fast-growing plant with grabbing roots to stabilize the soil. Ideally, you also want something that'll last a while, spread out, and cause you little trouble. If the plant excludes weeds by forming a mat, better still. Plants that meet this tall order include bearberry, creeping juniper, pachysandra, cotoneaster, and shrub or ground-cover roses.

If it's a large area, consider planting invasive groundcovers like snow-in-summer and goutweed. These plants may be unwelcome in other situations, but they shine in areas where you can let them roam free.

Day lilies also work well because they have fingerlike roots that really grab on. You can also look into having the slope terraced and planting each step or level. Or install a rock garden — the rocks may help hold the soil in place (besides, rock garden plants like quick-draining ground, and slopes fit the bill).

# How Do I Remove the Weeds from the Lawn without Pulling Them One by One?

In truth, you'll probably always have some weeds in your lawn, because nature favours diversity. Taking good care of the lawn — that is, not neglecting it — can help. Ultimately, if you must have a lawn that's close to being weed free, you'll probably want to resort to using some type of selective herbicide (weed killer). But first, check with your municipal government to find out what types of herbicides are approved for use in your area. Opt for liquid materials that you can surgically spray only on offending weeds and not on your entire lawn. Refer to Chapter 10 for more information on lawn care.

# *Is There Anything Deer Don't Eat?*

Deer will eat almost any plant if they're desperate! The problem is deer over-population due to a shrinking natural habitat and a lack of natural predators. Deer get hungry, they wander into your yard, and they dine on anything and everything (especially in winter, when natural food is even scarcer). One beleaguered homeowner isn't going to solve this problem. Although some repellents supposedly protect garden plants (noisemakers, foul-smelling sprays, bags of human hair from the local salon), the only sure deterrent is installing a 2.4-metre- (8-foot-) tall (possibly electrified) fence all the way around your yard.

You can try planting things that deer favour less — plants with thorns, for instance, or some bitter-tasting perennials and herbs. For complete lists, check with your nearest provincial ministry of agriculture office.

# Chapter 19

# Ten Quick, Fun, or Handy Garden Projects

. . . . . . . . . . . . . . . . . . . . . . . . . . . . . . . . . . . . . . . . . . . .

*In This Chapter*

▶ Adding useful structures to your yard or garden

▶ Beautifying your outdoor space

▶ Making your own compost and pest repellant

. . . . . . . . . . . . . . . . . . . . . . . . . . . . . . . . . . . . . . . . . . . .

S o your garden is all planted, the lawn is mowed, and everything is land-scaped to your satisfaction — and now you're itching for something else to do to your yard. Don't fret — you still have plenty of ways to make your yard even better and to help you enjoy it even more (preferably while sipping a cool lemonade). This chapter contains some fun ideas you can consider.

## Set Up a Hammock

You can string up a hammock between two strong trees or on the porch, or set up one of those free-standing hammocks in a shady spot. Then go take a well-deserved nap. After you mow the lawn. Before you shower. After you pour yourself a cold drink.

When stringing up a hammock, make sure you tie it very securely and stretch it *tight* between its two supports, whether they're trees or porch posts, so you don't hit the ground while taking an outdoor nap. And above all, make sure those trees or porch posts are very strong and secure and in no danger of breaking under your weight!

# Put Up a Rubber Tire Swing

What would summer be without a tire swing? What would childhood be without one? Just make certain to choose a limb that's strong and far enough away from the trunk and everything else to allow for swinging (and not for smacking into things). Also make sure the rope you use is stout and that the knots around the tree limb and tire are very, very secure. Using a strong chain may be a better idea, with large metal hooks to hold. Have a kid help you decide how high off the ground the swing should be. (And remember to dump the water out of the tire after a rain shower so mosquitoes and other bugs don't hang around.)

As with any swing, make sure that your kids know to play safely around the tire swing, and supervise them when they're using it. Check the rope or chain often to make sure it's still secure. Check the tree limb, as well — tire swing ropes have a habit of sawing through their tree limbs when used a lot.

# Install Stepping Stones

Stone paths lend architecture and accessibility to your garden and yard, and they make great projects. However, you have to do your planning beforehand to make sure you install your path right. Laying the stone atop the ground rarely works; you need to seat the stones in a base of sand or stone dust (which you can buy at the same place where you purchase the stones). Dig down a few centimetres — make the space slightly wider, too — and then add enough base material to fill the hole. Set the stones down and wiggle them into position. If you're laying a terrace or walkway, separate individual stones by a centimetre or two (½ to 1 inch). Pick up a copy of *Landscaping For Dummies* (Wiley) for more information.

# Set Up a Trellis

Like paths, trellises add architecture and functionality to many yards and make good weekend projects. The kind of trellis you choose and how securely you position it depends on what you plan to grow over it. Climbing roses, climbing hydrangea, wisteria, and grapevines are quite heavy — use stout wood, heavy-duty plastic, or cast iron for these, and plunge the "legs" deep into the ground so the trellis doesn't wobble. Clematis and morning glories can go on lighter structures. Refer to Chapter 12 to find out more about climbing vines.

If you're growing a vine that blooms and/or likes sun, don't set up a trellis completely flush against a house wall or a fence. Vines need space to grow and good air circulation, and too-close growth can damage the wood or paint of the backdrop. If you're setting your trellis against a wall or fence and anticipate wanting to paint or stain it every few years, pick up a trellis that's hinged near the base so it can be bent forward.

# Plant a Teepee

A teepee is a practical support that looks so much better than a regular pole. And if they're wide enough at the base, a small kid can hide inside.

The teepee ought to be at least 2 or 2.5 metres (6 or 8 feet) high, depending on what you're growing. Read the seed packet or the plant label for the plant's mature height and then plan accordingly. You don't have to use lumber — how about slender branches? Lash three or more tall branches or poles together, and stick them a few centimetres into the ground to make them stable. As for the climbing plant that will cloak it, you want something lush and fast growing. Try pole beans, scarlet runner beans, climbing nasturtium, or morning glory. Set at least one or two plants at the base of each support.

# Create Whimsical Garden Art from Castoffs

Make a "bouquet" of worn or discarded tools, cinched together with wire. Set the bouquet in the vegetable garden or flower bed, or mount it on a gate or fence. Or hang your old garden tools, with their handles painted the same colour as the trim of your house, in a pleasing pattern along your fence.

# Decorate the Front Steps with Potted Plants

Displaying potted plants is an easy way to add colour and beauty to front steps as well as to porches and balconies. If your steps are shady, use herbs or shade plants (or both). Colourful pots that match or contrast with their contents add a lot of splash and are a welcome sight. Move potted plants on and offstage as their prime comes and goes, and bring in replacement plants if the original ones fade or grow leggy. But above all, keep plants watered. Plants in pots dry out amazingly fast. Refer to Chapter 16 for more tips on container gardening.

Be sure to keep the plants out of the way of people climbing the stairs. You don't want anyone to trip and hurt themselves on your beloved plants!

# Make Some Plant Labels

Plant labels are important items that too many gardeners don't use. They're especially important when you're digging up or planting bulbs in the fall and you can't remember where you planted what! Make the labels out of Popsicle sticks, laminated seed packets, pieces of old mini-blinds, rocks — whatever you like. Use waterproof marker or acrylic paint. This project is great for one of those late-spring rainy days, when you or the kids are feeling antsy.

# Make a Simple Compost Bin for Your Own Organic Matter

Sure, you can buy a compost bin, but if you have an open spot that gets sun yet is out of the way, setting up a homemade one is easy. Plan for your bin to be about 1.2 metres (4 feet) in diameter; smaller piles don't heat up well, slowing decomposition.

Use about four wooden or metal stakes, and make sure they stand about a metre (3 feet) high (a size that keeps the bin manageable for maintenance) when plunged into the ground. Wrap galvanized chicken wire or snow fencing around these "corners," and then use lengths of wire to cinch the ends where they meet. Put a base of twigs or dried cornstalks on the bottom of the bin before beginning to add organic waste.

Refer to Chapter 4 for more information on using compost.

# Combat Garden Pests with Homemade Pepper Spray

Get white flies, mites, cucumber beetles, leaf hoppers, and cabbage loopers (those very hungry caterpillars) out of your yard with pepper spray. Pepper spray doesn't hurt your plants or the environment, but most insects and other pests don't like it. Consider it a temporary deterrent, not an insecticide, and be sure to spray all the leaves of your plants, or the little varmints will just move to an unsprayed one for a feast.

Here's the recipe: Mix together 3.8 litres (1 gallon) water, 6 drops dish soap, and 30 millilitres (2 tablespoons) dried hot red pepper flakes. (Alternatively, you can use 45 to 60 millilitres, or 3 to 4 tablespoons, of hot pepper sauce.) Let the pepper spray sit overnight, and then shake it well. Store the mixture in a spray bottle, and spray it on the vulnerable plants, covering every leaf. Respray after it rains, and make sure you rinse off your veggies very well after harvesting them — unless you want them to taste like hot peppers!

# Chapter 20

# Ten Garden Projects for Children

● ● ● ● ● ● ● ● ● ● ● ● ● ● ● ● ● ● ● ● ● ● ● ● ● ● ● ● ● ● ● ● ● ● ● ● ● ● ● ● ● ●

## *In This Chapter*

▶ Growing kid-friendly plants to play with and use

▶ Getting creative with seeds and sunlight

▶ Creating outdoor environments for watching birds and butterflies

● ● ● ● ● ● ● ● ● ● ● ● ● ● ● ● ● ● ● ● ● ● ● ● ● ● ● ● ● ● ● ● ● ● ● ● ● ● ● ● ● ●

**M**any kids are fascinated by how plants, birds, and butterflies grow and thrive in the world just outside their front doors. So why not give children the chance to play in the dirt and get up close and personal with insects and earthworms? Spending time outdoors teaches kids about science, gives them room to play and relax, and trains them to find entertainment beyond the warm glow of the computer or TV screen.

You can find easy ways to help your children love gardening just as much as you do! Here are some project ideas to get your budding botanists a good start in the world of gardening.

## *Create a Dinosaur Garden*

This time-honoured project will be around as long as there are small children with plastic dinosaur action figures. Just set aside a shady corner that includes ferns and some rocks. Your children can make their toy dinosaurs run rampant in the miniature jungle. While you're at it, try creating a designated dig area by burying some bones or other garden artifacts that are just waiting to be discovered.

## Grow a Sunflower Fort

Buy seeds for those huge, tall sunflower varieties, and plant them in a square or circle in a sunny spot in your yard. Water and fertilize the seeds often, and be amazed as they surge into growth. With luck, the plants may support one another, or you can provide support stakes. Your kids can spend hours playing inside the "rooms" the sunflowers create.

You can also create a teepee by growing climbing plants on several poles lashed together. Refer to Chapter 19 for details.

## Make Sunprints

Buy light-sensitive paper — many toy stores and school suppliers carry it. Have the kids go out in the yard and pick things — flowers, pinecones, seed pods, interesting leaves — and lay them on the paper in the sun for about seven minutes. Children can create patterns with the garden items if they'd like. Then rinse the paper with lukewarm water and let it dry. This nature-inspired art is suitable for framing!

## Plant Mini-Pumpkins

These cute little pumpkins are so much easier to grow to orange maturity than traditional jack-o'-lantern pumpkins, and many children love growing and playing with them. The vines ramble, like the vines of any squash-family plant, so make sure you give them enough room to grow. Organically rich soil is important, too. See your local nursery about getting varieties that do well in your area.

## Write with Seeds

It's fun to plant seeds in the pattern of letters and see how they grow to form living words. Radish seeds work great because they're easy to pour and manoeuvre (more so for little fingers than adult fingers, actually) and they germinate in a couple days. You and your child can do your names, your initials, or even a happy face.

# Trap a Zucchini

Take a see-through plastic bottle out to the garden when zucchini fruit are just forming, and slide the neck of the bottle over the little fruit. It'll keep growing inside the bottle, probably even filling it! Any size bottle will do. If the fruit fills the container, it'll stop growing.

Use plastic containers, not glass. A good approach is to cut the bottle in half lengthwise and then enclose the fruit with the two halves (like a mould), securing the container with rubber bands. When the plant fills the container, remove the bands and marvel at how the fruit has the container's shape. Try some fanciful containers, like the animal figures frequently used for honey or drinks.

# Make a Home-Grown Salad

Kids have fun trekking out to the vegetable garden with a big basket, and picking ingredients for the dinner salad. After bringing everything inside and washing it well, the kids can slice, tear, chop, and serve the salad to the grownups (and save some for themselves!). It's particularly fun for kids to make faces or patterns with cherry tomatoes or sliced big tomatoes.

Be sure to have the kids pick only what you need from the garden, and no more!

# Grow Paperwhites

These sweetly scented, white-flowered daffodils are very easy for children to grow. They don't even need soil — a dish of gravel will do. Just don't forget to keep paperwhites watered. Roots form and grab on to the gravel, green leaves shoot up, and those pretty, fragrant blossoms soon follow. The bulbs are usually for sale in the fall in stores that carry gardening supplies. Refer to Chapter 8 for more information on forcing bulbs.

# Set Up a Birdbath

Bring the kids along to the local nursery or hardware store to pick out a birdbath, and discuss the merits of size and style. Get the kids involved in picking out a good spot in the yard — in the open but not far from sheltering shrubs or trees so skittish birds can get to safety if need be. Kids can have fun spying on the birdbath from the house or from across the yard. The birds may be slow to discover and use the bath, but after they do, their antics can provide hours of entertainment.

Pick up a book on bird species so your kids can have fun identifying the various types of birds that visit the bath.

## Attract Butterflies to the Garden

Plant a guaranteed butterfly-magnet plant like butterfly bush *(Buddleia)* or butterfly weed *(Asclepias)*. Milkweed and lantana are other fine choices. Your kids can have lots of fun watching as the local butterflies, and possibly even hummingbirds, visit the bush.

Using pesticides in your garden will also kill the butterflies and other desirable insects. If you must use pesticides, use them with great care — only if they're approved for use in your area and only on plants where other methods have failed.

Look for a book about butterfly species so your kids can have fun learning about the butterflies that live in your area.

# Chapter 21

# Ten Ways to Be a Good Garden Citizen

- - - - - - - - - - - - - - - - - - - - - - - - - - - - - - - - - - - - - - - - - -

*In This Chapter*

▶ Using environmentally friendly gardening products

▶ Encouraging a balanced ecosystem and natural pest control

▶ Cutting down on waste

▶ Making your yard healthier and more beautiful

- - - - - - - - - - - - - - - - - - - - - - - - - - - - - - - - - - - - - - - - - -

**M**any gardening enthusiasts, quite naturally, are concerned with preserving a healthy outdoor environment and doing what they can to make the world a healthier and lovelier place through responsible gardening and yard care. You're holding this book, so we bet you're interested in being a Good Garden Citizen. Read on for some easy tips on how to do your part.

You might also want to check out *Organic Gardening For Dummies,* by Ann Whitman and The Editors of the National Gardening Association (Wiley). The book talks in-depth about sustainable gardening practices: building healthy soil, using organic weed and pest control, composting, and more.

## *Avoid Road Salt in Winter*

Many people reach for road salt when their cars are slippin' and slidin' on icy roads and driveways, but road salt damages plants growing not only in your yard but also on other properties. Salt leaches into the soil and damages plant roots, which in turn compromises plant health. If your car's wheels need traction, use sand or kitty litter instead.

# Add Birdhouses to Your Yard

Having birdhouses in your yard means that you'll attract birds, which add colour and song to your garden as well as natural insect control. Birdhouses also make your garden friendlier for local wildlife.

When we say to set up *birdhouses,* we mean real birdhouses — practical, not decorative ones. Different bird species prefer certain sizes or designs, so do your research to find out what birds are most common in your area. The local branch of a bird-watching club (www.web-nat.com/bic/society.html) will be happy to advise you.

# Fight Invasive Exotics

Many plants that you find in nurseries or through friends aren't native to your area, and some of them tend to take over the strange lands they find themselves in. These aggressive plants are known as *invasive exotics,* and by crowding out native plant life, they can disrupt entire ecosystems — plants, animals, and the physical environment.

You'll find a long list of invasive exotics that are threatening natural Canadian habitats at Environment Canada's Web site (www.cws-scf.ec.gc.ca/publications/inv/cont_e.cfm). Don't grow these plants in your garden, on the chance that they'll escape and cause problems in the wild. Don't even let these plants into your yard — the fewer areas they gain a foothold in, the better.

Invasive species show up a lot on provincial "noxious weeds" lists, and it's often a misdemeanor to grow any of the listed plants.

For more information on exactly what these plant villains are and what you can do to stop them, get in touch with your provincial ministry of agriculture or any local conservation agency, or do a Web search for the name of your province and the words "noxious weeds." You can also check out www.cws-scf.ec.gc.ca/publications/inv/23_e.cfm to find out what actions you're required to take if noxious weeds are growing on your property.

# Mulch to Conserve Water and Control Weeds

Mulch is for more than looks. The top layers of soil, when unprotected by mulch, dry out so fast that your plants can suffer very quickly. Exposed soil is such a waste. Mulch holds moisture in place longer, right where plants need it, and keeps your plants healthier.

Also, mulch cuts down on weeds, which can reduce the amount of herbicides you use (or how much pulling you have to do). For more benefits of mulch, refer to Chapter 4.

# Use Environmentally Friendly Lawn Care

Don't collect and dispose of your clippings; let them decompose naturally where they lie. Use fertilizer responsibly, not applying too much or adding it too late in the season. And use weed killer judiciously. Your local wildlife and groundwater will thank you.

# Seek Out the Least-Toxic Insect Controls

You have no need to poison everything in sight to get rid of your insect problems. Today, you can choose from many low-toxicity solutions for controlling pests. Search out these options, and always try them first.

And don't forget about the birdhouses that we mention earlier in the chapter — birds feast on insects.

For more information, here's a good site about biological pest control by Cornell University: www.nysaes.cornell.edu/ent/biocontrol.

# Build Up the Soil

Avid gardeners who amend or enrich the soil around their rented townhouses or homes should feel proud. Depleted soil is a major problem in many areas, leaving barely enough ground for things to grow well, if at all. Do your part and build up the soil, wherever you are! Improve it by adding compost or organic material of any kind every year. And if you're planning new-home construction, get to the contractor right away and forge an agreement that the topsoil on your property will be cleared and kept aside until after construction, then reapplied to your property. Don't let the builder bury or sell it off. It took hundreds of years for nature to produce this black gold — don't lose it!

# Recycle Plastic in Various Gardening Projects

Seems like half the stuff thrown away these days is made of plastic. Don't just recycle those containers — think about reusing them in your garden. Small yogurt cups, for example, are ideal for seedlings. Large milk jugs, with holes pierced in them and sunk into the ground near a thirsty plant, help water the plant slowly and deeply. Plastic tubes can work as stakes for floppy plants. Plastic can be a valuable resource, so take advantage of it when you can!

# Make Your Own Compost

Why buy compost when you can easily make it at home? Create a compost pile in your backyard, or buy an inexpensive composter to handle your kitchen scraps and grass clippings. And as all your kitchen waste goes into the pile instead of the household garbage, your family generates far fewer bags of trash. Refer to Chapter 4 for more information on compost.

# Plant a Tree

The annual Earth Day celebrations have been promoting this project all along, but you don't have to plant trees just on that day (though springtime is the best time). Just do it — on your property, or in a local park or school-yard or other public place in need of beautification and shade. Don't be a vigilante tree planter, though. Get permission if your area requires it, and while you're at it, ask a local nursery to donate trees. And get your friends and neighbours to help. Few acts promote "better days ahead" more than this simple act.

# Appendix

# Basic Gardening Resources

• • • • • • • • • • • • • • • • • • • • • • • • • • • • • • • • • • • • • • • • • • • • •

*S*o many resources for purchasing plants and tools or just gathering information are available that beginning gardeners are often intimidated by the vastness of it all. This appendix attempts to break down the sheer volume of gardening information into some links to simple, basic Web sites that you can use as a starting point for exploring the resources at your disposal. These recommended sites offer a wealth of info on many aspects of gardening, and they're ideal places to start when exploring the universe of gardening on the Web.

From practical tips to the latest research, universities offer valuable info and give a regional perspective. National organizations also have regional and local branches, and their sites tell you of events to attend, groups to join, and gardens to visit. If you have a particular plant passion, you're likely to find a plant association of like-minded gardeners on the Web. Many offer expert advice, publications, and regional gatherings. You can also find many sites on organic gardening, which can help you create a garden that's healthy for your family, for wildlife, and for the environment. And of course, you can search through numerous online mail-order companies that can supply you with what you need to get your garden started. Pull up a seat to your computer and get ready to explore! (In case the computer doesn't appeal to you today, we also give you the phone numbers and addresses of the mail-order companies so you can request a catalogue.)

## General Gardening Information

About.com: Gardening
`gardening.about.com`

GardenWeb
`www.gardenweb.com`

Internet Directory for Botany: Gardening
`herba.msu.ru/mirrors/www.helsinki.fi/kmus/bothort.html`

Plant Hardiness Zones of Canada 2000 Map
`nlwis-snite1.agr.gc.ca/plant00`

### University Resources: Canada

Memorial University of Newfoundland Botanical Garden
www.mun.ca/botgarden

University of Alberta Devonian Botanic Garden
www.devonian.ualberta.ca

University of British Columbia Botanical Garden and
Centre for Plant Research
www.ubcbotanicalgarden.org

University of Manitoba: Horticultural Inquiries
www.umanitoba.ca/afs/hort_inquiries

University of Saskatchewan: Gardenline
www.gardenline.usask.ca

### University Resources: United States

Ohio State University: Yard & Garden
ohioline.osu.edu/lines/hygs.html

Purdue University: Consumer Horticulture
www.hort.purdue.edu/ext/ConHort.html

University of Illinois Extension: Horticulture
web.extension.uiuc.edu/state/programarea.
cfm?ProgramAreaID=3

### Gardening Organizations

Arbor Day Foundation
arborday.org

British Columbia Council of Garden Clubs
www.bcgardenclubs.com

Canadian Botanical Conservation Network
www.rbg.ca/cbcn

*Canadian Gardening* Magazine
canadiangardening.com

Canadian Wildlife Federation
www.cwf-fcf.org

Cold Climate Gardening
www.coldclimategardening.com

Communities in Bloom
www.communitiesinbloom.ca

Composting Council of Canada
www.compost.org

Glendale Gardens & Woodland: Victoria Master Gardener Association
www.hcp.bc.ca/mg_MasterGardener.htm

Hobby Greenhouse Association
www.hobbygreenhouse.org

Master Gardeners Association of British Columbia
www.bcmastergardeners.org

Montreal Botanical Garden
www2.ville.montreal.qc.ca/jardin/en/menu.htm

National Gardening Association
www.garden.org

Northscaping
www.northscaping.com

Nova Scotia Association of Garden Clubs
www.nsagc.com

Ontario Horticultural Association: Garden Ontario
www.gardenontario.org

Plant a Row; Grow a Row
www.growarow.org

Royal Botanical Gardens
www.rbg.ca

Seeds of Diversity Canada
www.seeds.ca

Seed Savers Exchange
www.seedsavers.org

Toronto Botanical Garden
www.torontobotanicalgarden.ca

Toronto Master Gardeners: Factsheet Topics
www.torontobotanicalgarden.ca/mastergardener_
factsheets.shtml

## Plant Associations

Canadian Chrysanthemum and Dahlia Society
www.mumsanddahlias.com

Canadian Hemerocallis Society
www.distinctly.on.ca/chs

Canadian Horticultural Therapy Association
www.chta.ca

Canadian Peony Society
www.peony.ca

Canadian Rose Society
www.canadianrosesociety.org

Ikebana International
www.ikebanahq.org

International Waterlily & Water Gardening Society
www.iwgs.org

North American Rock Garden Society
nargs.org

### Organic Gardening Experts

Earthworm Digest
www.wormdigest.org

Everything Local & Organic
www.planetfriendly.net/organic.html

HowtoCompost.org
www.howtocompost.org

*Organic Gardening* Magazine: OG Solutions
www.organicgardening.com/channel/1,7502,s1-2,00.html

Rodale Institute
www.rodaleinstitute.org

### Mail-Order Companies: Flowers, Foliage, Trees, and Grasses

Acorus Restoration
722 Sixth Concession Rd., R.R. 1
Walsingham, ON N0E 1X0
Phone 519-586-2603
Web site www.ecologyart.com
Offers native plants and seed mixes.

Artemis Gardens
30182 Harris Rd.
Abbotsford, BC V4X 1Y9
Phone 604-856-0189
Web site www.artemisgardens.com
Growers of more than 900 day lilies suitable for Canadian climates.

Beaver Creek Greenhouses
P.O. Box 129
Fruitvale, BC V0G 1L0
Web site rockgardenplants.com
Specializes in hardy dwarf perennials, shrubs, and conifers.

Bluestem Nursery
1946 Fife Rd.
Christina Lake, BC V0H 1E3
Phone 250-447-6363
Web site www.bluestem.ca
Great for perennials, ornamental grasses, and willows.

Botanus
P.O. Box 3184
Langley, BC V3A 4R5
Phone 800-672-3413
Web site www.botanus.com
Shop for flowering bulbs, perennials, and roses.

Breck's
52429 Nova Scotia Ln.
Port Burnwell, ON N0J 1T0
Phone 800-644-5505
Web site www.brecksbulbs.ca
Get spring- and summer-flowering bulbs here.

Budd Gardens
2832 Innes Rd.
Ottawa, ON K1B 4K4
Phone 613-830-4328
Web site www.buddgardens.com
Check out their hostas and perennials.

Campbell River Garden Centre
673 Old Petersen Rd.
Campbell River, BC V9W 3N1
Phone 250-287-7645
Web site www.crgardencentre.com
Sells classic and rare bulbs.

Canada's Bamboo World
8450 Banford Rd.
Chilliwack, BC V2P 6H3
Phone 604-792-9003
Web site www.bambooworld.com
Try bamboo, giant canna, palms, bananas, or brugmansia for a
change of pace.

Canning Perennials
R.R. 2
Paris, ON N3L 3E2
Phone 519-458-4271
Web site www.canningperennials.com
Deals in perennials, grasses, groundcovers, and vines.

Cavendish Perennials
2451 Cavendish Dr.
Burlington, ON L7P 3T7
Phone 905-336-5107
Web site www3.sympatico.ca/semps
Offers winter-hardy succulent perennial plants.

Chuck Chapman Iris
8790 Wellington Rd., Highway 24, R.R. 1
Guelph, ON N1H 6H7
Phone 519-856-4424
Web site www.chapmaniris.com
Irises suitable for Canadian climate are found here.

Corn Hill Nursery
2700 Rte. 890
Corn Hill, NB E4Z 1M2
Phone 506-756-3635
Web site www.cornhillnursery.com
Check out their hardy roses, flowering shrubs, and vines.

Dominion Seed House
P.O. Box 2500
Georgetown, ON L7G 5L6
Phone 800-784-3037
Web site www.dominion-seed-house.com/en-CA
Seeds, seeds, and more seeds.

Erikson's Daylily Gardens
24642 Fifty-first Ave.
Langley, BC V2Z 1H9
Phone 604-856-575
Web site www.plantlovers.com/erikson
Offers day lilies.

Estate Perennials
P.O. Box 32, Site 103, R.R. 1
Stony Plain, AB T7Z 1X1
Phone 780-968-9199
Web site estateperennials.com
Deals in martagon lilies, Asiatic lilies, day lilies, and peonies.

Ferme les Champs Fleuris
993 Chemin Iberville
St-Lambert-de-Lauzon, QC G0S 2W0
Phone 418-889-9014
Web site www.champsfleuris.com
Sells lilies and Siberian irises.

Florabunda Seeds
P.O. Box 3
Indian River, ON K0L 2B0
Phone 705-295-6440
Web site www.florabundaseeds.com
Find untreated seeds for heirloom and unusual flowers.

Fraser's Thimble Farms
175 Arbutus Rd.
Salt Spring Island, BC V8K 1A3
Phone 250-537-5788
Web site www.thimblefarms.com
Order unusual and native plants, including hardy orchids, ferns, and bulbs.

Gardenimport
135 West Beaver Creek Rd., P.O. Box 760
Richmond Hill, ON L4B 1C6
Phone 905-731-1950 or 800-339-8314
Web site www.gardenimport.com
Find unusual perennials, flowering shrubs, David Austin roses, Raymond Evison clematis, and Sutton seeds here.

Gardens North
5984 Third Line Rd. N.
Gower, ON K0A 2T0
Phone 613-489-0065
Web site www.gardensnorth.com
Sells the seeds of rare, hardy, herbaceous, and woody species for northern gardens.

Golden Bough Tree Farm
P.O. Box 99
Marlbank, ON K0K 2L0
Web site www.goldenboughtrees.ca
Shop for rare native and hardy trees and shrubs.

Heirloom Roses
P.O. Box 9106, Station A
Halifax, NS B3K 5M7
Phone 902-471-3364
Web site www.oldheirloomroses.com
Offers winter-hardy Canadian roses.

Hillcrest Harmony Flowers
P.O. Box 24
Churchbridge, SK S0A 0M0
Phone 306-896-2992
Web site www.hillcrestharmony.com
Lots of lilies — Asiatic hybrids, orienpets, trumpet hybrids, martagons, and species.

Hole's Greenhouses and Gardens
101 Bellerose Dr.
St. Albert, AB T8N 8N8
Phone 888-884-6537
Web site www.holesonline.com
Order perennials, annuals, roses, fruit and shade trees, seeds, and accessories here.

Holt Geraniums
34465 Hallert Rd.
Abbotsford, BC V3G 1R3
Web site www.holtgeraniums.com
Shop for unusual pelargoniums.

Hortico Nurseries
723 Robson Rd., R.R. 1
Waterdown, ON L0R 2H
Phone 905-689-6984 or 905-689-3002
Web site www.hortico.com
Get perennials, roses, and shrubs here.

Humber Nurseries
8386 Hwy. 50
Brampton, ON L6T 0A5
Phone 416-798-8733
Web site www.humbernurseries.com
Get a range of products — perennials, ornamental grasses, hostas, bamboos, aquatics, ferns, and trees.

The Plant Farm
177 Vesuvius Bay Rd.
Salt Spring Island, BC V8K 1K3
Phone 250-537-5995
Web site www.theplantfarm.ca
A wide variety of plants — bamboo, phormiums, day lilies, hostas, rhodos, heathers, ornamental grasses, Siberian and Japanese water irises, and choice exotics.

Select Plus International Lilac Nursery
1510 Pine Rd.
Mascouche, QC J7L 2M4
Phone 450-477-3797
Web site spi.8m.com
Shop for heirloom and rare lilacs, peonies, Itoh peonies, lady slippers, day lilies, hostas, heucheras, and other rare plants.

Tropic to Tropic Plants
1170 Fifty-three A St.
South Delta, BC V4M 3E3
Phone 604-943-6562
Web site www.tropic.ca
Sells a variety of exotic plants.

Van Den Nest Nursery
9594 Somers Rd.
Eden, ON N0J 1H0
Phone 519-866-5269
Web site www.amtelecom.net/~edentree
Specializes in native and Carolinian trees and shrubs.

Whitehouse Perennials
594 Rae Rd., R.R. 2
Almonte, ON K0A 1A0
Phone 877-256-3406
Web site www.whitehouseperennials.com
Find rare and unusual perennials here.

Wildflower Farm
10195 Hwy. 12 W., R.R. 2
Coldwater, ON L0K 1E0
Phone 866-476-9453
Web site www.wildflowerfarm.com
Get native wildflowers and grasses here.

Wrightman Alpines
1503 Napperton Dr., R.R. 3
Kerwood, ON N0M 2B0
Phone 519-247-3751
Web site www.wrightmanalpines.com
Offers alpine and rock garden plants.

## Mail-Order Companies: Vegetables, Herbs, and Fruits

Agrestal Organic Heritage Seeds
P.O. Box 646
Gormley, ON L0H 1G0
Web site www.agrestalseeds.com
Find out-of-the-ordinary, heirloom varieties of vegetable, herb, fruit, and
flower seeds here.

Corn Hill Nursery Ltd.
2700 Rte. 890
Corn Hill, NB E4Z 1M2
Phone 506-756-3635
Web site www.cornhillnursery.com
Check out their fruit trees.

Grimo Nut Nursery
979 Lakeshore Rd., R.R. 3
Niagara-on-the-Lake, ON L0S 1J0
Phone 905-934-688
Web site www.grimonut.com
Shop for nut trees and related products here.

Halifax Seed Company
5860 Kane St., P.O. Box 8026, Station A
Halifax, NS B3K 5L8
Phone 902-454-7456
Web site shop2.itnweb.com/halifaxseed
Sells herb and organic vegetable seeds.

McKenzie Seeds
30 Ninth Street
Brandon, MB R7A 6E1
Phone 800-665-6340
Web site www.mckenzieseeds.com
Offers vegetable seeds and related gardening products.

OSC Seeds
330 Phillip St., P.O. Box 7
Waterloo, ON N2J 3Z6
Phone 519-886-0557
Web site www.oscseeds.com
Sells untreated vegetable and herb seeds.

Richters Herb Specialists
357 Hwy. 47
Goodwood, ON L0C 1A0
Phone 905-640-6677
Web site www.richters.com
Offers an extensive selection of herb seeds, plants, books, and products.

Salt Spring Seeds
P.O. Box 444, Ganges
Salt Spring Island, BC V8K 2W1
Phone 250-537-5269
Web site www.saltspringseeds.com
If you want to grow beans, grains, tomatoes, lettuce, garlic, amaranth, or quinoa, check for certified organic, untreated, open-pollinated, non-GMO seeds here.

Seeds of Diversity Canada
P.O. Box 36, Station Q
Toronto, ON M4T 2L7
Phone 905-623-0353
Web site www.seeds.ca
Seed exchange for heirloom, rare, and nonhybrid vegetables, fruits, and herbs.

Stellar Seeds
2750 Thirtieth Ave. N.E.
Salmon Arm, BC V1E 3L2
Phone 250-804-0122
Web site www.stellarseeds.com
Find locally grown, certified organic vegetable and herb seeds here.

Stokes Seeds
P.O. Box 10
Thorold, ON L2V 5E9
Phone 800-396-9238
Web site www.stokeseeds.com
Offers herb and vegetable seeds.

T & T Seeds
P.O. Box 1710
Winnipeg, MB R3C 3P6
Phone 204-895-9962
Web site www.ttseeds.com
Get early-season vegetable seeds here.

Veseys
P.O. Box 9000
Charlottetown, PEI C1A 8K6
Phone 800-363-7333
Web site www.veseys.com
Shop for vegetable seeds, some certified organic.

West Coast Seeds
3925 Sixty-fourth St., R.R. 1
Delta, BC V4K 3N2
Phone 604-952-8820
Web site www.westcoastseeds.com
Carries untreated and organic vegetable seeds, including Asian veggies.

William Dam Seeds
279 Hwy. 8, R.R. 1
Dundas, ON L9H 5E1
Phone 905-628-6641
Web site www.damseeds.com
Offers untreated and organic vegetable and herb seeds.

## Tools and Supplies

Backyard Greenhouses
2549 Dougall Ave.
Windsor, ON N8X 1T5
Phone 800-665-2124
Web site www.backyardgreenhouses.com
Carries hobby greenhouse kits, lean-to greenhouses, and accessories.

Bustan Urban Gardening Essentials
81 Harbord St.
Toronto, ON M5S 1G4
Phone 888-YOU-GROW or 416-922-6363
Web site www.bustan.ca
Buy grow lights and hydroponic supplies here.

Gardenscape Tools
2010A Queen St. E.
Toronto, ON M4L 1J3
Phone 888-472-3266
Website www.gardenscape.ca
Stocks fine garden tools and innovative and enabling gardening products.

Irrigro Canada
291 Riverview Blvd.
St. Catharines, ON L2T 3N3
Phone 905-688-4090
Web site ca.irrigro.com
Check out their drip irrigation systems.

Lee Valley Tools Ltd.
P.O. Box 6295, Station J
Ottawa, ON K2A 1T4
Phone 800-267-8767
Web site www.leevalleytools.com
Offers a variety of gardening tools and supplies.

Rittenhouse
1402 Fourth Ave., R.R. 3
St. Catharines, ON L2R 6P9
Phone 877-488-1914
Web site www.rittenhouse.ca
Sells gardening tools, sprayers, and accessories.

# Index

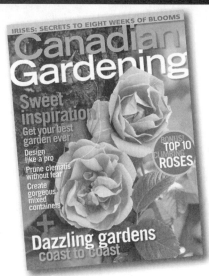